Great World Writers

TWENTIETH CENTURY

EDITOR
PATRICK M. O'NEIL

Index Volume

MARSHALL CAVENDISH
NEW YORK • TORONTO • LONDON • SYDNEY

Marshall Cavendish
99 White Plains Road
Tarrytown, New York 10591-9001

www.marshallcavendish.com

Project Editor:	Marian Armstrong
Development Editor:	Thomas McCarthy
Editorial Director:	Paul Bernabeo
Production Manager:	Michael Esposito

Designer: Patrice Sheridan

Photo Research: Anne Burns Images
                 Carousel Research, Inc.
                     Laurie Platt Winfrey
                     Elizabeth Meryman
                     Van Bucher
                     Cristian Pena

Indexing: AEIOU
           Cynthia Crippen

Library of Congress Cataloging-in-Publication Data

Great world writers : twentieth century / editor, Patrick M. O'Neil.
    p. cm.
    Vol. 13 is an index volume.
    Includes bibliographical references and index.
    ISBN 0-7614-7469-2 (v. 1)—ISBN 0-7614-7470-6 (v. 2)—
ISBN 0-7614-7471-4 (v. 3)—ISBN 0-7614-7472-2 (v. 4)—
ISBN 0-7614-7473-0 (v. 5)—ISBN 0-7614-7474-9
(v. 6)—ISBN 0-7614-7475-7 (v. 7)—ISBN 0-7614-7476-5
(v. 8)—ISBN 0-7614-7477-3 (v. 9)—ISBN 0-7614-7478-1
(v. 10)—ISBN 0-7614-7479-X (v. 11)—ISBN 0-7614-7480-3
(v. 12)—ISBN 0-7614-7481-1 (v. 13 —ISBN 0-7614-7468-4 (set)
    1. Literature—20th century—Bio-bibliography—Dictionaries.
    2. Authors—20th century—Biography—Dictionaries.
    3. Literature—20th century—History and criticism. I.
    O'Neil, Patrick M.

PN771.G73 2004
809'.04—dc21
[B]   200304092

Printed in China

09 08 07 06 05 04   6 5 4 3 2 1

Contents

Writers by Country of Origin   *1732*

Writers by Genre   *1734*

Winners of the Nobel Prize for Literature   *1737*

Glossary   *1740*

Further Reading   *1744*

Index of Literary Works   *1747*

Index of Visual Arts   *1771*

Index of Visual Artists   *1775*

Index of Films   *1780*

Index of Literary Characters   *1783*

Index of People, Places, Movements, and Events   *1798*

Comprehensive Index of Writers   *1818*

Writers by Country of Origin

AFRICA

Egypt
   Naguib Mahfouz
Kenya
   Ngũgĩ wa Thiong'o
Nigeria
   Chinua Achebe
   Buchi Emecheta
   Wole Soyinka
Senegal
   Mariama Bâ
South Africa
   J. M. Coetzee
   Athol Fugard
   Nadine Gordimer
   Alan Paton
Zimbabwe
   Tsitsi Dangarembga

ASIA

China
   Chou Shu-jen
   Gao Xingjian
India
   Anita Desai
   Bharati Mukherjee
   R. K. Narayan
   Salman Rushdie
   Rabindranath Tagore
Israel
   Imil Habibi
   Amos Oz
   A. B. Yehoshua
Japan
   Kōbō Abe
   Yasunari Kawabata
   Yukio Mishima
   Haruki Murakami
   Kōtarō Takamura
Pakistan
   Bapsi Sidhwa

Palestine
   Ghassan Kanafani

AUSTRALIA AND NEW ZEALAND

Australia
   Thomas Keneally
   Archie Weller
   Patrick White
New Zealand
   Katherine Mansfield

CENTRAL AMERICA AND THE CARIBBEAN

Antigua
   Jamaica Kincaid
Cuba
   Alejo Carpentier
   Nicolás Guillén
Dominica
   Jean Rhys
Martinique
   Aimé Césaire
Mexico
   Carlos Fuentes
St. Lucia
   Derek Walcott
Trinidad
   V. S. Naipaul

EUROPE

Austria
   Franz Kafka
Czech Republic
   Václav Havel
Denmark
   Isak Dinesen
France
   Albert Camus
   André Malraux
   Jean-Paul Sartre

Germany
  Bertolt Brecht
  Hermann Hesse
  Thomas Mann
  Erich Maria Remarque
  Rainer Maria Rilke
Greece
  Nikos Kazantzakis
Ireland
  Samuel Beckett
  James Joyce
  Frank O'Connor
  George Bernard Shaw
  John Millington Synge
  William Butler Yeats
Italy
  Italo Calvino
  Luigi Pirandello
Poland
  Joseph Conrad
Romania
  Eugène Ionesco
Russia
  Vladimir Nabokov
  Aleksandr Solzhenitsyn
Spain
  Federico García Lorca

UNITED KINGDOM

England
  W. H. Auden
  E. M. Forster
  William Golding
  Robert Graves
  Graham Greene
  Aldous Huxley

  D. H. Lawrence
  Doris Lessing
  C. S. Lewis
  Iris Murdoch
  George Orwell
  John Osborne
  Wilfred Owen
  J. R. R. Tolkien
  Evelyn Waugh
  H. G. Wells
  Virginia Woolf
Northern Ireland
  Seamus Heaney
Scotland
  Muriel Spark
Wales
  Dylan Thomas

NORTH AMERICA

Canada
  Farley Mowat
  Mordecai Richler
  Gabrielle Roy

SOUTH AMERICA

Argentina
  Jorge Luis Borges
Chile
  Isabel Allende
  Pablo Neruda
Colombia
  Gabriel García Márquez
Peru
  Mario Vargas Llosa

Writers by Genre

AUTOBIOGRAPHERS

Coetzee, J. M.
Conrad, Joseph
Dinesen, Isak
Emecheta, Buchi
Ionesco, Eugène
Lessing, Doris
Lewis, C. S.
Nabokov, Vladimir
Neruda, Pablo
O'Connor, Frank
Osborne, John
Paton, Alan
Rhys, Jean
Roy, Gabrielle
Soyinka, Wole
Vargas Llosa, Mario
Waugh, Evelyn
White, Patrick

CHILDREN'S BOOK AUTHORS

Achebe, Chinua
Desai, Anita
Emecheta, Buchi
Graves, Robert
Kazantzakis, Nikos
Lewis, C. S.
Mowat, Farley
Ngũgĩ wa Thiong'o
Richler, Mordecai
Tolkien, J. R. R.

ESSAYISTS

Achebe, Chinua
Auden, W. H.
Borges, Jorge Luis
Calvino, Italo
Camus, Albert
Carpentier, Alejo
Césaire, Aimé

Chou Shu-jen
Coetzee, J. M.
Conrad, Joseph
Desai, Anita
Dinesen, Isak
Forster, E. M.
Fuentes, Carlos
Gao Xingjian
Graves, Robert
Greene, Graham
Havel, Václav
Huxley, Aldous
Kanafani, Ghassan
Kazantzakis, Nikos
Kincaid, Jamaica
Lawrence, D. H.
Lewis, C. S.
Malraux, André
Mann, Thomas
Mishima, Yukio
Mukherjee, Bharati
Naipaul, V. S.
Ngũgĩ wa Thiong'o
Orwell, George
Oz, Amos
Paton, Alan
Richler, Mordecai
Rilke, Rainer Maria
Sartre, Jean-Paul
Shaw, George Bernard
Solzhenitsyn, Aleksandr
Synge, John Millington
Tagore, Rabindranath
Takamura, Kōtarō
Tolkien, J. R. R.
Vargas Llosa, Mario
Woolf, Virginia
Yeats, W. B.

FICTION WRITERS

Abe, Kōbō
Achebe, Chinua
Allende, Isabel

Bâ, Mariama
Beckett, Samuel
Borges, Jorge Luis
Brecht, Bertolt
Calvino, Italo
Camus, Albert
Carpentier, Alejo
Chou Shu-jen
Coetzee, J. M.
Conrad, Joseph
Dangarembga, Tsitsi
Desai, Anita
Dinesen, Isak
Emecheta, Buchi
Forster, E. M.
Fuentes, Carlos
Gao Xingjian
García Márquez, Gabriel
Golding, William
Gordimer, Nadine
Graves, Robert
Greene, Graham
Hesse, Hermann
Huxley, Aldous
Joyce, James
Kafka, Franz
Kanafani, Ghassan
Kawabata, Yasunari
Kazantzakis, Nikos
Keneally, Thomas
Kincaid, Jamaica
Lawrence, D. H.
Lessing, Doris
Lewis, C. S.
Mahfouz, Naguib
Malraux, André
Mann, Thomas
Mansfield, Katherine
Mishima, Yukio
Mowat, Farley
Mukherjee, Bharati
Murakami, Haruki
Murdoch, Iris
Nabokov, Vladimir
Naipaul, V. S.
Narayan, R. K.
Ngũgĩ wa Thiong'o
O'Connor, Frank
Orwell, George
Oz, Amos
Paton, Alan

Pirandello, Luigi
Remarque, Erich Maria
Rhys, Jean
Richler, Mordecai
Roy, Gabrielle
Rushdie, Salman
Sartre, Jean-Paul
Sidhwa, Bapsi
Solzhenitsyn, Aleksandr
Soyinka, Wole
Spark, Muriel
Tagore, Rabindranath
Thomas, Dylan
Tolkien, J. R. R.
Vargas Llosa, Mario
Waugh, Evelyn
Weller, Archie
Wells, H. G.
White, Patrick
Woolf, Virginia
Yeats, W. B.

JOURNALISTS

Calvino, Italo
Camus, Albert
Césaire, Aimé
García Márquez, Gabriel
Kanafani, Ghassan
Mahfouz, Naguib
Orwell, George
Richler, Mordecai
Roy, Gabrielle
Shaw, George Bernard
Waugh, Evelyn
Wells, H. G.

LYRICISTS

Brecht, Bertolt

PLAYWRIGHTS

Abe, Kōbō
Allende, Isabel
Auden, W. H.
Beckett, Samuel
Brecht, Bertolt

Camus, Albert
Carpentier, Alejo
Césaire, Aimé
Conrad, Joseph
Dangarembga, Tsitsi
Fugard, Athol
Gao Xingjian
García Lorca, Federico
Greene, Graham
Havel, Václav
Ionesco, Eugéne
Kazantzakis, Nikos
Keneally, Thomas
Lessing, Doris
Mishima, Yukio
Murdoch, Iris
Ngũgĩ wa Thiong'o
O'Connor, Frank
Osborne, John
Paton, Alan
Pirandello, Luigi
Sartre, Jean-Paul
Shaw, George Bernard
Solzhenitsyn, Aleksandr
Soyinka, Wole
Synge, John Millington
Tagore, Rabindranath
Thomas, Dylan
Vargas Llosa, Mario
Walcott, Derek
Weller, Archie
White, Patrick
Yeats, W. B.
Yehoshua, A. B.

POETS

Auden, W. H.
Borges, Jorge Luis
Carpentier, Alejo
Césaire, Aimé
Chou Shu-jen
García Lorca, Federico

Graves, Robert
Guillén, Nicolás
Heaney, Seamus
Hesse, Hermann
Joyce, James
Lawrence, D. H.
Nabokov, Vladimir
Neruda, Pablo
Owen, Wilfred
Paton, Alan
Rilke, Rainer Maria
Solzhenitsyn, Aleksandr
Soyinka, Wole
Synge, John Millington
Tagore, Rabindranath
Takamura, Kōtarō
Thomas, Dylan
Walcott, Derek
Weller, Archie
White, Patrick
Yeats, W. B.

SCREENWRITERS

Abe, Kōbō
Beckett, Samuel
Dangarembga, Tsitsi
Emecheta, Buchi
Fugard, Athol
García Márquez, Gabriel
Greene, Graham
Huxley, Aldous
Kawabata, Yasunari
Keneally, Thomas
Lessing, Doris
Mahfouz, Naguib
Nabokov, Vladimir
Osborne, John
Remarque, Erich Maria
Richler, Mordecai
Thomas, Dylan
Waugh, Evelyn

Winners of the Nobel Prize for Literature

The Nobel Prize for Literature is one of six prizes awarded annually from a fund established under the will of Alfred Bernhard Nobel (1833–1869), a Swedish chemist, engineer, and industrialist who had an abiding interest in literature. In his youth he had written poetry in English, and the beginnings of a novel were found among his papers. The Nobel Prize for literature, generally awarded to a writer for a body of work, has come to be one of the most highly regarded of international awards.

Names appearing in **boldface** indicate writers covered in this encyclopedia set.

2003	**J.M. Coetzee**	South Africa
2002	Imre Kertész	Hungarian
2001	**V. S. Naipaul**	British
2000	**Gao Xingjian**	Chinese
1999	Günter Grass	German
1998	José Saramago	Portuguese
1997	Dario Fo	Italian
1996	Wislawa Szymborska	Polish
1995	**Seamus Heaney**	Irish
1994	Kenzaburo Oe	Japanese
1993	Toni Morrison	American
1992	**Derek Walcott**	West Indian
1991	**Nadine Gordimer**	South African
1990	Octavio Paz	Mexican
1989	Camilo José Cela	Spanish
1988	**Naguib Mahfouz**	Egyptian
1987	Joseph Brodsky	Russian–American
1986	**Wole Soyinka**	Nigerian
1985	Claude Simon	French
1984	Jaroslav Siefert	Czechoslovakian
1983	**William Golding**	British
1982	**Gabriel Garcia Marquez**	Colombian–Mexican
1981	Elias Canetti	Bulgarian–British
1980	Czeslaw Milosz	Polish–American
1979	Odysseus Elytis	Greek
1978	Isaac Bashevis Singer	American
1977	Vicente Aleixandre	Spanish
1976	Saul Bellow	American
1975	Eugenio Montale	Italian
1974	Eyvind Johnson	Swedish
	Harry Edmund Martinson	Swedish
1973	**Patrick White**	Australian
1972	Heinrich Böll	German

1971	**Pablo Neruda**	Chilean
1970	**Aleksandr I. Solzhenitsyn**	Russian
1969	**Samuel Beckett**	Irish
1968	**Yasunari Kawabata**	Japanese
1967	Miguel Angel Asturias	Guatemalan
1966	Samuel Joseph Agnon	Israeli
	Nelly Sachs	Swedish
1965	Mikhail Sholokhov	Russian
1964	declined by **Jean-Paul Sartre**	French
1963	Giorgios Seferis	Greek
1962	John Steinbeck	American
1961	Ivo Andric	Yugoslavian
1960	Saint-John Perse	French
1959	declined by Salvatore Quasimodo	Italian
1958	Boris L. Pasternak	Russian
1957	**Albert Camus**	French
1956	Juan Ramón Jiménez	Spanish
1955	Halidor K. Laxness	Icelander
1954	Ernest Hemingway	American
1953	Sir Winston Churchill	British
1952	François Mauriac	French
1951	Par F. Lagerkvist	Swedish
1950	Bertrand Russell	British
1949	William Faulkner	American
1948	T. S. Eliot	American-British
1947	André Gide	French
1946	**Hermann Hesse**	German–Swiss
1945	Gabriela Mistral	Chilean
1944	Johannes V. Jensen	Danish
1940–1943	(not awarded)	
1939	Frans E. Sillanpää	Finn
1938	Pearl S. Buck	American
1937	Roger Martin du Gard	French
1936	Eugene O'Neill	American
1935	(not awarded)	
1934	**Luigi Pirandello**	Italian
1933	Ivan A. Bunin	Russian
1932	John Galsworthy	British
1931	Erik A. Karlfeldt	Swedish
1930	Sinclair Lewis	American
1929	**Thomas Mann**	German
1928	Sigrid Undset	Norwegian
1927	Henri Bergson	French
1926	Grazia Deledda	Italian
1925	**George Bernard Shaw**	Irish
1924	Wladyslaw S. Reymont	Polish
1923	**William Butler Yeats**	Irish
1922	Jacinto Benavente	Spanish
1921	Anatole France	French
1920	Knut Hamsun	Norwegian
1919	Carl F. G. Spitteler	Swiss

1918	(not awarded)	
1917	Karl A. Gjellerup	Danish
	Henrik Pontoppidan	Danish
1916	Verner von Heidenstam	Swedish
1915	Romain Rolland	French
1914	(not awarded)	
1913	**Rabindranath Tagore**	Indian
1912	Gerhart Hauptmann	German
1911	Maurice Maeterlinck	Belgian
1910	Paul J. L. Heyse	German
1909	Selma Lagerlöf	Swedish
1908	Rudolf C. Eucken	German
1907	Rudyard Kipling	British
1906	Giosuè Carducci	Italian
1905	Henryk Sienkiewicz	Polish
1904	Frédéric Mistral	French
	José Echegaray	Spanish
1903	Björnsterne Björnson	Norwegian
1902	Theodor Mommsen	German
1901	René F. A. Sully Prudhomme	French

Glossary

absurd: ridiculously unreasonable, unsound, or incongruous; having no rational or orderly relationship to human life; meaningless

aestheticism: a literary and artistic movement that began in nineteenth-century France whose followers believed that art should not be mixed with social, political, or moral teaching

alienation: a withdrawing or separation of a person or a person's affections from a person, an object, or a position of former attachment

allegory: the expression of truths or generalizations about human existence by the use of symbolic fictional figures and actions

alliteration: the repetition of initial consonant sounds in neighboring words

alliterative meter: the distinctive verse form of Old Germanic poetry, including Old English. It employed a long line divided by a caesura (a pause) into two balanced half-lines, each with a given number of stressed syllables and a variable number of unstressed symbols.

antihero: a protagonist or notable figure who is conspicuously lacking in heroic qualities

apartheid: a racial segregation, specifically a policy of segregation and political and economic discrimination against non-European groups in the Republic of South Africa

apologetics: a branch of theology devoted to the defense of the divine origin and authority of Christianity

assonance: the resemblance of sounds in words or syllables by the repetition of vowels without the repetition of consonants; used as an alternate to rhyme in verse

autobiography: a personal account of one's own life, especially for publication; a biography of oneself narrated by oneself

avant-garde: pioneers or innovators, especially in art and literature, who develop new or experimental concepts

bildungsroman: a novel dealing with one person's early life and development

blank verse: unrhymed verse; specifically, unrhymed iambic pentameter verse

boom novel (Latin American modernism): a Spanish-American novel written during the movement known as the Boom (which brought Spanish-American literature into the international limelight in the 1960s), which began in 1958 with Carlos Fuentes's novel *Where the Air Is Clear,* exploded in 1964 when Mario Vargas Llosa received the Biblioteca Breve Prize for his 1963 novel, *The Time of the Hero* (the first of five Biblioteca Breve Prizes awarded to Latin-American writers in the 1960s), and reached its definitive moment with the publication of Gabriel García Márquez's *One Hundred Years of Solitude* in 1967.

cinematic fiction: a novel relating to, suggestive of, or suitable for motion pictures or the filming of motion pictures; a novel filmed and presented as a motion picture

colonialism: control by one power over a dependent area or people

confessional literature: works that are intimately autobiographical

counterpoint: use of contrast or interplay of elements in a work of art in order to set off or emphasize by juxtaposition

creationist movement (literary): a short-lived avant-garde movement whose most vociferous exponent, and possible inventor, was Chilean writer Vicente Huidobro, a prominent figure in the post–World War I literary vanguard in Paris, Madrid, and Chile

demotic language: language derived from or using the language of the common people rather than the more formal style of a priesthood or other educated elite

dialect: a regional variety of language distinguished by features of vocabulary, grammar, and pronunciation from other regional varieties

dystopian fiction: works describing an anti-utopia, a place where people lead dehumanized and often fearful lives

dystopian novel: an anti-utopian novel where, instead of a paradise, everything has gone wrong in the attempt to create a perfect society

élan vital: the vital force or impulse of life, especially a creative principal held by the French philosopher Henri-Louis Bergson to be immanent in all organisms and responsible for evolution

epic poetry: long, narrative poems on a serious subject written in a grand or elevated style and centered on a larger-than-life hero or heroine

epistolary novel: a novel written in the form of a series of letters

existentialism: a twentieth-century philosophical movement embracing diverse doctrines but centering on the analysis of individual existence in an incomprehensible universe and the plight of the individual who must assume ultimate responsibility for his or her acts of free will without any certain knowledge of what is right or wrong or good or bad

extended metaphor: a figure of speech that makes an unusual and elaborately sustained comparison between two dissimilar things

fantastic literature: a mode of fiction in which the possible and the impossible are confounded so as to leave the reader (and often the narrator and/or central character) with no consistent explanation for the story's strange events

first-person narrator: "I," one of the characters involved in a story, narrates the story, and the story is thus seen from that character's point of view

flashbacks: interruptions of the chronological sequence in a story by the interjection of events that occurred earlier in the story

frame narrator: one who uses a literary device called a frame to provide a setting and exposition for the main narrative in a novel; the narrator will describe where he or she found the manuscript of the novel or where he or she heard someone tell the story the narrator is about to relate thus "framing" the narrative and giving credibility to the main section of the novel

free verse: poetry of any line length and any placement on the page, with no fixed measure or meter

futuristic satire: a satirical work—novel, movie, play, etc.—set in a futuristic society

gothic: a style of fiction characterized by the use of desolate or remote settings and ghastly, mysterious, or violent incidents

haiku: an unrhymed verse form of Japanese origin having three lines containing five, seven, and five syllables respectively; a poem in this form usually having a seasonal reference

half-rhyme: an imperfect rhyme in which the final consonants of stressed syllables agree but the vowel sounds do not match

historical fiction: a novel that has a period of history as its setting and that attempts to convey the spirit, manners, and social conditions of a past age with realistic detail and fidelity to historical fact

iambic tetrameter: an eight-syllable line of verse made up of four metrical feet, each metrical foot consisting of one short syllable followed by one long syllable or of one unstressed syllable followed by one stressed syllable

identity politics: signifies a wide range of political activity and theorizing founded in the shared experience of injustice of members of certain social groups

imagism: a twentieth-century movement in poetry advocating free verse and the expression of ideas and emotions through clear, precise images

irony: the use of words, often humorous or sarcastic, to express something other than, and especially the opposite of, literal meaning

Kafkaesque: of, relating to, or suggestive of Franz Kafka or his writings, especially having a nightmarishly complex, bizarre, or illogical quality

leitmotiv: an associated melodic phrase or figure that accompanies the reappearance of an idea, person, or situation; a dominant recurring theme

libretto: the text of a work (as an opera) for the musical theater

loco-descriptive poem (also called **topographical poem**): a poem devoted to the description of specific places, usually with additional meditative passages

magical realism: Latin-American literary phenomenon characterized by the incorporation of fantastic or mythical elements matter-of-factly into otherwise realistic fiction; a mingling of the mundane with the fantastic.

maqamat: an Islamic literary term usually translated as "assemblies" or "séances." Maqamat, cast in the ancient form of rhymed prose, are full of wit and learned allusions presupposing a knowledgeable audience that could appreciate them

memoirs: a narrative composed from personal experience; an autobiography

metafiction: fiction that refers to or takes as its subject fictional writing and its conventions

modernism: a practice, usage, or expression peculiar to modern times

multiple narrators: a story told by two or more narrators, not limited in viewpoint to any one character, and thus not limited in commenting on various aspects of the story

negritude: a consciousness of and pride in the cultural and physical aspects of the African heritage; the state or condition of being black

nihilism: a viewpoint that traditional values and beliefs are unfounded and that existence is senseless and useless; a perspective that denies moral truths and supports the belief that conditions in society are so bad as to make destruction desirable

oral tradition: the traditional knowledge and beliefs of cultures that are transmitted by word of mouth

paganism: the actions or beliefs of persons who have little or no religion and who delight in sensual pleasure and material goods

parables: short, fictitious stories that illustrate a moral attitude or a religious principle

patois: a dialect other than the standard or literary dialect; uneducated or provincial speech, often the special language of a social group

picaresque: a type of fiction dealing with the episodic adventures of a roguish protagonist who drifts from place to place and from one social milieu to another in an effort to survive

political correctness: a belief that language and practices that could offend political sensibilities, such as in matters of sex or race, should be eliminated

postcolonialism: a category of literature devised to replace and expand upon what was once called commonwealth literature. Postcolonial literature covers a wide range of writings from countries that were once colonies or dependencies of the European powers.

Pre-Raphaelites: a circle of writers and artists in mid-nineteenth-century England who valued the artistic qualities of religious symbolism, lavish pictorialism, and natural sensuousness and cultivated a sense of mystery and melancholy

protagonist: the principal character in a literary work

puns: the usually humorous use of a word in such a way as to suggest two or more of its meanings or the meaning of another word similar in sound

realism: a mode of writing that gives the impression of recording or "reflecting" faithfully an actual way of life

realismo mágico. See **magic realism**

real maravilloso: "the marvelous in the real"; enchanted worlds where the usual notions of modernity, progress, and rationality are challenged by magical attitudes and perceptions of reality bursting from folk wisdom, superstition, mysticism, etc.

rime couée: a tail rhyme; a stanza in which a usually closing short line rhymes with a previous short line and is separated from it by longer lines

romance **form:** in Spanish literature, a ballad composed in octosyllabic lines

samizdat literature: translated from two Russian words, *samizdat* means "self-publishing," and relates to manuscripts that were privately and illegally produced and circulated in the Soviet Union after the death of Joseph Stalin in 1953 and before glasnost in the 1980s

science fiction: a novel or story in which futuristic technology or otherwise altered scientific principles contribute in a significant way to the adventure

second-person voice: a narrative perspective wherein the author tells the story as if it is happening to the reader

social Darwinism: an extension of Darwinism to social phenomena; a theory in sociology that sociocultural advance is the product of intergroup conflict and competition and the socially elite classes (those possessing wealth and power) possess biological superiority in the struggle for existence

social realism (also known as **socialist realism**): a school of literary theory proposed by Maxim Gorky and established as a dogma by the first Soviet Congress of Writers that demanded adherence to a communist worldview in works of literature

social satire: a narrative form that uses cutting satire to highlight the foibles of society

stereotypes: a standardized mental picture that is held in common by members of a group and that represents an oversimplified opinion, prejudiced attitude, or uncritical judgment

stream of consciousness: narrative technique in nondramatic fiction intended to render the flow of a myriad of impressions—visual, auditory, physical, associative, and subliminal—that together with rational thought impinge on the consciousness of an individual

surrealism: the principles, ideals, or practice of producing fantastic or incongruous imagery or

effects in art, literature, film, or theater by means of unnatural juxtapositions and combinations

symbolism: the use of symbols to represent ideas; an artistic and poetic movement or style using symbols and indirect suggestions to express ideas, emotions, etc.

syncretism: the fusion of various religious forms and views

tanka: an unrhymed Japanese verse form of five lines containing five, seven, five, seven, and seven syllables respectively; a poem in this form

tragicomedy: a drama or a situation blending tragic and comic elements

utopianism: an idea or theory based on the principles of utopia, the imaginary, remote place of ideal perfection, especially in laws, government, and social conditions

vanguard movement: a phase in the world of art and literature that followed the modernist movement; also called the **avant-garde** movement

vernacular: a language or dialect native to a region or country rather than a literary, cultured, or foreign language; also a nonstandard language or dialect of a place, region, or country

zawen: a Chinese literary term for miscellaneous and/or random essays

Further Reading

MARILYN GADDIS ROSE

Distinguished Service Professor,
Department of Comparative Literature, Binghamton University

The Springs of Literary Culture. Resources for deepening the appreciation of literature; intended for selective browsing.

The Bible: Authorized Version (King James Version). Essential to an understanding of English-language authors and translators. Look for an edition with a concordance. For background on the books of the Old and New Testaments and the Apocrypha and a discussion of the various Bible translations, see *The Literary Guide to the Bible* (Robert Alter and Frank Kermode, eds.; Cambridge, MA: Belknap Press/Harvard, 1987).

Darwin, Charles. *The Darwin Reader.* New York: Scribners, 1968. Selections from the scientist whose insights underlie literary expressionism, naturalism, and realism.

Freud, Sigmund. *The Interpretation of Dreams.* Translated by Joyce Crick. New York: Oxford University Press, 1999. Where the key terms of serious and popular psychology begin.

Jung, Carl Gustave. *Man and His Symbols.* Edited by Marie-Luise von Franz. Garden City, NY: Doubleday, 1964. A primary source behind the meaning and origin of symbols used by writers and their critics.

Said, Edward. *Orientalism.* New York: Pantheon Books, 1978. Landmark study arguing that the West used the arts to "exoticize" the Middle East and North Africa.

Critical Background and Criteria for Evaluation. Resources to support understanding.

Bloom, Harold. *The Western Canon: Books and Schools of the Ages.* New York: Harcourt Brace, 1994. A time tour from Shakespeare to Beckett to see what makes great books great.

Draugsvold, Ottar G., ed. *Nobel Writers on Writing.* Jefferson, NC: McFarland, 2000. Lucid summary of Nobel election procedures with selected Nobelists through 1999 (including Camus, Golding, Mahfouz, Walcott, and Yeats) and excerpts from their acceptance addresses.

Hofstadter, Douglas. *Le Ton Beau de Marot: In Praise of the Music of Language.* New York: Basic Books, 1997. Celebration of the nature and creativity of language and the interactions of original text and translation by the author of the astonishingly imaginative *Gödel, Escher, Bach: An Eternal Golden Braid.*

Pound, Ezra. *ABC of Reading.* New Haven, CT: Yale University Press, 1934. Idiosyncratic with a personal stamp, Pound offers a set of terms that are still used 70 years later.

Critical Histories and Studies. Insight into specific areas, movements, and styles.

Applebaum, Anne. *Gulag. A History*. New York: Doubleday, 2003. The backdrop for the arts and clandestine literatures of Soviet Russia.

Bell, Quentin. *Bloomsbury Recalled*. New York: Columbia University Press, 1990. Bell, Virginia Woolf's nephew and Vanessa Bell's son, reconstructs the heady atmosphere of these major players in twentieth-century English arts.

Brater, Enoch, and Ruby Cohn, eds. *Around the Absurd: Essays on Modern and Postmodern Drama*. Ann Arbor: University of Michigan Press, 1995. Approaches to modern drama from the standpoint of both performance and substance.

Fallis, Richard. *The Irish Renaissance*. Syracuse, NY: Syracuse University Press, 1977. A masterly study on the flowering of the arts in Dublin in the early twentieth century.

Fraser, Nancy, and Sandra Lee Bartky, eds. *Revaluing French Feminism: Critical Essays on Difference, Agency and Culture*. Bloomington: Indiana University Press, 1990. Americans may have started the feminist movement, but the French have been better publicists.

Glotfelty, Cheryll, and Harold Fromm. *The Ecocriticism Reader*. Athens: University of Georgia Press, 1996. Especially good introduction linking literature to environmental activism.

Gorman, G. E. *The South African Novel in English since 1950*. Boston: G. K. Hall, 1978. Despite the title, Gorman begins this highly informative contextualizing with Alan Paton's *Cry the Beloved Country* (1942).

Gray, Stephen, ed. *The Picador Book of African Stories*. 5 vols. London: Picador, 2000. A thoughtful sampling of the continent by region: I, the North; II, the West; III, the East and the central region; IV, Indian Ocean and African island region; V, the South.

Montagu, Jemima. *The Surrealists: Revolution in Art and Writing 1919–1935*. London: Tate, 2002. How to understand the logic of illogic.

New, W. H. *Canadian Writers in 1984*. Vancouver: University of British Columbia Press, 1984. Essays and samples of literature by French and English writers (the former with translations) who have subsequently become established figures.

Summers, Claude J., ed. *The Gay and Lesbian Literary Heritage: A Reader's Companion to the Writers and Their Works from Antiquity to the Present*. New York: Henry Holt, 1995. The homosexual as observer, artist, and contributor to Western culture.

Watson, George. *British Literature since 1945*. New York: St. Martin's Press, 1991. This succinct review includes Golding, Graves, Greene, Lewis, Murdoch, Orwell, Osborne, Owen, Pinter, Spark, Stoppard, Tolkien, and Thomas.

Williams, Patrick, and Laura Chrisman, eds. *Colonial Discourse and Postcolonial Theory: A Reader*. New York: Columbia University Press, 1994. These excerpts from 32 postcolonial theorists provide useful sociohistorical context.

Zamora, Lois Parkinson, and Wendy R. Faris, eds. *Magic Realism: Theory, History, Community*. Durham, NC: Duke University, 1995. Background and insights on the Latin American contribution to the novel in the second half of the twentieth century.

The Author as Critic and Observer. Poaching on and enriching the territory of the historian.

Keneally, Thomas. *The Great Shame: And the Triumph of the Irish in the English-Speaking World*. New York: Random House, 1999. An inside view of the Irish diaspora during the nineteenth and twentieth century.

Levi, Primo. *Survival in Auschwitz: The Nazi Assault on Humanity*. Translated by Stuart Woolf. New York: Collier, 1961. An account of Auschwitz by a writer who survived it.

Richler, Mordecai. *Oh Canada, Oh Quebec: A Requiem for a Divided Country*. New York: Knopf, 1992. Acerbic, witty reporting on the language policy of Quebec and Richler's role in it.

Biography as History. Some biographies are so exhaustive that they present an entire era.

Bair, Deirdre. *Simone de Beauvoir: A Biography*. New York: Summit Books, 1990. A day-by-day account of the woman crucial to Sartre, existentialism, and poststructural criticism in France and the United States.

Ellman, Richard. *James Joyce*. Rev. ed. New York: Oxford University Press, 1982. From Dublin through Trieste, Zurich, and Paris, an encyclopedic record of an encyclopedic and inexhaustible writer, the defining figure of literary modernism.

Foster, R. F. *W. B. Yeats. A Life*. 2 vols. New York: Oxford University Press, 1997–2004. The man ultimately responsible for the Irish Renaissance.

Hayman, Ronald. *Thomas Mann: A Biography*. New York: Scribners, 1995. A great German writer remains loyal to his language and the best of his heritage during two world wars and exile.

Holroyd, Michael. *Bernard Shaw*. 4 vols. London: Chatto and Windus, 1988–1992. The activist-journalist-dramatist whose plays are perennial mainstays of the modern repertory.

King, James. *Virginia Woolf*. New York: Norton, 1995. Examines Woolf from her ancestors through her post-suicide heritage, with a full account of all the personalities who impinged upon hers.

Index of Literary Works

Numbers in **bold** indicate volumes.
Page numbers in *italic* indicate illustrations or illustration captions.

Abath al-aqdar (Mahfouz), **6**:825

Abbess of Crewe, The (Spark), **11**:1445, 1447, 1457–59

"Abencaján el Bojarí, Dead in His Labyrinth" (Borges), **1**:117

Abhijnana Shakuntalam (Narayan version), **8**:1044

Abinger Harvest (Forster), **3**:323

Abolition of Man, The (Lewis), **6**:811, 818

About the House (Auden), **1**:64

Acrobats, The (Richler), **9**:1260, 1261, 1262, 1264, *1265*, 1266, 1267, 1270–71, 1277

"Act of Union" (Heaney), **4**:572

Adah's Story (Emecheta), **3**:311, 318

Ada or Ardor: A Family Chronicle (Nabokov), **7**:990, 994, *1004*, 1005

Adrift on the Nile (Mahfouz), **6**:834, 835, 836

"Adulteress, The" (Camus), **2**:176

"Adventure of a Soldier, The" (Calvino), **2**:153

Adventures in the Skin Trade (Thomas), **11**:1524, 1527–28

Adventures of Huckleberry Finn, The (Twain), **1**:120

Adventures of Tom Bombadil, The (Tolkien), **11**:1532, 1534, 1535, 1538

Aeneid (Virgil), **4**:573; **11**:1576, 1577

"Aeroplanes of Brescia, The" (Kafka), **5**:662

Afrah al-qubbah (Mahfouz), **6**:835

African Laughter (Lessing), **6**:789

"After Death" (Chou), **2**:223

After Leaving Mr. Mackenzie (Rhys), **9**:1258

After Many a Summer Dies the Swan (Huxley), **5**:608, 616–17

Aftermath: Travels in a Postwar World (Mowat), **7**:928

"After the Race" (Joyce), **5**:637, 649

"Agamemnon Class of 1939" (Murdoch), **7**:969

Age of Anxiety, The: A Baroque Eclogue (Auden), **1**:63, 65, 66

Age of Iron (Coetzee), **2**:229, 231

Ah, but Your Land Is Beautiful (Paton), **9**:1183, 1184, 1186, 1197

"Ah Q zhenzhuan" (Chou), **2**:212, 219–21, 223

'*A'id ila Haifa* (Kanafani), **5**:687, 689, 691

Aiding and Abetting (Spark), **11**:1450, 1462

Aimé Césaire: The Collected Poetry (Césaire), **1**:200; **2**:200

"Ainulindalë" (Tolkien), **11**:1547, 1548

Aish fi al-haqiqa, Al- (Mahfouz), **6**:833

"Akai mayu" (Abe), **1**:14

"Akallabêth" (Tolkien), **11**:1548

Aka Weta (Achebe and Udechukwu, ed.), **1**:24

Aké (Soyinka), **10**:1428, 1431–32

Akhenaten: Dweller in Truth (Mahfouz), **6**:833

"Alabama Song" (Brecht and Weill), **1**:*138*

"Albergo Empedocle" (Forster), **3**:323

"Albino Gorilla, The" (Calvino), **2**:156

Albondocani (Dinesen unfinished work), **3**:307

Aleph, The (*Aleph, El*) (Borges), **1**:107, 117, 119, 120, 122

"Aleph, The" (Borges), **1**:117, *118*

Alice in Wonderland (Carroll), **7**:967, 973; **12**:1598

All about Mr. Hatterr (Desani), **10**:1325

"All at One Point" (Calvino), **2**:155

Allegory of Love, The (Lewis), **6**:806

All Quiet on the Western Front (Remarque), **9**:1217, *1218*, 1219, 1220, *1221*, 1222, 1224, 1227–30, 1231, 1233, 1235

All That Fall (Beckett; radio play), **1**:91, 92

All That's Left to You (Kanafani), **5**:686, 689, 691, 692

"All the Pretty Little Horses" (Weller), **12**:1618

"Allusions" (Borges), **1**:119

Almayer's Folly (Conrad), **2**:248, 249, 255

Almost a Gentleman: An Autobiography 1955–1966 (Osborne), **8**:1134

Altro figlio, L' (Pirandello), **9**:1206–7

Alturas de Macchu Picchu (Neruda), **8**:1063, 1064–66

"Amar Sonar Bangla" (Tagore), **11**:1493

Amédée (Ionesco), **5**:622, 624, 627

American Brat, An (Sidhwa), **10**:1380, 1382, 1385, 1393–95

American Scoundrel (Keneally), **6**:728

Amerika (Kafka), **5**:662, 664, 673, 674, 678–80

"Among School Children" (Yeats), **12**:1713

Among the Believers: An Islamic Journey (Naipaul), **8**:1017, 1021, 1030–32

Among the Believers (Naipaul), **8**:1017

Amor en los tiempos de cólera, El (García Márquez). *See Love in the Time of Cholera*

Anabasis (Xenophon), **7**:975

Anaforá stan Gréko (Kazantzakis), **5**:704

"And Death Shall Have No Dominion" (Thomas), **11**:1514

And No Birds Sang (Mowat), **7**:928

And the Dogs Were Silent: A Tragedy (Césaire), **2**:200

Anecdotes of Destiny (Dinesen), **3**:298, 299, 306–7

"Angel, The" (Rilke), **9**:1294

Angelic Avengers, The (Dinesen), **3**:297, 298

Angu shōden (Takamura). *See Brief History of Imbecility, A*

Animal Farm (Orwell), **8**:1109, 1113–15, 1116, 1117, 1119, 1120, 1122, 1125–27

Annie John (Kincaid), **6**:750, 754–56

Ann Veronica (Wells), **12**:1632, 1637

Another Mexico (Greene), **4**:498, 512, *513*

Another Time (Auden), **1**:64, 71

"Anthem for Doomed Youth" (Owen), **8**:1149

Anthills of the Savannah (Achebe), **1**:24, 25, 27, 28, 37, 38–39

Antic Hay (Huxley), **5**:603, 608

Anticipations (Wells), **12**:1632, 1633, 1639

Antilles, The: Fragments of Epic Memory (Walcott), **11**:1580–81

Antony and Clepatra (Shakespeare), **10**:1375

"Appeal to Reason, An" (Mann), **7**:872

"Appeli an die Vernunft, Ein" (Mann), **7**:872

Apple Cart, The (Shaw), **10**:1365

Apprenticeship of Duddy Kravitz, The (Richler), **9**:1266, 1271–72

Apprenticeship of Duddy Kravitz, The (Richler; screenplay), **9**:1261, 1264, *1271*

Arabian Nights, **1**:120; **3**:301, 302; **6**:833

Arabian Nights and Days (Mahfouz), **6**:833

"Araby" (Joyce), **5**:648, 649

Aran Islands, The (Synge), **11**:1466

Arch of Triumph (*Arc de Triomphe*) (Remarque), **9**:1221, 1224, *1225*, 1237

Area of Darkness, An (Naipaul), **8**:1016

Arms and the Man (Shaw), **10**:1360, 1362

Arrow of God (Achebe), **1**:24, 26, 37–38

Arthurian legends, **12**:1623

Artifices (Borges), **1**:116

Art of Fiction, The (James), **6**:770

"Art of Staying at the Seaside, The" (Wells), **12**:1631

Art of the Impossible, The (Havel), **4**:544

Art of the Theatre, The (O'Connor), **8**:1096

As Far As Thought Can Reach (Shaw), **10**:1375

Aspects of the Novel (Forster), **3**:323, 324

Astrologer's Day and Other Stories, An (Narayan), **8**:1040

"At a Potato Digging" (Heaney), **4**:569

"At Daybreak" (Calvino), **2**:155

At the Bottom of The River (Kincaid), **6**:749, 750, 758, 760–61

Audience (Havel), **4**:539, 541, 550

Aufstieg und Fall der Stadt Mahagonny (Brecht and Weill). *See Rise and Fall of the City of Mahgonny, The*

Aufzeichnungen des Malte Laurids Brigge, Die (Rilke). *See Notebooks of Malte Laurids Brigge, The*

August 1914 (Solzhenitsyn), **10**:*1417*

Auguste Rodin (Rilke), **9**:1283, 1292

Aunt Julia and the Scriptwriter (Vargas Llosa), **11**:1552, 1558, 1559, 1565–66

Aunt's Story, The (White), **12**:1653, 1659, 1664–65

Aura (Fuentes), **3**:339, 344, 345, 356–57, 358

"Author's notes" series (Conrad), **2**:255

"Author's Prologue" (Thomas), **11**:1521

Autobiography of My Mother (Kincaid), **6**:750, 756–58

Autres, Les (Sartre). *See No Exit*

Autumn of the Patriarch, The (García Márquez), **3**:411, 412, 414, 428

Autumn Quail (Mahfouz), **6**:828–29, 833, 834, 836

"Averroës' Search" (Borges), **1**:122, *123*

"Avventura di un soldato, L'" (Calvino), **2**:153

Awlad haratina (Mahfouz). *See Children of Gebalawi*

Babbling April (Greene), **4**:497

"Babette's Feast" (Dinesen), **3**:300, 306–7

"Babylon Lottery, The" (Borges), **1**:122

Bacchae, The (Euripides), **1**:76

Bacchae of Euripides, The (Euripides), **10**:1425, 1427, 1429

Bachelor of Arts, The (Narayan), **8**:1042

Back to Methuselah (Shaw), **10**:1358, 1361, 1365, 1375–76

Baines Avenue Way (Dangarembga), **2**:268

Bald Soprano, The (Ionesco), **5**:619, 622, 623, 624, *625*, 627, 628–30

"Ballad of Mack the Knife, The" (Brecht and Weill), **1**:*135*

Ballad of Peckham Rye, The (Spark), **11**:1453

Bapsi Sidhwa Omnibus (Sidhwa), **10**:1380

Baqi min al-zaman sa'a, Al- (Mahfouz), **6**:834

Baron in the Trees, The (*Barone rampante, Il*) (Calvino), **2**:153–54

Baroque Concert (Carpentier), **2**:183

Bassarids, The (Auden and Kallman; libretto), **1**:76

Baumgartner's Bombay (Desai), **2**:280, 281, 282, 283, 285–86

Bayn al-qasrayn (Mahfouz), **6**:832, 836, 842

Bayt sayye'al-sum'a (Mahfouz), **6**:831

"Beautiful Lofty Things" (Yeats), **12**:1714

"Beautiful Suit, The" (Wells), **12**:1641

Beauty and Sadness (Kawabata), **5**:696, 697, 698

"Before the Flood" (Brecht), **1**:126

"Before the Law" (Kafka), **5**:670

Beggar, The (Mahfouz), **6**:833

Beggar's Opera, The (Gay), **1**:135; **4**:558; **10**:1427

Beggar's Opera, The (Havel), **4**:539, 541, 558

Beginning and the End, The (Mahfouz), **6**:831, 836

Being and Nothingness (Sartre), **10**:1335–36, 1338, 1344–45

Bekenntnisse des Hochstaplers Felix Krull (Mann), **7**:873, 874

Bell, The (Murdoch), **7**:970, 982–83

Beloved Returns (*Lotte in Weimar*) (Mann), **7**:874

Bend in the River, A (Naipaul), **2**:233; **8**:1017, 1019, 1020, 1021, 1023, *1025*, 1028–30, 1032

Bend Sinister (Nabokov), **7**:992, 1002, *1003*, 1005

Beneath the Wheel (Hesse), **5**:585, 589, 591, 597–98

Beowulf (Anglo-Saxon epic), **1**:66; **11**:1533

Beowulf (Heaney translation), **4**:560, 562

Beowulf: The Monsters and the Critics (Tolkien), **11**:1532, 1533

Betrachtung (Kafka), **5**:662, 664, 676

Betrachtungen eines Unpolitischen (Mann), **7**:872, 873, 876

Better Class of Person, A: An Autobiography 1929–1956 (Osborne), **8**:1134

Between Life and Death (Gao), **3**:388

Between Right and Right (Yehoshua), **12**:1720, 1721

Between the Acts (Woolf), **12**:1677, 1687, 1691–92

Beware Soul Brother and Other Poems (Achebe), **1**:24

Beyond Belief (Naipaul), **8**:1021

Bi'an (Gao), **3**:382

Bible
    as Brecht influence, **1**:126, 133
    as Dinesen influence, **3**:301
    as Graves influence, **4**:487
    Joseph story, **7**:889
    as Kincaid influence, **6**:752
    as Paton influence, **9**:1188–89, 1190

as Soyinka influence, **10**:1429

as Spark influence, **11**:1458, 1460

Bidaya wa nihaya (Mahfouz), **6**:831, 836

Big Fellow, The (O'Connor), **8**:1096

Big Mama's Funeral (García Márquez), **3**:411, 412, 415, 426

Big Toys (White), **12**:1663

Billy Budd (Forster and Crozier; libretto), **3**:*321, 325*

"Blackberry-Picking" (Heaney), **4**:569

Black Box (Oz), **9**:1161

Black Hermit, The (Ngũgĩ), **8**:1074, 1075

Black Mischief (Waugh), **12**:1592, 1593

"Black Notebook" (Lessing), **6**:796

Black Obelisk, The (Remarque), **9**:1221, 1224

Black Prince, The (Murdoch), **7**:965, 973, 977, 978–80

Black Swan, The (Mann), **7**:873, 889

"Black Tower, The" (Yeats), **12**:1714

"Bliss" (Mansfield), **7**:905–6

Bliss, and Other Stories (Mansfield), **7**:895, 896

Blood Knot, The (Fugard), **3**:361–62, 366

Blood Wedding (Lorca), **3**:394, 397, 398, 406

"Blue Notebook" (Lessing), **6**:796

"Boarding House, The" (Joyce), **5**:649

Bodas de Sangre (García Lorca). *See Blood Wedding*

Boesman and Lena (Fugard), **3**:359, 362, 366, *367*

"Bog Queen" (Heaney), **4**:568

Bones of Contention and Other Stories (O'Connor), **8**:1096, 1108

Bonheur d'occasion (Roy). *See Tin Flute, The*

Book of Hours, The (Rilke), **9**:1282, 1283, 1288, 1290, 1293, 1294

Book of Images (Rilke), **9**:1283

Book of Lost Tales, The (Tolkien), **11**:1532, 1533, 1547

Book of Poems (García Lorca), **3**:398

"Borges and I" (Borges), **1**:121

Born Naked (Mowat), **7**:*930*

Box Man, The (Abe), **1**:20

Boyhood: Scenes from Provincial Life (Coetzee), **2**:229, 242, 243, *243*

Brass Butterfly, The (Golding), **4**:440, 444

Brave New World (Huxley), **5**:601, 604, 605, 608, 610, 612–14; **8**:1119

Bread and Butter Women (White), **12**:1662

Break My Heart (Golding: radio play), **4**:440

Bride, The (Sidhwa), **10**:1379, 1382, 1386, *1389*, 1396–98

Bride Price, The (Emecheta), **3**:310, 311, 313

Brideshead Revisited (Waugh), **12**:1589, 1592, 1593, 1594, 1595, 1596, 1597, 1598, 1599–1602, 1604, 1605

"Brief an den Vater" (Kafka), **5**:660–61, 662

Briefe an einen jungen Dichter (Rilke), **9**:1292–93

Brief History of Chinese Fiction, A (Chou), **2**:211

Brief History of Imbecility, A (Takamura), **11**:1503, 1505, 1507, 1510

Brief History of Imbecility, A: Poetry and Prose of Takamura Kōtarō (Satō translation), **11**:1506

Briefing for a Descent into Hell (Lessing), **6**:792

Brighton Rock (Greene; novel), **4**:495, 498, 500, 503, 505–7

Brighton Rock (Greene; screenplay), **4**:497, 502

Bring Larks and Heroes (Keneally), **6**:727, 728, 735

Buddenbrooks: The Decline of a Family (Mann), **7**:869, 872, 873, 875, 879–82, 883

Buddha (Kazantzakis), **5**:706, 708

Buile Suibhne (Irish story), **4**:573

Burger's Daughter (Gordimer), **4**:461, 463, 468–70, 475

Buried Mirror, The (Fuentes), **3**:344

Burmese Days (Orwell), **8**:1111, 1112, 1115, 1129

Burning Wheel, The (Huxley), **5**:603, 604, 608

Burnt Ones, The (White), **12**:1655

Burnt-Out Case, A (Greene), **4**:499, 500, 503, 510–12

"Burrow, The" (Kafka), **5**:662, 666

Bus Stop, The (Gao), **3**:379, 382, 385–86, 387, 388

Butterfly's Evil Spell, The (García Lorca), **3**:398

Caesar and Cleopatra (Shaw), **10**:1360, 1363, 1374–75

Cahier d'un retour au pays natal (Césaire). *See Notebook of a Return to the Native Land*

Cairo Trilogy, The (*Al-Thulathiyya*) (Mahfouz), **6**:825, 826, 828, 829, 830, 832, 833, 834, 842–44

Caitaani Mutharaba-ini (Ngũgĩ), **8**:1074, 1075, 1092

Caligula (Camus), **2**:161, 162, 163

Call to Arms (Chou), **2**:211, 212, 215–16, 218, 218–19, 219

Cancer Ward (Solzhenitsyn), **10**:1403, 1408, 1412–18, 1419

Canción de gesta (Neruda), **8**:1068–69

"Canción de la fiesta, La" (Neruda), **8**:1057

Canciones (García Lorca), **3**:408

Candida (Shaw), **10**:1360, 1362–63

Candide (Voltaire), **4**:534

Canopus in Argos series (Lessing), **6**:789, 791, 793, 796, 797–99

Canterbury Tales (Chaucer; Coghill transl.), **11**:1538

"Canto de amor para Stalingrado" (Neruda), **8**:1060

Canto general (Neruda), **8**:1060, 1061, 1063, 1066, 1069

"Canto general de Chile" (Neruda), **8**:1060

Cantos ceremoniales (Neruda), **8**:1069

Capital (Marx), **10**:1358, *1410*

Capodistria (Kazantzakis), **5**:708

Captain and the Enemy, The (Greene), **4**:495, 503

Captain Brassbound's Conversion (Shaw), **10**:1360

Captain Pantoja and the Special Service (Vargas Llosa), **11**:1558–59

Captain's Tiger, The (Fugard), **3**:362, 363, 374

Captain's Verses, The (Neruda), **8**:1059

"Capuchin from Toutes-Aides, The" (Roy), **10**:1313–14

"Caracola" (García Lorca), **3**:408

"Cardinal's First Tale, The" (Dinesen), **3**:307

"Cares of a Family Man, The" (Kafka), **5**:668

Carnival: Entertainments and Posthumous Tales (Dinesen), **3**:298

"Casada infidel, La" (García Lorca), **3**:401

Casa de Bernarda Alba, La (García Lorca), **3**:389, 395, 401–3

Casa verde, La (Vargas Llosa). *See Green House, The*

Cashier, The (Roy), **10**:1305, 1307, 1310–12

Castaway, The (Walcott), **11**:1570

Castle, The (Kafka), **4**:538; **5**:662, 665, 666, 673, 674, 674–76, 676

Catastrophe (Beckett), **4**:540

Catcher in the Rye, The (Salinger), **4**:446

Cathleen Ni Houlihan (Yeats), **12**:1698, 1699, 1715–16

Caucasian Chalk Circle, The (Brecht), **1**:126, 133, 141–42

"Celestial Omnibus, The" (Forster), **3**:330, 336, *337*

Celtic Twilight, The (Yeats), **12**:1696

Ceremonial Songs (Neruda), **8**:1069

Ceremony (Silko), **5**:690

"Cervantes, or the Critique of Reading" (Fuentes), **3**:344, 345

"Chac Mool" (Fuentes), **3**:*342*, 343

Chairs, The (Ionesco), **5**:622, 624, 627

Chamber Music (Joyce), **5**:637, 638, 644, 653

Chance (Conrad), **2**:248, 250, 252, 25229

Change of Skin, A (Fuentes), **3**:344, 345

Chant écarlate, Le (Bâ). *See Scarlet Song*

Chant of Jimmie Blacksmith, The (Keneally), **6**:728, 729, 734, 735, 740–42

Chant of Jimmie Blacksmith, The (Keneally; screenplay), **6**:729

Chase, The (Carpentier), **2**:*183*, 184, 185, *185*

"Chaucer as Philologist: The Reeve's Tale" (Tolkien), **11**:1533

"Cheese Museum, The" (Calvino), **2**:156

Cherry Orchard, The (Chekhov), **10**:1375

Chezhan (Gao). *See Bus Stop, The*

Chhelebela (Tagore), **11**:1486

Chieko and Other Poems of Takamura Kōtarō (Satō translation), **11**:1506

Chieko Poems, The (Takamura; Peters translation), **11**:1506–7

"Chieko Riding the Wind" (Takamura), **11**:*1509*

Chieko shō (Takamura), **11**:1501, 1503, 1505, 1506, 1507, 1508–9, 1510

Chieko shō sono go (Takamura), **11**:1501, 1503, 1505, 1506, 1507, 1509

Chieko's Sky (Takamura; Furuta translation), **11**:1506, 1507

Chike and the River (Achebe), **1**:28

Children of Gebalawi (Mahfouz), **6**:825, 828, 838–41

Children of My Heart (Roy), **10**:1305, 1315

Children of Violence series (Lessing), **6**:790, 791, 794, 795

Child's Christmas in Wales, A (Thomas), **11**:1524–26

Choice of Enemies, A (Richler), **9**:1265, 1267, 1277

"Christening, The" (Lawrence), **6**:773

Christopher Unborn (Fuentes), **3**:344

Christ Re-Crucified (Kazantzakis). *See Greek Passion, The*

Chronicle of a Death Foretold (García Márquez), **3**:412, 414, 426, 428

Chronicles of Narnia (Lewis), **11**:1538, 1540

Chronicles of Narnia, The (Lewis), **6**:806, 808, 810, *812*, 813, *816*, 818, *819*, 820

"Church and State" (Yeats), **12**:1703

"Churning Day" (Heaney), **4**:569

Chute, La (Camus). *See Fall, The*

"Ciaula Discovers the Moon" (Pirandello), **9**:1214–15, 1216

Cien anos de soledad (García Márquez). *See One Hundred Years of Solitude*

Cien sonetas del amor (Neruda), **8**:1060, 1061

"Circe" manuscript (Joyce), **5**:655

"Circular Ruins, The" (Borges), **1**:117, 119

Città invisibili, Le (Calvino), **2**:151, 154, 157–58

Ciudad y los perros, La (Vargas Llosa). *See Time of the Hero, The*

Claudius the God and His Wife Messalina (Graves), **4**:477, 479, 480, 482, 484, 488–91

"Clay" (Joyce), **5**:649

"Clearances" (Heaney), **4**:565, 566

Clear Light of Day (Desai), **2**:277, 278, 280, 281, 282, 284–85

Clergyman's Daughter, A (Orwell), **8**:1112, 1115

Close Quarters (Golding), **4**:445, 456

"Cobweb's Touch in the Dark, A" (Soyinka), **10**:1436

Cocksure (Richler), **9**:1262, 1263, 1264, 1273–74

Collected Essays (Orwell), **8**:1129

Collected Letters (Thomas), **11**:*1518*

Collected Letters of Wilfred Owen (H. Owen and Bell, ed.), **8**:1150

Collected Poems (Auden; Mendelson ed.), **1**:67

Collected Poems of Dylan Thomas, 1934–1952, The, **11**:1514, 1516, 1520–21

Collected Shorter Poems 1927–1957 (Auden), **1**:67

Collected Works (Guillén), **4**:520

Collected Works (Synge), **11**:1466

Collected Works of Oscar Wilde, The, 7:920

Collected Works of W. B. Yeats, The (Finneran and Harper, ed.), 12:1711

Collection Two (O'Connor), 8:1097

"Collier's Wife, A" (Lawrence), 6:773

"Colonel's Photograph, The" (Ionesco), 5:633

Comedians, The (Greene; novel), 4:499, 503, 515

Comedians, The (Greene; screen-play), 4:497, 502

Comforters, The (Spark), 11:1448, 1449, 1458, 1459–60

Coming Up for Air (Orwell), 8:1113, 1115

Common Chord, The (O'Connor), 8:1096, 1097

Common Reader, The: (Woolf), 12:1677, 1680–81

"Communist to Others, A" (Auden), 1:61

Complete Poems (Graves), 4:486–88

Complete Works (Césaire), 1:200; 2:200

"Conceptions of Travel in American Cinema" (Murakami), 7:957

Conclusive Evidence (Nabokov). See Speak Memory

Condemned of Altona, The (Sartre), 10:1338, 1340, 1353

Condition humaine, La (Malraux), 2:166

Condition humaine, La (Malraux). See Man's Fate

"Cone, The" (Wells), 12:1640

Confederates (Keneally), 6:728

Conference of Birds, The (Sufi poem), 10:1330

Confessions of a Mask (Mishima), 7:907, 910, 911, 922

Confessions of Felix Krull, Confidence Man (Mann), 7:873, 874

Conquerors, The (Les conquéants) (Malraux), 6:845, 847, 848, 853, 854, 855, 856–58

Conservationist, The (Gordimer), 4:461, 464, 467–68

Constantine Palaiologos (Kazantzakis), 5:708

Conversation in the Cathedral (Vargas Llosa), 11:1557

Cooley (Weller), 12:1614, 1616, 1627

Coral Island (Ballantyne), 4:446

"Cordilleras" (Neruda), 8:1069

Coronel no tiene quien le escriba, El (García Márquez). See No One Writes to the Colonel

Così è, se vi pare (Pirandello), 9:1203, 1208

Cosmicomics (Le Cosmicomiche) (Calvino), 2:151, 154, 155–56

"Counterparts" (Joyce), 5:649

Countess Cathleen, The (Yeats), 12:1699, 1702, 1705

Country Doctor, A (Kafka), 5:662

"Country of the Blind, The" (Wells), 12:1640–41

Country Sentiment (Graves), 4:486

Crab Apple Jelly (O'Connor), 8:1096

Cracking India (Sidhwa), 10:1377, 1378, 1380, 1382, 1385, 1388, 1390–93

film version, 10:1382, 1386, 1387

"Creative Unity" (Tagore), 11:1492

Crepusculario (Neruda), 8:1057

"Crime of S. Karma, The" (Abe), 1:19, 20

"Crist" (Cynewulf), 11:1531

Crome Yellow (Huxley), 5:603, 604, 608, 615, 616

Cronaca di una more annunciata (García Márquez). See Chronicle of a Death Foretold

"Crossbreed, A" (Kafka), 5:670

Cross Purposes (also The Misunderstanding) (Camus), 2:162, 177

Crossways (Yeats), 12:1701, 1702

Crow Comes Last, The (Calvino), 2:156

Crow Eaters, The (Sidhwa), 10:1379–80, 1385, 1393, 1395–96

Cry, the Beloved Country (Paton), 9:1179, 1180, 1181, 1182, 1183, 1186, 1187, 1189, 1190, 1191, 1192–95, 1197

Cry, the Peacock (Desai), 2:280, 281, 282

Cuadernos de Don Rigoberto, Los (Vargas Llosa), 11:1559

Cuchulain of Muirthemne (Irish myth), 11:1469

Curate's Friend, The (Forster), 3:326

Cure at Troy, The (Heaney), 4:562, 564

"Curse, The" (Synge), 11:1472

"Cyclical Night, The" (Borges), 1:121

Daily Daily, The (Guillén), 4:520, 526

Dai-yon kampyoki (Abe), 1:14, 20

Dance, Dance, Dance (Murakami), 7:959, 961–62

Dance of Death, The (Auden), 1:61

Dance of the Forests, A (Soyinka), 10:1423, 1424, 1427

"Dancing Girl of Izu, The" (Kawabata), 5:693, 694, 696, 698, 700

"Danny" (Synge), 11:1472, 1473

Darkness (Mukherjee), 7:940, 941

Darkness Visible (Golding), 4:445, 448, 455–56, 456

Dark Room, The (Narayan), 8:1042, 1048

Daughter of Fortune (Allende), 1:44, 46, 48, 55–56, 57

Day is Breaking (Kazantzakis), 5:705, 712

Day of the Dog, The (Weller), 12:1607, 1610, 1611, 1612, 1616, 1618, 1620–22

Days and Nights in Calcutta (Mukherjee and Blaise), 7:940, 949–50

Days of Wrath, The (Malraux), 6:848, 849, 861

"Day They Burned the Books, The" (Rhys), 9:1240, 1257

"Dead, The" (Joyce), 5:648, 649, 650–51

"Dead Dingo" (Weller), 12:1609, 1611, 1617

"Dead Fox Hunter, The" (Graves), 4:487

"Dead Man, The" (Borges), 1:117

Dead Roses (Weller), 12:1618

"Death and the Compass" (Borges), 1:116–17, 119

Death and the Compass (Borges), 1:109, 120

Death and the King's Horseman (Soyinka), 10:1427

Death in the Andes (Vargas Llosa), 11:1558

Death in Venice (Mann), 7:869, 870, 871, 873, 876, 882–84, 889

Death of a Naturalist (Heaney), 4:561, 562, 564, 565, 566, 569–70, 571

"Death of a Naturalist" (Heaney), 4:566–67

Death of Artemio Cruz, The (Fuentes), **3:**344, 345, 347, 352, *353*, 354–55

"Death of the Old Man" (Yehoshua), **12:**1718–19, 1720

Deaths and Entrances (Thomas), **11:**1514, 1515, 1526

"Debbie Go Home" (Paton), **9:**1195

"Decadence" (Takamura), **11:***1503*

"de Cats Family" (Dinesen), **3:**295

Decline and Fall (Waugh), **12:**1591, 1592, 1595, 1596, 1598, 1604

Decolonising the Mind: The Politics of Language in African Literature (Ngũgĩ), **8:**1074, 1076, 1082, 1090

Decorations of the Emotions (Kawabata), **5:**694

Defense, The (Nabokov), **7:**992

Deirdre of the Sorrows (Synge), **11:**1469, 1471, 1481

Déjàvu (Osborne), **8:**1134, 1140

"Deluge at Norderney, The" (Dinesen), **3:**302, 304

Demian (Sinclair; Hesse pseud.), **5:**586, 589, 591, 592–94, 595, 598

Démon de l'absolu, Le (Malraux unfinished novel), **6:**861

Descent into Hell (Williams), **6:**806

Descent of the Dove, The (Williams), **1:**61, 63

"Description of a Struggle" (Kafka), **5:**662, 664

Desirable Daughters (Mukherjee), **7:**940

Despair (Nabokov), **7:**992

Desperate People, The (Mowat), **7:**929, 930

Destination Biafra (Emecheta), **3:***311*, 312

Detained: A Writer's Prison Diary (Ngũgĩ), **8:**1074, 1076

Détresse et l'enchantement (Roy), **10:**1305, 1314, *1515*

"Deutsches Requiem" (Borges), **1:**122

Devi Bhagawatam (Hindu epic), **8:**1044

Devil and the Good Lord, The (Sartre), **10:**1353

Devil on the Cross (Ngũgĩ), **8:**1074, 1075, 1092

Devil's Disciple, The (Shaw), **10:**1360, 1363

"Dialogue of the Dead" (Borges), **1:**122

Diamond Dust: Stories (Desai), **2:**281, 286

Diaries of Jane Somers, The (Lessing), **6:**789, 796–97

Diary of a Good Neighbour, The (Lessing), **6:**791

"Diary of a Madman" (Chou), **2:**211–12, 213, 215, 216–18, 219, 221

"Diary of a Madman" (Gogol), **2:**217

"Diary of My Sixteenth Year" (Kawabata), **5:**694

Dictionary of National Biography (Stephen, ed.), **12:**1674

"Digging" (Heaney), **4:**569–70

Dimetos (Fugard), **3:**362, 363

"Dinosaurs, The" (Calvino), **2:**155

Dirty Hands (Sartre), **10:**1340, 1352

Discourse on Colonialism (*Discours sur le colonialisme*) (Césaire), **2:**200, *201*, 202–3

Disgrace (Coetzee), **2:**226, *226*, 228, *228*, 229, 231, 234, 240–42

Dispatch Edition (samizdat publication), **4:**548

"Distance of the Moon, The" (Calvino), **2:**155

Disturbing the Peace (Havel and Hvízdala), **4:**546–47

"Ditty of First Desire" (García Lorca), **3:***391*

Divine Comedy (Dante), **4:**567

Doctor and the Devils, The (Thomas; screenplay), **11:**1526, *1527*

Doctor Faustus (*Doktor Faustus*) (Mann), **4:**554; **7:**873, 874, 878, 888, 889

Doctor's Dilemma, The (Shaw), **10:**1355, 1361, 1363, 1375

Doctors of Philosophy (Spark), **11:**1448

Documents Relating to the Sentimental Agents in the Volyen Empire (Lessing), **6:**798

Dog Who Wouldn't Be, The (Mowat), **7:**936

Doktor Faustus (Mann), **4:**554

Dolce et decorum est (Owen), **8:**1148–49

Doll's House, A (Ibsen), **11:**1477

Domestic Relations (O'Connor), **8:**1097

Doña Rosita the Spinster (*Doña Rosita la soltera*) (García Lorca), **3:**397

"Do Not Go Gentle into That Good Night" (Thomas), **11:**1511, 1516, *1520*, 1521

Don Quixote (Cervantes), **1:**116, 120; **3:**345, 354, 356, 401

Don't Call It Night (Oz), **9:**1165, 1169, *1170*, 1171–72, 1174

"Door in the Wall, The" (Wells), **12:**1641

Door into the Dark (Heaney), **4:**561, 562, 565–66, 571

Doors of Perception, The (Huxley), **5:**604, 608, 617–18

Dōtei (Takamura), **11:**1501, 1503, 1505, 1506, 1508, 1510

Double Man, The (Auden), **1:**65

Double Tongue, The (Golding), **4:**441, 444

Double Yoke (Emecheta), **3:**312, 313, *316*

Dove of a Popular Flight, The, (Guillén), **4:**519, 525–26

"Dover Beach" (Arnold), **1:**72

Down and Out in Paris and London (Orwell), **8:**1112, 1115, 1119

"Dreamers, The" (Dinesen), **3:**302, 304

"Dreaming Child, The" (Dinesen), **3:**300

"Dreaming Child, The" (Pinter screenplay), **3:**300

Dream of Fair to Middling Women (Beckett), **1:**89–90, 94

Dream on Monkey Mountain (Walcott), **11:**1569–70, 1578–80

Dreamtigers (Borges), **1:**119, 121, 122, 123

"Dreamtigers" (Borges), **1:**119

Dreamtigers (Borges), **1:**119, 121, 122, 123

Drei Kameraden (Remarque), **9:**1220, 1224, 1235

Driver's Seat, The (Spark), **11:**1462

Drum, The (Achebe), **1:**29

Drums in the Night (Brecht), **1:**127

Dubliners (Joyce), **5:**637, 638, 639, 640, 641, 643, 648–51, 653; **12:**1707

"Duel, The" (Conrad), **2:**262
film adaptation, **2:**249

Duino Elegies (Rilke), **9:**1279, 1283, 1286–87, 1288, 1289, 1290, 1292, 1293, 1294

Dusklands (Coetzee), **2:**227, 229, 231, 234

Dutch Interior (O'Connor), **8:**1096, 1097

Dyer's Hand, The (Auden), **1:**62

Dylan Thomas Companion, A (Ackerman), **11:**1527

"Early Purges, The" (Heaney), **4:**569

East, West (Rushdie), **10:**1321, 1322

"East and West" (Tagore), **11:**1492

"Easter 1916" (Yeats), **12:**1700, 1710, 1712

Ecué-Yamba-O (Carpentier), **2:**182, 183, 193

Edice expedice (samizdat publication), **4:**548

Edice petlice (samizdat publication), **4:**548

Edmund Campion (Waugh), **12:**1592, 1593

Edward the Second (Brecht and Feuchtwanger), **1:***128*

Egyptian Journal, An (Golding), **4:**439

Ehrengard (Dinesen), **3:**295, 298

18 Poems (Thomas), **11:**1512, 1513, 1514, *1518*, 1526

Elder Edda, The: A Selection from the Icelandic (Auden and Taylor; transl.), **1:**66

Electric Light (Heaney), **4:**562, 563

Elegies (Guillén), **4:**519, 525–26

Elegies for Tiny Beings (Ionesco), **5:**623, 626

Elegy for Iris (Bayley), **7:**970, 971, 972

Elegy for Young Lovers (Auden, and Kallman; libretto), **1:**76

Elegy to Jesús Menéndez (Guillén), **4:**519

Elementary Odes (Neruda), **8:**1061, 1062, 1069–70

Elephant Vanishes, The (Murakami), **7:**963

Eleven Poems (Heaney), **4:**559, 561, 562

Elogio de la madrastra (Vargas Llosa), **11:**1559

Elsewhere, Perhaps (Oz), **9:**1165

Emerald Route, The (Narayan), **8:**1040

Eminent Victorians (Strachey), **12:**1685

"Emma Zunz" (Borges), **1:**117

"Empire of the Ants, The" (Wells), **12:**1636, 1640

En attendant Godot (Beckett). *See Waiting for Godot*

Enchafèd Flood, The (Auden), **1:**62

Enchantment and Sorrow: The Autobiography of Gabrielle Roy, **10:**1305, 1314, *1315*

"Encounter, An" (Joyce), **5:**648, 649

Endgame (Beckett), **1:**91, 92, *93*, 96, 102–3

End of the Affair, The (Greene), **4:**499, 500, 502, 513, *514*, 515

End of the Battle, The (Waugh). *See Unconditional Surrender*

"End of the Book" (Synge), **11:**1472

Enfants de ma vie, Ces (Roy), **10:**1305, 1315

English Literature in the Sixteenth Century (Lewis), **6:**806

English Teacher, The (Narayan), **8:**1040, 1042, 1047–49

Enigma of Arrival, The (Naipaul), **8:**1016, 1017, 1021, 1032

Enrico IV (Pirandello). *See Henri IV*

Entertainer, The (Osborne), **8:**1131, *1132*, 1133, 1134, 1135–36, 1139

"Errantry" (Tolkien), **11:**1538

España en el corazón (Neruda), **8:**1060

Espoir, L' (Malraux), **6:**848, 849, 861

Essays Presented to Charles Williams (Lewis, ed.), **11:**1540

"Essential Gesture, The" (Gordimer), **4:**475

Essential Gesture, The (Gordimer), **4:**473, 475

Este pueblo de mierda (García Márquez). *See In Evil Hour*

Étranger, L' (Camus). *See Stranger, The*

Être et le néant, L' (Sartre). *See Being and Nothingness*

Eugene Onegin (Pushkin; Nabokov translation), **7:**989, 990

Eva Luna (Allende), **1:***44*, 46

"Eveline" (Joyce), **5:**637, 649

Evening without Décor, An (Soyinka), **10:**1422

"Everlasting Voices, The" (Yeats), **12:**1710

"Ex-Africa" (Dinesen), **3:**297

Exile and the Kingdom Exil et le royaume, L' (Camus), **2:**163, 176

Exiles (Joyce), **5:**640, 644, 645–47, 650, 653

Exit the King (Ionesco), **5:**623, 624, 626, 627, 633–34

film version, **5:**621

Experiment in Autobiography (Wells), **12:**1633

Explosion in a Cathedral (Carpentier), **2:**183, 184, 191–93

Extravagaria (Estravagario) (Neruda), **8:**1059, 1060

Eye, The (Nabokov), **7:**994

Eyeless in Gaza (Huxley), **5:**604, 605, 608, 615–16

Eye of the Storm, The (White), **12:**1656

Fabian Essays in Socialism (Shaw), **10:**1359

Face of Another, The (Abe), **1:**17–18

Face of Another, The (Abe: screenplay), **1:**13, *17*

"Face of Evil, The" (O'Connor), **8:**1101

Face to Face (Gordimer), **4:**464

"Facing the Forests" (Yehoshua), **12:**1726

Facing the Forests (Yehoshua), **12:**1726

Fairly Honorable Defeat, A (Murdoch), **7:**974

Fairy and Folk Tales of the Irish Peasantry (Yeats), **12:**1696

Fall, The (Camus), **2:**159, 161, *161*, 162, 163, 167, 174–76

Fallen Idol, The (Greene), **4:**497, 502

Fallen Idol, The (Greene; screenplay), **4:**502

"Fan Ainong" (Chou), **2:**218

Fanfarlo and Other Verse, The (Spark), **11:**1449

"Farfetched Fables" (Shaw), **10:**1365

Farmer Giles of Ham (Tolkien), **11:**1532, 1533, 1548

Fasting, Feasting (Desai), **2:**277, 280, 281, 282, 283, 286

"Fate of the Daisy Lee, The" (Murdoch), **7:**967, 969

Faust (Goethe), **4:**554; **7:**888, 889

Faust legend, **4:**554

Havel modernization, **4:**554–56

Mann and, **4:**554; **7:**878, *888*, 889

"Fear" (Mahfouz), **6:**831

Feast of the Goat, The (Vargas Llosa), **11:**1554, 1558, 1566

Fellowship of the Ring, The (Tolkien), **11:**1531, 1543

"Fern Hill" (Thomas), **11:**1524, 1526

Fervor of Buenos Aires (*Fervor de Buenos Aires*) (Borges), **1**:107, 108, 110, 115

Fiabe italiane (Calvino), **2**:151

Ficciones (Borges), **1**:107, 116–17, 119, 120, 121–22

Field Work (Heaney), **4**:562, 563, 566, 572

Fiesta del chivo, La (Vargas Llosa), **11**:1554, 1558, 1566

Film (Beckett; screenplay), **1**:91

Fima (Oz), **9**:*1159*

Fin de partie (Beckett). *See Endgame*

Finders Keepers: Selected Prose, 1971–2001 (Heaney), **4**:564

Finnegans Wake (Joyce), **1**:89, 91; **5**:635, 639, 640, 643, 650, 653, 656–58

Fire Down Below (Golding), **4**:445, 456

Fire on the Mountain (Desai), **2**:280, 282, 283, 286

First Circle, The (Solzhenitsyn), **10**:1401, 1419

"First Confession" (O'Connor), **8**:1106–7

First Man, The (Camus), **2**:163, 176–77

First Men in the Moon, The (Wells), **12**:1632

"Fish" (Lawrence), **6**:770

Five (Lessing), **6**:799

Five Modern No Plays (Mishima), **7**:911

Five Seasons (Yehoshua), **12**:1720, 1723

Flag on the Island, A (Naipaul), **8**:1016

Flaws in the Glass: A Self-Portrait (White), **12**:1655, 1656, 1671–72

Flies, The (Sartre), **10**:1336, 1340, 1348–50

Flight from the Enchanter, The (Murdoch), **7**:974, 980–82

Flight of the Inca, The (Vargas Llosa), **11**:1552

Flotsam (Remarque), **9**:1220, 1224, 1237

"Flowering of the Strange Orchid, The" (Wells), **12**:1641

Flush (Woolf), **12**:1681

Flute, The (Achebe), **1**:29

Foe (Coetzee), **2**:229, 231, 234, 237, 237, 238

Food of the Gods, The (Wells), **12**:1632

Forbidden Colors (Mishima), **7**:910, 911, 916, 923–25

Forewords and Afterwords (Auden), **1**:68

"Forging the Swords" (Chou), **2**:212, 223–24

Forgiveness of Sins, The (Williams), **11**:1540

"Forms of a Legend" (Borges), **1**:121

"For the Commander of the 'Eliza'" (Heaney), **4**:569

For the Time Being (Auden), **1**:60, 65

"For W. H. A." (Tolkien), **1**:66

Fountain and Tomb (Mahfouz), **6**:835

Fountain of Magic, The (O'Connor translation), **8**:1096, *1102*

"Fountain of Mankind" (Takamura), **11**:*1504*

"Four Archetypes" (Soyinka), **10**:1436

Four-Gated City, The (Lessing), **6**:792, 793, 794, 795

Four Plays (White), **12**:1662

"Fourth Stage, The" (Soyinka), **10**:1429

Franz Kafka: Representative Man (Karl), **5**:668

Fraticides, The (Kazantzakis), **5**:711, 712, 718

"Frederick the Great and the Grand Coalition" (Mann), **7**:873

Freedom or Death (Kazantzakis), **5**:704, 708, 710, 711, 712, 717–18

Free Fall (Golding), **4**:447, 454

"Freud" (Mann), **7**:872

Friedrich und die grosse Koalition (Mann), **7**:873

Friends (Abe), **1**:18–19

Friends (Abe; screenplay), **1**:13

"Frog and the Golden Ball, The" (Graves), **4**:488

Ftohúlis tou Théu, O (Kazantzakis), **5**:708, 709, 717

Fugitives, The (Gao), **3**:381

Full Circle (Remarque), **9**:1221

Full Moon in March, A (Yeats), **12**:1715

Fu Mattia Pascal, Il (Pirandello). *See Late Mattia Pascal, The*

"Funeral Rites" (Heaney), **4**:572

"Funes the Memorious" (Borges), **1**:116

Funke Leben, Der (Remarque). *See Spark of Life*

Fun with Dick and Jane (Richler; screenplay), **9**:1264

Fury (Rushdie), **10**:1321, 1322, 1324, 1330–31

Future in America, The (Wells), **12**:1639

"Gadabouts, The" (Roy), **10**:1313

Galileo (Brecht). *See Life of Galileo, The*

Game of the Parts, The (Pirandello), **9**:1203

Garden of Forking Paths, The (Borges), **1**:107, 116, 120

"Garden of Forking Paths, The" (Borges), **1**:117, 119

Garden Party, The (Havel), **4**:538, 541, 544, 556

"Garden Party, The" (Mansfield), **7**:904–5

Garden Party and Other Stories, The (Mansfield), **7**:895, 896, *900*

General in His Labyrinth, The (*El General en su laberinto*) (García Márquez), **3**:412, 426

George Orwell: A Life (Crick), **8**:1120

"Germans at Meat" (Mansfield), **7**:901–3

Gertrude (*Gertrud*) (Hesse), **5**:589, 591

Geschichten Jaakobs, Die (Mann), **7**:874

Getting Married (Shaw), **10**:1363

Ghare-Baire (Tagore), **11**:1490, 1492, 1494–96

Ghost Is Here, The (Abe), **1**:19–20

Ghosts (Ibsen), **10**:1359

Giara, La (Pirandello), **9**:1215–16

"Gift, The" (Kincaid), **6**:759

Giganti delle montagne, I (Pirandello), **9**:1204

Gioco delle parti, Il (Pirandello), **9**:1203

Giornata d' uno scrutatore, La (Calvino), **2**:156

"Girl" (Kincaid), **6**:758, 760

Girls at War and Other Stories (Achebe), **1**:24

Girls of Slender Means, The (Spark), **11**:1447, 1450

Gitanjali (Tagore), **11**:1489, *1495*, 1496–98

Giving Offense: Essays on Censorship (Coetzee), **2**:242, 244

"Glanmore Sonnets" (Heaney), **4**:566

Glass Bead Game, The (*Glasperlenspiel, Das*) (Hesse), **5**:585, 586, 591, 600

"Glencullen" (Synge), **11**:1472

Glory (Nabokov), **7**:991, 994

Gods, Demons and Others (Narayan), **8**:1042, 1044

"Goethe" (Mann), **7**:872

Going Home (Lessing), **6**:789

Going Home (Weller), **12**:1611, 1611–12, 1612, 1614, 1624, 1627

"Going Home" (Weller), **12**:1624, 1626–27

"Golden Key, The" (MacDonald), **11**:1549

Golden Notebook, The (Lessing), **6**:785, 789, 791, 792, 796–97, 797

Golem, Der (Meyrink), **1**:120

"Goliath and David" (Graves), **4**:487

"Goodbye Marcus, Goodbye Rose" (Rhys), **9**:1257

Good-Bye to All That (Graves), **4**:477, 478, 479, 480, 491, 493–94

Good Conscience, The (Fuentes), **3**:344, 345

Good Morning, Midnight (Rhys), **9**:1242, 1246, 1248, 1249, 1252, *1253*, 1254

Good Person of Setzuan, The (Brecht), **1**:133, 139–40

Gospel of the Brothers Barnabas, The (Shaw), **10**:1375

Gossip from the Forest (Keneally), **6**:728, 734

"Grace" (Joyce), **5**:649

Grain of Wheat, A (Ngũgĩ), **8**:1074, 1075, 1078–79, 1084–86

Grandmother, The (Nemcová), **5**:673

Grandmother's Tale, The (Narayan), **8**:1040, 1052–53

Grass Is Singing, The (Lessing), **6**:785, 789, 791, 793, 800, *801*

"Grauballe Man, The" (Heaney), **4**:568

Great Divorce, The (Lewis), **6**:821–22

Great Shame, The: And the Triumph of the Irish in the English-Speaking World (Keneally), **6**:728, 734, 744, 745, 746

"Great Wall of China, The" (Kafka), **5**:662, 664, 670

Great Zoo, The (Guillén), **4**:526

Greek Passion, The (Kazantzakis), **5**:706, 708, 710, 711, 712, 715, 717

Greek tragedy
    Sartre adaptation, **10**:1348–50
    Soyinka adaptation, **10**:1425, 1427, 1429

Green House, The (Vargas Llosa), **11**:1553, 1554, 1557, 1564–65

Green Sailed Vessel, The (Graves spoken-word album), **4**:487

Grimus (Rushdie), **10**:1320, 1321, 1330

Ground beneath Her Feet, The (Rushdie), **10**:1321, 1322, 1324, 1331

Guerra del fin del mundo, La (Vargas Llosa), **11**:*1554*, 1558

Guerrillas (Naipaul), **8**:1016, 1019, 1020, 1021, 1026–28, 1030, 1032

"Guest, The" (Camus), **2**:176

Guests of the Nation (O'Connor), **8**:1096, 1097

"Guests of the Nation" (O'Connor), **8**:1104–5

Guide, The (Narayan), **8**:1039, 1042, 1050–51

Gulag Archipelago (Solzhenitsyn), **10**:*1400*, 1402, 1405–6, 1419–20

"Gulliver" (Soyinka), **10**:1429, 1436

Gulliver's Travels (Swift), **8**:1119; **10**:1436

Gun for Sale, A (Greene), **4**:500, *502*

Gushi xinbian (Chou). *See Old Stories Retold*

Gute Mensch von Sezuan, Der (Brecht), **1**:133, 139–40

Guy Domville (James), **10**:*1361*

Gypsy Ballads (García Lorca), **3**:397, 399, *400*, 401

Habitante y su esperanza, El (Neruda), **8**:1058

Hablador, El (Vargas Llosa), **11**:1558, 1562–64

"Hacedor, El" (Borges), **1**:119

Hadrat al-muhtaram (Mahfouz), **6**:833

Hako otoko (Abe), **1**:20

Hakufu (Takamura), **11**:1504

Half a Life (Naipaul), **8**:1017, 1019, 1021, 1023

Ham Funeral, The (White), **12**:1662, *1663*

Hamlet (Shakespeare), **7**:979; **9**:1211; **10**:1429

"Hamlet" (Soyinka), **10**:1429, 1436

Hams al-junun (Mahfouz), **6**:828

"Hanazakari no mori" (Mishima), **7**:909

Hanazakari no mori (Mishima), **7**:910, 911

Handful of Dust, A (Waugh), **12**:1592, 1596–97, 1604–5

"Hand in the Grave, A" (Kanafani), **5**:692

"Hanging, A" (Orwell), **8**:1111, 1129

Hangmen Also Die (Brecht; screenplay), **1**:129, *130*

Hanye de xingchen (Gao), **3**:381

Happy Days (Beckett), **1**:91, 92, 93

Happy Death, The (Camus), **2**:177

"Happy Prince, The" (Wilde; Borges translation), **1**:114, 120

Happy Valley (White), **12**:1653, 1655

Harafish, The (Mahfouz), **6**:838, *839*

Hard-Boiled Wonderland and the End of the World, The (Murakami), **7**:961

Haroun and the Sea of Stories (Rushdie), **10**:1321–22, 1331

Harp and the Shadow, The (Carpentier), **2**:183

Harvest of Thorns (Chinodya), **2**:275

Haw Lantern, The (Heaney), **4**:562, 563, 566

Head above Water (Emecheta), **3**:311, 312, 318

Heart and Mind (Guillén), **4**:518

Heartbreak House (Shaw), **10**:1355, 1358, 1361, 1363, 1375

Heart of Darkness (Conrad), **2**:49, 245, 248, 249, 250, 259–60; **4**:446, 470; **8**:1021, *1080*
    film adaptation, **2**:249

Heart of the Matter, The (Greene), **4**:498–99, 500, 502, 503, 507–10

Heather Field, The (Martyn), **12**:1705

Heaven Has No Favorites (Remarque), **9**:1221

Heights of Macchu Picchu, The (Neruda), **8**:1063, 1064–66

Heilige Johanna der Schlachthöfe, Die (Brecht), **1**:132, 133

"Heizer, Der: Ein Fragment" (Kafka), **5**:662, 664, 676

Helena (Waugh), **12**:1592, 1594, 1605–6

"He Mourns for the Change That Has Come upon Him and His Beloved, and Longs for the End of the World" (Yeats), **12**:1702

Henri Christophe (Walcott), **11**:1569, 1570, *1575*

Henry IV (Pirandello), **9**:*1200*, 1202, 1203, *1205*

Herland (Gilman), **3**:317

Hermit, The (Ionesco), **5**:624, 627

"Hermits, The" (Dinesen), **3**:295, 297

"He Wishes for the Cloths of Heaven" (Yeats), **12**:1710

"He Wishes His Beloved Were Dead" (Yeats), **12**:1710

"High Road of Saint James , The" (Carpentier), **2**:187, 193

High Wind in Jamaica (Hughes), **4**:446

Hikayat haritina (Mahfouz), **6**:835

Hill of Evil Counsel, The (Oz), **9**:1161

Himmel kennt heine Günstlinge, Der (Remarque), **9**:1221

Hindu epics, Narayan and, **8**:*1041*, 1042, 1044–45

"Hint of an Explanation, A" (Greene), **4**:500

Historia de Mayta (Vargas Llosa), **11**:1558

History of African Civilization (Froebenius), **2**:196

History of Middle-earth, The (Tolkien), **11**:1533, 1535, 1540, 1547

History of Mr. Polly, The (Wells), **12**:1632, 1636

Hobbit, The (Tolkien), **11**:1529, 1532, 1533, 1534, 1535, 1536, 1537, 1542–43, 1544, 1545, 1548, 1549

Hofmeyr (Paton), **9**:1183, 1184

Hojarasca, La (García Márquez). *See Leaf Storm*

Holder of the World, The (Mukherjee), **7**:940, 943, 950, 952

Holy Place (Fuentes), **3**:344, 345

Holy Sinner, The (Mann), **7**:873

Homage to Catalonia (Orwell), **8**:1109, 1113, *1117*, 1119, *1121*, 1122, 1124–25

Home and Exile (Achebe), **1**:24, 33

Home and the World, The (Tagore), **11**:1490, 1492, 1494–96

Homecoming: Essays on African and Caribbean Literature, Culture and Politics (Ngũgĩ), **8**:1074

Home Sweet Home: My Canadian Album (Richler), **9**:1264

Hondero entusiasta, El (Neruda), **8**:1058

Honorary Consul, The (Greene), **4**:499, 503

"Honour and Arms" (Lawrence). *See* "Prussian Officer, The"

"Hope and the Absurd in the Work of Franz Kafka" (Camus), **5**:667

Hopes and Impediments: Selected Essays, 1965–1987 (Achebe), **1**:24

Horse and Two Goats, A (Narayan), **8**:1040

"Hosting of the Sidhe, The" (Yeats), **12**:1709

"Host of the Air, The" (Yeats), **12**:1709

"Hôte, L'" (Camus), **2**:176

Hotel in Amsterdam, The (Osborne), **8**:1136

Hot Gates, The (Golding), **4**:440

Hothouse by the East River, The (Spark), **11**:1450

House for Mr. Biswas, A (Naipaul), **8**:1016, 1018, *1019*, 1020, 1022, 1024–26

House Gun, The (Gordimer), **4**:461, 463, 472–73

House of Bernarda Alba, The (García Lorca), **3**:389, 395, 401–3

House of the Sleeping Beauties and Other Stories, The (Kawabata), **5**:696

House of the Spirits, The (Allende), **1**:41, 44, 45, 47, 48, 50–52, 53, 54, 56

Howards End (Forster), **3**:320, 322, 323, 326, 330, 334, *335*, 336

How Many Rainbows (Kawabata), **5**:697

How the Leopard Got His Claws (Achebe and Iroaganachi), **1**:28

Hristós ksanastavrónetai, O (Kazantzakis). *See Greek Passion, The*

"Huaijiu" (Chou), **2**:210

Hubb tahta al-matar, Al- (Mahfouz), **6**:835

Huida del Inca, La (Vargas Llosa), **11**:1552

Huis clos (Sartre). *See No Exit*

Hullabaloo in the Guava Orchard (K. Desai), **2**:281

Human Factor, The (Greene), **4**:499

"Hunger" (Lessing), **6**:799

"Hunger Artist, A" (Kafka), **5**:662, 681

Hungerkünstler, Ein: Vier Geschichten (Kafka), **5**:665, 676, 681

Hunting Tigers under Glass: Essays and Reports (Richler), **9**:1264

"Hunt of the Stone" (Soyinka), **10**:1436–37

Hurry On Down (Wain), **11**:1539

Hydra Head (Fuentes), **3**:344

Ibn Battuta's Travels (Arabic classic), **6**:833

Ice-Candy-Man (Sidhwa). *See Cracking India*

I, Claudius (Graves), **4**:477, 479, 480, 488–91

"If all our acts are conditioned behaviour" (Auden), **1**:63

"If I Were Tickled by the Rub of Love" (Thomas), **11**:1526

If on a Winter's Night a Traveler (Calvino), **2**:151

I Have (Guillén), **4**:520, 526

"I hear an army charging upon the land" (Joyce), **5**:638

Ikhtayyi (Habibi), **4**:532, 535

Iliad (Homer; Kazantzakis translation), **5**:708

Iliad (Virgil), **11**:1576, *1577*

Imaginary Homelands (Rushdie), **10**:1321

"Imaginary Homelands" (Rushdie), **10**:1323

Imagistes, Des (anthology), **5**:638

"Immortal, The" (Borges), **1**:117

"Immortal Story, The" (Dinesen), **3**:300, 300278

"Imperial Message, An" (Kafka), **5**:670

Impressions and Landscapes (*Impresiones y paisajes*) (García Lorca), **3**:392

Im Westen nichts Neues (Remarque). *See All Quiet on the Western Front*

Inadmissible Evidence (Osborne), **8**:1131, 1134, 1135, 1136, 1138

In a Free State (Naipaul), **8**:1016, 1018, 1020, 1021, 1023

In a German Pension (Mansfield), **7**:893, 895

In a Green Night (Walcott), **11**:1569

"Incident at Krechetovka Station, An" (Solzhenitsyn), **10**:1418–19

Incomparable Atuk, The (Richler), **9**:1263, 1272–73

Increased Difficulty of Concentration, The (Havel), **4**:541, 544, 557–58

In Custody (Desai), **2**:277, 280, 281, 282, 283

Inde française, L' (Burnouf), lithograph from, **3**:322

India: A Wounded Civilization (Naipaul), **8**:1016

Indian Epics Retold, The (Narayan), **8**:1044

In Evil Hour (García Márquez), **3**:411, 412, 415, 418, 419, 424, 428, *429*, 430

"Inexperienced Ghost, The" (Wells), **12**:1641

Inferno (Dante), **4**:*455*, 573; **10**:1419

Infinite Plan, The (Allende), **1**:*46*, 47, 48, *50*, 57–58

"In Good King Charles's Golden Days" (Shaw), **10**:1365

Inheritors, The (Conrad and Ford), **2**:249

Inheritors, The (Golding), **4**:442, 447, 453

Inklings, The (Carpenter), **11**:1539, 1540–41

"In My Craft or Sullen Art" (Thomas), **11**:1515, 1526

"Innocence of Father Brown, The" (Chesterton), **12**:1600

Innommable, L' (Beckett). *See Unnamable, The*

"In Praise of Limestone" (Auden), **1**:67, 72–74

In Praise of the Stepmother (Vargas Llosa), **11**:1559

Instrument of Thy Peace (Paton), **9**:1183

Intelligent Woman's Guide to Socialism and Capitalism, The (Shaw), **10**:1355, 1358, 1361, 1376

Inter Ice Age Four (Abe), **1**:14, 20

Interpreters, The (Soyinka), **10**:1423, 1424, 1428, 1429, 1432–33

In the Beginning (Shaw), **10**:1375

In the Days of the Comet (Wells), **12**:1632

In the Ditch (Emecheta), **3**:311, 312, 313, 316, 318

In the Heart of the Country (Coetzee), **2**:229, 231

"In the Penal Colony" (Kafka), **5**:662, 664, 680–81; **10**:1436

In the Shadow of the Glen (Synge). *See Shadow of the Glen*

In the Train (O'Connor and Hunt), **8**:1096, 1107–8

"Intruder, The" (Borges), **1**:117

Invención de Morel, La (Bioy Casares), **1**:115

"Investigations of a Dog" (Kafka), **5**:662

Invincibles, The (O'Connor and Hunt), **8**:1096

Invisible Cities (Calvino), **2**:151, 154, 157–58

Invisible Man, The (Wells), **12**:1631, 1635

Invitation to a Beheading, **7**:992

Invitation to a Beheading (Nabokov), **7**:992

Irish Miles (O'Connor), **8**:1096

Island (Huxley), **5**:608, 614–15

Island, The (Fugard), **3**:363

Island of Dr. Moreau, The (Wells), **12**:1631, 1635

Island of Statues, The (Yeats), **12**:1697

Isla Negra: A Notebook (Neruda), **8**:1059, 1061

Italian Folktales (Calvino), **2**:151

"Iurokusai" (Kawabata), **5**:694

"I've Thirty Months" (Synge), **11**:1473

"Ivy Day in the Committee Room" (Joyce), **5**:649

I Will Marry When I Want (Ngũgĩ and Ngũgĩ), **8**:1074, 1075

"Izu no odoriko" (Kawabata). *See* "Dancing Girl of Izu, The"

Jack, or The Submission (Ionesco), **5**:622, 624

Jack Rivers and Me (Radley), **12**:1610

Jackson's Dilemma (Murdoch), **7**:971

Jacob's Room (Woolf), **12**:1677, 1678

Jacob Two-Two and the Dinosaur (Richler), **9**:1264

Jacob Two-Two Meets the Hooded Fang (Richler), **9**:1264

Jaguar Smile, The: A Nicaraguan Journey (Rushdie), **10**:1321, 1331

"Jana Gana Mana Adhinayaka" (Tagore), **11**:1493

Jane Eyre (Brontë), **9**:1248–49, 1254, 1256

    Huxley screenplay, **5**:605, 608

Jar, The (Pirandello), **9**:1215–16

Jardin de senderos que se bifurcan, El (Borges), **1**:107, 116, 120

Jardin des rochers, Le (Kazantzakis), **5**:506

Jasmine (Mukherjee), **7**:940, 948–49

Jefes, Los (Vargas Llosa), **11**:1553, 1554

Jero Chronicles (Soyinka), **10**:1437

Jero's Metamorphosis (Soyinka), **10**:1425

Jiban Smriti (Tagore), **11**:1486

Job, Book of, as Spark influence, **11**:1458, 1460

John Bull's Other Island (Shaw), **10**:1363

"Johnny Blue" (Weller), **12**:1627

"Jonah" (Camus), **2**:176

"Joseph" (Soyinka), **10**:1429, 1436

Joseph and His Brothers (Joseph und seine Brüder) (Mann), **7**:874, 887, 889

Joseph in Egypt (Joseph in Agypten) (Mann), **7**:874

"Josephine the Singer" (Kafka), **5**:662, 668

Joseph the Provider (Joseph der Ernährer) (Mann), **7**:874

Joshua Then and Now (Richler), **9**:1264, *1265*, 1277–78

Joshua Then and Now (Richler; screenplay), **9**:1261, 1263, 1264

Journal of the Plague Year, A (Defoe), **2**:172

"Journey Back to the Source" (Carpentier), **2**:187, 193

Journey of Ibn Fattouma, The (Mahfouz), **6**:833

Journeys among the Dead (Ionesco), **5**:624

Journey to a War (Auden and Isherwood), **1**:*61*, 62, 63

Journey to Ithaca (Desai), **2**:281, 283

Journey to the East, The (Hesse), **5**:591, 598, 600

Journey to the End of the Millennium, A (Yehoshua), **12**:1720

Journey to the West (Chinese classic novel), **2**:213

Joys of Motherhood, The (Emecheta), **3**:309, 313, 315–16

"Judgment, The" (Kafka), **5**:662, 664, 670, 673

Julius Caesar (Shakespeare), **10**:1375

July's People (Gordimer), **4**:461, 462, 463, 470–72

Junge Joseph, Der (Mann), **7**:874

Jungle, The (Sinclair), **4**:459

Jungle Book, The (Kipling), **2**:156

"Jurokusai no nikki" (Kawabata), **5**:694

Kabe (Abe), **1**:13, 19

Kabikahini (Tagore), **11**:1487

Kafka's Narrators (Pascal), **5**:671

Kamera Obskura (Nabokov). *See Laughter in the Dark*

Kangaroo Notebook (*Kangaru noto*) (Abe), **1**:15

Kanjo soshoku (Kawabata; screenplay), **5**:694

Kapetán Mihális, O (Kazantzakis). *See Freedom or Death*

Kapodístrias, O (Kazantzakis), **5**:708

"Karain" (Conrad), **2**:253

Karnak, Al- (Mahfouz), **6**:831

Kaukasische, Der (Brecht). *See Caucasian Chalk Circle, The*

Kaze no uta o kike (Murakami), **7**:955, 957, 961

Keep the Aspidistra Flying (Orwell), **8**:1112, 1115

Kehinde (Emecheta), **3**:312, 318

Kew Gardens (Woolf), **12**:1677

Khan al-khalili (Mahfouz), **6**:833, 835

"Khawf, Al-" (Mahfouz), **6**:831

Kifah Tiba (Mahfouz), **6**:825, 828

Killer, The (Ionesco), **5**:624, 626, 627, 632–33

Kim (Kipling), **7**:967

King, Queen, Knave (*Korol', Dama, Valet*) (Nabokov), **7**:992

Kingdom of This World, The (Carpentier), **2**:183, 184, 187, 187, 188–89

King James Version of Bible, Paton and, **9**:1188–89, 1190

King Jesus (Graves), **4**:491

King of the Great Clock Tower, The (Yeats), **12**:1715

Kipps: The Story of a Simple Soul (Wells), **12**:1631, 1632

Kiroku (Takamura), **11**:1505, 1510

"Kitosch's Story" (Dinesen), **3**:304, 305

Klass and the Devil (Fugard), **3**:362

Kongi's Harvest (Soyinka), **10**:1425, 1427

"Kong Yiji" (Chou), **2**:212, 223

Konstandinos o Palaiológos (Kazantzakis), **5**:708

Kontakion for You Departed (Paton), **9**:1180, 1195

Koto (Kawabata), **5**:696, 697

Krapp's Last Tape (Beckett), **1**:91, 92, 103–4

Ksimeróne (Kazantzakis), **5**:705, 712

"Kuangren riji" (Chou). *See* "Diary of a Madman"

Kurutta ippeji (Kawabata; screenplay), **5**:694, 696

Kyoko's House (Mishima), **7**:912

Labels (Waugh), **12**:1592

Lady Chatterley's Lover (Lawrence), **6**:763, 766, 767–68, 768, 769, 770, 771, 777, 779–81

"Lagarto está Ilorando, El" (García Lorca), **3**:408

"Lagoon, The" (Conrad), **2**:253

"Lake Isle of Innisfree, The" (Yeats), **12**:1702

Lament for Art O'Leary, A (O'Connor translation), **8**:1099

Land and People of South Africa, The (Paton), **9**:1183

Landarzt, Ein: Kleine Erzählungen (Kafka), **5**:662, 676

Landlocked (Lessing), **6**:794

Land of Heart's Desire, The (Yeats), **12**:1698, 1715

Land of the Golden Clouds (Weller), **12**:1611, 1613, 1616, 1618, 1622–24

Largo Desolato (Havel), **4**:540, 541, 544, 557

Last Poems and Two Plays (Yeats), **12**:1714

Last Tales (Dinesen), **3**:298, 307

Last Temptation of Christ, The (Kazantzakis), **5**:703, 707, 708, 711, 716

Late Bourgeois World, The (Gordimer), **4**:461

Late Divorce, A (Yehoshua), **12**:1720, 1722

Late Mattia Pascal, The (Pirandello), **9**:1202, 1203, 1209–11

Laughing Anne (Conrad), **2**:250, 250

Laughter in the Dark (Nabokov), **7**:987, 990, 991, 992, 994, 997, 999, 1005

Lauriers sont coupés, Les (Dujardin), **5**:650

Lawless Roads, The (Greene), **4**:498, 513

Lawley Road and Other Stories (Narayan), **8**:1040

Lawrence and the Arabs (Graves), **4**:480, 492–93

Layali alf-layla (Mahfouz), **6**:833

Lay of the Love and Death of the Cornet Christoph Rilke, The (Rilke), **9**:1293

"Leaf by Niggle" (Tolkien), **11**:1534, 1548–49

Leaf Storm (García Márquez), **3**:411, 412, 415, 425–26

"Learning to be Dead" (Calvino), **2**:157

Leave It to Me (Mukherjee), **7**:940

Leaves of Grass (Whitman), **1**:120; **3**:394

Leben des Galilei (Brecht). *See Life of Galileo, The*

Left Bank and Other Stories, The (Rhys), **9**:1242, 1257

"Legend of the Dead Soldier, The" ("Legende vom toten Soldaten, Die") (Brecht), **1**:126, 127

Lesson, The (Ionesco), **5**:622, 623, 624, 625, 627

Lesson from Aloes, A (Fugard), **3**:359, 362, 363, 365, 371–73, 375

"Letter, The" (Dangarembga), **2**:269

Letters from Africa (Dinesen), **3**:298, 304

Letters from Iceland (Auden and MacNeice), **1**:61, 62, 65

Letters from the Hunt (W. Dinesen), **3**:294

Letters to a Young Poet (Rilke), **9**:1292–93

Letters to Olga (Havel), **4**:537, 544, 546

"Letter to His Father" (Kafka), **5**:660–61, 662

"Letter to Lord Byron" (Auden), **1**:65

Letter to Maurice Thorez (Césaire), **1**:200; **2**:200

"Let Them Call It Jazz" (Rhys), **9**:1257

Letzte Akt, Der (Remarque; screenplay), **9**:1219, 1224

Letzte Station, Die (Remarque), **9**:1221

Lezioni americane: Sei proposte per il prossimo millennio (Calvino), **2**:152

Liberating Bride, The (Yehoshua), **12**:1720

"Library of Babel, The" (Borges), **1**:116, 119

Libro de poemas (García Lorca), **3**:398

Liebe deinen Nächsten (Remarque), **9**:1220, 1224, 1237

Life and Songs (Rilke), **9**:1281, 1283

Life and Times of Michael K, The (Coetzee), **2**:229, *230*, 231, 235–36, 238

Life at the Top (Richler; screenplay), **9**:1262, 1264

"Life for a Life" (Paton), **9**:1195

Life of Galileo, The (Brecht), **1**:129, 130, *131*, 132, *134*, 140

Life to Come, The (Forster), **3**:323, 327

"Light-Years, The" (Calvino), **2**:155

"Limes of Sicily, The" (Pirandello), **9**:1203

"Lines Composed a Few Miles above Tintern Abbey" (Wordsworth), **1**:72

Lingshan (Gao). *See Soul Mountain*

Lion, the Witch and the Wardrobe, The (Lewis), **6**:808, 813, 818, 820; **11**:1538

Lion and the Unicorn, The (Orwell), **8**:1115

Lis wal-kilab, Al- (Mahfouz), **6**:833

Literatura y conciencia política en América Latina (Carpentier), **2**:183

"Literature on the Eve of Revolution" (Chou), **2**:212

"Little Cloud, A" (Joyce), **5**:649

Little Herr Friedemann (Mann), **7**:870, 873, 876

Little Monasteries, The (O'Connor), **8**:1097

"Little Mother, The" (O'Connor), **8**:1107

Little Women (Alcott), **10**:1386, *1387*

Lituma en los Andes (Vargas Llosa), **11**:1558

Living and the Dead, The (White), **12**:1653

"Living in the Interregnum" (Gordimer), **4**:475

Loitering with Intent (Spark), **11**:1447

Lolita (Nabaokov), **7**:985, 988–89, 990, 991, 992, 997–1000

Lolita (Nabokov; screenplay), **7**:989, *991*, 994

Lonely Voice, The (O'Connor), **8**:1097

Long Day's Journey into Night (O'Neill), **3**:366

Longest Journey, The (Forster), **3**:320, 323, 330

"Long View, The" (Paton article series), **9**:1183

Look at the Harlequins (Nabokov), **7**:990

Look Back in Anger (Osborne), **8**:1131, 1132, 1133, 1134, 1135, 1137–38, 1140

Look Stranger! (Auden), **1**:69

Lord Jim (Conrad), **2**:245, 248, 250, 252, 260–63; **8**:*1080*

Lord of the Flies (Golding), **4**:437, 439–40, 441, 442, *443*, 444, 446, 447, 448, 449–51; **7**:922–23

Lord of the Rings, The (Tolkien), **1**:66; **6**:806, *810*; **11**:1529, *1530*, 1532, 1533, 1535, 1536, 1537, 1538, 1540, *1541*, 1542, 1543–47, 1548, 1549; **12**:1616, 1623

Loss of El Dorado, The (Naipaul), **8**:1016, 1020

Lost Childhood, The (Greene), **4**:496

Lost Horizon (Hilton), **3**:317

Lost in the Barrens (Mowat), **7**:929, 930, 936

Lost in the Stars (musical), **9**:1182, *1191*, 1194

Lost of the Soil, The (Dangarembga), **2**:269

Lost Steps, The (Carpentier), **2**:183, 184, 187, 189–90

Lotte in Weimar (The Beloved Returns) (Mann), **7**:874

Love among the Ruins (Waugh), **12**:1592, 1595

Love and Mr. Lewisham (Wells), **12**:1631, 1636

Love and Other Demons (García Márquez), **3**:412

Loved One, The (Waugh), **12**:1592, 1594, 1597, 1605

Love in the Time of Cholera (García Márquez), **3**:412, 414, 422, *423*, 425

Love Poems (Guillén), **4**:520

Love Poems and Others (Lawrence), **6**:765

Lover, The (Yehoshua), **12**:1720, 1722–23

Love Respelt (Graves), **4**:488, *489*

Love's Labour's Lost (Auden and Kallman; libretto), **1**:76

"Love Song of J. Alfred Prufrock, The" (Eliot), **7**:*900*

Lucy (Kincaid), **6**:751, 752, 756, 761

"Lullaby" (Auden), **1**:64

Luna de enfrente Inquisiciones (Borges), **1**:115

Luther (Osborne), **8**:1131, *1132*, 1133, 1134, 1136, 1138, 1139

"Luzina Takes a Holiday" (Roy), **10**:1313

Lying Days, The (Gordimer), **4**:459, 460–61

"Machine Stops, The" (Forster), **3**:336

Magic Flute, The: An Opera in Two Acts (Auden and Kallman; libretto), **1**:75–76

Magic Mountain, The (Mann), **7**:869, 876, 884–86

"Magic Shop, The" (Wells), **12**:1640

Mahabharata (Hindu epic), **8**:*1041*, 1042, 1044–45

Mahabharata, The: A Shortened Modern Prose Version, **8**:1042, 1044–45

Mahagonny (Brecht and Weill). *See Rise and Fall of the City of Mahagonny, The*

Mains sales, Les (Sartre), **10**:1340, 1352

Maitu Njugira (Ngũgĩ), 1076; **8**:1074

"Majesty of the Law, The" (O'Connor), **8**:1108

Major Barbara (Shaw), **10**:1355, 1361, 1363, *1369*, 1370–72

"Maker, The" (Borges), **1**:119

Making of the Representative for Planet 8, The (Lessing), **6**:798

Mala hora, La (García Márquez). *See In Evil Hour*

Maleficio de la mariposa, El (García Lorca), **3**:398

Malentendu, Le (Camus), **2**:162, 177

Malgudi Days (Narayan), **8**:1040

Malhamat al-harafish (Mahfouz), **6**:838, *839*

Malone Dies (Malone meurt) (Beckett), **1**:90, 100, 101

"Management of Grief, The" (Mukherjee), **7:**951, 952

"Man and Bat" (Lawrence), **6:**770

"Man and Boy" (Heaney), **4:**573

Man and Superman (Shaw), **10:**1355, 1358, 1360, 1363, 1364, 1368–70

Man and Two Woman, A (Lessing), **6:**799

Mandarins, The (Beauvoir), **10:**1342

Mandelbaum Gate, The (Spark), **11:**1450

Man Died, The: Prison Notes of Wole Soyinka (Soyinka), **10:**1423, 1424, 1425, 1428, 1434

Man-Eater of Malgudi, The (Narayan), **8:**1042, 1046–47

Man of Destiny, The (Shaw), **10:**1360

Man of the People, A (Achebe), **1:**24, 27, 39–40

Man's Fate (Malraux), **2:**166; **6:**845, 848, 849, 852, 854, 855, 858–59, 861

Man's Hope (Malraux), **6:**848, 849, 861

Man Within, The (Greene), **4:**496, 497, 503

Map of Love, The (Thomas), **11:**1514, 1515

Maraya, Al- (Mahfouz), **6:**835

Marcovaldo, or the Seasons in the City (Marcovaldo, ovvero le staioni in città) (Calvino), **2:**153, 156

"Marcovaldo al supermarket" (Calvino), **2:**153

Mariana Pineda (García Lorca), **3:**395, 398

Marianne Thornton: A Domestic Biography (Forster), **3:**323

Mario and the Magician (Mario und der Zauberer) (Mann), **7:**872

"Markings" (Heaney), **4:**573

Mark on the Wall, The (Woolf), **12:**1677

Marriages between Zones Three, Four and Five, The (Lessing), **6:**798

Martha Quest (Lessing), **6:**794

"Martín Fierro" (Borges), **1:**123

Mary (Mashen'ka) (Nabokov), **7:**987, 991

Maschere nude (Pirandello), **9:**1203

Masked Days, The (Fuentes), **3:**343, 344

Master and Margarita, The (Bulgakov), **10:**1325

Master Harold…and the Boys (Fugard), **3:**359, 360, 362, 363, 365, 366, 368–71

Master of Go, The (Kawabata), **5:**699

Master of Petersburg, The (Coetzee), **2:**231

Ma tabbaqa lakum (Kanafani). See All That's Left to You

"Matryona's House" (Solzhenitsyn), **10:**1418

Maurice (Forster), **3:**321, 322, 323, 327

"Meaning of Art, The" (Tagore), **11:**1491

"Medicine" (Chou), **2:**218–19

Meditation (Kafka), **5:**662, 664, 676

"Meditation for a Young Boy Confirmed" (Paton), **9:**1197

"Meditations in Time of Civil War" (Yeats), **12:**1700, 1713–14

Meiyou zhuyi (Gao), **3:**384

Melancholia (Sartre). See Nausea

Memento Mori (Spark), **11:**1461–62

Memoirs (Neruda), **8:**1060

Memoirs of Many in One (White), **12:**1655

Memorandum, The (Havel), **4:**538, 539, 541, 556–57

Memorial de Isla Negra (Neruda), **8:**1059, 1061

"Memory Lapses" (Fuentes), **3:**354

Men at Arms (Waugh), **12:**1592, 1602, 1603

Men in the Sun (Kanafani), **5:**683, 686, 688, 690–91

"Metalogue" (Auden), **1:**76

"Metamorphosis, The" (Kafka), **3:**410; **5:**662, 664, 665, 667, 668, 670, 673, 676–78

Michael Robartes and the Dancer (Yeats), **12:**1710–12, 1714

Midaq Alley (Mahfouz), **6:**830, 833

Middleman and Other Stories, The (Mukherjee), **7:**947, 952

Middle Pasaage, The (Naipaul), **8:**1016, 1018, 1020

Midnight Court, The (Merriman; O'Connor translation), **8:**1096, 1099

Midnight's Children (Rushdie), **10:**1317, 1318, 1320, 1321, 1324–25, 1326–28, 1331

Midsummer Night's Dream, A (Shakespeare), **9:**1211

Miguel Street (Naipaul), **8:**1016, 1018, 1020

Mimic Men, The (Naipaul), **8:**1016, 1019, 1020, 1021, 1023, 1032

Mind at the End of Its Tether (Wells), **12:**1634

Miracles (Lewis), **1:**63; **6:**806

Miramar (Mahfouz), **6:**836, 842

Mirror in the Roadway, The (O'Connor), **8:**1097

"Mirror of an Evening Scene" (Kawabata), **5:**695

Misalliance (Shaw), **10:**1363

"Mis ojos" (Neruda), **8:**1057, 1062

Miss Pulkinhorn (Golding; radio play), **4:**440

Mister Johnson (Cary), **1:**33

Misunderstanding, The (also called Cross Purposes) (Camus), **2:**162, 177

Mkhumbane (Paton and Matshikiza), **9:**1183

Modern Utopia, A (Wells), **12:**1632, 1649

"Modest Attempt to Set Forth a Theory, A" (Oz), **9:**1166, 1167

"Modest Proposal, A" (Swift), **9:**1167

Moetsukita chizu (Abe), **1:**14

Molloy (Beckett), **1:**90, 95–96, 98, 100, 101

Monday or Tuesday (Woolf), **12:**1677

"Monkey, The" (Dinesen), **3:**302

Monsters and the Critics and Other Essays, The (Tolkien), **11:**1536

Moonlight Bride, The (Emecheta), **3:**314

Moor's Last Sigh, The (Rushdie), **10:**1322, 1324, 1325, 1331

More Pricks Than Kicks (Beckett), **1:**90, 91, 94

More Stories (O'Connor), **8:**1096

Morgenlandfahrt, Erzählung, Die (Hesse), **5:**591, 598, 600

Mort heureuse, La (Camus), **2:**177

Moscou a Crié (Kazantzakis), **5:**706

Moses' Rock (O'Connor and Hunt), **8:**1096

"Mossbawn: Two Poems in Dedication for Mary Heaney" (Heaney), **4:**571

"Mother" (Gao), **3:**384

"Mother, A" (Joyce), **5:**649

Mother, Sing for Me (Ngũgĩ), **8:**1074, 1076

Mother Courage and Her Children (Brecht), **1:**129, 130, 137–39

Motives for Son (*Motivos de Son*) (Guillén), **4**:518–19, 520, 523

Motor Show, The (Ionesco), **5**:622

Mouches, Les (Sartre), **10**:1336, 1340, 1348–50

Mountain Giants, The (Pirandello), **9**:1204

Movements in European History (Lawrence), **6**:766

Moving the Centre: The Struggle for Cultural Freedoms (Ngũgĩ), **8**:1076

Mr. Britling Sees It Through (Wells), **12**:1633, 1639

Mr. Mani (Yehoshua), **12**:1717, 1718, 1720, 1722, 1723, 1724–25

Mrs. Dalloway (Woolf), **9**:1163; **12**:1676, 1677, *1679*, 1686–89

"Mr. Skelmersdale in Fairyland" (Wells), **12**:1641

Mr. Stone and the Knight's Companion (Naipaul), **8**:1016

Mrs. Warren's Profession (Shaw), **10**:1360, 1362, 1373–74

Muerte y la brújula, La (Borges), **1**:109, 120

"Municipal Gallery Revisited, The" (Yeats), **11**:1477

"Municipal Gallery Revisted, The" (Yeats), **12**:1714

"Muñoz Marín" (Neruda), **8**:1068–69

Murphy (Beckett), **1**:90, 91, 94, 101

Music in Cuba (Carpentier), **2**:183

"Music of the Ainur, The" (Tolkien), **11**:1547

"Mute, The" (Camus), **2**:176

Mutter Courage und thre Kinder (Brecht). *See Mother Courage and Her Children*

My Boyhood Days (Tagore), **11**:1485

My Brother (Kincaid), **6**:750, 752, 753, 760, 761–62

My Children! My Africa! (Fugard), **3**:362, 363, *366*

"My Da" (O'Connor), **8**:*1105*

My Dateless Diary (Narayan), **8**:1040

My Days (Narayan), **8**:1040

My Discovery of America (Mowat), **7**:932

My Father's Son: Memories of War and Peace (Mowat), **7**:928

My Garden (*Book*) (Kincaid), **6**:751–52

My Head! My Head! (Graves), **4**:480, 484

My Life (Fugard), **3**:363

My Lost City (Fitzgerald; Murakami transl.), **7**:957

My Michael (Oz), **9**:1157, 1159, 1160, *1164*, 1165, 1168–69

"My Oedipus Complex" (O'Connor), **8**:1099, 1105–6

My Reminiscences (Tagore), **11**:1485

My Son's Story (Gordimer), **4**:461

Mystic Masseur, The (Naipaul), **8**:1016, 1018, 1020

Myth, Literature, and the African World (Soyinka), **10**:1425

"Myth of Sisyphus, The" (Camus), **1**:162; **2**:161, 162

Myth of Sisyphus, The (Camus), **5**:667

Nacht und Träume (Beckett), **1**:91

Nacht von Lissabon, Die (Remarque)., **9**:1221, 1224, 1237

Naga (Narayan), **8**:*1042*, 1053

Nahan (Chou). *See Call to Arms*

Naira Power (Emecheta), **3**:312

Naked Masks (Pirandello), **9**:1203

Name of the Rose, The (Eco), **1**:116

Narcissus and Goldmund (*Narziss und Goldmund*) (Hesse), **5**:585, 586, 591, 598–600

Narnia chronicles (Lewis). *See Chronicles of Narnia, The*

Nature of a Crime, The (Conrad and Ford), **2**:249

Nausea (*La Nausée*) (Sartre), **10**:1333, 1336, 1337, 1338, 1340, 1341, 1346–48

Nervous Conditions (Dangarembga), **2**:267, 269, 270, 271, 272, 273–75

Netherwood (White), **12**:1663

Never Cry Wolf (Mowat), **7**:927, 929, 930, 935

"New Advocate, The" (Kafka), **5**:670

"New Hispanic American Novel, The" (Fuentes), **3**:344, 345, 348

New Machiavelli, The (Wells), **12**:1639

New Poems (Rilke), **9**:1282, 1283, 1294

New Poems (Thomas), **11**:1514

"New Refutation of Time, A" (Borges), **1**:121

New Tribe, A (Emecheta), **3**:312

New Worlds for Old (Wells), **12**:1637

"New Year Letter" (Auden), **1**:65

"New Year's Sacrifice" (Chou), **2**:212, 221, 221–22, 222

Ngaahika Ndeendai (Ngũgĩ), **8**:1074, 1075

Ngũgĩ wa Thiong'o, *Trial of Dedan Kimathi, The* (Ngũgĩ and Mugo), **8**:1074, 1075

Nidjera (Weller), **12**:1612

Nigger of the "Narcissus", The (Conrad), **2**:250, 253, 255–58

Night and Day (Woolf), **12**:1677

Night and Dream (Beckett), **1**:91

Night in Lisbon, The (Remarque), **9**:1221, 1224, 1237

Night of the Prowler, The (White), **12**:1663

Niji ikutabi (Kawabata), **5**:697

1973 nen no pinbooru (Murakami), **7**:959

1984 (Orwell), **7**:1002; **8**:1109, 1115, 1116, 1117, 1119, 1120, 1122, 1127–28

"Nineteen Hundred and Nineteen" (Yeats), **12**:1713, 1714

Ninety-two Days (Waugh), **12**:1592

No! (*Nu*) (Ionesco), **5**:621, 626

No Exit (Sartre), **10**:1335, 1336, 1340, 1341, 1350–52

No-Good Friday (Fugard), **3**:361, 362

No Longer at Ease (Achebe), **1**:24, 27, 32–36

"Nomad and Viper" (Oz), **9**:1174–77

Nones (Auden), **1**:72

Nongogo (Fugard), **3**:361, 362

No One Writes to the Colonel (García Márquez), **3**:411, 412, 415, 418, 426, 427, *429*

Nordic Twilight (Forster), **3**:323

Norse sagas, Auden and, **1**:66

North (Heaney), **4**:562, 563, 568, 570–72

Norwegian Wood (Murakami), **7**:953, 954, 956, 957, 960–61

Nostromo (Conrad), **2**:248, 250, 252, 264, 265; **8**:1020
  film adaptation, **2**:249

Notebook of a Return to the Native Land (Césaire), **2**:195, 198, 200, 201–2, 203

Notebooks of Don Rigoberto, The (Vargas Llosa), **11**:1559

Notebooks of Malte Laurids Brigge, The (Rilke), **9**:1279, 1282, 1283, 1288–90, 1293

Notes and Counter Notes (Ionesco), **5**:623, 624, 625, 626

Notes on an Endangered Species and Others (Richler), **9**:1264

Not I (Beckett), **1**:91

"Notion Club Papers, The" (Tolkien), **11**:1540

Not to Disturb (Spark), **11**:1462

Novelle per un anno (Pirandello), **9**:1203

Nowhere to Play (Emecheta), **3**:314

Noyers d'Altenburg, Les (Malraux), **6**:850

Nürnberger Reise, Die (Hesse), **5**:586

Occasion for Loving, An (Gordimer), **4**:461

Odas elementales (Neruda), **8**:1061, 1062, 1069–70

"Ode to Salvador Dali" (García Lorca), **3**:397

"Ode to Walt Whitman" (García Lorca), **3**:394, *399*

Odissia (Kazantzakis). *See Odyssey, The: A Modern Sequel*

"Odour of Chrysanthemums" (Lawrence), **6**:766, 773–74

Odyssey (Homer), **10**:1429; **11**:1576
    as Joyce model, **5**:654–55
    as Kazantzakis model, **5**:710, 716–17
    Walcott adaptation, **11**:1571
    as White influence, **12**:1665

Odyssey, The: A Modern Sequel (*Odissia*) (Kazantzakis), **5**:703, 706, 707, 711, 716–17

Oedipus at Colonus (Sophocles; Murdoch translation, **7**:969

Oedipus Rex (Sophocles), **7**:920, **11**:1480

Officers and Gentlemen (Waugh), **12**:1592, 1602, 1603

Ofis ke krino (Kazantzakis), **5**:705

Of Love and Other Demons (García Márquez), **3**:412, 426

Of Love and Shadows (Allende), **1**:46, 48, 54, 56

"Of the Rings of Power and the Third Age" (Tolkien), **11**:1548

Ogun Abibiman (Soyinka), **10**:1428

Ōinaru hi ni (Takamura), **11**:1505, 1510

Ojisan no shi (Takamura), **11**:1505, 1510

Old Capital, The (Kawabata), **5**:696, 697

"Old Chevalier, The" (Dinesen), **3**:302

"Old Chief Mshlanga, The" (Lessing), **6**:799

"Old Fellows" (O'Connor), **8**:1101

Old Gringo, The (Fuentes), **3**:*340*, 344, 345, 355–56

Old Stories Retold (Chou), **2**:210, *210*, 216, 223–24

Omeros (Walcott), **11**:1571, 1576–78

"On an Anniversary" (Synge), **11**:1473

On Being a Woman (Kawabata), **5**:697

One Day in the Life of Ivan Denisovich (Solzhenitsyn), **10**:*1400*, 1401, 1402, 1403, 1408, 1410–12, 1414, 1419

One Day More (Conrad), **2**:*250*

One Hundred Love Sonnets (Neruda), **8**:1060, 1061

One Hundred Years of Solitude (García Márquez), **3**:347, 409, 412, 413, 416, 417, 420–22, 424, 426; **10**:1325

One Man's Bible (Gao), **3**:381, 382, 384, 388

"On Fairy–Stories" (Tolkien), **1**:66; **11**:1532, 1533, 1534, 1536, 1540

On Humor (Pirandello), **9**:1209

Only Child, An (O'Connor), **8**:1097

Only Problem, The (Spark), **11**:1458

Onna de aru koto (Kawabata), **5**:697

"On Parables" (Kafka), **5**:670

"On the Circuit" (Auden), **1**:63, 66

"On the Knocking at the Gate in *Macbeth*" (De Quincey), **6**:782

On This Island (Auden), **1**:64

Open Heart (Yehoshua), **12**:1720, 1725–26

Open Sore of a Continent, The (Soyinka), **10**:1424, 1426, 1434–36

Optimist, The (Habibi), **4**:*534*

Ordeal of Gilbert Pinfold, The (Waugh), **12**:1592, 1594

Orient Express (Greene), **4**:497, 498, 503

Orlando (Woolf), **12**:1677, 1678, *1680*, 1681, 1687

Orwell: Wintry Conscience of a Generation (Myers), **8**:1116

Other Man, The: Conversations with Graham Greene (Allain), **4**:496

Other Shore, The (Gao), **3**:382

Other Son, The (Pirandello), **9**:1206–7

Otono del patriarca, E. (García Márquez). *See Autumn of the Patriarch, The*

Our Man in Havana (Greene; novel), **4**:499

Our Man in Havana (Greene; screenplay), **4**:497, 502

Our Republic (Keneally), **6**:728, 730

Outcast of the Islands, An (Conrad), **2**:255

Outline of History, The (Wells), **12**:1629, 1633, *1637*

Out of Africa (Dinesen), **3**:293, 296, 297, 298, 299, 301, 304–5

Out of Exile (Dangarembga), **2**:268

Out of Isak Dinesen in Africa (Donelson), **3**:298, *300*

Out of the Silent Planet (Lewis), **1**:*120*; **6**:808, 811, 814–17

Overcrowded Barracoon and Other Articles, The (Naipaul), **8**:1016

Over the Brazier (Graves), **4**:480

"Over the Rainbow" (Rushdie), **10**:1319, 1331

Owarishi michi no shirube ni (Abe), **1**:12

"Oxen of the Sun" chapter (Joyce), **5**:656

Oxford Book of Modern Verse, The (anthology), **11**:1489

Oxford English Dictionary, **11**:1531, 1532, 1548

Padlock Edition (samizdat publication), **4**:548

Page of Madness, A (Kawabata; screenplay), **5**:694, 696

Paid on Both Sides (Auden), **1**:66

"Painful Case, A" (Joyce), **5**:649

Palace of Desire (Mahfouz), **6**:830, 834, 842–43

Palace Walk (Mahfouz), **6**:*832*, 836, 842

Pale Fire (Nabokov), **7**:989, 992, 1002

Palm-of-the-Hand Stories (Kawabata), **5**:698, 699, 702

Palomar (Calvino), **2**:154, 156–57, 158, *158*

Pantaleón y las visitadoras (Vargas Llosa), **11**:1558–59

"Panther, The" (Rilke), **9**:1294

Panther in the Basement (Oz), **9**:*1172*

Paradise Lost (Milton), **4**:455;
  6:752

title page, **6**:*761*

Paraíso en la otre esquina, El (Vargas
  Llosa), **11**:1554

"Parrot's Training, The" (Tagore),
  11:1499

*Parrot's Training and Other Stories,
  The* (Tagore), **11**:1499

Passage to India, A (Forster), **2**:283;
  3:322, 323, 326, 330, 331–34;
  7:944; **8**:1129; **9**:1174–75

"Passerby, The" (Chou), **2**:223

"Passion for Buenos Aires" (Borges).
  See Fervor of Buenos Aires

Path to the Spiders' Nest, The
  (Calvino), **2**:150, 153, 154

Patrick White Letters (Marr, ed.),
  12:1657

Patrick White Speaks (White),
  12:1657

Patriot for Me, A (Osborne), **8**:1131,
  1134, 1136, 1139–40

Paula (Allende), **1**:42, 44, 46, 48,
  52–53, 54, 55, 57

Paul Bunyan: An Operetta in Two Acts
  (Britten and Auden; libretto), **1**:74

"Pearl of Love, The" (Wells),
  12:1641

Pedestrian of the Air (Ionesco),
  5:624, 626, 627, 632, 633

*Penpoints, Gunpoints, and Dreams:
  Towards a Critical Theory of the
  Arts and the State in Africa*
  (Ngũgĩ), **8**:1076

"Pension Day" (Weller), **12**:1627

People of the Abyss (London),
  8:1119

People of the Deer (Mowat), **7**:927,
  929, 930, 931, 933–35

Perelandra (Lewis), **6**:813, 814, *815*,
  816–17; **11**:1540

Perennial Philosophy, The (Huxley),
  5:604, 608

Perfect Peace, A (Oz), **9**:1169, 1171,
  1172, *1173*, 1174

Perfect Wagnerite, The (Shaw),
  10:1364

Personal Anthology, A (Borges), **1**:121

"Personal Helicon" (Heaney), **4**:564,
  568, 570

Personal Record, A (Conrad), **2**:257

Peste, La (Camus). *See Plague, The*
  (Camus)

Petals of Blood (Ngũgĩ), **8**:1074,
  1075, 1079, 1081, 1086, *1087*,
  1088, 1090

Peter Camenzind (Hesse), **5**:583,
  585, 587–88, 591, 592–93, 594

Petite poule d'eau, La (Roy). *See
  Where Nests the Water Hen*

Phaedo (Plato), **12**:1659

Philanderer, The (Shaw), **10**:1360,
  1362

Philoctetes (Sophocles; Heaney version), **4**:562, 564

Philosopher's Pupil, The (Murdoch),
  7:973–74

"Phoenix-Hearted, The" (Murdoch),
  7:969

Pickup, The (Gordimer), **4**:461, 463,
  476

"Pierre Menard, Author of Don
  Quixote" (Borges), **1**:116

Piers Plowman (Langland), **1**:64

Pilgrim's Regress, The (Lewis), **6**:806,
  808, 810, 813

Pincher Martin (Golding), **4**:447,
  451–52, 454

"Pitchfork" (Heaney), **4**:573

Place at Whitton, The (Keneally),
  6:726, 728

Place of the Lion, The (Williams),
  11:*1541*

Plague, The (Camus), **2**:159, 161,
  162, 163, 166, 167, 172–74,
  173, 176

Playboy of the Western World, The
  (Synge), **11**:1463, 1466, 1467,
  1468, *1469*, 1471, 1472, 1477,
  1478–81, 1484; **12**:1698, 1699,
  1702, 1703, 1704, 1715, 1716

  significance of, **12**:1706

Playing the Game (Lessing and
  Adlard), **6**:789

Playland (Fugard), **3**:362, 363, 373

Plays Pleasant and Unpleasant
  (Shaw), **10**:1358, 1360

Play with a Tiger (Lessing), **6**:791

Plough and the Stars, The (O'Casey),
  12:1699, 1706–7

Ploughman and Other Poems, The
  (White), **12**:1652, 1655, 1662

Plumed Serpent, The (Lawrence),
  6:766, 767, 767–68, 768,
  781–82

Pnin (Nabokov), **7**:989, 994,
  1000–1002

Podvig (Nabokov), **7**:991, 994

Poems (Auden), **1**:*60*, 62, 64, 69

Poems (Owen), **8**:1148–50

Poems (*Poemas*) (Borges), **1**:107

Poems (Yeats), **12**:1701

Poems and Ballads of Young Ireland
  (Yeats, ed.), **12**:1698

Poems and Translations (Synge),
  11:1472

"Poet, The" (Dinesen), **3**:302,
  304

Poetic Diction: A Study in Meaning
  (Barfield), **11**:1538

Poet in New York (*Poeta en Nueva
  York*) (García Lorca), **3**:392, 394,
  403–4

"Poet's School, A" (Tagore),
  11:1499–1500

Point Counter Point (Huxley), **5**:604,
  605, 608, 611–12

"Politics and Conscience" (Havel),
  4:541, 544

"Politics and the English Language"
  (Orwell), **8**:1117, 1129

"Politics vs. Literature: An
  Examination of *Gulliver's Travels*"
  (Orwell), **8**:1120

Pomes Penyeach (Joyce), **5**:644, 653

Pornography and Obscenity
  (Lawrence), **6**:766

Portrait in Sepia (Allende), **1**:56–57

Portrait of the Artist as a Young Dog
  (Thomas), **11**:1514, 1523–24,
  1525, 1527

*Portrait of the Artist as a Young Man,
  A* (Joyce), **5**:635, 636, 637, 638,
  639, 640, 643, 646, 651–53,
  654; **6**:782; **11**:1523

"Poseidon" (Kafka), **5**:670

Possessed, The (*Les possédés*) (Camus
  adaptation of Dostoyevsky),
  2:162, 163

Post Office, The (Tagore),
  11:1498–99

"Postscript: Astrafiammante to the
  translators" (Auden and
  Kallman), **1**:76

Postures (Rhys). *See Quartet: A Novel*

Power and the Glory, The (Greene),
  4:498, 512–13

"Power of Mara Poetry, The" (Chou),
  2:210

"Power of the Powerless, The"
  (Havel), **4**:541, 544

"Prayer for My Daughter, A" (Yeats),
  12:1712

*PRB: An Essay on the Pre-Raphaelite
  Brotherhood* (Waugh), **12**:1591

"Preciosa y el aire" (García Lorca), **3**:399

Preface to *Call to Arms* (Chou), **2**:212, 215–16, 218, 218–19, 219

"Prelude" (Mansfield), **7**:895, 896, 903–4

Premier homme, Le (Camus), **2**:163, 176–77

Present Past, Past Present: A Personal Memoir (Ionesco), **5**:623, 624

Pride and Prejudice (Huxley screenplay), **5**:605

Priglashenie na Kazin' (Nabokov), **7**:992

Prime of Miss Jean Brodie, The (Spark), **11**:1445, 1446, 1448, 1454–56, 1458

Princess and Curdie, The (Macdonald), **11**:1542

Princess and the Goblin, The (Macdonald), **11**:1542

Principia Ethica (Moore), **12**:1683

Private View (Havel). See *Unveiling*

Problem of Pain, The (Lewis), **6**:806; **11**:1540

"Proem" (Auden), **1**:76

Progress and Poverty (George), **10**:1358

Prometheus (Promithéas) (Kazantzakis), **5**:708

Proper Marriage, A (Lessing), **6**:794

Protest (Havel), **4**:550, 552

"Protestant Mystics, The" (Auden), **1**:68

Prozess, Der (Kafka). *See Trial, The*

"Prussian Officer, The" (Lawrence), **6**:782

Prussian Officer and Other Stories, The (Lawrence), **6**:766

Psychoanalysis and the Unconscious (Lawrence), **6**:766

Public Image, The (Spark), **11**:1458

"Punishment" (Heaney), **4**:568, 572

"Purgatory" (Soyinka), **10**:1436

Purgatory (Yeats), **12**:1715

Purple Dreams (Weller), **12**:1611

Putain respectususe, La (Sartre), **10**:1340, 1352

Pygmalion (Shaw), **10**:1355, 1358, 1361, 1363
　film and musical adaptations, **10**:1366–67

Pyramid, The (Golding), **4**:*448*, 455

Qahira al-jadida, Al- (Mahfouz), **6**:830, 835

Qasr al-shawq (Mahfouz), **6**:830, 834, 842–43

Quartet: A Novel (Rhys), **9**:1242, 1257–58

"Quenta Silmarillion: The History of the Silmarils" (Tolkien), **11**:1547–48, 1549

"Question, A" (Synge), **11**:1472–73

Quiet American, The (Greene), **4**:499, 500, 502

Quintessence of Ibsenism, The (Shaw), **10**:1359

Qushtumur (Mahfouz), **6**:835

Rabindrasangit (Tagore song), **11**:1493

Radubis (Mahfouz), **6**:825, 828

Rainbow, The (Lawrence), **6**:763, 766, 770, 771, 775–77, 782

Rake's Progress, The: A Fable (Auden and Kallman; libretto), **1**:74, 75, 76

Ramayana (Hindu epic), **8**:1042, 1045; **11**:1581

Ramayana, The: A Shortened Modern Prose Version (Narayan), **8**:*1039*, 1042, 1044, 1045

Ramila (Hindu pantomimes), **8**:1032

Rape of Shavi, The (Emecheta), **3**:312, 316–18

"Reading and Writing" (Naipaul), **8**:1032

Reading and Writing: A Personal Account (Naipaul), **8**:1032, *1033*

Real Life of Alejandro Mayta, The (Vargas Llosa), **11**:1558

Real Life of Sebastian Knight, The (Nabokov), **7**:988, 990, 991, 994, 995–97

Reasons of State (Carpentier), **2**:183, 193–94

Rebel, The (Camus), **2**:162, 163, 166, 174

"Rebuilding" (Paton), **9**:1192

"Red Cocoon" (Abe), **1**:14

"Red Notebook" (Lessing), **6**:796

Redress of Poetry, The (Heaney), **4**:562

Reflections of a Non-Political Man (Mann), **7**:872, 873, 876

Règne du malin, Le (Malraux unfinished novel), **6**:861

"Religion of the Artist, The" (Tagore lecture), **11**:1491

"Reluctant Dragon, The" (Grahame), **11**:1548

"Remembrance of the Past" (Chou), **2**:210

Remote People (Waugh), **12**:1593

"Renegade, The" (Camus), **2**:176

"Report to an Academy, A" (Kafka), **5**:662, 666, 668

Report to Greco (Kazantzakis), **5**:704

Residence on Earth (*Residencia en la tierra*) (Neruda), **8**:1058, 1059, 1061

Respected Sir (Mahfouz), **6**:833

Respectful Prostitute, The (Sartre), **10**:1340, 1352

"Return, The" (Conrad), **2**:253

Return of the King, The (Tolkien), **11**:1543

Return to Abyssinia (White), **12**:1662

Return to Haifa (Kanafani), **5**:687, 689, 691

Rhinoceros (Ionesco), **5**:619, 621, 623, 624, 626, 627, 630–32, 633

Rhlat ibn Battuta (Arabic classic), **6**:833

Riders in the Chariot (White), **12**:1659, 1667–69

Riders to the Sea (Synge), **11**:1463, 1465, 1467, 1471, 1474–75; **12**:1704

Right You Are, If You Think You Are (Pirandello), **9**:1203, 1208

Rihlat ibn Fattouma (Mahfouz), **6**:833

Rijal fi al-shams (Kanafani). *See Men in the Sun*

"Rime of the Ancient Mariner" (Coleridge), **3**:308

Ripple from the Storm, A (Lessing), **6**:794

Rise and Fall of the City of Mahagonny, The (Brecht and Weill), **1**:*127*, 128, 133, *138*, 140–41

Rites of Passage (Golding), **4**:441, 444, 445, 456

Rites of Spring, The (Carpentier), **2**:183

River Between, The (Ngũgĩ), **8**:1074, 1075, 1078, 1090, 1092

Road, The (Soyinka), **10**:1427

Road Back, The (Remarque), **9**:1220, 1222, 1224, 1231, 1235

Road past Altamont, The (Roy), **10**:1307

"Roads of Life, The" (Dinesen), **3**:304

"Roads Round Pisa, The" (Dinesen), **3**:302, 304

Road to Mecca, The (Fugard), **3**:362, 363, *371*

Road to Wigan Pier, The (Orwell), **8**:1109, 1112, 1115, 1117, 1120, 1122, 1130

Robbery under Law: The Mexican Object-Lesson (Waugh), **12**:1592, 1593

Robinson (Spark), **11**:1460

Robinson Crusoe (Defoe), **2**:231, 237, 238

Rock Garden, The (Kazantzakis), **5**:706

"Rocking-Horse Winner, The" (Lawrence), **6**:782

"Rocky Acres" (Graves), **4**:486

Roger Fry: A Biography (Woolf), **12**:1677

Romance (Conrad and Ford), **2**:249
film adaptation, **2**:249

Romancero (García Lorca). *See Gypsy Ballads*

Romantische Lieder (Hesse), **5**:585, 588, 591

Room of One's Own, A (Woolf), **12**:1677, 1680, 1692–93

Room with a View, A (Forster), **3**:320, 323, 326, 328, *329*, 330, 331, *333*

Rose, The (Yeats), **12**:1701

Rosshalde (Hesse), **5**:584, 589, 591

Rover, The (Conrad), **2**:*251*, 262

Roverandom (Tolkien), **11**:1535

Royal Highness (Mann), **7**:887

Royal Way, The (Malraux), **6**:848, 849, 860–61

Rue Deschambault (Roy). *See Street of Riches*

Ruined Map, The (Abe), **1**:14

Ruined Map, The (Abe; screenplay), **1**:13, 17

Runaway Horses (Mishima), **7**:911, *913*

Russia in the Shadows (Wells), **12**:1639

Sacred and Profane Love Machine, The (Murdoch), **7**:965, 966, 970, 982

"Sailing to Byzantium" (Yeats), **12**:1712, 1713

"Sailor-Boy's Tale, The" (Dinesen), **3**:307–8

Sailor's Graveyard, The (Valéry), **7**:975

Sailor Who Fell from Grace with the Sea, The (Mishima), **7**:911, 913, 914, 915, 920–23

Saint and Mary Kate, The (O'Connor), **8**:1096

Saint Francis (Kazantzakis), **5**:708, 709, 717

Saint Joan (Shaw), **10**:1355, 1358, 1361, 1365, 1372–73

St. Joan of the Stockyards (Brecht), **1**:132, 133

St. Mawr (Lawrence), **6**:768

St. Urbain's Horseman (Richler), **9**:1262, 1263–64, *1265*, 1266, 1274–75, 1277

Saison au Congo, Une (Césaire), **2**:204

Salvatores Dei: Askitikí (Kazantzakis), **5**:706, 709, 715

Sandcastle, The (Murdoch), **7**:974

Sanity of Art, The (Shaw), **10**:1364

Satanic Verses, The (Rushdie), **10**:1317, *1318*, 1320, 1321, 1323, 1324, 1325, 1328, *1329*, 1331

"Saturday Night and Sunday Morning" (Weller), **12**:1618, 1627

Saving the Appearances: A Study in Idolatry (Barfield), **11**:1538

Saviors of God, The: Spiritual Exercises (Kazantzakis), **5**:706, 709, 715

Scarlet Song (Bâ), **1**:79, 80, 81, 82, 85, 86

Scarlet Woman, The (Waugh; screenplay), **12**:1591, 1597

Schatten im Paradies (Remarque). *See Shadows in Paradise*

Schindler's Ark (Keneally), **6**:725, 728, 731, 733, 736–37, 738–40

Schloss, Das (Kafka). *See Castle, The*

School for Friends, The (White), **12**:1662

"School on the Little Water Hen, The" (Roy), **10**:1313

Schwarze Obelisk, Der (Remarque), **9**:1221, 1224

Scoop (Waugh), **12**:1592, 1593, 1598, 1604

Scorpion God, The (Golding), **4**:441

Scott-King's Modern Europe (Waugh), **12**:1592

Screwtape Letters, The (Lewis), **6**:806, 820–21; **11**:1533

Sea, the Sea, The (Murdoch), **7**:965, 970, 975–76, 978

"Sea and the Mirror, The: A Commentary on Shakespeare's *The Tempest*" (Auden), **1**:65

Sea of Fertility, The (Mishima tetralogy), **7**:911, 912, 916

"Sea Raiders, The" (Wells), **12**:1640

Search, The (Mahfouz), **6**:833

"Search, The" (Paton), **9**:1190

Season at Sarsaparilla, The (White), **12**:1655, 1662

Season in the Congo, A (Césaire), **2**:204

Season of Anomy (Soyinka), **10**:1424, 1428

Secondary Worlds (Auden), **1**:62, 76

Second-Class Citizen (Emecheta), **3**:311, 312, 313, 318

"Second Coming, The" (Yeats), **1**:32; **12**:1695, 1703, 1712, 1715

Second Sex, The (Beauvoir), **10**:*1342*

"Secret Agent, The" (Auden), **1**:66, 67, 69, 70

Secret Agent, The (Conrad), **2**:248, 250, 252, 264–65
film adaptation, **2**:249

Secret Life of Saeed, the Ill-Fated Pessoptimist, The (Habibi), **4**:*529*, 530, 532, 533–35

Secret Lives (Ngũgĩ), **8**:1074, 1075

"Secret Sharer, The" (Conrad), **2**:248, 250, 263–64, 265
film adaptation, **2**:249

"Secret Vice, A" (Tolkien), **11**:1536

Sectret Defector, The (Sigal), **6**:789

"Seed Cutters, The" (Heaney), **4**:571

Seeing Things (Heaney), **4**:562, 563, 572–73

Sei personaggi in cerca d'autore (Pirandello). *See Six Characters in Search of an Author*

Sentiero dei nidi di ragno, Il (Calvino), **2**:150, 153, 154

"September 1913" (Yeats), **12**:1703

Séquestrés d'Altona, Les (Sartre), **10**:1338, 1340, 1353

"Seraph and the Zambesi, The" (Spark), **11**:1449

Serpent and Lily (Kazantzakis), **5**:705

Serrated Wheel, The (Guillén), **4**:520

Se una notte d'inverno un viaggiatore (Calvino), **2**:151

Seven Gothic Tales (Dinesen), **3**:293, 296, 297, 299, 302, *303*, 304

Seven Letters to Melin (Šafařík), **4**:552

Severed Head, A (Murdoch), **7**:967, 970, 974

Sextet of the Six Days (Habibi), **4**:531–32, 535–36

"Shades of Darkness: Three Impressions" (Richler), **9**:1261

Shadow Line, The (Conrad), **2**:248, 250, 265–66

Shadow of the Glen, The (Synge), **11**:1463, 1466, 1467, *1470*, 1471, 1475–78

"Shadow's Farewell, The" (Chou), **2**:223

Shadows in Paradise (Remarque), **9**:1221, 1224, *1232*, 1233–35, 1237

Shadows on the Grass (Dinesen), **3**:298

Shahhadh, Al-) (Mahfouz), **6**:833

Shahhadh, Al- (Mahfouz), **6**:833

Shame (Rushdie), **10**:1320, 1321, 1324, 1330

Shape of Things to Come, The (Wells), **12**:1633, *1634*, 1648–49

Shengsijie (Gao), **3**:384, 388

She No Longer Weeps (Dangarembga), **2**:269, 270

Shikasta (Lessing), **6**:792, 798

Shiva Purana (Narayan version), **8**:1044

Shoemaker's Prodigious Wife, The (García Lorca), **3**:394, 406, *407*, 408

"Shokonsai ikkei" (Kawabata), **5**:696

"Shooting an Elephant" (Orwell), **8**:1111, 1129

"Short Ode to a Philologist, A" (Auden), **1**:66

Shovelling Trouble (Richler), **9**:1264

"Show, The" (Owen), **8**:1147

Shuttle in the Crypt, A (Soyinka), **10**:1429, 1436–37

"Sick Collier, A" (Lawrence), **6**:773

Siddhartha (Siddharta) (Hesse), **5**:585, 586, 589, 593–95

Signal Driver: A Morality Play for the Times (White), **12**:1663

"Sign in Space, A" (Calvino), **2**:155

Silapaddikaram (Narayan version), **8**:1044

Silmarillion, The (Tolkien), **11**:1529, 1531, 1532, 1533, 1535, *1546*, 1547–48

Si longue lettre, Une (Bâ). See *So Long a Letter*

"Singing School" (Heaney), **4**:572

"Sirens" chapter (Joyce), **5**:656

Sir Gawain and the Green Knight (Tolkien and Gordon, ed.), **11**:1531, 1532, *1533*

Sirian Experiments, The (Lessing), **6**:798

"Sisters, The" (Joyce), **5**:637, 648–50

Six Characters in Search of an Author (Pirandello), **9**:1199, 1202, 1203, 1204, 1211–14, 1216

Six Memos for the Next Millennium (Calvino), **2**:152

Sizwe Bansi Is Dead (Fugard), **3**:361, 363

Slave Girl, The (Emecheta), **3**:313

Sleep It Off Lady (Rhys), **9**:1243

Slum Clearance (Havel), **4**:541, 544

Small Place, A (Kincaid), **6**:758, 760

Smile Please: An Unfinished Autobiography (Rhys), **9**:1242, 1243–44

Smith of Wootton Major (Tolkien), **11**:1532, 1534, 1549

"Snail" (García Lorca), **3**:408

"Snake" (Lawrence), **6**:770–71

Snow Country (Kawabata), **5**:693, 695, 696, 698, 699, 702

Soglyadataj (Nabokov), **7**:994

Soldier Miguel Paz and Sergeant José Inés (Guillén), **4**:519

Solid Mandala, The (White), **12**:1655, 1670–71

Solomon Gursky Was Here (Richler), **9**:1263, 1264, 1275–76

So Long a Letter (Bâ), **1**:77, 78–79, 80, 81, 82, 84–86

"Song of Despair, A" (Neruda), **8**:1068

Song Offerings (Tagore), **11**:1489, *1495*, 1496–98

Song of Protest (Neruda), **8**:1068–69

Song of Solomon (Hebrew Bible), **5**:644

"Song of the Faeries" (Yeats), **12**:1697

"Song of the Great Capitulation" (Brecht), **1**:137

Sóngoro Cosongo: Mulatto Poems (Guillén), **4**:519, 520, 523–24

Songs (García Lorca), **3**:408

Songs for Soldiers and Sones for Tourists (Guillén), **4**:519

Songs of Africa (Paton), **9**:1197

Songs of the Sea (Weller), **12**:1618

"Song to David, A" (Smart), **1**:69

Sonnets from the Portuguese (Browning; Rilke, transl.), **9**:1287

Sonnets to Orpheus (Rilke), **9**:1279, 1283, 1288, 1292, 1293

Son of a Smaller Hero (Richler), **9**:*1265*, 1266, 1267, 1277

Sons and Lovers (Lawrence), **6**:764, 765, 766, 769, 770, 773, 782–84

"Sorrow-Acre" (Dinesen), **3**:306

Sorrow and the Terror, The: The Haunting Legacy of the Air India Tragedy (Mukherjee and Blaise), **7**:940

Sorrows and Rejoicings (Fugard), **3**:362, 363, 375

Sorrows of Young Werther, The (Goethe), **7**:874

Sorry… (Havel), **4**:550

Soul Mountain (Gao), **3**:379, 381, 382, 384, 386–87, 388

Sound and the Fury, The (Faulkner), **5**:689

Sound of the Mountain, The (Kawabata), **5**:696, 697, 698–99, 702

Sound of Waves, The (Mishima), **7**:907, 911, 912, 913, 915

"South, The" (Borges), **1**:107, 112, 120

space trilogy (Lewis), **6**:813, 814–18

Spain: Poem in Four Notes of Anguish and One of Hope (Guillén), **4**:519, 525

Spain in My Heart (Neruda), **8**:1060

Spark of Life (Remarque), **9**:1221, 1224, 1230, 1232–33, 1235, *1236*

Speak, Memory (Nabokov), **7**:986, 988, 991, 994, 995–96

"Spiral, The" (Calvino), **2**:155

Spire, The (Golding), **4**:442, 444–45, 454–55

Spirit Level, The (Heaney), **4**:562, 563

Spiritual Exercises (Ignatius Loyola), **5**:706

Sponono (Paton and Shah), **9**:1183

Sport of Nature, A (Gordimer), **4**:461, 463, 475–76

Spring Snow (Mishima), **7:**911, 916–17

"Squarings" (Heaney), **4:**572

Stamboul Train (Greene), **4:**497, 498, 503

"Star, The" (Wells), **12:**1636, 1640

Stars on a Cold Night (Gao), **3:**381

Statements after an Arrest under the Immorality Act (Fugard), **3:**363

Statements plays (Fugard), **3:**360, 362, 363

Station Island (Heaney), **4:**562, 563, 567

Statue's Daughter, The (O'Connor), **8:**1096

Stephen Hero (Joyce). *See Portrait of the Artist as a Young Man, A*

Steppenwolf (Hesse), **5:**585, 586, 588, 589–91, 595–97

Stick Your Neck Out (Richler). *See Incomparable Atuk, The*

Stirrings Still (Beckett), **1:**91

"Stoker, The" (Kafka), **5:**662, 664

"Stolen Child, The" (Yeats), **12:**1702

"Stone That Grows, The" (Camus), **2:**176

Stories of Eva Luna, The (Allende), **1:**44, 46

Stories of Frank O'Connor, The (O'Connor), **8:**1096

Story of an African Farm (Schreiner), **6:**793

Story of a Panic, The (Forster), **3:**326

"Story of Frankie…My Man, The" (Weller), **12:**1611

"Story of the Warrior and the Captive Woman, The" (Borges), **1:**117

Storyteller, The (Vargas Llosa), **11:**1558, 1562–64

"Strange Meeting" (Owen), **8:**1149

Strange Pilgrims (García Márquez), **3:**412

Stranger, The (Camus), **2:**159, 161, 162, 164, 166, 167, 168–72, 169, 177

translations of, **2:**168–69

Street, The: A Memoir (Richler), **9:**1263, 1264

Street of Riches (Roy), **10:**1305, 1307, 1312–13

"Strike Pay" (Lawrence), **6:**773

Strong Breed, The (Soyinka), **10:**1425, 1427

Studies in Classic American Literature (Lawrence), **6:**766, 768

Stunde hinter Mitternacht, Eine (Hesse), **5:**585, 588

Stunden-Buch, Das. See Book of Hours, The (Rilke)

"Such Were the Joys" (Orwell), **8:**1110

Sudasiyat al-ayyam al-sitta (Habibi), **4:**531–32, 535–36

Suffrage of Elvira, The (Naipaul), **8:**1016, 1018, 1020

Sugar Street (Mahfouz), **6:**830, 843–44

Sukariyya, Al- (Mahfouz), **6:**830, 843–44

Summan wal-kharif, Al– (Mahfouz). *See Autumn Quail*

Summer before the Dark, The (Lessing), **6:**791

"Summer Night, A" (Auden), **1:**67, 68–69

Sun Also Rises, The (Hemingway), **9:**1249

Suna no onna (Abe). *See Woman in the Dunes, The*

Sunday Sun (Guillén), **4:**520

"Sunlight" (Heaney), **4:**571

Sunset and Shadows (Weller), **12:**1611, 1612

"Supper at Elsinore, The" (Dinesen), **3:**301, 302

Suppressing Bandits (Chinese classic novel), **2:**213

"Sur, El" (Borges), **1:**107, 112, 120

Surprised by Joy (Lewis), **6:**806

Survivor, The (Keneally), **6:**728

Suspense (Conrad), **2:**250, 262

Swami and Friends (Narayan), **8:**1039, 1042, 1051–52

Swamp Dwellers, The (Soyinka), **10:**1422, 1424, 1427

Sweeney Astray (Heaney version), **4:**560, 573–74

"Sweet Dancer" (Yeats), **12:**1714

Sword of Honour, The (trilogy) (Waugh), **12:**1589, 1592, 1594, 1596, 1597, 1602–4

Taht al-midhallah (Mahfouz), **6:**828, 832

Taido (Young Samurai: Bodybuilders of Japan) (Mishima, intro.), **7:**911

Tale of Genji, The, **5:**699

Tales from a Troubled Land (Paton), **9:**1195

Tales of Jacob, The (Mann), **7:**874

Talk Stories (Kincaid), **6:**751

Tamaño de mi esperanza, El (Borges), **1:**115

"Tango, The" (Borges), **1:**121

Tanin no kao (Abe), **1:**17–18

Tariq, Al- (Mahfouz), **6:**833

Teleftaios pirasmós,O (Kazantzakis). *See Last Temptation of Christ, The*

Tempest, A: After the Tempest of Shakespeare (Une Tempête) (Césaire), **2:**195, 199, 204

Tempest, The (Shakespeare)
as Huxley title source, **5:**614
as Walcott influence, **11:**1573

"Tempests" (Dinesen), **3:**301

Temple of Dawn, The (Mishima), **7:**911, 912

Temple of the Golden Pavilion, The (Mishima), **7:**911, 912

Temps du mépris, Le (Malraux), **6:**848, 849, 861

Temptation (Havel), **4:**540, 541, 544, 554–56

Temptation of the West, The (La tentation de l'occident) (Malraux), **6:**845, 848, 854, 860

"Tenant, The" (Mukherjee), **7:**940

Tenkei (Takamura), **11:**1503, 1505

Tenth Man, The (Greene; screenplay), **4:**502

Tentiva del hombre infinito (Neruda), **8:**1058

Terra Nostra (Fuentes), **3:**339, 344, 345, 354, 357–58

"Thanksgiving, A" (Auden), **1:**63

Tharthara fawq al-Nil (Mahfouz), **6:**834, 835, 836

That Hideous Strength (Lewis), **6:**813, 814, *815*, 817–18; **11:**1540

"Theologians, The" (Borges), **1:**117

Thief and the Dogs, The (Mahfouz), **6:**833

Thing Happens, The (Shaw), **10:**1375

Things Fall Apart (Achebe), **1:**25, 26, 27, 30–32, 33, 37

Third Man, The (Greene), **4:**502

Third Man, The (Greene; screenplay), **4:**497, 502

Third One, The (Dangarembga), **2:**269

"Third Resignation, The" (García Márquez), **3:**415

Thirst for Love (Mishima), **7:**907, 910, 911, 913–14, 915, 918–20

Thirteen Poems (White), **12:**1655, 1662

This Gun for Hire (Greene), **4:**500, 502

This Town of Shit (García Márquez). *See In Evil Hour*

This Was the Old Chief's Country (Lessing), **6**:789, 799

This Year in Jerusalem (Richler), **9**:1263

Those Barren Leaves (Huxley), **5**:603, 608

Thousand and One Nights, The, **1**:120; **3**:301, 302; **6**:833

Thousand Cranes (Kawabata), **5**:696, 697

Three Cheers for the Paraclete (Keneally), **6**:728, 742–44

Three Comrades (Remarque), **9**:1220, 1224, 1235

Three Essays (Mann), **7**:873

Three Guineas (Woolf), **12**:1677, 1678, 1681, 1693–94

Threepenny Opera, The (Brecht and Weill), **1**:125, 128, 129, 133, 134, 135–37; **10**:1427, 1429

Three Plays for Puritans (Shaw), **10**:1358, 1360

Three Tales (O'Connor), **8**:1096

Three Uneasy Pieces (White), **12**:1657

Through the Looking Glass (Carroll), **7**:967, 980

Through the West Indian Sea Sails a Paper Boat (Guillén), **4**:520

Thulathiyya, al-. *See* Cairo Trilogy, The

Tía Julia y el escribidor, La (Vargas Llosa). *See Aunt Julia and the Scriptwriter*

Tibetan Book of the Dead, **5**:617

Tiempo de morir (Fuentes and García Márquez; screenplay), **3**:341, *343*, 345

Tientos y diferencias (Carpentier), **2**:183

Tiger's Daughter, The (Mukherjee), **7**:940, 943

Till We Have Faces: A Myth Retold (Lewis), **6**:806, 813, 822–24

Time and the Place, The (Mahfouz), **6**:834

Time Machine, The (Wells), **12**:1629, 1631, 1633, 1639, 1642–44, 1646

Time Must Have a Stop (Huxley), **5**:608, 617

Time of the Hero, The (Vargas Llosa), **11**:1553, 1554, 1557, 1559, 1560–62

Time Present (Osborne), **8**:1134, 1135, 1136

Time's Pocket (O'Connor), **8**:1096

Time to Die (Fuentes and García Márquez; screenplay), **3**:*343*, 345

Time to Love and a Time to Die, A (Remarque), **9**:1221, 1224, *1226*, 1235, 1237

Tin Drum, The (Grass), **10**:1325

Tin Flute, The (Roy), **10**:1301, 1303, 1304, 1305, 1307, 1309–10

Tinker's Wedding, The (Synge), **11**:1471, 1483–84

"To a Picture" (Paton), **9**:1183

"To Be Carved on a Stone at Thoor Ballylee" (Yeats), **12**:*1713*

Tobias Makombe (Dangarembga), **2**:268

Toda-Raba (Kazantzakis), **5**:706

Tod in Venedig, Der (Mann). *See Death in Venice*

Tokyo People (*Tokyo no hito*) (Kawabata), **5**:697

Tom Jones (Fielding; Osborne screenplay), **8**:*1133*, 1134

Tomorrow (Conrad), **2**:*250*

Tonio Kröger (Mann), **7**:870–71, 873

Tono-Bungay (Wells), **12**:1629, 1632, 1633, 1644–46

Tōō o yuku (Abe), **1**:13

Too True to Be Good (Shaw), **10**:1365

"To Room 19" (Lessing), **6**:799–800

To the Lighthouse (Woolf), **9**:1163; **12**:1676, 1677, 1678, 1679, *1688*, 1689–90

"To the Oaks of Glencree" (Synge), **11**:1473

Towards Asmara (Keneally), **6**:744

Towards the Mountain (Paton), **9**:1188

"Tower, The" (Yeats), **12**:1703, 1712–13

Tower, The (Yeats), **12**:1712–14

Tragedy of an Elderly Gentleman, The (Shaw), **10**:1375

Tragedy of King Christophe, The (*Tragédie du Roi Christophe, La*) (Césaire), **2**:195, 199, 204

Transparent Things (Nabokov), **7**:990

Traumbude, Die (Remarque), **9**:1220, 1221

Traveller's Samples, **8**:1096, 1097, 1106

Travels (Polo), **2**:157–58

Travels with My Aunt (Greene), **4**:500, 502

Treasure Island (Stevenson), **7**:967, 973

Tree and Leaf (Tolkien), **11**:1532, 1534, 1536, 1548

Tree of Man, The (White), **12**:1653, 1654, 1670

Trespasser, The (Lawrence), **6**:782

Trial, The (Kafka), **2**:236; **5**:662, 664, 666, 670, 672–74, 680, 681

"Trial and Reconciliation" (Paton), **9**:1190, 1192

Trial of Dedan Kimathi, The (Ngũgĩ and Mugo), **8**:1074, 1075

Trials of Brother Jero, The (Soyinka), **10**:1425, 1427, 1437

Trilogy, The: *Molloy; Malone Dies; The Unnamable* (Beckett), **1**:90, 91, 95, 96, 100–102

Trip to Nuremberg, The (Hesse), **5**:586

Tristan (Mann), **7**:871, 873, 886–87

Trommeln in der Nacht (Brecht), **1**:127

Trouble with Nigeria, The (Achebe), **1**:24, 25

"True Story of Ah Q, The" (Chou), **2**:212, 219–21, 223

"Trust the People" (Brecht; screenplay). *See Hangmen Also Die*

"Truth about My Adventure, The" (Velasco), **3**:418

Turn in the South, A (Naipaul), **8**:1017

"TV People" (Murakami), **7**:963

25 Poems (Thomas), **11**:1513–14

Twenty-five Poems (Walcott), **11**:1570

Twenty Love Poems and a Song of Despair (Neruda), **8**:1055, 1057–58, 1059, 1063, 1066–68

Twilight (Neruda), **8**:1057

Two Cheers for Democracy (Forster), **3**:323

"Two Gallants" (Joyce), **5**:649

"Two Kings and the Two Labyrinths, The" (Borges), **1**:117

Two Towers, The (Tolkien), **11**:1543

Twyborn Affair, The (White), **12**:1656, 1671

"Typhoon" (Conrad), **2**:250, 253

Ultimo viene il corvo (Calvino), **2**:156

Ulyesses (Joyce), **10**:1429

Ulysses (Joyce), **3**:428; **4**:535; **5**:635, 637, 639, 640, *642*, 643, 645, 646, 650, 653, 654–56, 717; **10**:*1371*

significance of, **12**:1704, 1707

Woolf's assessment of, **12**:1685

"Ulysses" (Soyinka), **10**:1429, 1436

"Um al Rubabeeka" (Habibi), **4**:*530*

Umm Saad (Kanafani), **5**:688, 691

Umorismo, L' (Pirandello), **9**:1211

Uncle Tom's Cabin (Stowe), **9**:1193, 1194

Unconditional Surrender (The End of the Battle) (Waugh), **12**:1592, 1602–4

Underground: The Tokyo Gas Attack and the Japanese Psyche (Murakami), **7**:956, 958

Under Milk Wood (Thomas; radio play), **11**:1514, 1516, *1517*, 1521, *1522*, 1523, 1525

Under My Skin (Lessing), **6**:789

Under the Net (Murdoch), **7**:969, 970, 974, *978*, 980

Under This Blazing Light (Oz), **9**:1166, *1167*

Under Western Eyes (Conrad), **2**:248, 250, 265

"Unfaithful Wife, The" (García Lorca), **3**:401

Unfinished Tales (Tolkien), **11**:1535

Unicorn, The (Murdoch), **7**:974

"Unknown Citizen, The" (Auden), **1**:67, 71–72

Unnamable, The (Beckett), **1**:90, 96, 100, 101–2

Unterm Rad (Hesse). *See Beneath the Wheel*

Unveiling (Havel), **4**:541, 550, 552

Upanishads (Hindu text), **11**:1498

Us Fellas: An Anthology of Aboriginal Writing (Weller contributions.), **12**:1611, 1612

Utsukushisa to kanashimi (Kawabata), **5**:696, 697, 698

"Valaquenta" (Tolkien), **11**:1547

Valley Song (Fugard), **3**:362, 363, 373–74

Vaněk Plays, The), **4**:544, 550–54, 557

"Veiled Mirrors, The" (Borges), **1**:119

Veinte poemas de amor y una canción desesperada (Neruda). *See Twenty Love Poems and a Song of Despair*

Versos del capitán, Los (Neruda), **8**:1059

"Verwandlung, Die" (Kafka). *See* "Metamorphosis, The"

"Vice, The" (Pirandello), **9**:1203

Victims of Duty (Ionesco), **5**:622, 624

Victory (Conrad), film adaptation, **2**:249

"Vienne" (Rhys), **9**:1257

"View from a Window, A" (Kafka), **5**:661

"View of Yasukuni Festival, A" (Kawabata), **5**:696

Vile Bodies (Waugh), **12**:*1590*, 1591, 1592, 1595, 1596, 1597

Village by the Sea, The (Desai), **2**:280, 281, 286

Víos ke politía tu Aléksi Zorbá (Kazantzakis). *See Zorba the Greek*

Viper of Milan, The (Bowen), **4**:496

Vision, A (Yeats), **12**:1703, 1714–15

Viva Sandino (García Márquez; screenplay), **3**:414

"Voices" (Yeats), **12**:1697

Voices in the City (Desai), **2**:281, 282

Voices of the Heroic Dead (Mishima), **7**:*910*

Voie royale, La (Malraux), **6**:848, 849, 860–61

Von der Freuden und Mühen der Jugendwehr (Remarque), **9**:1220

"Vor der Sintflut" (Brecht), **1**:126

Voss (White), **12**:1654, 1655, 1659, 1665–67

Voyage in the Dark (Rhys), **9**:1240, 1242, 1246, 1248, 1257

"Voyage of Éarendel the Evening Star, The" (Tolkien), **11**:1547

Voyage Out, The (Woolf), **12**:1676, 1677

Vúdas (Kazantzakis), **5**:706, 708

"Wagner" (Mann), **7**:872

Waiting for Godot (Beckett), **1**:87, 90, 91, 92, 95, 96, 97–100, 102, 103; **3**:386, 387

Waiting for the Barbarians (Coetzee), **2**:229, 231, 232, 234, 238–40

Walking in the Shade (Lessing), **6**:789

Walls (Abe), **1**:13, 19

Walnut Trees of Altenburg, The (Malraux), **6**:850

Wanderings of Oisin and Other Poems, The (Yeats), **12**:1698

Waqa'i al-ghariba fi ikhtifa' Sa'id abi al-nahs al-mutasha'il, Al- (Habibi). *See Secret Life of Saeed, the Ill-Fated Pessoptimist*

War in Heaven (Williams), **11**:1544

War in the Air, The (Wells), **12**:1632

War of the End of the World, The (Vargas Llosa), **11**:*1554*, 1558

War of the Worlds, The (Wells), **12**:1631, 1635–36, 1646–48

War of Time: Three Short Stories and a Novella (Carpentier), **2**:183, 184, 193

"Wasteland" (Paton), **9**:1195

Waste Land, The (Eliot), **12**:1604

Watcher, The (Calvino), **2**:156

Watt (Beckett), **1**:91, 101

Waugh in Abyssinia (Waugh), **12**:1592, 1593

Waves, The (Woolf), **12**:1677, 1680

Way in the World, A (Naipaul), **8**:1017, 1021

"Way of the Wind, The" (Oz), **9**:1166–67, *1176*, 1177

Ways of Escape (Greene), **4**:506, *508*

We (Zamatin), **8**:1119

Wedding Song (Mahfouz), **6**:835

Weep Not, Child (Ngũgĩ), **8**:1074, 1075, 1078, 1090, *1091*

Weg zurück, Der (Remarque). *See Road Back, The*

Well of the Saints, The (Synge), **11**:1463, 1467, 1471, 1481–83, 1484

"Welsh Incident" (Graves), **4**:482

We Never Make Mistakes (Solzhenitsyn), **10**:1418

"West Indian Weekend" (Kincaid), **6**:751

West Indies, Ltd. (Guillén), **4**:519, 524–25

West of Suez (Osborne), **8**:1134, 1135, 1136

"Whatever You Say, Say Nothing" (Heaney), **4**:572

"What Is the Word" (Beckett), **1**:91

"What's Wrong with the Country?" (O'Connor), **8**:1108

"What Then?" (Yeats), **12**:1714

"When I Was Seventeen" (Kincaid), **6**:749, 750

When the Going Was Good (Waugh), **12**:1592

When the Moon Has Set (Synge), **11**:1466

When We Dead Awaken (Ibsen), **5:**637, 646

Where Angels Fear to Tread (Forster), **3:**323, 326, 330

Where Nests the Water Hen (Roy), **10:**1305, 1307, 1313–14

Where Shall We Go This Summer? (Desai), **2:**282

Where the Air Is Clear (Fuentes), **3:**339, 344, 345, 347, 351–52, 354

Where the Jackels Howl (Oz), **9:**1159, 1161, 1162, 1174, 1177

White Goddess, The (Graves), **4:**477, 480, 481, 484, 487, 491–92

White Peacock, The (Lawrence), **6:**764, 765, 766, 770, 782

Whole Son, The (Guillén), **4:**519, 525

Whoroscope (Beckett), **1:**89, 91, 93–94

"Who's Who When Everybody is Somebody Else" (Glasheen), **5:**658

"Why I Write" (Orwell), **8:**1117, 1120

Why She Would Not (Shaw), **10:**1362

Wide Sargasso Sea (Rhys), **9:**1239, 1240, 1242, 1243, 1246, 1248–49, 1250, 1251, 1254–56

Widowers' Houses (Shaw), **10:**1358, 1359–60, 1362

Wife (Mukherjee), **7:**940, 943, 944, 946–48

Wife of Sir Isaac Harman, The (Wells), **12:**1637

Wijhat nazar (Mahfouz newspaper column), **6:**831

Wild Bird's Nest, The (O'Connor, transl.), **8:**1096

Wild Grass (Chou), **2:**212, 223

Wild Sheep Chase, A (Murakami), **7:**953, 956, 957

Wilfred Owen: Selected Letters (Bell, ed.), **8:**1150

"Williams and the Arthuriad" (Lewis), **11:**1540

Wind among the Reeds, The (Yeats), **12:**1697, 1701, 1702, 1708–10

Wind Blows Away Our Words, The (Lessing), **6:**789

Windflower (Roy), **10:**1314

Wind in the Willows, The (Grahame), **11:**1542

Wind-up Bird Chronicle, The (Murakami), **7:**956, 957, 963–64

Wintering Out (Heaney), **4:**562, 571

"Winter's Tale, A" (Thomas), **11:**1515

Winter's Tales (Dinesen), **3:**296, 297, 299, 306

"Wisdom of the King, The" (Yeats), **12:***1701*

"Wishing Gate, The" (Wordsworth), **1:**69

"Without Colors" (Calvino), **2:**155

Without Isms (Gao), **3:**384

"Without Isms" (Gao), **3:**384

Without Isms (Gao), **3:**384

"Without Isms" (Gao), **3:**384

Wizard of Oz, The (Rushdie), **10:**1321, 1331

Woman in the Dunes (Abe; screenplay), **1:**13, 15, *16*, 17

Woman in the Dunes, The (Abe), **1:**11, 13, 15, 16–17, 18

Women in Love (Lawrence), **6:**763, 766, 767, 767–68, 769, 771, 777–79, 782

Wonyosi (Soyinka), **10:**1427, 1429

"Word about Words, A" (Havel), **4:**544

World I Breathe, The (Thomas), **11:**1514

World of William Clissold, The (Wells), **12:**1633, 1639

World Set Free, The (Wells), **12:**1632

"World Split Apart, A" (Solzhenitsyn), **10:**1402

Worm Ouroboros, The (Eddison), **11:**1539

Wrestling Match, The (Emecheta), **3:**314

Wretched of the Earth, The (Fanon), **2:**275

"Writer and India, The" (Naipaul), **8:**1032

Writers in Politics: A Reengagement with Issues of Literature and Society (Ngugi), **8:**1074, 1076, 1082

Writing and Being (Gordimer), **4:**460, 472

"Writing and Being" (Gordimer Nobel Prize lecture), **4:**470

"Yao" (Chou), **2:**218–19

Years, The (Woolf), **12:**1677

Years with Laura Díaz, The (Fuentes), **3:**344, 345, 349–50

Yecao (Chou), **2:**212, 223

"Yellow Notebook" (Lessing), **6:**796

Yerma (García Lorca), **3:**394, 404, 405, 406

Yi ge ren de shenjing (Gao). *See One Man's Bible*

You Never Can Tell (Shaw), **10:**1360, 1363

Young Joseph (Mann), **7:**873, 874

Young Man Luther (Erikson), **8:**1138

"Youth" (Conrad), **2:**250

"Yugeshiki no kagami" (Kawabata), **5:**695

Yukiguni (Kawabata). *See Snow Country*

Zapatera prodigiosa, La (García Lorca), **3:**394, 406, *407*, 408

Zaschita Luzhina (Nabokov), **7:**992

Zauberflöte, Die (Auden and Kallman; libretto). *See Magic Flute, The: An Opera in Two Acts*

Zeit zu leben und Zeit zu sterben (Remarque). *See Time to Love and a Time to Die, A*

"Zhufu" (Chou), **2:**212, 221–22

Zorba the Greek (Kazantzakis), **5:**703, 705, *707*, 708, 710, 711, 713–15, 716, 717

Zuqaq al-Midaq (Mahfouz), **6:**830, 833

Index of Visual Arts

Numbers in **bold** indicate volumes.
Page numbers in *italic* indicate illustrations or illustration captions.

Aboriginal Family in Alice Springs, Australia (painting), **12:***1609*
Adventurer (painting), **9:***1173*
Alarm, The (artwork), **10:***1418*
Allegory of Death (painting), **11:***1461*
aloe plant (photograph), **3:***372, 373*
Alpine Meadow, An (painting), **5:***592*
Amour et Psyche (Cupid and Psyche) (sculpture), **6:***823*
Archangel Gabriel (painting), **7:***983*
Argenteuil in the Snow, Setting Sun (painting), **11:***1525*
Ascent, The (painting), **2:***257*
Attack on the People, The (painting), **11:***1473*
At the Border II (painting), **2:***177*
Autobiography: Air/CS 560 (artwork), **10:***1435*
Awakening Conscience, The (painting), **3:***324*
Azazel's Revenge (painting), **1:***49*

balloon flight at Versailles (print), **12:***1645*
Balseros (painting), **2:***192*
Barren Land, The (painting), **12:***1623*
Barricades (artwork), **3:***429*
Basket of Eggs (painting), **9:***1170*
Beata Beatrix (painting), **12:***1715*
Bedouin from the Sahara Desert Making Enquiries at Gaza (watercolor), **7:***887*
Bedouin nomad (photograph), **9:***1175*
Beethoven's Death Mask, Variation #7 (painting), **2:***263*
Between a Mulatto and a Quadroon (artwork), **4:***524*
Bird Pull Toy (artwork), **7:***964*
Black Girl with Wings (painting), **6:***761*
Black Man Always Hides His Left Hand, The (painting), **8:***1085*
Bound (artwork), **10:***1394*

British Commonwealth of Nations—Together, The (poster), **12:***1617*
Business City (painting), **7:***959*

Café (artwork), **3:***417*
Cantando el Corrido (artwork), **3:***396*
Ceremony Cousin Zaka (Voodoo Scene) (painting), **2:***188*
Chapter Meeting of Nuns (gouache), **11:***1457*
Childhood of Cain and Abel (painting), **6:***840*
Claude Monet Painting at the Edge of a Wood (painting), **11:***1549*
Cleave (painting), **12:***1621*
Cobbler and His Family, The (painting), **3:***407*
Confession Scene, A (painting), **8:***1106*
Continental Divide (artwork), **1:***26*
Convalescent (Emma) (color chalk-on-paper), **7:***877*
Costume Designs for Pamina and Monostatos in "The Magic Flute" (artwork), **7:***981*
Cotopaxi (painting), **8:***1069*
Courtesan, The (painting), **5:***654*
Crouching Girl (painting), **11:***1509*
Cuatro Santos (painting), **2:***187*
Cuba Libre (gouache-and-ink), **4:***523*

Day's End (artwork), **3:***317*
Days of Small Sorrows (artwork), **8:***1105*
Death of a Capitalist (mural), **3:***353*
Descent, The (painting), **3:***337*
Desperation (painting), **9:***1277*
Diptych: Interior with Couple (painting), **11:***1565*
Disappointed Love (painting), **9:***1168*
Don Juan Discovered by Haydee (painting), **5:***714*
Dream Play, A (painting), **12:***1724*
Dreams about Japan (painting), **5:***698*
Dreams No. 2 (painting), **2:***273*

Drunkard, The (painting), **5:***675*
Duelo a Garrozatos (painting), **3:***406*
Duino Castle etching, **9:***1293*

Echelle de feu, L' (The Ladder of Fire) (painting), **7:***995*
Embrace, The (artwork), **8:***1061*
Empire des lumières, L' (Empire of light) (painting), **12:***1658*
End of Dinner, 1913 (painting), **3:***306*
Enigma of the Hour (painting), **10:***1339*
Eskimo (painting), **9:***1272*

Face in Mirror (artwork), **1:***119*
Falconer, The (painting), **3:***307*
False Prophet, The (painting), **8:***1091*
Family in Interior (painting), **6:***753*
Fang mask, **11:***1579*
Farmstead in Russia, A (artwork), **10:***1414*
Father and Daughter (ink and prismacolor on paper), **2:***222*
Faust and Mephistopheles (untitled lithograph), **7:***888*
Favorite Piece, A (painting), **3:***329*
Federico García Lorca (painting), **3:***393*
fighting cock (mosaic), **3:***427*
"Figure Inside Box, Number 2" (artwork), **1:***18*
Fire Man, The (El Hombre de fuego) (artwork), **8:***1029*
fire-walking festival in India (lithograph), **3:***322*
Five Centuries Later (painting), **2:***259*
Five Eunuchs (painting), **2:***210*
Four Women at Trouville (watercolor), **7:***960*
Francis Noel Clarke Mundy and His Grandson, William Mundy (painting), **7:***880*
French school, **12:***1635*
From Here I Saw What Happened and I Cried (artwork series), **4:***462*
Funeral in Connaught (painting), **5:***657*

Funeral Procession, The (painting), 3:425

Gallery of HMS Calcutta (Portsmouth), The (painting), 3:332
Game, The (painting), 4:555
Game of Universal History (artwork), 12:1637
Germans Eating Sour-Krout (etching), 7:901
Gitanos in Alcala de Jenarez (painting), 3:400
Golden Hind (engraving), 4:441
Grand Marshals, The (artwork), 1:34
Graveyard in Snow (painting), 5:651
Greed (artwork), 1:135
Green Turban, The (painting), 2:1687
Grosstadt (Big Town) (painting), 5:616
Grosstadt (Metropolis) (artwork), 1:127

Hadatu (Syria) statuary fragment, 6:819
Hammer and Sickle (image), 7:1003
Head of a Woman (watercolor), 11:1493
Heads and Hands I (artwork), 4:463
Head with Hand (artwork), 8:1063
henta (wooden board), 8:1049
"Hillside with Flowering Azalea" (painting), 11:1504
Hindu illustrated page (artwork), 7:938
Hitching the Sleigh (painting), 7:933
Holy Bible frontispiece (engraving), 9:1189
Homer (painting), 5:717
House of Death, The (painting), 10:1409

Illustration of the Mahabharata: Combat with Arches and Swords with Four People (gouâche), 8:1041
Imprison (painting), 2:220
In a Refugee's Camp (painting), 4:529
Incognito (acrylic-on-canvas), 4:504
Incredulity of Saint Thomas (painting), 11:1452
Innocence (pastel), 2:218
Inside Story (painting), 10:1314
Inside the Tower of Babel (painting), 1:116
Instrument, The (painting), 2:155

Interior (artwork), 6:755
In the Ferryman's (painting), 11:1479

James Joyce (portrait), 1:95
January Sunrise, Quebec City (painting), 10:1306
Jeantaud, Linet and Lainé, Friends of the Artist (painting), 3:327
Jenny Cassatt with Her Son (painting), 6:783
Jewish Funeral, A (painting), 7:905
J. M. Coetzee (painted portrait), 2:228
Jodhpur Blue (artwork), 10:1327
John Butler Yeats (portrait), 12:1709

Kiss, The (painting), 4:489; 6:776
Kizette in Pink (Kizette en rose) (painting), 7:998
Knight on a Galloping Charger, A (painting), 9:1274
Known Faces of Unknown People (oil-on-linen), 4:553

Laguna Que Espera (painting), 2:184
Landscape with Large Plants and People (artwork), 3:420
Last Train to Atlith (painting), 12:1719
Lenin on an Armored Car During the October Revolution (painting), 10:1413
Letter, The (painting), 11:1503
Lipsos Room (artwork), 1:114
Loch Duich, Summer Moonlight (watercolor), 9:1214
Love Letter 2 (artwork), 10:1431
Lovers with Daisies (Les Amoreux aux Marguerites) (artwork), 8:1062
Lunch (painting), 12:1661
Lu Xun (head sculpture), 2:209
Lu Xun (painted portrait), 2:208

Mad Woman (painting), 9:1255
Male Nude with Red Cloth (artwork), 2:175
Man Walking in the Sky (painting), 5:633
Man with a Bib (painting), 7:885
Many Dinners: Old Wood (painting), 3:375
Maria and Her Mother (painting), 3:357
Martians (engraving), 12:1635
Mascara de la Locura, La (The Mask of Madness) (painting), 9:1164

Massacre of Turkish Soldiers (woodcut), 5:709
Maternity (painting), 4:565
Meeting Between Solzhenitsyn and Böll at Rostropovich's Country House (painting), 10:1406
Memento Mori (artwork), 1:70
Millworkers Landscape (artwork), 6:772
Misses Hunter, The (painting), 10:1374
Mixed Messages (installation), 4:469
Moghul miniature painting, 7:942, 943
Moonlight—Dance of the Aboriginees of van Diemen Land, Tasmania (painting), 12:1612
Mosque al-Azher at Cairo, The (artwork), 6:839
Mother Courage II (painting), 6:759
Mother's Kiss (painting), 6:795
Mouthful of Words, A (artwork), 4:556
Muerte de Capitalista, La (mural), 3:353
Musical Chairs (artwork), 12:1597

Naga protecting Buddha statue (photograph), 8:1053
Nazi Insignia (image), 7:1003
Neruda on His Island (Neruda En Sur Isla) (artwork), 3:423
New Baby (painting), 9:1270
New Planet, The (painting), 12:1643
Night in Bologna, A (painting), 2:153
No Apartheid Anywhere (painting), 4:473
"No Parking Anytime" (art portfolio), 10:1394
#83 Hollandsche Spoor (image), 5:679

On the Street (painting), 11:1482
Operatic Duet #3 (artwork), 7:977
Orgy—Night of the Rich (La Orgia) (painting), 5:611
Otago (drawing), 2:258
Our Waiting (painting), 1:123
Out of the Woods (painting), 12:1666
Outside the Ale House Door (painting), 11:1476
Oval of Apparitions (painting), 12:1664

Painter's Family, The (artwork), 12:1660
Parachutist (crayon and pastel), 9:1176

Parade of the Red Army, The (painting), **10:**1415

Parrot: Lory or Collared (artwork), **11:**1499

Passing Time (painting), **12:**1679

Patrick White (sketches), **12:**1668, 1670

People Walking (photograph), **9:**1263

Pit of Disease, The: The Falsifiers (watercolor), **4:**455

Pity (painting), **12:**1708

Playful Fight (painting), **4:**443

Politicians, The (painting), **4:**549

Poor Woman with the Children (painting), **9:**1247

Portrait of Dona Carmen Alcalde Velasco de Cazotte (painting), **3:**395

Portrait of Joseph Conrad (lithograph), **8:**1080

Portrait of Rani Jindan Singh (painting), **11:**1494

portrait of Robert Graves (artwork), **4:**483

portrait of Toussaint-Louverture (painting), **11:**1575

Portrait of V. S. Eliseyeva (sculpture), **9:**1285

Posies Already Prepared (artwork), **1:**51

Priest at the Altar (artwork), **6:**743

Primavera, La (artwork), **7:**1004

Radha and Krishna in the Grove (gouache-on-paper painting), **7:**946

Rake's Progress, The (etchings), **1:**74

Rama and Lakshmana Shooting Arrows at the Demon Ravana (artwork), **8:**1045

"Ra-Ra" Haitian Carnival Scene (painting), **9:**1257

Reading (The Politicians) (painting), **4:**549

Red Head (artwork), **11:**1561

Red Ship (oil and acrylic), **2:**261

Rendering of Sakyamuni Buddha (artwork), **3:**383

Revolt of the Prisoners (sculpture), **9:**1269

Revolutionary (painting), **2:**271

rock paintings, **12:**1615, 1626

Romeo and Juliet balcony scene (book illustration), **8:**1067

"Rower, The" (artwork), **1:**73

Sacred and Profane Love (painting), **7:**982

St. George slaying the dragon (medieval artwork), **11:**1534

Saint-Sauveur (painting), **10:**1311

Saint Sebastian (painting), **7:**909

Schistos (artwork), **1:**20

Sculpture de Nord (Sculpture of the North) (sculpture), **9:**1276

Sea-piece by Moonlight (painting), **2:**253

Seated Man (Oceanside) (painting), **2:**156

Secret Door in Bramham Park (photograph), **12:**1641

Secret Lives (painting), **7:**924

Self-Portrait (Bacon painting), **4:**454

Set: From the Series Equilibrium (artwork), **8:**1031

Seven Red Flowers (painting), **8:**1087

Shape of the Universe, The (collage), **1:**118

Shout #16 (artwork), **2:**233

Silence (painting), **7:**919

Silhouette and Shadow (oil-on-canvas), **1:**37

Slave of Love and Light of Eyes: Abdel Gheram and Nouri el-Din (painting), **6:**843

Sleeper, The (painting), **5:**613

So Be It! (painting), **4:**471

Sorciere, La (The Sorceress) (pastel), **3:**303

Soulmates (painting), **2:**254

souls and outer space (untitled artwork), **6:**815

"Soviet is the Achievement of October, The" (political poster), **6:**788

Stalin and the Muses (painting), **10:**1404

Standing Woman (sculpture), **12:**1681

Star Shell, A (painting), **9:**1229

Still Life with Salad (painting), **9:**1170

Stirling Station (painting), **7:**899

Stone-Age Dike on the Island of Ruegen, Germany (painting), **11:**1537

Street Scene (painting), **5:**599; **6:**760

Study for Political Prisoner (charcoal-and-pencil-on-paper), **1:**39

Study for Portrait II after the Life Mask of William Blake (artwork), **8:**1137

Study of White Horse (Dappled Gray) (artwork), **6:**822

Sueno (Dream; Eve before Adam) (painting), **2:**201

Sueno de una Tarde (fresco), **3:**351

Sun in Pink Sky (photograph), **9:**1167

Swimmer #16 (painting), **2:**190

Taking Tea (painting), **7:**951

Tempest, The (artwork), **11:**1573

Tiresia (painting), **4:**501

Tomorrow I May Be Far Away (collage), **8:**1079

Topsy-Turvy Doll (artwork), **1:**36

Tramp, The (painting), **11:**1470

Translucent (painting), **12:**1663

Tree (artwork), **8:**1027

Two Fridas, The (painting), **3:**350

Two Suitors, The (painting), **5:**647

Unison of Many Hearts (painting), **1:**68

Untitled #13 from Visual Haiku Series (artwork), **2:**220

"Untitled" (painting), **1:**71

Untitled Suit (oil and charcoal on paper), **2:**272

Vecchio col nipotino (Old Man with Nephew) (painting), **5:**648

Venice, La Salute (artwork), **7:**883

View of the Plaza from Central Park, A (painting), **3:**404

View of the World, A (painting), **6:**798

Virginia Woolf at the Hogarth Press (sketch), **12:**1676

Visit to the Grandparents, The (lithograph), **7:**875

Vita Sackville-West (studio photograph), **12:**1678

Voice 1 (artwork), **4:**557

Wanderer above the Sea of Clouds, The (painting), **5:**652

Watching (artwork), **4:**474

We Shall Return (painting), **4:**536

What Is the Truth? (painting), **10:**1407

Who Is to Say? (painting), **2:**230

Wildeview (painting), **2:**158

Window X (painting), **1:**85

Winter in Broceliande (painting), **11:**1520

Index of Visual Artists

Numbers in **bold** indicate volumes.
Page numbers in *italic* indicate illustrations or illustration captions.

Adlard, Charlie, **6:**789
Akhal, Tamam Al-
 In a Refugee's Camp, **4:***529*
Allen, Harry Epworth
 Funeral in Connaught, **5:***657*
Andreas, Carl B.
 Wolf, A, **5:***596*
Anthony, Carol
 Lipsos Room, **1:***114*
Antunez, Nemesio
 Neruda on His Island (Neruda En Sur Isla), **3:***423*
Anwar, Ahmad Zakii
 Incognito, **4:***504*
Arreguin, Alfredo
 Sueno (Dream; Eve before Adam), **2:***201*
Aufiery, Dennis
 Balseros, **2:***192*

Bacon, Francis
 Self-Portrait, **4:***454*
 Study for Portrait II after the Life Mask of William Blake, **8:***1137*
Bacon, John Henry Frederick
 balcony scene from *Romeo and Juliet,* **8:***1067*
Bakst, Leon
 Costume Designs for Pamina and Monostatos in "The Magic Flute", **7:***981*
Balla, Giacomo
 Mad Woman, **9:***1255*
Barbier, Charles
 Father and Daughter, **2:***222*
Barraband, Jacques
 Parrot: Lory or Collared, **11:***1499*
Barton, Glenys
 Within, **8:***1033*
Bearden, Romare
 Tomorrow I May Be Far Away, **8:***1079*
Beers, Jan van
 The Courtesan, **5:***654*
Bell, Clive
 Woolf and, **12:***1675, 1677, 1685*

Bell, Vanessa Stephen
 Woolf and, **12:***685, 1674, 1675, 1677, 1678, 1683–84*
Bergner, Yosi
 Last Train to Atlith, **12:***1719*
Bergt, Michael
 Out of the Woods, **12:***1666*
 Rower, The, **1:***73*
Bigaud, Wilson
 "Ra-Ra" Haitian Carnival Scene, **9:***1257*
Binzen, Bill
 black-and-white photograph, **9:***1162*
Birch, Willie
 Grand Marshals, The, **1:***34*
Bittar, Antoine
 January Surprise, Quebec City, **10:***1306*
Blake, William
 House of Death, The, **10:***1409*
 Pit of Disease, The: The Falsifiers, **4:***455*
 Pity, **12:***1708*
 as Yeats influence, **12:***1709*
Blanche, Jacques Émile
 portrait of James Joyce, **1:***95*
Böcklin, Arnold, **9:***1222*
Boel, Cornelius
 Holy Bible frontispiece engraving, **9:***1189*
Borglum, Gutzon, **11:***1502*
Borofsky, Jonathan
 Man Walking in the Sky, **5:***633*
Boudin, Eugène
 Four Women at Trouville, **7:***960*
Boys, Michael
 Secret Door in Bramham Park, **12:***1641*
Brown, Ford Madox
 Convalescent (Emma), **7:***877*
 Don Juan Discovered by Haydee, **5:***714*

Cadmus, Paul
 Night in Bologna, A, **2:***153*

Calder, Alexander
 Bird Pull Toy, **7:***964*
Canova, Antonio
 Amour et Psyche (Cupid and Psyche, **6:***823*
Cariou, Thierry
 People Walking, **9:***1263*
Carolus-Duran, Charles Emile
 Kiss, The, **6:***776*
Carra, Carlo
 Oval of Apparitions, **12:***1664*
Carreno, Mario
 Cuba Libre, **4:***523*
Carriere, Eugene
 Maternity, **4:***565*
Carrière, Eugène
 Mother's Kiss, **6:***795*
Carrington, Dora
 Bloomsbury group and, **12:***1682, 1683, 1684*
Carus, Carl Gustav
 Stone Age Dike on the Island of Ruegen, Germany, **11:***1537*
Casorati, Felice
 Woman with a Bowl, **3:***405*
Cassatt, Mary
 Jenny Cassatt with Her Son, **6:***783*
Castañeda, Alfredo
 Our Waiting, **1:***123*
Cézanne, Paul
 as Rilke influence, **9:***1287*
Chagall, Marc
 Lovers with Daisies (Les Amoreux aux Marguerites), **8:***1062*
Chance, Jane Linnell
 Adventurer, The, **9:***1173*
Chin-Cheng Hung
 Innocence, **2:***218*
Chirico, Giorgio de, **8:***1032*
 Enigma of the Hour, **10:***1339*
 Painter's Family, The, **12:***1660*
Church, Frederick Edwin
 Cotopaxi, **8:***1069*
Chvostenko, Vassilli
 Lenin on an Armored Car During the October Revolution, **10:***1413*

Ciacelli, Arturo
  Parachutist, **9:**1176
Cienfuegos, Gonzalo
  Diptych: Interior with Couple,
    11:1565
  *Landscape with Large Plants and
    People*, **3:**420
Clark, Alex
  Inside the Tower of Babel, **1:**116
Colquhoun, Robert
  Barren Land, The, **12:**1623
Correco, Alvin
  Illustration of *War of the Worlds*,
    12:1647
Couture, Thomas
  Falconer, The, **3:**307
Cremer, Fritz
  Revolt of the Prisoners,
    9:1269
Crespi, Giovanni Battista
  Confession Scene, **8:**1106
Crook, P. J.
  Passing Time, **12:**1679

Dalí, Salvador
  García Lorca friendship, **3:**391,
    392, 394, 397, 401, 403
Danby, Francis
  Disappointed Love, **9:**1168
Dauzat, Adrien
  Mosque al-Azher at Cairo, The,
    6:839
Dean, Graham
  Red Head, **11:**1561
Degas, Edgar
  *Jeantaud, Linet and Lainé, Friends
    of the Artist*, **3:**327
Delaporte, Henri
  Basket of Eggs, **9:**1170
Dill, Lesley
  Mouthful of Words, A, **4:**556
Dinet, Etienne
  *Slave of Love and Light of Eyes:
    Abdel Gheram and Nouri el-
    Din*, **6:**843
Dinnerstein, Simon
  Dream Play, A, **12:**1724
Dix, Otto
  Grosstadt (Big Town), **5:**616
Donghi, Antonio
  Woman in a Café, **11:**1447
Dumont, Jacques
  Poor Woman with the Children,
    9:1247
Dunne, George E.
  In the Ferryman's, **11:**1479

El Greco, **5:**710
Ernst, Max
  self-portrait, **9:**1253
Esbens, Emile-Etienne
  Gitanos in Alcala de Jenarez, **3:**400
Escoffery, Michael
  Embrace, The, **8:**1061
Eveleth, Emily
  "Untitled," **1:**71
Eyck, Hubert and Jan van,
  2:174–75

Fenton, Terry
  Inside Story, **10:**1314
Fesca, A.
  etching of Castle Duino, **9:**1293
Frank, Mary
  Cleave, **12:**1621
  Head with Hand, **8:**1063
  Red Ship, **2:**261
  Standing Woman, **12:**1681
Freeman, Michael
  photograph of *Naga* protecting
    Buddha statue, **8:**1053
Freeman, Pearl
  photographic portrait of Rhys,
    9:1241
Friedrich, Caspar David
  Graveyard in Snow, **5:**651
  Sea-piece by Moonlight, **2:**253
  *Wanderer above the Sea of Clouds,
    The*, **5:**652
Frost, George Albert
  Hitching the Sleigh, **7:**933
Fry, Roger
  Bloomsbury group and,
    12:1676, 1677, 1678, 1682,
    1685

Gamarra, José
  Five Centuries Later, **2:**259
Gao Xingjian
  bird painting, **3:**379
Ge, Nikolai
  What Is the Truth?, **10:**1407
Gerasimov, Alexander
  Attack on the People, The,
    11:1473
Géricault, Jean Louis Théodore
  *Study of White Horse (Dappled
    Gray)*, **6:**822
Ghirlandaio, Domenico
  *Vecchio col nipotino (Old Man with
    Nephew)*, **5:**648
Gillray, James
  Germans Eating Sour-Krout, **7:**901

Glover, John
  *Moonlight—Dance of the
    Aboriginees of van Diemen
    Land, Tasmania*, **12:**1612
Goncharova, Natalia
  Funeral Procession, The, **3:**425
Goodman, Sidney
  Study for Political Prisoner, **1:**39
Goodwin, Arthur Clifton
  *View of the Plaza from Central
    Park, A*, **3:**404
Gordin, Misha
  Shout #16, **2:**233
Goya, Francisco de
  Duelo a Garrozatos, **3:**406
Goya y Lucientes, Francisco José de
  Reading (The Politicians), **4:**549
Granet, François Marius
  Priest at the Altar, **6:**743
Grant, Duncan
  Bloomsbury group and,
    12:1682, 1684, 1685
Greve, Gerit
  Many Dinners: Old Wood, **3:**375
Greve, Gerrit
  Unison of Many Hearts, **1:**68
Gromaire, Marcel
  Tramp, The, **11:**1470
Grosz, George
  looking at painting with Brecht
    and Charles Laughton, **1:**131
  Grosstadt (Metropolis), **1:**127
  Street Scene, **5:**599
Groux, Charles de
  Drunkard, The, **5:**675
Grun, Jules Alexandre
  End of Dinner, 1913, **3:**306

Haacke, Hans
  Mixed Messages, **4:**469
Haag, Carl
  *Bedouin from the Sahara Desert
    Making Enquiries at Gaza*,
    7:887
Halloran, Thomas
  *Beethoven's Death Mask, Variation
    #7*, **2:**263
Hannah, Duncan
  Days of Small Sorrows, **8:**1105
Henri, Robert
  portrait of John Butler Yeats,
    12:1709
Hocks, Teun
  untitled artwork, **4:**452
  untitled oil on silver print, **4:**533
  untitled painting, **7:**975

Hodalic, Arne
  photograph of *sadhu*, **8:***1050*
Hogarth, William, **1:**74
  Tempest, The, **11:***1573*
Hope, G. F. W.
  Otago, **2:***258*
Hoppé, E. O.
  studio photograph of Vita
    Sackville-West, **12:***1678*
Hoyningen-Huene, George
  photograph of Paris street scene,
    10:*1309*
Huang Chih-Yang
  Imprison, **2:***220*
Hung Liu
  Five Eunuchs, **2:***210*
Hunt, Charles
  Two Suitors, The, **5:***647*
Hunt, William Holman
  Awakening Conscience, The,
    3:*324*
Hurley, Frank
  photograph of eastern view of
    Perth, **12:***1608*

Ilina, Irina
  Dreams about Japan, **5:***698*
Illanes, Maria
  Desperation, **9:***1277*
Indermaur, Robert
  At the Border II, **2:***177*

Jacklin, Bill
  Man with a Bib, **7:***885*
Jacobi, Kathryn
  Operatic Duet #3, **7:***977*
Jakobson, Janis
  Set: From the Series Equilibrium,
    8:*1031*
James, Laura
  Black Girl with Wings, **6:***761*
Jarrell, Wadsworth
  Revolutionary, **2:***271*
John, Augustus
  Thomas and, **11:***1514–15*
Judkins, Rod
  Descent, The, **3:***337*

Kahan, Louis
  sketches of Patrick White,
    12:*1668, 1670*
Kahlo, Frida
  Fuentes and, **3:***350*
  Mascara de la Locura, La (*The
    Mask of Madness*), **9:***1164*
  Two Fridas, The, **3:***350*

Kaneko
  Crouching Girl, **11:***1509*
Kangra School of miniature painting
  Radha and Krishna in the Grove,
    7:*946*
Kaufmann, Ruprecht von
  Soulmates, **2:***254*
Kennedy, Richard
  Virginia Woolf at the Hogarth Press
    (sketch), **12:***1676*
Kennedy, William
  Stirling Station, **7:***899*
Kennington, Eric
  portrait of Graves, **4:***483*
Kent, Rockwell
  Eskimo, **9:***1272*
Kirby, John
  Secret Lives, **7:***924*
Kisseleff, Alexander
  Farmstead in Russia, A, **10:***1414*
Klee, Paul
  Wise Man, A, **4:***545*
Klimt, Gustav
  Kiss, The, **4:***489*
Komar, Vitaly
  *Meeting Between Solzhenitsyn and
    Böll at Rostropovich's Country
    House*, **10:***1406*
  Stalin and the Muses, **10:***1404*
Kozloff, Joyce
  Jodhpur Blue, **10:***1327*
Kronberg, Louis
  Maria and Her Mother, **3:***357*

Laboureur, Jean-Emile
  Letter, The, **11:***1503*
Laetitia
  Street Scene, **6:***760*
Lancaster, Osbert
  caricature of Waugh, **12:***1595*
Lawrence, Jacob
  Dreams No., 2 **2:***273*
Lee-Smith, Hughie
  Silhouette and Shadow, **1:***37*
Lempicka, Tamara de
  Green Turban, The, **12:***1687*
  Kizette in Pink (*Kizette en rose*),
    7:*998*
Lévy-Dhurmer, Lucien
  Silence, **7:***919*
Lévy-Dhurmer, Lucien
  Sorciere, La (*The Sorceress*), **3:***303*
Linn, David
  Ascent, The, **2:***257*
Liu Chunhua
  oil painting, **3:***382*

Long, Terry
  "Figure inside Box, Number 2,"
    1:18
Lovell, Whitfield
  Tree, **8:***1027*
  Untitled Suit, **2:***272*

MacDonald, Sonny
  Sculpture de Nord (*Sculpture of the
    North*), **9:***1276*
Madrazo, Raimondo de
  Favorite Piece, **3:***329*
Magee, Alan
  Schistos, **1:***20*
Magritte, René
  Echelle de feu, L' (*The Ladder of
    Fire*), **7:***995*
  Empire des lumières, L' (*Empire of
    light*), **12:***1658*
  Posies Already Prepared, **1:***51*
Master of Processions
  Cobbler and His Family, The,
    3:*407*
Mathey, Paul
  Woman and Child in a Room,
    8:*1100*
Maynard, Valerie
  No Apartheid Anywhere, **4:***473*
McMahon, Franklin
  *Aboriginal Family in Alice Springs,
    Australia*, **12:***1609*
McPhedran, Russell
  photograph of National
    Aborigine Day marchers,
    12:*1610*
McWirter, John
  Alpine Meadow, An, **5:***592*
Melamid, Alex
  *Meeting Between Solzhenitsyn and
    Böll at Rostropovich's Country
    House*, **10:***1406*
  Stalin and the Muses, **10:***1404*
Merry, Tom
  untitled lithograph, **5:***672*
Michelangelo
  Forster on, **3:***326, 331*
Miesenberger, Maria
  untitled artwork, **4:***459*
Moghul School of miniature paint-
    ing, **7:***942, 943*
Monet, Claude
  Argenteuil in the Snow, Setting Sun,
    11:*1525*
Monvoisin, Raymond
  *Portrait of Dona Carmen Alcalde
    Velasco de Cazotte*, **3:***395*

Mora, Heriberto
  Instrument, The, **2:***155*
Morland, George
  Outside the Ale House Door,
    11:*1476*
Murray, Kenneth
  photograph of Macchu Picchu
    ruins, **8:***1064*

Nash, John Northcote
  Millworkers Landscape,
    6:*772*
Nasogaluak, Eli
  *Sculpture de Nord (Sculpture of the
    North),* **9:***1276*
Natal, J.
  Memento Mori, **1:***70*
Nevay, Heather
  The Tribe, **4:***442*
Nevinson, Christopher R. W.
  Star Shell, A, **9:***1229*
No, Abdim Dr
  Day's End, **3:***317*
Nolan, Sidney
  White and, **12:***1656, 1671*
Noter, David Emil Joseph de
  Taking Tea, **7:***951*

O'Neill, Daniel
  Interior, **6:***755*
Orlik, Emil
  sketch of Rilke, **9:***1282*
Orozco, José Clemente
  *Fire Man, The (El Hombre de
    fuego),* **8:***1029*

Petrov-Vodkin, Kuzma
  Alarm, The, **10:***1418*
  Primavera, La, **7:***1004*
Pierre, A.
  *Ceremony Cousin Zaka (Voodoo
    Scene),* **2:***188*
Pindell, Howardena
  Autobiography: Air/CS 560,
    10:*1435*
Poisson, L'Ouverture
  Family in Interior, **6:***753*
Porter-Brown, Catherine
  Azazel's Revenge, **1:***49*
Portinar, Candido
  Café, **3:***417*
Poulton, Michael
  Shape of the Universe, The,
    1:*118*
Preti, Mattia
  Homer, **5:***717*

Pugliese, Christopher
  Greed, **1:***135*

Querfurt, August
  Knight on a Galloping Charger, A,
    9:*1274*

Regamey, Frederic
  Visit to the Grandparents, The,
    7:*875*
Regierungszeit, Georg I.
  woodcut of massacre of Turkish
    soldiers, **5:***709*
Reinagle, Ramsay Richard
  *Francis Noel Clarke Mundy and
    His Grandson, William Mundy,*
    7:*880*
Reni, Guido
  Saint Sebastian, **7:***909*
Ribera Gomez, Francisco
  Barricades, **3:***429*
Richmond, George
  Portrait of Rani Jindan Singh,
    11:*1494*
Rivera, Diego
  Cantando el Corrido, **3:***396*
  Fuentes and, **3:***349, 350*
  Muerte de Capitalista, La, **3:***353*
  mural painting, **3:***349, 350, 353*
  *Orgy—Night of the Rich (La
    Orgia),* **5:***611*
  Sueno de una Tarde, **3:***351*
  Xochipilli and His Votaries,
    11:*1563*
  Zapotec Civilization, **3:***342*
Roberts, Warren
  photograph of Kiowa Ranch
    chapel, **6:***771*
Roche-Rabell, Arnaldo
  *Black Man Always Hides His Left
    Hand, The,* **8:***1085*
  False Prophet, The, **8:***1091*
Rodin, Auguste
  photograph of, **9:***1286*
  Portrait of V. S. Eliseyeva, **9:***1285*
  Rilke and, **9:***1279, 1282, 1283,
    1285, 1286, 1287, 1292,
    1294*
  as Takamura influence, **11:***1502*
Romano, Giulio
  Achilles dragging body of
    Hector, **11:***1577*
Rossetti, Dante Gabriel
  Beata Beatrix, **12:***1715*
Rothenstein, Sir William
  Portrait of Joseph Conrad, **8:***1080*

Rowlandson, Thomas
  Witches in a Hayloft, **6:***821*
Rozot, Isabelle
  Musical Chairs, **12:***1597*
Rubens, Peter Paul
  Incredulity of Saint Thomas,
    11:*1452*
Ruthart, Carl B. Andreas
  Wolf, A, **5:***596*

Saar, Betye
  Watching, **4:***474*
Saar, Lezley
  *Between a Mulatto and a
    Quadroon,* **4:***524*
Sabourin, John
  *Sculpture de Nord (Sculpture of the
    North),* **9:***1276*
Salez, Claude
  Winter in Broceliande, **11:***1520*
Sanchez, Angel Ramiro
  Tiresia, **4:***501*
Sargent, John Singer
  *Claude Monet Painting at the Edge
    of a Wood,* **11:***1549*
  Misses Hunter, The, **10:***1374*
Savage, Anne
  Saint-Sauveuv, **10:***1311*
Schaaf, C.
  #83 Hollandsche Spoor, **5:***679*
Schiele, Egon
  Male Nude with Red Cloth, **2:***175*
Schuenke, Susanne
  Sleeper, The, **5:***613*
Sell, Michael
  untitled work, **2:***170*
Shammout, Ismail
  We Shall Return..., **4:***536*
Sickert, Walter Richard
  Venice, La Salute, **7:***883*
Sierra, Paul
  Cuatro Santos, **2:***187*
  Swimmer #16, **2:***190*
Sikander, Shahzia
  Bound, **10:***1394*
  untitled phantasmagoria,
    10:*1329*
Skinner, Victoria
  untitled work, **2:***284*
Soindra, Tómas
  Laguna Que Espera, **2:***184*
Solomon, Maxine
  So Be It!, **4:***471*
  Who Is to Say?, **2:***230*
Stivers, Robert
  Face in Mirror, **1:***119*

Stora, Jean-Pierre
Business City, **7:**959
Sturzenegger, Hans
Hesse and, **5:**585
Sultan, Donald
Seven Red Flowers, **8:**1087

Tagore, Jyotirindranath, **11:**1486, 1488
Tagore, Rabindranath, **11:**1490
Head of a Woman (watercolor), **11:**1493
Takamura, Kōun, **11:**1502
Tansey, Mark
Continental Divide, **1:**26
Tardieu, Ambroise
Woman in a Straightjacket, **9:**1208
Terzic, Zoran
Game, The, **4:**555
untitled oil-on-canvas, **4:**551
Tissot, James Jacques Joseph
Gallery of HMS Calcutta (Portsmouth), The, **3:**332
Titian
Sacred and Profane Love, **7:**982
Toledo, Gregorio
Federico García Lorca, **3:**393
Tooker, George
Lunch, **12:**1661
Voice I, **4:**557
Window X, **1:**85

Turner, J. M. W.
Loch Duich, Summer Moonlight, **9:**1214

Vaillancourt, Armand
Sculpture de Nord (Sculpture of the North), **9:**1276
Valdés Leal, Juan de
Allegory of Death, **11:**1461
Valerio, James
Translucent, **12:**1663
Vannucci, Pietro
Archangel Gabriel, **7:**983
Vaughan, Helen J.
Woman Sitting on a Quilt, **6:**800
Vuillard, Edouard
Still Life with Salad, **9:**1170

Warhol, Andy
Hammer and Sickle, **7:**1003
Weems, Carrie Mae
untitled work, **4:**462
Westhoff, Clara, **9:**1282, 1283, 1285, 1287
Wheeler, Nik
photograph of Habash, **5:**688
White, Charles Wilbert
Love Letter 2, **10:**1431
Mother Courage II, **6:**759

Wilde, John
Wildeview, **2:**158
Williams, Evelyn
New Baby, **9:**1270
Wilmer, Val
photograph of Emecheta, **3:**314
Winship, John
Seated Man (Oceanside), **2:**156
Wojcik, Deborah
Playful Fight, **4:**443
Wood, Roger
photograph of Beirut street scene, **5:**688
Wright, Liz
View of the World, A, **6:**798

Yarde, Richard
Heads and Hands I, **4:**463
Yoshida, Hiroshi
"Hillside with Flowering Azalea," **11:**1504
Yuon, Konstantin
New Planet, The, **12:**1643
Parade of the Red Army, The, **10:**1415

Zadorine, A.
Known Faces of Unknown People, **4:**553

Index of Films

Numbers in **bold** indicate volumes.
Page numbers in *italic* indicate illustrations or illustration captions.

Abbess of Crewe, The, **11**:1445

Affair of Honror, An, **7**:987

African Queen, The, **8**:1018

Age of Reason, The (television), **10**:1335

All Quiet on the Western Front, **9**:1219, *1220, 1223, 1226,* 1228

Amant de Lady Chatterley, L' (*Lady Chatterley's Lover*), **6**:765, 771, *780*

Amerika (*Class Relations*), **5**:667

Animal Farm, **8**:1114, *1116*

Animal Farm (television), **8**:*1123, 1126*

Apocalypse Now, **2**:249

Apprenticeship of Duddy Kravitz, The, **9**:1261, 1264, *1271*

Arch of Triumph, **9**:1219

As You Desire Me, **9**:1201, *1202*

Babette's Feast, **3**:295, 300, *306*

Balcón abierto, El, **3**:391

Bald Soprano, The, **5**:621

Bend Sinister (*Das Bastardzeichen*), **7**:987

Blackfellas, **12**:1607, *1611, 1612*

Blood Wedding, **3**:391

Bobby Deerfield, **9**:1219

Body Snatchers, The, **11**:*1526, 1527*

Boesman and Lena (1973; 2000), **3**:361, *367*

Brideshead Revisited (television miniseries), **12**:1591, *1597, 1600, 1601*

Brighton Rock, **4**:497, 502

Caesar and Cleopatra, **10**:1357

Caifanes, Los, **3**:341

Carrington, **12**:1684, *1685*

Castle, The, **5**:667

Celui qui doit mourir, **5**:705, 708, 715

Chant of Jimmie Blacksmith, The, **6**:727, *729*

Chaos, **9**:1201, *1206, 1215*

Chips Are Down, The, **10**:1335

Chronicle of a Death Foretold, **3**:411, *428*

Citizen Kane, **5**:616

Class Relations, **5**:667

Comediens, The (television), **4**:497, 502

Condemned of Altona, The, **10**:1335

Confessions of Felix Krull, **7**:871

Confidential Agent, The, **4**:497

Coronel no tiene quien le escriba, El, **3**:411

Cronaca di una more annunciata, **3**:411

Cry, the Beloved Country (1952), **9**:1181, 1182, *1193, 1194*

Cry, the Beloved Country (1995), **9**:1181, *1185,* 1195

Dancing Girl of Izu (1954; 1967), **5**:695

Dangerous Paradise, **2**:249

Deadfall, **4**:479

Death in Venice, **7**:871

Decline and Fall of a Bird Watcher, **12**:1591, *1596*

Despair, **7**:987

Devil's Disciple, **10**:1357

Devil's Playground, The, **6**:729

Dias del odio, **1**:107

Doctor and the Devils, The, **11**:*1526, 1527*

Doctor Faustus, **7**:871

Doctor's Dilemma, **10**:1357

Driver's Seat, The, **11**:1447

Duellists, The, **2**:249

Earth, **10**:1380, 1382, 1386, 1387, *1391*

Ehrengard, **3**:295

Einladung zur Enthauptung, **7**:987

Emma Zunz, **1**:107, 117

End of the Affair, The, **4**:497, 502, *514*

Entertainer, The, **8**:1133

Entertainer, The (television), **8**:*1139*

Eréndira, **3**:411

Eugène Ionesco: Voices Silences, **5**:621

Everyone's Child, **2**:267, 270, 275–76

Eyes of a Blue Dog, **3**:411

Face of Another, The, **1**:13, *17*

Face to Face, **2**:249

Facing the Forest (television), **12**:1719

Faith under Fire (television documentary), **4**:542

Fallen Idol, The, **4**:497, 502

Fire, **10**:1387

First Men in the Moon, The, **12**:1631, 1632

Food of the Gods, **12**:1631

Friends, **1**:13

Fugitive, The, **4**:497

Fun with Dick and Jane, **9**:1264

Gallo de Pelea, **3**:341

Girls of Slender Means (television), **11**:1447

God or Politics: Tom Keneally in Eritrea, **6**:727

Golven (based on *The Waves*), **12**:1675

Good Morning, Midnight (television), **9**:1241, 1242

Grass is Singing, The, **6**:787

Guide, The, **8**:1042

Handful of Dust, A, **12**:1591, *1605*

Hangmen Also Die, **1**:129, *130*

Heartbreak House (television), **10**:1357

Heart of Darkness (television; 1955, 1958, 1994), **2**:249

Heart of the Matter, The, **4**:497, 502, 508, 510

Henry IV, **9**:1201, *1205*

He Who Must Die (*The Greek Passion*), **5**:705, 708, 715

Historia del guerrero y la cautiva, **1**:107

History of Mr. Polly, The, **12**:1631
Hobbit, The (cartoon), **11**:*1542*
Hombre de la esquina rosada, **1**:107
Homme et Deux Femmes, Un, **6**:787, 793
House of Bernarda Alba, The, **3**:391
House of Spirits, **1**:44
Howards End, **3**:321, *325*

I, Claudius (television miniseries), **4**:490–91
Immortal Story, The, **3**:295, 300
Inadmissible Evidence, **8**:1133
In Custody, **2**:279, 281
Intrusa, La, **1**:107
Invisible Man, The, **12**:1631
Invitation to a Beheading, **7**:987
I Return to the House, **5**:621
Iris, **7**:974
Island of Dr. Moreau, The (1977; 1996), **12**:1631, *1636*
Island of Lost Souls, **12**:1631
Izo no odoriko (1954; 1967), **5**:695

Jacob Two-Two Meets the Hooded Fang, **9**:1261, 1264
Jane Eyre, **5**:605, 608
Joshua Then and Now, **9**:1261, 1263, 1264

King, Queen, Knave, **7**:987
Kipps, **12**:1631

Lady Chatterley's Lover, **6**:765, 771
Lady Chatterley's Lover (television), **6**:765, 771
Largo Desolato, **4**:540, 557
Last Temptation of Christ, The, **5**:705, 716
Laughing Anne, **2**:249
Laughter in the Dark (1969; 1999), **7**:987, 992, 994
Lawrence of Arabia, **4**:493
Lesson, The, **5**:621
Letzte Akt, Der, **9**:1219, 1224
Life at the Top, **9**:*1262*, 1264
Lion, the Witch and the Wardrobe, The (animated, television), **6**:805
Lion, the Witch and the Wardrobe, The (BBC), **6**:805
Lion, the Witch and the Wardrobe, The (television), **6**:805
Lolita (1962; 1997), **7**:985, 987, 991, 994
Look Back in Anger, **8**:1133
Look Back in Anger (television), **8**:1133

Lord Jim, **2**:249
Lord of the Flies (1963; 1990), **4**:440, 444, 446, 447, *449*
Lord of the Rings, The, **11**:1544, *1546*
Lost in the Barrens (television), **7**:929
Lost in the Stars, **9**:1181, 1194
Lost Lover, The (television), **12**:1719
Lotte, **7**:871
Loved One, The, **12**:1591, 1597
Lurjus, **7**:987
Luzhin Defense, The, **7**:987

Mademoiselle O, **7**:987
Magic Mountain, The, **7**:871
Major Barbara, **10**:1357
Man Who Could Work Miracles, The, **12**:1631
Man Within, The, **4**:497
María de mi corazán (*Maria My Dearest*), **3**:411
Maschenka, **7**:987
Master Harold…and the Boys, **3**:361
Master Harold…and the Boys (television), **3**:369
Maurice, **3**:321, 327
Memento Mori (television), **11**:1447
Memoirs of a Survivor, **6**:787
Men in the Sun, **5**:683
Metamorphosis, The, **5**:667
Metamorphosis, The (television), **5**:667
Michael, **9**:1159
Ministry of Fear, The, **4**:497
Modern Times, **10**:1338
Mr. Mani (television), **12**:1719
Mrs. Dalloway, **12**:1675, *1686*
Muerto cacique Bandeira, El, **1**:107
Mujer que llegaba a las seis, **3**:411
My Fair Lady, **10**:1357, 1367

Nasty Habits, **11**:1447, *1459*
Never Cry Wolf, **7**:929, 930
New Tenant, The, **5**:621
1984, **8**:*1118*, 1128
No Exit, **10**:1335, *1341*
No One Writes to the Colonel, **3**:411
Nostromo (television), **2**:249

Old Gringo, The, **3**:341, 345, *355*
Olympic Glory, **6**:727
Orient Express, **4**:497
Orlando, **12**:1675, *1680*
Other Love, The, **9**:1219
Our Man in Havana, **4**:497, 502
Outcast of the Islands, **2**:249
Out of Africa, **3**:295, 301, 305
Outpost of Progress, An, **2**:249

Page of Madness, A, **5**:694, 696
Passage to India, A, **3**:321, 334
Passionate Friends, The, **12**:1631
Pedro Paramo, **3**:341
Penal Colony, The, **5**:667
Plague, The, **2**:173
Power and the Glory, The (television), **4**:497
Pride and Prejudice, **5**:605, 608
Prime of Miss Jean Brodie, The, **11**:1445, 1447, *1455*, 1456
Prime of Miss Jean Brodie, The (television), **11**:1447
Prince Caspian (BBC), **6**:805
Proud and the Beautiful, The, **10**:1335
Pygmalion, 10.1357, 10.*1363*, 10.*1366*, 10.*1367*. *See also My Fair Lady*
Pygmalion (television), **10**:1357

Quartet, **9**:1241, *1245*
Quiet American, The, **4**:497, 502

Rainbow, The, **6**:765, 771
Reprieve, The (television), **10**:1335
Rescue, The, **2**:249
Respectable Prostitute, The, **10**:1335
Rhinoceros, **5**:621
Rising of the Moon (television), **8**:1095
Road Back, The, **9**:1219, 1220, *1222*
Roads to Freedom, The (television miniseries), **10**:1335
Road to Romance, The, **2**:249
Room of One's Own, A (television), **12**:1675
Room with a View, A, **3**:321, 331
Rover, The (television), **2**:249
Ruined Map, The, **1**:13, *17*

Sabotage, **2**:249
Sailor Who Fell from Grace with the Sea, The, **7**:921, 923
Saint Joan, **10**:1357
Scarlet Woman, The, **12**:1591, 1597
Schindler's List, **6**:725, 727, 728, 730, 736–37
Scoop (television), **12**:1591
Secret Agent, The, **2**:249
Secret Agent, The (television; 1967, 1975, 1992), **2**:249
Secret Sharer, The (television), **2**:249
Sembazuru, **5**:695
Señor muy viejo con unas alas enormes, Un, **3**:411
Seven Deadly Sins, **5**:621

Severed Head, A (film), **7**:974
Shadow Line, The (television), **2**:249
Siddharta (*Siddhartha*), **5**:587
Sierra de Teruel, **6**:848, 849
Silence of the Poet, The, **12**:1719
Silent Song (television), **8**:1095
Silver Chair, The (BBC), **6**:805
Silver City, **6**:727
Silver Treasure, The, **2**:249
Simbene: The Making of African Cinema, **8**:1076
Sing Characters in Search of an Author, **9**:1201
Sizwe Bansi Is Dead, **3**:361
Snow Country, **5**:695
Snow Goose, The (television), **8**:1095
So Ends Our Night, **9**:1219
Sons and Lovers, **6**:765
Sound of the Mountain, The, **5**:695
Steppenwolf, Der (*Steppenwolf*), **5**:587
Stranger, The, **2**:169
Strategia de la ragna, La, **1**:107
Summer of Miss Forbes, The, **3**:411
Swept from the Sea, **2**:249
Sword of Honour, **12**:1591

Tenth Man, The, **4**:502
Things to Come, **12**:1631, *1634*, 1649

Third Man, The, **4**:497, 502
This Gun for Hire, **4**:497, *502*
Thousand Cranes, **5**:695
Three Comrades, **9**:1219
Three Days and a Child, **12**:1719
Tiempo de morir, **3**:341, *343*, 345
Time Machine, The (1960, 2002), **12**:1631
Time Machine, The (television), **12**:1631
Time to Die, **3**:341, *343*, 345
Time to Love and a Time to Die, **9**:1219, 1221, *1226*
Tom Jones, **8**:*1133*, 1134
To the Lighthouse (television), **12**:1675, *1688*, 1690
Travels with My Aunt (television), **4**:497, 502
Trial, The, **5**:667
Troubled Sleep (television), **10**:1335
Tune in Tomorrow, **11**:1566
Two Lives of Mattia Pascal, The, **9**:1201, *1210*

Under Western Eyes (television), **2**:249

Verano de la señora Forbes, El, **3**:411
Very Old Man with Enormous Wings, A, **3**:411

Victory, **2**:249
Victory (television), **2**:249
Village by the Sea, The (television), **2**:279, 281
Viva Sandino, **3**:414
Voyage of the Dawn Treader, The (BBC), **6**:805

War of the Worlds, The, **12**:1631
Water, **10**:*1386*, 1387
Whale for the Killing, A (television), **7**:929
Wheels of Chance, The, **12**:1631
Where Angels Fear to Tread, **3**:321
Wide Sargasso Sea, **9**:1241, *1243*, 1256
Wizard of Oz, The, **10**:1331
Woman in the Dunes, **1**:13, 15, *16*, 17
Woman Who Arrive at Six, The, **3**:411
Women in Love, **6**:765, 771, *778*
Wordsmith, The, **9**:1261

Yama no oto, **5**:695
Yukiguni, **5**:695

Zorba the Greek, **5**:705, 715

Index of Literary Characters

Note: Character names are listed uninverted
Numbers in **bold** indicate volumes.
Page numbers in *italic* indicate illustrations or illustration captions.

Abd al-Jawwad, Aisha (The Cairo Trilogy), **6**:834, 842, 843

Abd al-Jawwad, Amina (The Cairo Trilogy), **6**:834, 842, 843

Abd al-Jawwad, Fahmi (The Cairo Trilogy), **6**:834, 842

Abd al-Jawwad, Kamal (The Cairo Trilogy), **6**:834, 842, 843, 844

Abd al-Jawwad, Khadija (The Cairo Trilogy), **6**:834, 842, 844

Abd al-Jawwad, Radwan (The Cairo Trilogy), **6**:843–44

Abd al-Jawwad, Sayyed Ahmad (The Cairo Trilogy), **6**:834, 842, 843–44

Abd al-Jawwad, Yacine (The Cairo Trilogy), **6**:834, 842–43, 844

Abd al-Munem (The Cairo Trilogy), **6**:844

Abdu (The Pickup), **4**:476

Abdulla (Petals of Blood), **8**:1079, 1081, 1088

Abul Khaizuran (Men in the Sun), **5**:690–91

Abu Qais (Men in the Sun), **5**:690, 691

Achille (Omeros), **11**:1576, 1577

Ackermann, Paul (Mahagonny), **1**:140, 141

A. D. (The Temptation of the West), **6**:860

Adah (Adah's Story), **3**:318

Adah (In the Ditch), **3**:311

Adaku (The Joys of Motherhood), **3**:315

Adam (The Lover), **12**:1722–23

Adham (Children of Gebalawi), **6**:840–41

Adler, Noah (Son of a Smaller Hero), **9**:1277

Agamemnon (The Flies), **10**:1349

Agrippina (I, Claudius/Claudius the God), **4**:490

Ahmad (Sugar Sweet), **6**:844

Ah Q ("True Story of Ah Q"), **2**:219–21

Ainnle (Deidre of the Sorrows), **11**:1481

Aissatou (So Long a Letter), **1**:84–86

Alans, Miss (A Room with a View), **3**:328

Alba, Adela (The House of Bernarda Alba), **3**:402

Alba, Angustias (The House of Bernarda Alba), **3**:401–2

Alba, Bernarda (The House of Bernarda Alba), **3**:395, 401–2

Alba, Martirio (The House of Bernarda Alba), **3**:402

Albert (Kehinde), **3**:318

Alberto (The Time of the Hero), **11**:1560

Albinus (Laughter in the Dark), **7**:1005

Alcasan (That Hideous Strength), **6**:817

Alexandria, Abbess (The Abbess of Crewe), **11**:1453, 1457–58

Alf (Smith of Wootton Major), **11**:1549

Ali (The Heart of the Matter), **4**:507, 508

Ali, Sherif (Lord Jim), **2**:261–62

Al-Ith (The Marriages between Zolnes, Three, Four and Five), **6**:798

Allison (Sorrows and Rejoicings), **3**:375

Al-Naji, Ashur (The Harafish), **6**:838

Al-Naji family (The Harafish), **6**:838, 839

ALP (Finnegans Wake), **5**:657

Alpha Plus group (Brave New World), **5**:613–14

Alwan, Rauf (The Thief and the Dogs), **6**:834

Alyosha (One Day in the Life of Ivan Denisovich), **10**:1411

Amaechina (Anthills of the Savannah), **1**:39

Amal (The Post Office), **11**:1499

Ambien II (The Sirian Experiments), **6**:798

Angel, Father (In Evil Hour), **3**:430

Angel, Father (No One Writes to the Colonel), **3**:426

Anna (The Rainbow), **6**:775, 776

Anna (Voyage in the Dark), **9**:1248

Annette (The Flight from the Enchanter), **7**:980, 981

Annie John (Annie John), **6**:754–55

Antoinette (Wide Saragasso Sea), **9**:1243, 1246, 1249, 1251, 1254–56

Antonia (The Conservationist), **4**:468

Apthorpe (Sword of Honour), **12**:1596, 1604

Arafa (Children of Gebalawi), **6**:841

Aragorn (The Lord of the Rings), **11**:1544, 1545

Ardan (Deidre of the Sorrows), **11**:1481

Ariza, Florentino (Love in the Time of Cholera), **3**:422, 423

Arrowby, Charles (The Sea, the Sea), **7**:975–76, 978

Arrowby, James (The Sea, the Sea), **7**:975–76

Arroyo, Tomas (The Old Gringo), **3**:355, 356

Aschenbach, Gustav (Death in Venice), **7**:876, 882–83

Ashley, Brett (The Sun Also Rises), **9**:1249

Aslan the Lion (Narnia books), **6**:813, 818, 819

Asogba, Prince (The Rape of Shavi), **3**:317

Assad (Men in the Sun), **5**:690

Astrafiammante, Queen (The Magic Flute), **1**:75, 76

Atuk (The Incomparable Atuk), **9**:1272, 1273

Augustus (I, Claudius/Claudius the God), **4**:489, 490

Aunt Mira (*Clear Light of Day*),
2:284

Aura (*Aura*), 3:356–57

Author (*Valley Song*), 3:373

Awasin (*Lost in the Barrens*), 7:936

Ayah (*Cracking India*), **10**:1390

Ayoko (*The Rape of Shavi*), 3:317

Azariah, (*A Perfect Peace*), **9**:1174

Aziz (*A Passage to India*), 3:326,
332, 333–34

Aziz ("Nomad and Viper"), **9**:1175

Baba (*Clear Light of Day*), 2:284

Babamukuru (*Nervous Conditions*),
2:271, 273, 274, 275

Babette ("Babette's Feast"), 3:306–7

Baffin, Arnold (*The Black Prince*),
7:979

Baffin, Julian (*The Black Prince*),
7:979

Baffin, Rachel (*The Black Prince*),
7:979

Baker, Mr. (*Nigger of the "Narcissus"*),
2:255

Bakul (*Clear Light of Day*), 2:284

Baldwin, Mr. (*Scoop*), **12**:1604

Balrog (*The Lord of the Rings*),
11:1545

Bankes, Mr. (*To the Lighthouse*),
12:1690

Bard (*The Hobbit*), **11**:1543

Barlow, Dennis (*The Loved One*),
12:1605

Baroka (*The Lion and the Jewel*),
10:1437

Baron Wrangtel (*The Days of Wrath*),
6:861

Bartlett, Charlotte (*A Room with a
View*), 3:325, 328, 331, 332

Bartley (*Rider to the Sea*), **11**:1474

Barton, Susan (*Foe*), 2:238

Basil (*Unnamable*), 1:102

Bast, Jack (*Howard's End*), 3:334

Bast, Leonard (*Howard's End*), 3:325,
326, 334, 336

Bast family (*Howard's End*), 3:334

Basu, Amit (*Wife*), 7:947, 948

Bäumer, Paul (*All Quiet on the
Western Front*), **9**:1228, *1229,*
1230

Baumgartner, Hugo (*Baumgartner's
Bombay*), 2:283, 285–86

Beatrice (*Anthills of Savannah*), 1:37,
38, 39

Beaver, Mrs. (*Narnia* chronicles),
6:806

Beavis, Anthony (*Eyeless in Gaza*),
5:615–16

Beebe, Mr. (*A Room with a View*),
3:325, 328, 331

Begbick, Mrs. (*Mahagonny*), 1:133,
140

Behrens, Hofrat (*The Magic
Mountain*), 7:884

Belcher ("Guests of the Nation"),
8:1105

Belfounder, Hugo (*Under the Net*),
7:980

Belle (*Voss*), **12**:1665

Beltran, Irene (*Of Love and Shadows*),
1:48, 56

Ben Ata (*The Marriages between
Zolnes, Three, Four and Five*),
6:798

Benazir (*Clear Light of Day*), 2:284

Bendemann, George (*The Judgment*),
5:670

Bendrix, Maurice (*The End of the
Affair*), 4:500, 513, *514,* 515

Bennet, André (*The Acrobats*),
9:1270, 1277

Bennet, Samuel (*Adventures in the
Skin Trade*), **11**:1528

Benny, Ben (*Paul Bunyan*), 1:74

Beorn (*The Hobbit*), **11**:1542

Beren (*The Silmarillion*), **11**:1531

Berenger (*Exit the King*), 5:626, 627,
633–34

Berenger (*Pedestrian in the Air*),
5:626, 627, 632, 633

Berenger (*Rhinoceros*), 5:626, 627,
630, 632, 633

Berenger (*The Killer*), 5:626, 627,
632–33

Berger, Moses (*Solomon Gursky Was
Here*), **9**:1275–76, 1278

Bernard (*Brave New World*),
5:612–13, 614

Beryl (*Brideshead Revisited*), **12**:1599

Beton, Mary (*A Room of One's Own*),
12:1692–93

Betty (*The Captain's Tiger*), 3:374

Bezeidenhout, Gladys (*A Lesson from
Aloes*), 3:372, 373

Bezeidenhout, Piet (*A Lesson from
Aloes*), 3:372, 373

Bhave, Shaila (*The Management of
Grief*), 7:952

Bidlake, Walter (*Point Counter
Point*), 5:611

Bierce, Ambrose (*The Old Gringo*),
3:355, 356

Big Brother (*1984*), **8**:1109, 1123,
1127–28

Big Man (*Bend in the River*), **8**:1029,
1030

Bilbo Baggins (*The Hobbit*),
11:1536–37, 1542, 1543, 1544

Bilbo Baggins (*The Lord of the Rings*),
11:1546

Bim (*Clear Light of Day*), 2:282,
284, 285

Bimala (*The Home and the World*),
11:1494–96

Binetou (*So Long a Letter*), 1:84–85,
86

Birkholz, Ernst (*The Road Back*),
9:1235

Birkin (*Women in Love*), **6**:769, 777,
778–79, 782

Bishop, Clare (*The Real Life of
Sebastian Knight*), 7:995, 996

Biswas, Anand (*House for Mr.
Biswas*), **8**:1026

Biswas, Mohun (*House for Mr.
Biswas*), **8**:1024–26

Biswas, Raghu (*House for Mr.
Biswas*), **8**:1025

Black Riders (*The Lord of the Rings*),
11:1544

Blacksmith, Jimmie (*The Chant of
Jimmie Blacksmith*), **6**:735,
740–42

Blacksmith, Mort (*The Chant of
Jimmie Blacksmith*), **6**:741–42

Black Woman ("High Road of Saint
James"), 2:193

Blanche, Anthony (*Brideshead
Revisited*), **12**:1596

Bloom, Leopold (*Ulysses*), 5:637,
642, 654, 655, 656

Bloom, Molly (*Ulysses*), 5:654, 655

Blount, Colonel (*Vile Bodies*),
12:1596

Bluntschli, Captain (*Arms and the
Man*), **10**:*1362*

Bobby Watsons family (*The Bald
Soprano*), 5:629

Boesman (*Boesman and Lena*), 3:367

Boeuf, Mrs. (*Rhinoceros*), 5:630, 632

Bonaparte ("Guests of the Nation"),
8:1104

Bonifacia (*The Green House*),
11:1565

Bons, Mr. ("The Celestial
Omnibus"), 3:336, 337

Boot, John Courteney (*Scoop*),
12:1604

Boot, William (*Scoop*), **12**:1604

Boppi (*Peter Camenzind*), **5**:593

Boro (*Weep Not, Child*), **8**:1078, 1090

Boromir (*The Lord of the Rings*), **11**:1545

Boss (*Zorba the Greek*), **5**:713, 714

Botard (*Rhinoceros*), **5**:630, 632

Botkin, V.(*Pale Fire*), **7**:1002

Bouckman (*Kingdom of This World*), **2**:189

Boxer (*Animal Farm*), **8**:1126

Brackel, Baron von ("The Old Chevalier"), **3**:302

Bradshaw, Sir William (*Mrs. Dalloway*), **12**:1688

Brangwen, Gudrun (*Women in Love*), **6**:777, 778

Brangwen, Lydia (*The Rainbow*), **6**:775

Brangwen, Tom (*The Rainbow*), **6**:775, 776, 782

Brangwen, Ursula (*The Rainbow*), **6**:775, 776–77

Brangwen, Ursula (*Women in Love*), **6**:769, 777, 778–79

Brangwen family (*The Rainbow*), **6**:775

Brewmaster (*The Vaněk Plays*), **4**:554

Bride, Dan ("Majesty of the Law"), **8**:1108

Brigge (*The Notebooks of Malte Laurid's Brigge*), **9**:1282, 1288–90

Briscoe, Lily (*To the Lighthouse*), **12**:1689, 1690

Britling, Hugh (*Mr. Britling Sees It Through*), **12**:1639

Britomart, Lady (*Major Barbara*), **10**:1371

Britomart, Stephen (*Major Barbara*), **10**:1371

Brodie, Jean (*The Prime of Miss Jean Brodie*), **11**:1446, 1453, 1454, *1455*, 1456

Brother Jeroboam (Jero) (*The Trials of Brother Jero*), **10**:1437

Brother Leo (*Saint Francis*), **5**:717

Brown (*The Comedians*), **4**:515

Brown, Mr. (*Things Fall Apart*), **1**:32

Brown, Pinkie (*Brighton Rock*), **4**:498, 500, *505*, 506–7

Brown, Tiger (*Threepenny Opera*), **1**:136

Brown, Waldo and Arthur (*The Solid Mandala*), **12**:1670–71

Brunelda (*Amerika*), **5**:680

Bruner, Egon (*Mr. Mani*), **12**:1724

Bruno (*Time Must Have a Stop*), **5**:617

Bucher (*Spark of Life*), **9**:1233

Buddenbrooks, Antonie (Tony) (*Buddenbrooks*), **7**:879

Buddenbrooks, Chlotilde (*Buddenbrooks*), **7**:879–80

Buddenbrooks, Christian (*Buddenbrooks*), **7**:879

Buddenbrooks, Elisabeth (*Buddenbrooks*), **7**:879

Buddenbrooks, Gerda (*Buddenbrooks*), **7**:879

Buddenbrooks, Gotthold (*Buddenbrooks*), **7**:879

Buddenbrooks, Hanno (Johannes) (*Buddenbrooks*), **7**:875, 879, 880, 881

Buddenbrooks, Johann (*Buddenbrooks*), **7**:879

Buddenbrooks, Johann, Jr. (*Buddenbrooks*), **7**:879

Buddenbrooks, Thomas (*Buddenbrooks*), **7**:879, 880–81

Buddenbrooks family (*Buddenbrooks*), **7**:875, 879–82

Buendia family (*One Hundred Years of Solitude*), **3**:420, 421

Bunyan, Paul (*Paul Bunyan*), **1**:74

Bürgel (*The Castle*), **5**:674

Burger, Rosa (*Burger's Daughter*), **4**:468–69

Burke, Dan (*The Shadow of the Glen*), **11**:1471, *1476*, 1477, 1478

Burke, Nora (*The Shadow of the Glen*), **11**:1471, *1476*, 1477–78

Burnell family ("Prelude"), **7**:904

Byrne, Mary (*The Tinker's Wedding*), **11**:1483, 1484

Byrne, Michael (*The Tinker's Wedding*), **11**:1483

Caesar (*Caesar and Cleopatra*), **10**:*1362*, 1375

Caliban (*Tempest: After the Tempest of Shakespeare*), **2**:204

Caligula (*I, Claudius/Claudius the God*), **4**:488, 490

Camacho, Pedro (*Aunt Julia and the Scriptwriter*), **11**:1565

Camenzind, Peter (*Peter Camenzind*), **5**:592–93

Capran, Hillela (*Sport of Nature*), **4**:475–76

Captain (*Shadow Line*), **2**:265, 266

Captain Cat (*Under Milk Wood*), **11**:1523

Cardinal ("The Cardinal's First Tale"), **3**:307

Carlos (*Explosion in a Cathedral*), **2**:191, 192, 193

Carmichael, Mr. (*To the Lighthouse*), **12**:1689, 1690

Casey, Sarah (*The Tinker's Wedding*), **11**:1471, 1483–84

Castorp, Hans (*The Magic Mountain*), **7**:876, 884, *885*, 886

Catalina (*The Death of Artemio Cruz*), **3**:354

Cathleen (*Riders to the Sea*), **11**:1475

Cauchon, Bishop (*Saint Joan*), **10**:1373

Cava (*The Time of the Hero*), **11**:1560

Celestina (*Terra Nostra*), **3**:357

Chamcha, Saladin (*The Satanic Verses*), **10**:1328

Chandran, Willie Somerset (*Half a Life*), **8**:1021

Charles VII (*Saint Joan*), **10**:1372, 1373

Chatterley, Constance (*Lady Chatterley's Lover*), **6**:769, 777, 779–81

Chatterley, Sir Clifford, **6**:779, 780, 781

Chauchet, Clavdia (*The Magic Mountain*), **7**:884

Ch'en (*Man's Fate*), **6**:852, 858, 859

Chenevert, Alexandre (*The Cashier*), **10**:1310–11

Chief Inspector Wanja (*Petals of Blood*), **8**:1079, 1081, 1088

Chief Mate (*Shadow Line*), **2**:265

Chike (*Chike and the River*), **1**:28

Christine (*Street of Riches*), **10**:1312–13

Christophe, King Henri. *See* King Henri Christophe (*below*)

Christophine (*Wide Saragasso Sea*), **9**:1240, 1243, 1256

chronicler (*Terra Nostra*), **3**:357

Chui (*Petals of Blood*), **8**:1079, 1081

Ciaula (*ciaula Discovers the Moon*), **9**:1214–15

Cienfuegos, Ixca (*Where the Air Is Clear*), **3**:351

Circumference, Lady (*Decline and Fall*), **12**:1604

Civario, Angela (*Chronicle of a Death Foretold*), **3**:426, 428

Clair, Ivor (*Sword of Honour*), **12**:1602

Clamence, Jean-Baptiste (*Fall*), **2**:174, *175, 176*

Clara (*Love among the Ruins*), **12**:1595

Clara (*No Longer at Ease*), **1**:33–36

Clarke (*Arrow of God*), **1**:37

Claudius (*I, Claudius/Claudius the God*), **4**:488–91

Clayton (*Ah but Your Land Is Beautiful*), **9**:1186

Cleopatra (*Caesar and Cleopatra*), **10**:1362, 1375

Clissold, William, (*The World of William Clissold*), **12**:1639

Clive (*Maurice*), **3**:321, 327

Clov (*Endgame*), **1**:96, 102–3

Clytemnestra (*The Flies*), **10**:1349

Coldridge, Lynda (*The Four-Gated City*), **6**:792, 794, 795

Coldridge, Mark (*Children of Violence*), **6**:794

Colin, Dr. (*A Burnt-Out Case*), **4**:512

Colleoni (*Brighton Rock*), **4**:506

Colonel (*No One Writes to the Colonel*), **3**:426

Colonel Pickering (*Pygmalion*), **10**:*1367*

Conchubor (*Deirdre of the Sorrows*), **11**:1469, 1471, 1481

Consuelo Llorente (*Aura*), **3**:356–57

Copper, Lord (*Scoop*), **12**:1604

Cornelius (*Lord Jim*), **2**:261, 262

Côté, Mademoiselle (*Where Nests the Water Hen*), **10**:1313

Cranley (*Portrait of the Artist as a Young Man*), **5**:636

Crichton, Gerald (*Women in Love*), **6**:777–78

Crouchback, Guy (*Sword of Honour*), **12**:1596, 1602–4

Crouchback, Virginia (*Sword of Honour*), **12**:1602, 1603

Cruso, Robinson (*Foe*), **2**:238

Crusoe, Robinson (*Robinson Crusoe*), **2**:237

Cruz, Artemio (*The Death of Artemio Cruz*), **3**:345, 352, 353, 354, 355

Cruz, Lorenzo (*The Death of Artemio Cruz*), **3**:354

Cusins, Adolphus (*Major Barbara*), **10**:1371, 1372

Cyrus (*The Infinite Plan*), **1**:*58*

Daisy (*Rhinoceros*), **5**:630, 632

Dalloway, Clarissa (*Mrs. Dalloway*), **12**:1680, 1686–89

Dalloway, Elizabeth (*Mrs. Dalloway*), **12**:1686, 1688

Dalloway, Richard (*Mrs. Dalloway*), **12**:1686, 1688

Dame Hortense (*Zorba the Greek*), **5**:713

Dara, Michael (*The Shadow of the Glen*), **11**:*1476*, 1478

Darcy (*Towards Asmara*), **6**:744

Darcy, Patch (*The Shadow of the Glen*), **11**:1478

Dark, Johanna (*St. Joan of the Stockyards*), **1**:133

Darkblom, Vivian (*Lolita*), **7**:997

D'Arraste ("Stone That Grows"), **2**:176

Daru ("Guest"), **2**:176

Das, Ila (*Fire on the Mountain*), **2**:286

Dasguta, Dimple (*Wife*), **7**:946–47, 948

Daughter (*Misunderstanding*), **2**:177

Daza, Fermina (*Love in the Time of Cholera*), **3**:422

De Coninck, Eliza and Fannie ("The Supper at Elsinore"), **3**:302

Dedalus, Stephen (*Portrait of the Artist as a Young Man*), **5**:636, 641, 643, 644, 653; **11**:1523

Dedalus, Stephen (*Ulysses*), **5**:654, 655, 656

Deirdre (*Deirdre of the Sorrows*), **11**:1469, 1481

Delamarche (*Amerika*), **5**:680

Delaura, Father Cayetano (*Of Love and Other Demons*), **3**:426

del Valle, Aurora (*Portrait in Sepia*), **1**:56056

del Valle, Clara (*The House of Spirits*), **1**:48, 50, 52

del Valle, Paulina (*Portrait in Sepia*), **1**:57

Demian, Max (*Demian*), **5**:592, 598

Deo Gratias (*A Burnt-Out Case*), **4**:512

Detering (*All Quiet on the Western Front*), **9**:1228

Deven (*In Custody*), **2**:283

Devine (*Out of the Silent Planet*), **6**:814

Devine, Dick (*That Hideous Strength*), **6**:817

Díaz, Laura (*The Years with Laura Díaz*), **3**:349, 350

Didi (*Waiting for Godot*). *See* Vladimir

Dietrich zur Linde, Otto ("Deutsches Requiem"), **1**:122

Dimble, Professor (*That Hideous Strength*), **6**:817

Doctor (*Exit the King*), **5**:634

Doctor Urbino (*Love in the Time of Cholera*), **3**:422

Dodge, William (*Between the Acts*), **12**:1692

Dolores (Lolita) (*Lolita*), **7**:991, 997, 998, 999

Donaghue, Jake (*Under the Net*), **7**:980

Don Cipriano (*The Plumed Serpent*), **6**:781, 782

Don Juan (*Man and Superman*), **10**:1368, 1369, 1370

Donkeyman (*The Captain's Tiger*), **3**:374

Donkin (*Nigger of the "Narcissus"*), **2**:256

Donovan, Jeremiah ("Guests of the Nation"), **8**:1104, 1105

Don Ramon (*The Plumed Serpent*), **6**:781, 782

Dontsova, Ludmila Afanasyevna (*The Cancer Ward*), **10**:1414, 1416

Dooligan, Doug (*Day of the Dog*), **12**:1616, 1621

Doolittle, Eliza (*Pygmalion*), **10**:1366

Dora (*The Bell*), **7**:982–83

Doramin (*Lord Jim*), **2**:261–62

Dori (*Open Heart*), **12**:1725, 1726

Doul, Martin and Mary (*The Well of the Saints*), **11**:1471, 1481, *1482*, 1483

Drakos (*The Fratricides*), **5**:711,718

Dr. Obispo (*After Many a Summer Dies the Swan*), **5**:616

Dr. Ravic (*Arch of Triumph*), **9**:1237

Dr. Rieux (*Plague*), **2**:161, 166, 172, 173–74

Dubbo, Alf (*Riders in the Chariot*), **12**:1669

Dudard (*Rhinoceros*), **5**:630, 632

Dunois (*Saint Joan*), **10**:1372

Duval (*All Quiet on the Western Front*), **9**:1230

Dyomka (*The Cancer Ward*), **10**:1416, 1417

Earwicker, Humphrey Chimpden (*Finnegans Wake*), **5**:657

Edmund (*The Lion, the Witch and the Wardrobe*), **6**:813, 818, 820

Edouard (*The Killer*), 5:632–33

Effendi (*Children of Gebalawi*), 6:841

Eilif (*Mother Courage and Her Children*), 1:137

Electra (*The Flies*), 10:1349, 1350

Electric Aunt (*Cracking India*), 10:1385

Elizabeth (*Peter Camenzind*), 5:593

Eloi (*The Time Machine*), 12:1642

Elvis (Wolf) (*Going Home*), 12:1614, 1616

Emerson, George (*A Room with a View*), 3:326, 328, 331

Emerson, Mr. (*A Room with a View*), 3:328, 331

Emerson family (*A Room with a View*), 3:328, 331

Enno (*Good Morning, Midnight*), 9:1252, *1253*, 1254

Enoch ("Life for a Life"), 9:1195

ents (*The Lord of the Rings*), 11:1537, 1545

Eric (*The Lord of the Flies*), 4:450

Erlanger (*The Castle*), 5:674

Erminé (*Freedom or Death*), 5:711, 718

Ernst (*A Choice of Enemies*), 9:1277

Esteban (*Explosion in a Cathedral*), 2:191, 192, 193

Estelle (*No Exit*), 10:1340, *1341*, 1350, 1351

Estragon (Gogo) (*Waiting for Godot*), 1:96, *97*, 98–99, 102

Etkin ("Nomad and Viper"), 9:1176

Etsuko (*Thirst for Love*), 7:913–14, 915, 918, *919*

Eustace, Uncle (*Time Must Have a Stop*), 5:617

Evans (*Mrs. Dalloway*), 12:1686, 1688

Eynesford-Hill, Freddy (*Pygmalion*), 10:1366, *1367*

Ezelulu (*Arrow of God*), 1:26, 37–38

Farishta, Gibreel(*The Satanic Verses*), 10:1328

Farmer Giles (*Farmer Giles of Ham*), 11:1548

Farnaby, Will (*Island*), 5:615

Farrell (*The Chant of Jimmie Blacksmith*), 6:741

Father (*Boyhood*), 2:242

Father Angel (*In Evil Hour*), 3:430

Father Angel (*No One Writes to the Colonel*), 3:426

Father Cayetano Delaura (*Of Love and Other Demons*), 3:426

Father Jacoby (*The Philosopher's Pupil*), 7:974

Father James Maithland (*Three Cheers for the Paraclete*), 6:742–43

Father Joseph-Marie (*Where Nests the Water Hen*), 10:1313

Father Paneloux (*Plague*), 2:172, 173, 174

Father Reilly (*The Playboy of the Western World*), 11:1471

Father Rothschild (*Vile Bodies*), 12:1595

Father Thomas (*A Burnt-Out Case*), 4:512

Father Yánaros (*The Fratricides*), 5:718

Fawley, Catherine (*The Bell*), 7:983

Fawley, Nick (*The Bell*), 7:982, 983

Felicity, Sister (*The Abbess of Crewe*), 11:1457–58

Fergus (*Deidre of the Sorrows*), 11:1481

Feroza (*Cracking India*), 10:1385

Feverstone, Lord (*That Hideous Strength*), 6:817

Fielding, Cyril (*A Passage to India*), 3:326, 332, 333–34

Filostrato (*That Hideous Strength*), 6:817, 818

Finnegan, Tim (*Finnegans Wake*), 5:656–58

Fire Chief (*The Bald Soprano*), 5:629

Fistula (*Temptation*), 4:555

Flaherty, Margaret ("Pegeen Mike") (*The Playboy of the Western World*), 11:1471, 1479–80, 1481

Flaherty, Michael James (*Playboy of the Western World*), 11:1471

Flip (*The Rape of Shavi*), 3:317

Flory, John (*Burmese Days*), 8:1112, 1129

Flyte, Bridey (*Brideshead Revisited*), 12:1599, 1600

Flyte, Cordelia (*Brideshead Revisited*), 12:1599, 1600

Flyte, Julia (*Brideshead Revisited*), 12:1599, 1600

Flyte, Sebastian (*Brideshead Revisited*), 12:1599, 1600

Foe, Daniel (*Foe*), 2:238

Forsner, Lincoln ("The Dreamers"), 3:302

Foustka (*Temptation*), 4:554–56

Fox, Mischa (*The Flight from the Enchanter*), 7:980, 982

Franz (*The Condemned of Altona*), 10:1340

Freddy (*A Room with a View*), 3:328

Freddy (*The Crow Eaters*), 10:1385, 1393, 1395, 1396

Friday (*Foe*), 2:231, 234, 237, 238

Frieda (*The Castle*), 5:674

Frodo Baggins (*The Lord of the Rings*), 11:1536, 1537, 1544, *1544*, 1545, 1546

Fusuako (*The Sailor Who Fell from Grace with the Sea*), 7:914, 920, 922, 923

Gabriel (*The Dead*), 5:651

Gamboa, Lieutenant (*The Time of the Hero*), 11:1560

Gandalf (*The Hobbit*), 11:1542–43

Gandalf (*The Lord of the Rings*), 11:1544, 1545, 1546

Gangart, Vera Kornilyevna (*The Cancer Ward*), 10:1414, 1415, 1416, 1417

García, Estaban (*The House of Spirits*), 1:50, 52

Garcin (*No Exit*), 10:1340, *1341*, 1350, 1351

Garine (*The Conquerors*), 6:853, 856–58

Gavender, Blaise (*The Sacred and Profane Love Machine*), 7:982

Gavender, Harriet (*The Sacred and Profane Love Machine*), 7:982

Gebalawi (*Children of Gebalawi*), 6:840–41

Gebel (*Children of Gebalawi*), 6:841

Gentleman Brown (*Lord Jim*), 2:262

Gerlach, Franz von (*The Condemned of Altona*), 10:1353

Gerlach, Johanna von (*The Condemned of Altona*), 10:1353

Gerlach, Leni von (*The Condemned of Altona*), 10:1353

Gertrude, Sister (*The Abbess of Crewe*), 11:1459

Geula ("Nomad and Viper"), 9:1175–77

Gideon (*Playland*), 3:373

Gideon (*The Way of the Wind*), 9:1176

Giebenrath, Hans (*Beneath the Wheel*), 5:598

Gikonyo (*A Grain of Wheat*), 8:1078, 1079, 1084, 1085, 1086

Gilda (*The Chant of Jimmie Blacksmith*), **6**:741, 742

Gillane, Michael (*Cathleen Ni Houlihan*), **12**:1716

Gimli (*The Lord of the Rings*), **11**:1545

Gino (*Where Angels Fear to Tread*), **3**:326

Ginwalla, Feroza (*An American Brat*), **10**:1393, *1394*, 1395

Godbold, Ruth (*Riders in the Chariot*), **12**:1669

Godbole, Professor (*A Passage to India*), **3**:325, 332, 333, 334

Godfrey, Chief Inspector (*Petals of Blood*), **8**:1088

Goeth, Amon (*Schindler's Ark*), **6**:737, 739, 740

Goetz (*The Devil and the Good Lord*), **10**:1353

Gogo (*Waiting for Godot*). See Estragon

Goldmund (*Narcissus and Goldmund*), **5**:598

Goldstein, Emmanuel (*1984*), **8**:1122, 1127, 1128

Gollum (*The Hobbit*), **11**:1542

Gollum (*The Lord of the Rings*), **11**:1544, 1545, 1546

Gondor (*The Lord of the Rings*), **11**:1545

Goodman, Mr. (*The Real Life of Sebastian Knight*), **7**:995, 996

Goodman, Theodora (*The Aunt's Story*), **12**:1664–65

Gotama (*Siddhartha*), **5**:595

Gould, Charles (*Nostromo*), **2**:264

Govinda (*Siddhartha*), **5**:595

Gräber, Ernst (*A Time to Love and a Time to Die*), **9**:1237

Grabot (*The Royal Way*), **6**:860–61

Grace-Groundling-Marchpole, Colonel (*Sword of Honour*), **12**:1602

Gradus (*Pale Fire*), **7**:1002

Graf, Miss (*The Chant of Jimmie Blacksmith*), **6**:742

Grand (*Plague*), **2**:172, 173, 174

Grandma ("First Confession"), **8**:1107

Greenspan, Raya ("The Way of the Wind"), **9**:1177

Gregor Samsa ("The Metamorphosis"), **5**:667, 668, 670, 673, 676–78

Grete ("The Metamorphosis"), **5**:678

Grey, Jack (Gradus) (*Pale Fire*), **7**:1002

Griffin (*War of the Worlds, The*), **12**:1635

Griffin, Mortimer (*Cocksure*), **9**:1273

Grimes, Captain (*Decline and Fall*), **12**:1596, 1604

Grünlich (*Buddenbrooks*), **7**:879

Grünlich, Erica (*Buddenbrooks*), **7**:879

Grusha (*Caucasian Chalk Circle*), **1**:142

Gursky, Bernard (*Solomon Gursky Was Here*), **9**:1263

Gursky, Ephraim (*Solomon Gursky Was Here*), **9**:1276

Gursky, Solomon (*Solomon Gursky Was Here*), **9**:1275, 1276

Guzman (*Terra Nostra*), **3**:357

Haines, Rupert (*Between the Acts*), **12**:1692

Haldin, Victor (*Under Western Eyes*), **2**:265

Haldin's mother (*Under Western Eyes*), **2**:265

Haller, Harry (*Steppenwolf*), **5**:590, 595–97

Hally (*Master Harold…and the Boys*), **3**:365, *368*, 369, 370, 371

Hally's father (*Master Harold…and the Boys*), **3**:370, 371

Hally's mother (*Master Harold…and the Boys*), **3**:370, 371

Hamdans (*Children of Gebalawi*), **6**:841

Hamid (*All That's Left To You*), **5**:692

Hamm (*Endgame*), **1**:102–3

Hand, Bertha (*Exiles*), **5**:646

Hand, Georgie (*A Severed Head*), **7**:967

Hand, Robert (*Exiles*), **5**:646

Hannah (*My Michael*), **9**:*1164*, 1165, 1168–69

Hardcastle, Major "Fairy" (*That Hideous Strength*), **6**:817

Hare, Mary (*Riders in the Chariot*), **12**:1669

Hari (*Village by the Sea*), **2**:286

Harriet (*The Sacred and Profane Love Machine*), **7**:956

Hartley, Mary (*The Sea, the Sea*), **7**:976

Hartley, Titus (*The Sea, the Sea*), **7**:976

Hatsue (*The Sound of Waves*), **7**:913, 915

Hatsumi (*Norwegian Wood*), **7**:960

Hawkins ("Guests of the Nation"), **8**:1104–5

Hawkins, Nanny (*Brideshead Revisited*), **12**:1599, 1600

Haze, Charlotte (*Lolita*), **7**:997

HCE (*Finnegans Wake*), **5**:640, 657

He (*Boyhood*), **2**:242

Healy, Mr. (*The Chant of Jimmie Blacksmith*), **6**:741, 742

Healy, Mrs. (*The Chant of Jimmie Blacksmith*), **6**:742

Hector (*Omeros*), **11**:1576, *1577*

Heinrich, Klaus (*Royal Highness*), **7**:887

Helen (*Omeros*), **11**:1576, 1577

Helena (*Helena*), **12**:1605–6

Helena (*Look Back in Anger*), **8**:1137

Helena, Sister (formerly Sandy) (*The Prime of Miss Jean Brodie*), **11**:1454

Helholtz (*Brave New World*), **5**:613–14

Hella (*Sport of Nature*), **4**:463

Heng (*The Quiet American*), **4**:500

Henri Christophe (*Kingdom of This World*), **2**:189

Henri Christophe (*Tragedy of King Christophe*), **2**:204

Hermann (*The Journey to the East*), **5**:598, 600

Hermine (*Steppenwolf*), **5**:597

Hersh, Jake (*St. Urbain's Horseman*), **9**:1274–75, 1277

Hesse, Anton (*Children of Violence*), **6**:794

Higgins, Henry (*Pygmalion*), **10**:1366

Hilda (*Master Harold…and the Boys*), **3**:368, 369, 370

Hilda (*The Years with Laura Díaz*), **3**:349, *350*

Himmelfarb, Mordecai, (*Riders in the Chariot*), **12**:1667, 1669

Hingest (*That Hideous Strength*), **6**:818

Hirsh, Helen (*Schindler's Ark*), **6**:737

Hoederer (*Dirty Hands*), **10**:1352

Holland, Ruth (*Flotsam*), **9**:1237

Holstius (*The Aunt's Story*), **12**:1664–65

Honda (*Spring Snow*), **7**:916–17

Honeychurch, Freddy (*A Room with a View*), **3**:328

Honeychurch, Lucy (*A Room with a View*), **3**:326, 328, *329*, 331, 332

Honeychurch family (*A Room with a View*), **3**:328, 331

Honor (*A Severed Head*), **7**:974

Hook-finger Jacob (*Threepenny Opera*), **1**:136

Hooper (*Brideshead Revisited*), **12**:1599

Horowitz, Ivor (*Mr. Mani*), **12**:1724

Houlihan, Cathleen Ni (*Cathleen Ni Houlihan*), **12**:1716

Hound, Major "Fido" (*Sword of Honour*), **12**:1602

Hugho (*Dirty Hands*), **10**:1340, 1352

Hugo (*The Garden Party*), **4**:556

Hugues, Victor (*Explosion in a Cathedral*), **2**:191–92, 193

Humaam (*Children of Gebalawi*), **6**:841

Humbert, Humbert (*Lolita*), **7**:*991*, 992, 997, 998, 999

Huml (*The Increased Difficulty of Concentration*), **4**:557–58

Hyder Ali (*Clear Light of Day*), **2**:284

"I" (*Dance, Dance, Dance*), **7**:961–62

Ibn Fattouma (*The Journey of Ibn Fattouma*), **6**:833

Idrees (*Children of Gebalawi*), **6**:841

Ikemefuna (*Things Fall Apart*), **1**:30, 31, 33

Ilgar (*Land of the Golden Clouds*), **12**:1624

Indar (*Bend in the River*), **8**:1030

Inez (*No Exit*), **10**:1340, 1350, 1351

Isabel (*Terra Nostra*), **3**:357

Issy (*Finnegans Wake*), **5**:657

Ivan Denisovich Shukhov (*One Day in the Life of Ivan Denisovich*), **10**:1410–11

Jabavu ("Hunger"), **6**:799

Jack (*The Lord of the Flies*), **4**:444, 450, 451

Jackie ("First Confession"), **8**:1106–7

Jackson, Snowy, **12**:1616

Jacob (*The Secret Life of Saeed, the Ill-Fated Pessoptimist*), **4**:533

Jacob, Edward (*Amerika*), **5**:678, 680

Jacob, Uncle (*Amerika*), **5**:680

Jacobo (*Weep Not, Child*), **8**:1078

Jacobus (*The Conservationist*), **4**:467–68

Jacoby, Father (*The Philosopher's Pupil*), **7**:974

Jamie (*Lost in the Barrens*), **7**:936

Jan (*Misunderstanding*), **2**:177

Jane (*Guerrillas*), **8**:1026, 1028

Jane/Jyoti/Jasmine (*Jasmine*), **7**:948–49

Jansen, Sasha (*Good Morning, Midnight*), **9**:1246, 1252, *1253*, 1254

Jarvis, Arthur (*Cry, the Beloved Country*), **9**:1192, 1194

Jarvis, James (*Cry, the Beloved Country*), **9**:*1185*, 1189, 1190, 1192, 1194, 1195

Jarvis, Margaret, **9**:1192

Jawwad, Sayyed Ahmad Abd al- (The Cairo Trilogy), **6**:826

Jean (*Rhinoceros*), **5**:630, 632

Jennie (*The Prime of Miss Jean Brodie*), **11**:1454

Jeroboam (Jero), Brother (*The Trials of Brother Jero*), **10**:1437

Jewel (*Lord Jim*), **2**:263

Jim (*Lord Jim*), **2**:260–63

Joan of Arc (*Saint Joan*), **10**:1372–73

Joaquín (*Daughter of Fortune*), **1**:55

Jocelin, Dean (*The Spire*), **4**:444–45, 454–55

John (*Brave New World*), **5**:613–14

John (*The Pilgrim's Regress*), **6**:813

Joll, Colonel (*Waiting for the Barbarians*), **2**:239, 240

Jones (*The Comedians*), **4**:515

Jones, Farmer (*Animal Farm*), **8**:1125

Jonkers, Abraam (*Valley Song*), **3**:373

Josef K., (*The Trial*), **2**:236; **6**:666, 672–74

Joseph-Marie, Father (*Where Nests the Water Hen*), **10**:1313

Joshua (*The River Between*), **8**:1078

Joyboy, Mr. (*The Loved One*), **12**:1605

Joyce Emily (*The Prime of Miss Jean Brodie*), **11**:1454

Juan ("High Road of Saint James"), **2**:193

Juan (*Yerma*), **3**:404, 406

Judd (*Voss*), **12**:1667

Judge Othon (*Plague*), **2**:173, 174

Julia (*1984*), **8**:1128

Julian (*Terra Nostra*), **3**:357

Junglewalla, Faredoon (Freddy) (*The Crow Eaters*), **10**:1385, 1393, 1395, 1396

K. (*The Castle*), **5**:666, 674–76

Kabonyi (*The River Between*), **8**:1078, 1092

Kaburagi, Mrs. (*Forbidden Colors*), **7**:916, 925

Kahn, Harry (*Shadows in Paradise*), **9**:1234

Kamala (*Siddhartha*), **5**:595

Kamal Abd al-Jawwad, Kamal (*Palace of Desire*), **6**:834

Kamaswami (*Siddhartha*), **5**:595

Kamau (*Weep Not, Child*), **8**:1090

Kantorek (*All Quiet on the Western Front*), **9**:1228, 1230

Kanyi, Mr. and Mrs. (*Unconditional Surrender*), **12**:1603

Karanja (*A Grain of Wheat*), **8**:1078, 1079, 1084, 1085, 1086

Karega (*Petals of Blood*), **8**:1079, 1081, 1088

Karima (*Sugar Sweet*), **6**:844

Kassner (*The Days of Wrath*), **6**:861

Kätchen (*Scoop*), **12**:1604

Katczinsky, Stanislaus (*All Quiet on the Western Front*), **9**:1228, *1229*

Kate (*The Plumed Serpent*), **6**:781–82

Katov (*Man's Fate*), **6**:859

Kattrin (*Mother Courage and Her Children*), **1**:137

Kaul, Nanda (*Fire on the Mountain*), **2**:283, 286

Keepers of the Trees (*Land of the Golden Clouds*), **12**:1624

Kehinde (*Kehinde*), **3**:318

Kemmerich (*All Quiet on the Western Front*), **9**:1228

Keogh, Shawn (*The Playboy of the Western World*), **11**:1471, 1479, 1480

Kern, Ludwig (*Flotsam*), **9**:1237

Kestner, Lotte (*The Beloved Returns*), **7**:874

Khadija (The Cairo Trilogy), **6**:834

Khaizuran, Abul (*Men in the Sun*), **5**:688

Kihika (*A Grain of Wheat*), **8**:1084, 1085, 1086

Kiki (*Dance, Dance, Dance*), **7**:962

Killer (*The Killer*), **5**:633

Kilman, Miss (*Mrs. Dalloway*), **12**:1688

Kimeria, (*Petals of Blood*), **8**:1079, 1081

Kimeria, Chief Inspector (*Petals of Blood*), **8**:1088

Kinanjui, Chief (*Out of Africa*), **3**:304

Kinbote, Charles (*Pale Fire*), **7**:1002

King ("Forging Swords"), **2**:223, 224

King Henri Christophe (*Kingdom of This World*), **2**:189

King Henri Christophe (*Tragedy of King Christophe*), **2**:204

King of Zembla (*Pale Fire*), **7**:1002

Kitosch ("Kitosch's Story"), **3**:304

Kiyoaki (*Spring Snow*), **7**:916–17

Klamm (*The Castle*), **5**:674

Klopstock, Baron and Baroness (*Not to Disturb*), **11**:1462

Kloterjahn, Frau (*Tristan*), **7**:886

Knecht, Joseph (*The Glass Bead Game*), **5**:600

Knight, Sebastian (*The Real Life of Sebastian Knight*), **7**:995, 996

Knowell, Douglas (*Children of Violence*), **6**:794

Komako (*Snow Country*), **5**:701

Kong Yiji ("Kong Yiji"), **2**:212, 223

Kori (*Weep Not, Child*), **8**:1090

Kostoglotov, Oleg (*The Cancer Ward*), **10**:1412, 1414, 1414–18

Krapp (*Krapp's Last Tape*), **1**:103, 104

Kravitz, Duddy (*The Apprenticeship of Duddy Kravitz*), **9**:1266, 1271–72

Krishnan (*The English Teacher*), **8**:1047–48

Kropp, Albert (*All Quiet on the Western Front*), **9**:1228

Krug, Dr. Adam (*Bend Sinister*), **7**:1002, 1005

Kublai Khan (*Invisible Cities*), **2**:157, 158

Kumalo, Absalom (*Cry, the Beloved Country*), **9**:1190, 1192, *1193*, 1194

Kumalo, Gertrude (*Cry, the Beloved Country*), **9**:1190, 1192, 1194

Kumalo, John (*Cry, the Beloved Country*), **9**:1190, 1192, 1194

Kumalo, Matthew (*Cry, the Beloved Country*), **9**:1190

Kumalo, Rev. Stephen (*Cry, the Beloved Country*), **9**:*1185*, 1186, 1189, 1190, 1192, *1193*, 1194, 1195

Kuno ("The Machine Stops"), **3**:336

Kurt (*Baumgartner's Bombay*), **2**:285

Kurtz (*Heart of Darkness*), **2**:259–60

Kyo Gisors (*Man's Fate*), **6**:859

LaBatte, Monsieur (*Autobiography of My Mother*), **6**:756

Lacasse, Azarius (*Tin Flute*), **10**:1312

Lacasse, Daniel (*The Tin Flute*), **10**:1310

Lacasse, Florentine (*The Tin Flute*), **10**:1310

Lacasse, Rose-Anna (*The Tin Flute*), **10**:1310

Lachmann, Kurt (*Shadows in Paradise*), **9**:1234

Lackersteen, Elizabeth (*Burmese Days*), **8**:1129

Lactantius, Bishop (*Helena*), **12**:1605–6

Lakunle (*The Lion and the Jewel*), **10**:1437

Larry ("My Oedipus Complex"), **8**:1099, 1105, 1106

Last, Tony (*A Handful of Dust*), **12**:1596, 1604–5

La Trobe, Miss (*Between the Acts*), **12**:1691, 1692

Laura (*The Death of Artemio Cruz*), **3**:354

Laura (*The Years with Laura Díaz*), **3**:349, 350

Lavarcham (*Deidre of the Sorrows*), **11**:1481

Lavish, Miss (*A Room with a View*), **3**:328

Lazar (*Open Heart*), **12**:1725, 1726

Leal, Francisco (*Of Love and Shadows*), **1**:56

Lecerf, Madame (*The Real Life of Sebastian Knight*), **7**:995, 996

Leer (*All Quiet on the Western Front*), **9**:1228

Leggatt ("Secret Sharer"), **2**:263, 264

Legolas (*The Lord of the Rings*), **11**:1545

Lena (*Boesman and Lena*), **3**:366, 367

Lenina (*Brave New World*), **5**:612–13, 614

Lenio (*The Greek Passion*), **5**:711

Lenny (*Cracking India*), **10**:1385, 1390, 1391

Leo, Brother (*Saint Francis*), **5**:717

Leonardo (*Blood Wedding*), **3**:406

Leonidovich, Lev (*The Cancer Ward*), **10**:1416

Létourneau, Emmanuel (*The Tin Flute*), **10**:1310

Leung, Jimmy (*Guerrillas*), **8**:1026, 1028

Leverkühn, Adrian (*Doctor Faustus*), **7**:874, 889

Levesque, Jean (*The Tim Flute*), **10**:1310

Lila (*Village by the Sea*), **2**:286

Lilia (*The Death of Artemio Cruz*), **3**:354

Linda (*Brave New World*), **5**:613

Ling (*The Temptation of the West*), **6**:860

Lingard, Duncan (*The House Gun*), **4**:472–73

Lingard, Harald and Claudia (*The House Gun*), **4**:472–73

Lise (*The Driver's Seat*), **11**:1462

Lituma (*The Green House*), **11**:1565

Livia (*I, Claudius/Claudius the God*), **4**:488–91

Liza (*Pnin*), **7**:1000

Lizzie (*The Respectful Prostitute*), **10**:1340, 1341, 1352

Llorente, Consuelo (*Aura*), **3**:356–57

Llorente, General (*Aura*), **3**:356, 357

Lloyd, Teddy (*The Prime of Miss Jean Brodie*), **11**:1454

Lockit (*The Beggar's Opera*), **4**:558

Loewienthal, General ("Babette's Feast"), **3**:307

Lok (*The Inheritors*), **4**:453

Lolita (Dolores) (*Lolita*), **7**:991, 997, 998, 999

Lowther, Gordon (*The Prime of Miss Jean Brodie*), **11**:1454

Luca (*The Sacred and Profane Love Machine*), **7**:982

Lucan, Lord (*Aiding and Abetting*), **11**:1462

Lucia (*Nervous Conditions*), **2**:272, 274, 275

Lucky (*Waiting for Godot*), **1**:97, 99–100

Lucy (*A Room with a View*), **3**:326, 328, 329, 331, 332

Lucy (*Disgrace*), **2**:240

Lucy (*Lucy*), **6**:761

Lucy (*The Lion, The Witch and the Wardrobe*), **6**:818, 820

Ludovic, Corporal-Major (*Sword of Honour*), **12**:1602, 1603, 1604

Ludovico (*Terra Nostra*), **3**:357

Lurie, David (*Disgrace*), **2**:226, 228, 240–41

Luther, Martin (*Luther*), **8**:1138

Lúthien (*The Silmarillion*), **11**:1531

MacCool, Finn (mythic character), **5**:656

Macgregor, Mary (*The Prime of Miss Jean Brodie*), **11**:1454

Macheath (*The Beggar's Opera*), **4**:558

MacHugh, Emily (*The Sacred and Profane Love Machine*), **7**:982

Mackandal (*Kingdom of This World*), **2**:*188*, 189

Mackay, Miss (*The Prime of Miss Jean Brodie*), **11**:1454

Mackie the Knife (*Threepenny Opera*), **1**:133, 135–36

Madama Pace (*Six Characters in Search of an Author*), **9**:1211

Mad Lady (*Terra Nostra*), **3**:357

Madou, Dr. Joan (*Arch of Triumph*), **9**:1237

Magistrate (*Waiting for the Barbarians*), **2**:239, 240

Maguire, Helena (*In the Train*), **8**:1107–8

Mahon, Christy (*The Playboy of the Western World*), **11**:1471, 1478–79, 1480, 1481

Mahood (*Unnamable*), **1**:102

Maiguru (*Nervous Conditions*), **2**:275

Main, Avraham (*Mr. Mani*), **12**:1725

Maithland, Father James (*Three Cheers for the Paraclete*), **6**:742–43

Maitland, Bill (*Inadmissible Evidence*), **8**:1136, 1138

Makak (*Dream on Monkey Mountain*), **11**:1570, 1578, *1579*

Maleldil (*Out of the Silent Planet*), **6**:816

Malone (*Malone Dies*), **1**:96, 101, 102

Malopo, Willie (*Master Harold...and the Boys*), **3**:365, 366, 368, 369, 370

Mama Fresia (*Daughter of Fortune*), **1**:56

Manek (*An American Brat*), **10**:1393, 1395

Mani (*Swami and Friends*), **8**:1052

Mani, Gavriel (*Mr. Mani*), **12**:1724

Mani, Moshe (*Mr. Mani*), **12**:1724

Mani, Yosef (*Mr. Mani*), **12**:1724

Mani family (*Mr. Mani*), **12**:1724–25

Man in black ("Forging Swords"), **2**:223–24

Manolakas (*Zorba the Greek*), **5**:713

Manolios (*The Greek Passion*), **5**:710, 711, 715

Manresa, Mrs. (*Between the Acts*), **12**:1692

Manuel (*Man's Hope*), **6**:861

Marangrazia (*The Other Son*), **9**:1206, 1207

Marchmain, Lady (*Brideshead Revisited*), **12**:1599, 1600

Marchmain, Lord (*Brideshead Revisited*), **12**:1599, 1600–1601

Marcial, Marquis de Capellanías ("Journey Back to the Source"), **2**:193

Marcovaldo (*Marcovaldo*), **2**:153

Marguerite, Queen (*Exit the King*), **5**:634

Maria (*Steppenwolf*), **5**:597

María Josefa (*The House of Bernarda Alba*), **3**:401, 403

Marie (*Stranger*), **2**:171

Marie, Queen (*Exit the King*), **5**:634

Mario (*Aunt Julia and the Scriptwriter*), **11**:1565

Marketa (*Temptation*), **4**:554

Marlow, Charlie (*Heart of Darkness*), **2**:259, 260

Marlow, Charlie (*Lord Jim*), **2**:252, 261, 262–63

Marlow, January (*Robinson*), **11**:1460

Marta (*Sorrows and Rejoicings*), **3**:375

Martin, Christopher (*Pincher Martin*), **4**:451–52

Martin, Julia (*After Leaving Mr. Mackenzie*), **9**:1258

Martin, Mr. and Mrs. (*The Bald Soprano*), **5**:627, 629, 630

Martine ("Babbette's Feast"), **3**:306–7

Martinus (*Playland*), **3**:373

Marwan (*Men in the Sun*), **5**:690, 691

Mary (*The Bald Soprano*), **5**:629

Maryam (*All That's Left to You*), **5**:689, 692

Maryam (*Palace of Desire*), **6**:842–43

Mary Macgregor (*The Prime of Miss Jean Brodie*), **11**:1454

Ma'Shingayi (*Nervous Conditions*), **2**:271, 272, 274, 275

Master of the Game (*The Glass Bead Game*), **5**:600

Masters, Beigh (*The Holder of the World*), **7**:950

Masud (*Sextet of the Six Days*), **4**:535–36

Mathias (*The Interpreters*), **10**:1433

Mattia (*The Late Mattia Pascal*), **9**:1209–10

Matty (*Darkness Visible*), **4**:445, 455–56

Mauler, Pierpont (*St. Joan of the Stockyards*), **1**:133

Maura, Jorge (*The Years with Laura Díaz*), **3**:350

Maurice (*Maurice*), **3**:327

Maurya (*Riders to the Sea*), **11**:1471, 1474

Mavrandoni (*Zorba the Greek*), **5**:713

Mawdo (*So Long a Letter*), **1**:84–85, 86

Maya (*Cry, the Peacock*), **2**:282

Mbanta (*Things Fall Apart*), **1**:32, 33

McCreadie (*The Chant of Jimmie Blacksmith*), **6**:742

McPhee (*That Hideous Strength*), **6**:818

Meade, Michael (*The Bell*), **7**:982, 983

Mehring (*The Conservationist*), **4**:467–68

Melanie (*Disgrace*), **2**:240

Melchor ("Journey Back to the Source"), **2**:193

Mellors (*Lady Chatterley's Lover*), **6**:769, 779–81

Melville, Mr. (*The Chant of Jimmie Blacksmith*), **6**:741

Menegildo (*Ecué-Yamba-O*), **2**:193

Mercy (*Voss*), **12**:1667

Merry (*The Lord of the Rings*), **11**:1544, 1545

Messalina (*I, Claudius/Claudius the God*), **4**:490

Metroland, Margot (*Decline and Fall*), **12**:1604

Meursault (*Happy Death*), **2**:177

Meursault (*Misunderstanding*), **2**:177

Meursault (*Stranger*), **2**:168–69, 170, 171, 172

Mezy, Lenormand de (*Kingdom of This World*), **2**:189

Michael (*Caucasian Chalk Circle*), **1**:142

Michael (*My Michael*), **9**:1168–69

Michael (*Riders to the Sea*), **11**:1475

Michael (*The Dead*), **5**:651

Michael K (*Life and Times of Michael K*), **2**:230, 235–36

Midori (*Norwegian Wood*), **7**:960

Miguel (*The House of Spirits*), **1**:50

Mihális, Kapetán (*Freedom or Death*), **5**:704, 710, 711, 1717–18

Mildred, Sister (*The Abbess of Crewe*), **11**:1459

Miles (*Love among the Ruins*), **12**:1595

Miller, Dr. (*Eyeless in Gaza*), **5**:615–16

Mireille (*Scarlet Song*), **1**:85, 86

Miriam (*Sons and Lovers*), **6**:765, 770, 782

Misra sisters (*Clear Light of Day*), **2**:285

Miss O'Rorke (*Where Nests the Water Hen*), **10**:1313

Mitzelbach, Grete (*Amerika*), **5**:680

Miyo (*Thirst for Love*), **7**:913, 914, 915, 918

Modou (*So Long a Letter*), **1**:84–85

Molkho (*Five Seasons*), **12**:1723

Moller (*Shadows in Paradise*), **9**:1234

Molloy (*Molloy*), **1**:95–96, 101, 102

Mond, Mustapha (*Brave New World*), **5**:613–14

Money Matthew (*Threepenny Opera*), **1**:136

Monica (*The Prime of Miss Jean Brodie*), **11**:1454

Montero, Felipe (*Aura*), **3**:356–57

Monteros family (*Nostromo*), **2**:264

Mookerjis, the (*Wife*), **7**:947

Moore, Mrs. (*A Passage to India*), **3**:325, 332, 333, 334

Moore, Ralph (*A Passage to India*), **3**:333

Moore, Ronny (*A Passage to India*), **3**:332, 333

Moore, Stella (*A Passage to India*), **3**:333

Morales, Pedro and Immaculada (*The Infinite Plan*), **1**:58

Morante, Gustavo (*Of Love and Shadows*), **1**:56

Moreau, Dr. (*The Island of Dr. Moreau*), **12**:1636

Morel, Gertrude (*Sons and Lovers*), **6**:782

Morel, Paul (*Sons and Lovers*), **6**:765, 770, 782

Morel, Walter (*Sons and Lovers*), **6**:773, 784

Morgan, Anna (*Voyage in the Dark*), **9**:1240, 1257

Morlocks (*The Time Machine*), **12**:1642

Morrie (*The Blood Knot*), **3**:361, 366

Moses (*The Grass Is Singing*), **6**:800

Mother (*Boyhood*), **2**:242

Mother (*Life and Times of Michael K*), **2**:235–36

Mother (*Misunderstanding*), **2**:177

Mother Courage (*Mother Courage and Her Children*) 1.137, l, **1**:10, 138, 139

Mother Saad (*Umm Saad*), **5**:688

Mottram, Rex (*Brideshead Revisited*), **12**:1596, 1599

Mouche (*Lost Steps*), **2**:190

Mountjoy, Sammy (*Free Fall*), **4**:454

Mr. and Mrs. Kanyi (*Unconditional Surrender*), **12**:1603

Mr. and Mrs. Martin (*The Bald Soprano*), **5**:627, 629, 630

Mr. and Mrs. Smith (*The Bald Soprano*), **5**:627, 629, 630

Mr. Baker (*Nigger of the "Narcissus"*), **2**:255

Mr. Baldwin (*Scoop*), **12**:1604

Mr. Bankes (*To the Lighthouse*), **12**:1690

Mr. Beebe (*A Room with a View*), **3**:325, 328, 331

Mr. Bons ("*The Celestial Omnibus*"), **3**:336, 337

Mr. Brown (*Things Fall Apart*), **1**:32

Mr. Carmichael (*To the Lighthouse*), **12**:1689, 1690

Mr. Emerson (*A Room with a View*), **3**:328, 331

Mr. Goodman (*The Real Life of Sebastian Knight*), **7**:995, 996

Mr. Healy (*The Chant of Jimmie Blacksmith*), **6**:741, 742

Mr. Joyboy (*The Loved One*), **12**:1605

Mr. Melville (*The Chant of Jimmie Blacksmith*), **6**:741

Mr. Newby (*The Chang of Jimmie Blacksmith*), **6**:741, 742

Mr. Palomar (*Palomar*), **2**:156–57, 158

Mr. Pollunder (*Amerika*), **5**:680

Mr. Ramsay (*To the Lighthouse*), **12**:1679, 1689, 1690

Mr. Rochester (*Jane Eyre*), **9**:1248–49, 1254

Mr. Samgrass (*Brideshead Revisited*), **12**:1599

Mrs. Healy (*The Chant of Jimmie Blacksmith*), **6**:742

Mrs. Moore (*A Passage to India*), **3**:325, 332, 333, 334

Mrs. Newby (*The Chang of Jimmie Blacksmith*), **6**:742

Mrs. Ponza (*Right You Are, If You Think You Are*), **9**:1208

Mrs. Prothero (*A Child's Christmas in Wales*), **11**:1525

Mrs. Qamar (*Children of Gebalawi*), **6**:841

Mrs. Ramsay (*To the Lighthouse*), **12**:*1688*, 1690

Mrs. Sheridan ("*The Garden Party*"), **7**:904, 905

Mrs. Vhd (*Distance of the Moon*), **2**:155

Mr. Todd (*A Handful of Dust*), **12**:1604–5

Msimangu, Theophilus (*Cry, the Beloved Country*), **9**:1186, 1190, 1192, *1193*, 1194

Mugo (*A Grain of Wheat*), **8**:1079, 1084

Mulcaster, Celia (*Brideshead Revisited*), **12**:1599

Müller (*All Quiet on the Western Front*), **9**:1228

Mulligan, Buck (*Ulysses*), **5**:643

Mumbi (*A Grain of Wheat*), **8**:1078, 1079, 1084, 1085, 1086

Munira (*Petals of Blood*), **8**:1079, 1081, 1088

Murphy (*Murphy*), **1**:94, 101

Murugan (*Island*), **5**:615

Musicologist (*Lost Steps*), **2**:190

Mutt (*The Dog Who Wouldn't Be*), **7**:936

Mwihaki (*Weep Not, Child*), **8**:1078

Mzigo (*Petals of Blood*), **8**:1079, 1081, 1088

Nabil (*A Hand in the Grave*), **5**:692

Nagasawa (*Norwegian Wood*), **7**:960

Nagg (*Endgame*), **1**:102–3

Naima (*Sugar Sweet*), **6**:843, 844

Naisi (*Deirdre of the Sorrows*), **11**:1469, 1481

Nanga (*Man of the People*), **1**:27

Nanga, M. A. (*Man of the People*), **1**:40

Naoko (*Norwegian Wood*), **7**:960

Naphta (*The Magic Mountain*), **7**:884, 886

Napoleon (*Animal Farm*), **8**:1125–26

Narcissus (*Narcissus and Goldmund*), **5**:598

Natalia (*Under Western Eyes*), **2**:265

Nataraj (*Man-Eater of Malgudi*), **8**:1042, 1047

Nat-og-Dag, Malin ("Deluge at Norderney"), **3**:304

Neanderthals (*The Inheritors*), **4**:453

Nell (*Endgame*), **1**:102–3

Nero (*I, Claudius/Claudius the God*), **4**:490

Neubauer (*Spark of Life*), **9**:1232–33

Newby, Mr. (*The Chant of Jimmie Blacksmith*), **6**:741, 742

Newby, Mrs. (*The Chant of Jimmie Blacksmith*), **6**:742

New Captain ("Secret Sharer"), **2**:263, 264

Ngotho (*Weep Not, Child*), **8**:1078, 1090

Nhamo (*Nervous Conditions*), **2**:273

Nicolaieff (*The Conquerors*), **6**:857

Niggle ("Leaf by Niggle"), **11**:1548, *1549*

Nightstalkers (*Land of the Golden Clouds*), **12**:1624

Nikhil (*The Home and the World*), **11**:1494–96

Nikita (*Under Western Eyes*), **2**:265

Njoroge (*Weep Not, Child*), **8**:1078, 1084, 1090

Nnaife (*The Joys of Motherhood*), **3**:315

Nnu Ego (*The Joys of Motherhood*), **3**:315–16

Noa (*Don't Call It Night*), **9**:1165, 1169, *1170*, 1171

Noaks (*Smith of Wootton Major*), **11**:1549

Noble ("Guests of the Nation"), **8**:1104–5

Noboru (*The Sailor Who Fell from Grace with the Sea*), **7**:914–15, 920, 921, 922, 923

Noel, Ti (*Kingdom of This World*), **2**:189

Nora ("First Confesson"), **8**:1106–7

Nora (*Riders to the Sea*), **11**:1475

Nora (*The Shadow of the Glen*), **11**:*1470*

Norman, Robert (*The Conquerors*), **6**:856

Nostromo (*Nostromo*), **2**:264

Nuri Bey (*Freedom or Death*), **5**:711, 717–18

Nwoye (*Things Fall Apart*), **1**:30, 31, 32, 33, 35

Nyambura (*The River Between*), **8**:1078, 1092

Nyasha (*Nervous Conditions*), **2**:271, 272, 273–74, 275

Obispo, Dr. (*After Many a Summer Dies the Swan*), **5**:616

O'Brien (*1984*), **8**:1128

Octavius (*Man and Superman*), **10**:1369

Odradek ("The Cares of a Family Man"), **5**:668, 671

Ogedembge, Debbie (*Destination Biafra*), **3**:311

Old Husband (*Cracking India*), **10**:1385

Old Major (*Animal Farm*), **8**:1119

Oliver, Bartholomew (*Between the Acts*), **12**:1691, 1692

Oliver, Dawid (*Sorrows and Rejoicings*), **3**:375

Oliver, George (*Between the Acts*), **12**:1691, 1692

Oliver, Giles (*Between the Acts*), **12**:1691, 1692

Oliver, Isa (*Between the Acts*), **12**:1691, 1692

Oliver family (*Between the Acts*), **12**:1691–92

Omeros (*Omeros*), **11**:1576, 1577

Ona (*The Joys of Motherhood*), **3**:315

Orestes (*The Flies*), **10**:1340, 1348–50

O'Rorke, Miss (*Where Nests the Water Hen*), **10**:1313

Orual (*Till We Have Faces*), **6**:824

Owen (*Deidre of the Sorrows*), **11**:1481

Oyarsa (*Out of the Silent Planet*), **6**:813, 814, 816–17

Oyé (*Explosion in a Cathedral*), **2**:191

Pablo (*Steppenwolf*), **5**:597

Pace, Madama (*Six Characters in Search of an Author*), **9**:1211

Palomar, Mr. (*Palomar*), **2**:156–57, 158

Paneloux, Father (*Plague*), **2**:172, 173, 174

Papillon (*Rhinoceros*), **5**:630, 632

Parish ("Leaf by Niggle"), **11**:1548

Parker, Stan and Amy (*The Tree of Man*), **12**:1670

Parkinson (*A Burnt-Out Case*), **4**:512

Pavlis (*Zorba the Greek*), **5**:713, *714*

Pavlo (*One Day in the Life of Ivan Deniisovich*), **10**:1411

Peachum (*The Beggar's Opera*), **4**:558

Pearson, Bradley (*The Black Prince*), **7**:973, 979–80

Pearson, Christian (*The Black Prince*), **7**:979

Pedro (*Terra Nostra*), **3**:357

Peeperkorn, Mynheer (*The Magic Mountain*), **7**:884

Pegeen (*The Playboy of the Western World*), **11**:1471, 1479–80, 1481

Pellegrini, Leona ("The Dreamers"), **3**:302, 304

Pennyfeather, Paul (*Decline and Fall*), **12**:1595–96, 1604

Perken (*The Royal Way*), **6**:860–61

Permaneder (*Buddenbrooks*), **7**:879

Pete (*After Many a Summer Dies the Swan*), **5**:616

Peter (*The Lion, The Witch and the Wardrobe*), **6**:818, 820

Peters, Margot (*Laughter in the Dark*), **7**:1005

Pétion (*Tragedy of King Christophe*), **2**:204

Petrovna, Natasha (*Shadows in Paradise*), **9**:1234–35

Petrus (*Disgrace*), **2**:240

Phelim (*Bring Larks and Heroes*), **6**:735

Philip (*Where Angels Fear to Tread*), **3**:326

Philip II, King of Spain (*Terra Nostra*), **3**:357

Philippa ("Babbette's Feast"), **3**:306–7

Philip the Fair (*Terra Nostra*), **3**:357

Philoctetes (*Omeros*), **11**:1576

Pickering, Colonel (*Pygmalion*), **10**:*1367*

Piggy (*The Lord of the Flies*), **4**:444, 450, 451

Pin (*Path to the Spiders' Nest*), **2**:153

Pineda, Mariana (*Mariana Pineda*), **3**:395

Pinfold, Gilbert (*The Ordeal of Gilbert Pinfold*), **12**:1594

Pinkie (*Brighton Rock*), **4**:498, 500, 505, 506–7

Pippin (*The Lord of the Rings*), **11**:1544, 1545

Plunkett, Sergeant Major Dennis (*Omeros*), **11**:1577

Plurabell, Anna Livia (*Finnegans Wake*), **5**:657

Pnin, Timothy (*Pnin*), **7**:1000–1001

Pohlmann (*A Time to Love and a Time to Die*), **9**:1226

Pollunder, Mr. (*Amerika*), **5**:680

Polo, Marco (*Invisible Cities*), **2**:157–58

Ponderevo, Edward (*Tono-Bungay*), **12**:1644, 1645, 1646

Ponderevo, George (*Tono-Bungay*), **12**:1632, 1644–46

Ponza, Mrs. (*Right You Are, If You Think You Are*), **9**:1208

Porter, Alison (*Look Back in Anger*), **8**:1137

Porter, Jimmy (*Déjavu*), **8**:1134, 1140

Porter, Jimmy (*Look Back in Anger*), **8**:1133, 1137

President (*Reasons of State*), **2**:193–94

Price, Norman (*A Choice of Enemies*), **9**:1277

Prince Asogba (*The Rape of Shavi*), **3**:317

Prison Chaplain (*Stranger*), **2**:169, 171

Professor (*The Lion, the Witch and the Wardrobe*), **6**:813

Professor Godbole (*A Passage to India*), **3**:325, 332, 333, 334

Proper, Mr. (*After Many a Summer Dies the Swan*), **5**:617

Prospero (*Tempest: After the Tempest of Shakespeare*), **2**:204

Prothero, Mrs. (*A Child's Christmas in Wales*), **11**:1525

Proust, Adrien (*Love in the Time of Cholera*), **3**:422

Psyche (*Till We Have Faces*), **6**:813

Qaasim (*Children of Gebalawi*), **6**:841

Qadri (*Children of Gebalawi*), **6**:841

Qamar, Mrs. (*Children of Gebalawi*), **6**:841

Qasim (*The Bride*), **10**:1397–98

Qfwfq (*Cosmicomics*), **2**:155, 156

Querry (*A Burnt-Out Case*), **4**:500, 510, *511*, 512

Quest, Martha (*Children of Violence*), **6**:791, 794, *795*

Quested, Adela ("Nomad and Viper"), **9**:1175

Quilty, Clare (*Lolita*), **7**:997, 999

Raina (*Arms and the Man*), **10**:*1362*

Raja (*Clear Light of Day*), **2**:284

Raja ("The Parrot's Training"), **11**:1499

Rajam (*Swami and Friends*), **8**:1052

Raju (*The Guide*), **8**:1042, 1050–51

Raka (*Fire on the Mountain*), **2**:286

Ralph (*The Lord of the Flies*), **4**:444, 450

Rambert (*Plague*), **2**:172, 174

Ramboat, Marion (*Tono-Bungay*), **12**:1646

Rampions (*Point Counter Point*), **5**:611, 612

Ramsay, James (*To the Lighthouse*), **12**:1679, *1688*, 1690

Ramsay, Mr. (*To the Lighthouse*), **12**:1679, 1689, 1690

Ramsay, Mrs. (*To the Lighthouse*), **12**:*1688*, 1690

Ramsay family, **12**:1689–90

Ramsden (*Man and Superman*), **10**:1369

Rangi (*Man-Eater of Malgudi*), **8**:1047

Ransom, Dr. Elwin (*Out of the Silent Planet*), **6**:813, 814, 815–17

Ransom, Dr. Elwin (*That Hideous Strength*), **6**:817

Ras Tafarians (*Land of the Golden Clouds*), **12**:1624

Raven (*A Gun for Sale*), **4**:500, *502*

Ravic, Dr. (*Arch of Triumph*), **9**:1237

Rawlings, Susan ("To Room 19"), **6**:799–800

Raymond (*Bend in the River*), **8**:1030

Raymond (*Stranger*), **2**:168, 171, 172

Razumov (*Under Western Eyes*), **2**:265

Rechnoy, Nina (*The Real Life of Sebastian Knight*), **7**:995, 996

Redl, Alfred (*Patriot for Me*), **8**:1140

Regina (*The Death of Artemio Cruz*), **3**:354

Reiko (*Norwegian Wood*), **7**:960

Reilly, Father (*The Playboy of the Western World*), **11**:1471

Remington, Richard (*The New Machiavelli*), **12**:1639

Rendang (*Island*), **5**:615

Rex, Axel (*Laughter in the Dark*), **7**:1005

Ribiera (*Nostromo*), **2**:264

Ricardo (*The Time of the Hero*), **11**:1560

Rice, Archie (*The Entertainer*), **8**:1133, 1139

Richard (*Peter Demian*), **5**:592

Richardson, Xuela Claudette (*Autobiography of My Mother*), **6**:756, 757, 758

Rieux, Dr. (*Plague*), **2**:161, 166, 172, 173–74

Rifaa (*Children of Gebalawi*), **6**:841

Rilke, Cristoph (*The Lay of the Love and Death of the Cornet Christoph Rilke*), **9**:1293

Rimona (*A Perfect Peace*), **9**:1171, 1172, 1174

Ritchie-Hooke, Brigadier Ben (*Sword of Honour*), **12**:1596, 1602, 1603

Robartes, Michael (*Michael Robartes and the Dancer*), **12**:1710–11

Robbertse ("Life for a Life"), **9**:1195

Robinson (*Amerika*), **5**:680

Robinson (*Robinson*), **11**:1460

Roche, Peter (*Guerrillas*), **8**:1026, 1028

Rochester (unnamed) (*Wide Saragasso Sea*), **9**:1254, 1255, 1256

Rochester, Bertha (*Jane Eyre*), **9**:1248–49, 1251, 1254

Rochester, Mr. (*Jane Eyre*), **9**:1248–49, 1254

Rodichev (*The Cancer Ward*), **10**:1415, 1417

Roger (*The Lord of the Flies*), **4**:450

Rolt, Helen (*The Heart of the Matter*), **4**:509–10

Romano, Pepe el (*The House of Bernarda Alba*), **3**:401, 402

Ronje (*The Rape of Shavi*), **3**:317

Roquentin, Antoine (*Nausea*), **10**:1340, 1346–48

Rosa (*Burger's Daughter*), **4**:463

Rosalie (*The Black Swan*), **7**:889

Rosario (*Lost Steps*), **2**:190

Rose (*Brighton Rock*), **4**:506–7

Rose (*The Prime of Miss Jean Brodie*), **11**:1454

Rose, Caroline (*The Comforters*), **11**:1459–60

Ross, Robert (*Shadows in Paradise*), **9**:1234–35

Rossmann, Karl (*Amerika*), **5**:673, 674, 678, 679, 680–81

Rothschild, Father (*Vile Bodies*), **12**:1595

Rowan, Richard (*Exiles*), **5**:646

Rubin, Benjamin (Benjy) (*Open Heart*), **12**:1725–26

Rusanov, Kapitolina Matveyevna (*The Cancer Ward*), **10**:1412

Rusanov, Pavel Nikolayevich (*The Cancer Ward*), **10**:1412, *1413*, 1414–18

Rusanov, Yuri (*The Cancer Ward*), **10**:1412

Ruth (*Lost Steps*), **2:**190

Ruth (*Spark of Life*), **9:**1233

Rycker (*A Burnt-Out Case*), **4:**512

Ryder, Charles (*Brideshead Revisited*), **12:**1596, 1599–1602

Ryder, John and Caroline (*Brideshead Revisited*), **12:**1599

Saad, Mother (*Umm Saad*), **5:**688

Sabas (*No One Writes to the Colonel*), **3:**426

Sabir (*The Search*), **6:**833

Saburo (*Thirst for Love*), **7:**913–14, 915, 918

Saeed (*The Secret Life of Saeed, the Ill-Fated Pessoptimist*), **4:**532, 533, 534–35

Sagoe (*The Interpreters*), **10:**1432

Sa'id Mahran (*The Thief and the Dogs*), **6:**833–34

Salem Bibi (*The Holder of the World*), **7:**950

Salim (*Bend in the River*), **8:**1028, 1029–30

Sally (*A Choice of Enemies*), **9:**1277

Sam (*The Lord of the Flies*), **4:**450

Samgrass, Mr. (*Brideshead Revisited*), **12:**1599

Samsa, Gregor ("The Metamorphosis"), **5:**667, 668, 670, 673, 676–78

Samurai (*A Modern Utopia*), **12:**1649

Sandip (*The Home and the World*), **11:**1494–96

Sandy (*The Prime of Miss Jean Brodie*), **11:**1454, 1456

San Roman, Bayardo (*Chronicle of a Death Foretold*), **3:**428

Santiago (*The Years with Laura Díaz*), **3:**349, 350

Sarah (*The End of the Affair*), **4:**513, 514, 515

Sarn (*The Lord of the Rings*), **11:**1536, 1537, 1544, 1545, 1546

Saruman (*The Lord of the Rings*), **11:**1545, 1546, 1547

Sastri (*Man-Eater of Malgudi*), **8:**1047

Satoko (*Spring Snow*), **7:**916

Sauron (*The Hobbit*), **11:**1542

Sauron (*The Lord of the Rings*), **11:**1544, 1545, 1546, 1547

Saward, Peter (*The Flight from the Enchanter*), **7:**782, 980

Sawsan (*Sugar Sweet*), **6:**844

Schimmelman, Augustus von ("The Roads Round Pisa"), **3:**302

Schindler, Emilie (*Schindler's Ark*), **6:**739

Schindler, Oskar (*Schindler's Ark*), **6:**738–40

Schlegel, Helen (*Howard's End*), **3:**334, 336

Schlegel family (*Howard's End*), **3:**326, 334

Schneils (*The Storyteller*), **11:**1564

Scobie, Louise (*The Heart of the Matter*), **4:**507, 509–10

Scobie, Major Henry (*The Heart of the Matter*), **4:**498–99, 500, 502, 507–9

Screwtape (*The Screwtape Letters*), **6:**820–21

Scudder, Alec (*Maurice*), **3:**327

Sebastian (*Time Must Have a Stop*), **5:**617

Selina ("Let Them Call It Jazz"), **9:**1257

Semela, Sam (*Master Harold…and the Boys*), **3:**365, 368, 369–70

Sen, Meena and Jyoti (*Wife*), **7:**947

Servant (*Misunderstanding*), **2:**177

Seton, Sally (*Mrs. Dalloway*), **12:**1686, 1687, 1688

Settembrini (*The Magic Mountain*), **7:**884, 886

Seven Seas (*Omeros*), **11:**1576

Shade, John (*Pale Fire*), **7:**1002

Shahrayar (*Arabian Nights and Days*), **6:**833

Shakespeare, Judith (*A Room of One's Own*), **12:**1693

Shapiro, Efrayim (*Mr. Mani*), **12:**1724

Shapiro, Joshua (*Joshua Then and Now*), **9:**1277–78

Shaun (*Finnegans Wake*), **5:**657

Shawkat, Mrs. (The Cairo Trilogy), **6:**842

Sheinbaum, Shimson ("The Way of the Wind"), **9:**1177

Shem (*Finnegans Wake*), **5:**657

Shenhav, Gideon ("The Way of the Wind"), **9:**1166–67, 1171, 1177

Sheridan, Laura ("The Garden Party"), **7:**904, 905

Sheridan, Mrs. ("The Garden Party"), **7:**904, 905

Sherif Ali (*Lord Jim*), **2:**261–62

Shiloh, Hagar (*Mr. Mani*), **12:**1724

Shimamura (*Snow Country*), **5:**699, 701

Shingo (*The Sound of the Mountain*), **5:**698–99

Shinji (*The Sound of Waves*), **7:**913, 914

Shiva (*Midnight's Children*), **10:**1326, 1328

Shudha (*The Post Office*), **11:**1499

Shukhov, Ivan Denisovich (*One Day in the Life of Ivan Denisovich*), **10:**1410–11

Shunsuké (*Forbidden Colors*), **7:**923, 925

Siddhartha (*Siddhartha*), **5:**594–95

Sidi (*The Lion and the Jewel*), **10:**1437

Sierva María (*Of Love and Other Demons*), **3:**426

Silvers (*Shadows in Paradise*), **9:**1234

Simon (*Terra Nostra*), **3:**357

Simon (*The Lord of the Flies*), **4:**444, 450

Sinai, Saleem (*Midnight's Children*), **10:**1324, 1326–28

Sinclair, Eric (*Demian*), **5:**598

Singh, Ralph (*Mimic Man*), **8:**1021

Singleton (*Nigger of the "Narcissus"*), **2:**256, 258

Sister Gertrude (*The Abbess of Crewe*), **11:**1459

Sister Helena (formerly Sandy) (*The Prime of Miss Jean Brodie*), **11:**1454

Sister Mildred (*The Abbess of Crewe*), **11:**1459

Sister Winifrede (*The Abbess of Crewe*), **11:**1459

Slavesister (*Cracking India*), **10:**1385

Sluzick, Nick (*Where Nests the Water Hen*), **10:**1313

Smale, Bam (*July's People*), **4:**470–71

Smale, Maureen (*July's People*), **4:**463, 470–71

Smaug (*The Hobbit*), **11:**1537, 1542, 1543

Smith (*Smith of Wootton Major*), **11:**1549

Smith, Lucrezia (*Mrs. Dalloway*), **12:**1687, 1688

Smith, Mr. and Mrs. (*The Bald Soprano*), **5:**627, 629, 630

Smith, Septimus (*Mrs. Dalloway*), **12:**1686, 1687–89

Smith, Winston (*1984*), **8:**1127–28

Snowball (*Animal Farm*), **8:**1122, 1123, 1125–26

Sofía (*Explosion in a Cathedral*), **2:**191–92, 193

Solanka, Malik (*Fury*), **10**:1330–31
Son ("Forging Swords"), **2**:223–24
Sophie (*Too Late the Phalarope*), **9**:1195, 1197
Sophy (*Darkness Visible*), 445; **4**:456
Spinell, Detlev (*Tristan*), **7**:886
Spoelmann, Imma (*Royal Highness*), **7**:887
Spruce, Everard (*Sword of Honour*), **12**:1603
S'shony (*Land of the Golden Clouds*), **12**:1624
Staněk (*Protest*), **4**:552, 553
Stavridakis (*Zorba the Greek*), **5**:713, 714
Stein (*Lord Jim*), **2**:261
Stein, Betty (*Shadows in Paradise*), **9**:1234
Steinbrenner (*Flotsam*), **9**:1237
Steiner, Josef (*Flotsam*), **9**:1237
Stephanie (*Two Late the Phalorope*), **9**:1195, *1196*
Stern, Itzhak (*Schindler's Ark*), **6**:737
Stern, Thomas (*Children of Violence*), **6**:794
Steve (*A Lesson from Aloes*), **3**:372
Stevie (*Secret Agent*), **2**:265
Stitch, Lady Julia (*Sword of Honour*), **12**:1596, 1602
Stoyte, Jo (*After Many a Summer Dies the Swan*), **5**:616
Straik (*That Hideous Strength*), **6**:817, 818
Studdock, Jane (*That Hideous Strength*), **6**:813, 817
Studdock, Mark (*That Hideous Strength*), **6**:813, 817
Student (*Reasons of State*), **2**:194
Suhail (*A Hand in the Grave*), **5**:692
Summer, Julie (*The Pickup*), **4**:476
Susan (*The Lion, The Witch and the Wardrobe*), **6**:818, 820
Susila (*The English Teacher*), **8**:1048
Swami (*Swami and Friends*), **8**:1052
Sweeney (*Sweeney Astray*), **4**:560, 574
Swithin, Lucy (*Between the Acts*), **12**:1691–92

Tadzio (*Death in Venice*), **7**:870, 876, 882, 883
Talbot, Edmund (*Rites of Passage/Close Quarters/Fire Down Below*), **4**:445, 456
Tali (*Don't Call It Night*), **9**:1171
Tambu (*Nervous Conditions*), **2**:271, 272, 273, 274–75

Tambu's father (*Nervous Conditions*), **2**:274
Tangent, Lord (*Decline and Fall*), **12**:1604
Tanner, Jack (*Man and Superman*), **10**:1368, 1369, 1370
Tansley, Mr. (*To the Lighthouse*), **12**:1690
Tara (*Clear Light of Day*), **2**:284, 285
Tarrou (*Plague*), **2**:172, 173, 174
Tekla (*Under Western Eyes*), **2**:265
Templeton, Judith (*The Management of Grief*), **7**:952
Terry (*The Conservationist*), **4**:468
Thakurda (*The Post Office*), **11**:1499
Thanatogenos, Aimée (*The Loved One*), **12**:1605
Theo (*Don't Call It Night*), **9**:1165, 1169, 1174
Thomas, Father (*A Burnt-Out Case*), **4**:512
Thought Police (*1984*), **8**:1127, 1128
Tia (*Wide Saragasso Sea*), **9**:1240, 1243, 1246, 1254, 1255, 1256
Tiberius (*I, Claudius/Claudius the God*), **4**:488, 490
Tiger (*The Captain's Tiger*), **3**:374
Time Traveller (*The Time Machine*), **12**:1642
Ti Noel (*Kingdom of This World*), **2**:189
Tinúviel (*The Silmarillion*), **11**:1531
Tjaden, Albert (*All Quiet on the Western Front*), **9**:1228
Toby (*The Bell*), **7**:982–83
Todd, Mr. (*A Handful of Dust*), **12**:1604–5
Tomas Arroyo (*The Old Gringo*), **3**:355, 356
Toni (*Darkness Visible*), **4**:456
Toribio (*Terra Nostra*), **3**:357
Tousignant, Luzina (*Where Nests the Water Hen*), **10**:1313, 1314
Tramp (*The Shadow of the Glen*), **11**:1471, *1476*, 1477–78
Treebeard (*The Lord of the Rings*), **11**:1540, 1545
Trevelyan, Laura (*Voss*), **12**:1665, 1667
Trimmer (*Sword of Honour*), **12**:1602, 1603
Tsezar (*One Day in the Life of Ivan Deniisovich*), **10**:1411
Tuami (*The Inheritors*), **4**:453

Tulsi, Seth (*House for Mr. Biswas*), **8**:1026
Tulsi, Shama (*House for Mr. Biswas*), **8**:1024, 1025, 1026
Tulsi family (*House for Mr. Biswas*), **8**:1024–25
Turner, Mary (*The Grass is Singing*), **6**:800
Tveritinov ("An Incident at Krechetovka Station"), **10**:1418–19
Twyborn, Eddie (*The Twyborn Affair*), **12**:1671
Tzukazaki (*The Sailor Who Fell from Grace with the Sea*), **7**:914, 915, 922, 923

Uma (*Fasting, Feasting*), **2**:283
Umar (*The Beggar*), **6**:833
Umaya (*Children of Gebalawi*), **6**:841
Undershaft, Andrew (*Major Barbara*), **10**:1371–72
Undershaft, Barbara (*Major Barbara*), **10**:1371, 1372
U Po Kyin (*Burmese Days*), **8**:1129
Urania (*The Feast of the Goat*), **11**:1566
Urbino, Doctor (*Love in the Time of Cholera*), **3**:422

V. (*The Real Life of Sebastian Knight*), **7**:995, 996
Vaněk, Ferdinand (*The Vaněk Plays*), **4**:550, 552–54
Vannec (*The Royal Way*), **6**:860–61
Van Vlaanderen, Nella (*Two Late the Phalorope*), **9**:1195
Van Vlaanderen, Pieter (*Two Late the Phalorope*), **9**:1195, *1196*
Vashti ("The Machine Stops"), **3**:336
Vasu (*Man-Eater of Malgudi*), **8**:1042, 1046, 1047
Veen, Ivan and Ada Demonovich (*Ada or Ardor: A Family Chronicle*), **7**:1004, 1005
Veraswami, Dr. (*Burmese Days*), **8**:1129
Verloc (*Secret Agent*), **2**:265
Veronica (*Valley Song*), **3**:373–74
Vhd, Mrs. (*Distance of the Moon*), **2**:155
Victor (*Pnin*), **7**:1000
Victor Hugues (*Explosion in a Cathedral*), **2**:191–92, 193
Vincent (*Cry, the Beloved Country*), **9**:1186

Virginia (*After Many a Summer Dies the Swan*), **5**:616

Virginia (*The Years with Laura Díaz*), **3**:349, *350*

Vojh, Prakash (*Jasmine*), **7**:949

Volkovoy, Lieutenant (*One Day in the Life of Ivan Deniisovich*), **10**:1411

Volodin (*The First Circle*), **10**:1419

Voss, Johann, **12**:1665, *1666, 1667*

Vriesländer (*Shadows in Paradise*), **9**:1234

Vyse, Cecil (*A Room with a View*), **3**:328, 331

Wait, James (*Nigger of the "Narcissus"*), **2**:255–56, 258

Waiyaki (*The River Between*), **8**:1078, 1084, 1090, 1092

Walburga, Sister (*The Abbess of Crewe*), **11**:1459

Walsh, Peter (*Mrs. Dalloway*), **12**:1686, 1687, 1688

Walter ("Odour of Chrysanthemums"), **6**:773

Wanja, Chief Inspector (*Petals of Blood*), **8**:1079, 1081, 1088

Wargs (*The Hobbit*), **11**:1542, 1543

Watanabe, Toru (*Norwegian Wood*), **7**:960

Watkins, Charles (*Briefing for a Descent into Hell*), **6**:792

Weil (*The Road Back*), **9**:1222

Westhus, Haier (*All Quiet on the Western Front*), **9**:1228

Weston (*Out of the Silent Planet*), **6**:811, 814, 816

Weston (*That Hideous Strength*), **6**:818

Whitefield, Ann (*Man and Superman*), **10**:*1368, 1369, 1370*

White Witch (*The Lion, the Witch and the Wardrobe*), **6**:813, 818, 820

Widow Quin (*The Playboy of the Western World*), **11**:1480

Wife (*Misunderstanding*), **2**:177

Wilcox, Charles (*Howard's End*), **3**:336

Wilcox, Margaret (*Howard's End*), **3**:334, 336

Wilcox, Paul (*Howard's End*), **3**:334

Wilcox family (*Howard's End*), **3**:334, 336

Will (*The Rainbow*), **6**:775, 776

Willie Malopo (*Master Harold…and the Boys*), **3**:365, 366, 369, 370

Wilma (*Temptation*), **4**:555

Wind, Eric (*Pnin*), **7**:1000

Winifrede, Sister (*The Abbess of Crewe*), **11**:1459

Winnie (*Secret Agent*), **2**:265

Winslow, Harriet (*The Old Gringo*), **3**:355, 356Winston Smith (*1984*), **8**:1127–28

Wither (*That Hideous Strength*), **6**:817, 818

Wolf ("Saturday Night and Sunday Morning"), **12**:1627

Wolf, Dr. Hildegard (*Aiding and Abetting*), **11**:1462

Woodhouse, Colonel Michael (*Mr. Mani*), **12**:1724

Woodward, Billy ("Going Home"), **12**:1624, 1626

Wormwood (*The Screwtape Letters*), **6**:820

Wrangtel, Baron (*The Days of Wrath*), **6**:861

Wulf, Anna (*The Golden Notebook*), **6**:791, 796

Xianglin's wife ("New Year's Sacrifice"), **2**:221, 222

Yakichi (*Thirst for Love*), **7**:914, 918

Yánaros, Father (*The Fratricides*), **5**:718

Yasuko (*Forbidden Colors*), **7**:923, 925

Yasuo (*The Sound of Waves*), **7**:915

Yerma (*Yerma*), **3**:404, *405, 406*

Yolek (*A Perfect Peace*), **9**:1172, *1173,* 1174

Yonathan (*A Perfect Peace*), **9**:1169, 1171, 1172, 1174

Yonathan (*Elsewhere, Perhaps*), **9**:1165

Young, Bertha ("Bliss"), **7**:906

Yuaad (*The Secret Life of Saeed, the Ill-Fated Pessoptimist*), **4**:535

Yuichi (*Forbidden Colors*), **7**:923, 925

Yumiyoshi (*Dance, Dance, Dance*), **7**:962

Yvette (*Bend in the River*), **8**:1030

Zach (*The Blood Knot*), **3**:361, 362, 366

Zagreus (*Happy Death*), **2**:177

Zahra (*Miramar*), **6**:836, 842

Zaitoon (*The Bride*), **10**:1397–98

Zakaria (*All That's Left To You*), **5**:692

Zannuba (*Palace of Desire*), **6**:843

Zeitblom, Serenus (*Doctor Faustus*), **7**:889

Zelli, Marya (*Quartet*), **9**:*1245, 1257–58*

Zembla, King of (*Pale Fire*), **7**:1002

Zeus (*The Flies*), **10**:1348, 1349, 1350

Ziemssen, Joachim (*The Magic Mountain*), **7**:884, 886

Zogoiby, Moraes (*The Moor's Last Sigh*), **10**:1331

Zorba (*Zorba the Greek*), **5**:713–15

Zotov, Lieutenant ("An Incident at Krechetova Station"), **10**:1418–19

Zoya (*The Cancer Ward*), **10**:1415, 1416, 1417

Zuratas, Saúl (*The Storyteller*), **11**:1564

Index of People, Places, Movements, and Events

Numbers in **bold** indicate volumes.

Page numbers in *italic* indicate illustrations or illustration captions.

Abacha, Sani, **10:**1428, 1435, 1436

Abba, Marta, **9:**1202, 1203

Abbey Theatre (Dublin)
    O'Connor and, **8:**1093, 1094, 1096, 1097, 1099, 1107
    Synge and, **11:**1466, 1467, 1468
    Yeats and, **12:**1697, 1699, 1705–6

Abe, Machi (Machiko Yamada), **1:**12, 15

Abeokuta (Nigeria), Soyinka and, **10:**1421, 1422, 1423

aborigines, Australian, **12:**1610
    Keneally and, **6:**740, 741–42, 741
    Weller and, **12:**1607, 1608–28

absurdism
    Abe and, **1:**13
    Beckett and, **1:**93; **2:**227
    Camus and, **2:**159
    Gao Xingjian and, **3:**385–86
    Havel and, **4:**552
    Ionesco and, **5:**619, 625, 628–32, 628
    Murakami and, **7:**953, 956

Academy of Irish Letters, **12:**1698, 1699

Achebe, Christie Chinwe Okoli, **1:**23, 24

Acre (Palestine), **5:**683, 684, 685, 686

Acton, Lord, **11:**1547

Adjani, Isabelle, **9:**1245

aestheticism, **12:**1701

Africa
    Achebe and, **1:**21–40
    Bâ and, **1:**77–86
    Césaire and, **2:**202
    colonialism and, **1:**78; **2:**239, 241, 259–60
    Conrad and, **2:**247, 248, 249, 259–60; **8:**1080
    Dangarembga and, **2:**267–76

Dinesen and, **3:**295–96, 299, 301, 304–5

Emecheta and, **3:**309–18

Greene and, **4:**498–99, 503, 507–12

Lessing and, **6:**799

Naipaul's writings on, **8:**1023

Ngũgĩ and, **8:**1071–92

postcolonial writers and, **2:**233, 274

Soyinka and, **10:**1421–27

Waugh in, **12:**1592

See also Kenya; Nairobi; North Africa; South Africa; Zaire; Zimbabwe

African National Congress, **4:**462, 465, 466

African Presence, The (journal), **2:**199, 200

African Theatre Workshop, Fugard and, **3:**361

Afrikaans language, **2:**226–27, **2:**233

Afro-Caribbean traditions
    Carpentier and, **2:**181–82, 189, 192, 193
    Césaíre and, **2:**195

Afro-Cuban culture, Guillén and, **4:**517–26

Agrigento (formerly Girgenti) (Italy), Pirandello and, **9:**1199, 1201, 1202

Aguirre Cerda, Pedro, **8:**1060

Aguiyi-Ironsi, Johnson, **1:**23

AIDS crisis, as Dangarembga film topic, **2:**270, 275, 276

Akey, Ahmad, **6:**835

Akihito, Crown Prince (Japan), **7:**908

Akutagawa Prize, **1:**13

Aldeburgh Festival, **3:**321

Algeria
    Camus and, **2:**159, 160, 161, 162, 163, 164, 165, 166, 170, 171, 174, 176, 177

Sartre and, **10:**1338, 1340, 1353

Algiers (Algeria), **2:**164, 170, 171, 177

Allen, Woody, **9:**1208

Allende, Salvador
    Isabel Allende and, **1:**43, 44, 45, 52, 54
    Neruda and, **8:**1060

Allende, Tomás, **1:**42, 52, 57

Allende Frias, Nicolás, **1:**43, 44, 53

Allende Frias, Paula, **1:**43, 44, 46, 52, 53, 54, 55

Allgood, Molly, **11:**1467, 1468, 1472–73

Alternativa (newspaper), **3:**412, 414

Amazon jungle, Carpentier and, **2:**189

America. *See* United States

Amiel, Jon, **11:**1566

Amin, Idi, **8:**1023

Amritsar massacre, **11:**1488, 1489

Amsterdam (Netherlands), Camus and, **2:**174

Andalucía (Spain), **3:**390, 392, 392, 394, 395, 399, 401, 403

Anderson, Maxwell, **9:**1191

Andreas-Salomé, Lou, **9:**1281, 1282, 1284, 1287

Andrews, Anthony, **12:**1600

Andrews, Julie, **10:**1367

Anglicanism
    Paton and, **9:**1186, 1187
    See also Christianity

Anglo-Saxon language
    Auden and, **1:**60, 66
    Tolkien and, **1:**66; **11:**1530–31, 1532, 1533

anticommunism
    Havel and, **4:**438–40, 543–44, 556
    Mann and, **7:**872
    Orwell and, **8:**1113, 1115, 1117, 1120, 1122–23, 1125–27

antifascism
    Calvino and, **2**:150, *151*, 154
    Ionesco and, **5**:624, 627
    Orwell and, **8**:1112–13, 1127
Antigua, **6**:*748*, 752, 754–55, 758,
    760–61
anti-Nazism
    Borges and, **1**:122
    Brecht and, **1**:126, 128, 129
    Calvino and, **2**:150, *151*
    Forster and, **3**:323
    Hesse and, **5**:585, 586
    Ionesco and, **5**:622, 624, 626,
        627, 630
    Mann and, **7**:872, 889
    Remarque and, **9**:1220, 1222,
        1223, 1224, 1230, 1232–35
anti-Semitism
    Mann polemic against, **7**:876
    Richler and, **9**:1268–69
    See also Holocaust
apartheid
    background and history,
        4:465–66
    Coetzee and, **2**:225, 226, 227,
        229, 231, 232, 233–34, 235,
        236, 241, 242, 244
    Fugard and, **3**:362–63, 365,
        367, 368, 370, 372, 373,
        374, 375
    Gordimer and, **4**:457, 458,
        459–61, 464, 467–76
    history of, **3**:364–65
    Lessing and, **6**:785, 800
    Paton and, **9**:1179, 1186, *1187*
Apollo (deity), **7**:979
Arab-Israeli conflict, **5**:*684*; **12**:*1722*
    Habibi and, **4**:530, 534
    Kanafani and, **5**:684, 686, 690
    Mahfouz and, **6**:828, 834
    Oz and, **9**:1159, *1160*, 1161
    See also Israel; Palestinians
Arab nationalism
    Camus and, **2**:161, *165*
    Kanafani and, **5**:685–86
    Mahfouz and, **6**:825, 829, 830,
        833
Arab Nationalist Movement, **5**:685,
    686
Aracataca (Colombia), García
    Márquez and, **3**:409, 410,
    411, 412, 415, 424, 425
Arafat, Yasir, **4**:*531*; **10**:*1430*
Aran Islands, Synge and, **11**:1465,
    1466, 1467, *1468*, 1474,
    1475, 1477, *1477*

Arcand, Adrien, **9**:1268
Arctic region, Mowat and, **7**:927,
    928–29, *931*, 933–34, 935,
    936
Arequipa (Peru), Vargas Llosa and,
    11:1551, *1553*, 1554
Argentina
    Borges and, 105–24
    Calvino and, **2**:152
    García Lorca and, **3**:394, 398
Arnold, Thomas, **12**:1685
Arthurian legend, **6**:817
Ashcroft, Peggy, **3**:334
Asquerosa (Spain), García Lorca
    and, **3**:390
Association irlandaise, L', **11**:1466,
    1467
Augustine, Saint, **2**:166
Aum Shinrikyō subway terrorism,
    7:956, *956*, 957, 958
Auschwitz, **9**:*1236*
Austin (Texas), Coetzee and, **2**:227
Australia
    Keneally and, **6**:725–46
    Weller and, **12**:1607–28
    White and, **12**:1651–72
Australian National Screenwriters
    Conference, **6**:729–30
Australian Republican Movement,
    6:730
Austria
    Auden and, **1**:62, 63
    Camus and, **2**:162
avant-garde
    Abe and, **1**:14
    Beach's Paris bookstore and,
        5:638
    Beckett and, **1**:87, 100–102
    Ionesco and, **5**:619, 625,
        628–32, *628*
Axel, Gabriel, **3**:300, *306*
Aylwin, Patricio, **1**:46
Aztec culture, Fuentes and, **3**:339,
    342, 343, 345, 354

Badminton School (Bristol,
    England), Murdoch and,
    7:967, 969, 970
Badshai Mosque (Lahore, Pakistan),
    10:*1384*
ballad. *See romance* form
banana strike massacre (1928),
    3:410, 424
Bangladesh, **6**:851; **11**:1493
Banteal Srey temple (Cambodia),
    Malraux and, **6**:847, *847*, 848

Bard College, Achebe and, **1**:22, 23,
    25
Barnacle, Nora, **5**:637–38, 639,
    640, 645
Barraca, La (theater group), García
    Lorca and, **3**:394, 398
Barranquilla (Colombia), García
    Márquez and, **3**:410, 411,
    412
Barrault, Jean-Louis, **5**:632
Barros Moreira, Isabel (Allende's
    grandmother), **1**:42, 54,
    57
Basle (Switzerland), Hesse and,
    5:582, 583, 585
Basse-Pointe (Martinique), **2**:*196*
    Césaire and, **2**:195, 196, 200
Bassett, Angela, **3**:367
Bataille, Nicolas, **5**:623, 629
Bates, Alan, **5**:715
Bateson, Timothy, **1**:97
Batista, Fulgencio, **3**:348; **4**:519,
    520
Bauer, Felice, **5**:660, 662, 664, 666,
    673, 681
Bavaria (Germany)
    Brecht and, **1**:127–28, 129,
        133
    Mansfield and, **7**:893, 895,
        901–3
BBC (British Broadcasting
    Corporation)
    Naipaul and, **8**:1016, 1018
    O'Connor and, **8**:1096, 1097,
        1098
    Orwell and, **8**:1113, 1115
Beach, Sylvia, **5**:638, *640*
Beatles, **7**:956
Beauchamp, Jeanne, **7**:*894*
Beauchamp, Leslie, **7**:895, 896
Beckett, Maria (May) Roe, **1**:88
Beckett, William, **1**:88
Beijing (China)
    Chou and, **2**:211
    Gao Xingjian and, **3**:380, 381,
        387, 388
Beijing People's Art Theater (China),
    3:379, 381
Beirut (Lebanon), Kanafani and,
    5:685–86, *688*
Belfast (Northern Ireland)
    Heaney and, **4**:560, 561, 562,
        563
    Lewis and, **6**:803, 804
    Royal Avenue, **6**:*804*
    violence, **4**:*571*

Belgian Congo
  Conrad and, **2:**248, 249,
    259–60
  as *Heart of Darkness* setting,
    2:259–60
Bell, Julian, **12:**1678
Belvedere College (Dublin), Joyce
    and, **5:**636, 639
Bengal
  Mukherjee and, **7:**938, 945,
    946–48
  Tagore and, **11:**1487–90, 1491,
    1492–93, 1494, 1497, 1498,
    1500
Bengali language, **11:**1485,
    1492–93, 1496, 1497–98
Ben-Gurion University, Oz and,
    9:1159, 1161
Berdyczów (Ukraine), Conrad and,
    2:245, 248
Bergman, Ingmar, **9:**1208
Bergmann, Hugo, **5:**661
Berlin (Germany)
  Brecht and, **1:**125, 127, 128,
    129, 130, *132*, 133, 139
  Dangarembga and, **2:**270
  Desai and, **2:**285
  Lustgarten, **1:***128*
Berliner Ensemble, **1:**129, 130, *134*
Bern (Switzerland), Hesse and,
    5:584, 585
Bevan, Aneurin, **6:***790*
Bhutto, Benazir, **10:**1379
Biafran war
  Achebe and, **1:**23, 24, 25, 28;
    3:*311*, 312
  Emecheta and, **3:***311*, 312
  Soyinka and, **10:**1423, 1424,
    1426
Bihl, Esmerelda, **3:***374*
Bishopsbourne (England), Conrad
    and, **2:**245
blacklisting, Richler novel on,
    9:1277
Black Orpheus (journal), **10:**1423
Black Student, The (journal), **2:**196,
    199, 200
Blake, Larry, **9:***1222*
Blake, Patricia, **2:**163
Blixen-Finecke, Bror, **3:**295–96,
    297, 298
Bloom, Claire, **7:**974; **8:***1135*
Bloomsbury (London neighbor-
    hood), **12:**1675
Bloomsbury group
  Forster and, **3:**320, 321

Woolf and, **12:**1673, 1676,
    1677, 1682–85
Bloomsday (June 16), **5:**637, *642*;
    12:1707
Blum, Léon, **2:**162
Boat Shed (Laugharne), **11:***1517*,
    1518
Bobrowski, Tadeusz (Conrad's
    uncle), **2:**246–47, 248
Bogotá (Colombia), García Márquez
    and, **3:**410, 411, 412, 414,
    415, 418
Bolívar, Simon, **3:**426
Bolivia, Vargas Llosa and, **11:**1552,
    1554
Bolshevik Revolution (1917), **2:**179;
    8:*1123*, 1125
  Nabokov as exile from, **7:**987,
    988, 989, 990, 992
  Orwell's view of, **8:***1123*;
    8:1125–27
  Soviet poster, **6:***788*
Bombay (India)
  Conrad and, **2:**255
  Desai and, **2:**285
  Rushdie and, **10:**1317, 1318,
    1319, *1320*, 1321, 1326
Bonner, Elena, **10:***1405*
boom writers (Latin America)
  Borges and, **1:**105
  Fuentes and, **3:**346–47, 348;
    11:1557
  García Márquez and, **3:**415
  Vargas Llosa and, **11:**1557
Boston University, Walcott and,
    11:1571
Bowden, George, **7:**893, 894, 895
Brahmin caste, **8:**1036
Brahms, Johannes, **1:**122
Brandenburg Gate (Berlin), **1:***132*
Brazil, Camus and, **2:**163, 176
Bredel, Willy, **6:**861
Brennan, Walter, **1:***130*
Brighton (England), **4:***505*
Britain. *See* Great Britain
British Broadcasting Corporation.
    See BBC
British East Africa. *See* Kenya
Britten, Benjamin, **1:**74; **3:***321*, *325*;
    8:1147
Broadbent, Jim, **7:**974
Broderick, Matthew, **3:***369*
Brussels (Belgium), Conrad and, **2:**259
Brustein, Robert, *1212*
Bucharest (Romania), Ionesco and,
    5:620, 621

Buddhism
  Gao and, **3:**383, 384, 386
  Hesse and, **5:**586, 595
  Kazantzakis and, **5:**706, 710
  Mishima and, **7:**917
Buenos Aires (Argentina), Borges and,
    1:105, 106, 107, 108, 109,
    115
Bulith Wells (Wales), **11:***1524*
Bull, Peter, **1:**97
Bungei Jidai (journal), **5:**694
Buñuel, Luis, García Lorca friend-
    ship, **3:**391, 401
Burma, Orwell and, **8:**1111, 1117,
    1119, 1129
Burton, Richard (actor), **8:***1135*;
    11:*1513*
Bushnellville (N.Y.), García Lorca
    and, **3:**403

Caballo Verde para la Poesía, La
    (Chilean literary magazine),
    8:1059, 1060
Cacoyannis, Michael, **5:**715
Cairo (Egypt)
  Egyptian Museum, **6:***829*
  hospital, **6:***831*
  Mahfouz and, **6:**830, 836
  street scenes, **6:***826*, *827*, *829*,
    837
  student unrest, **6:***832*
Cairo University, **6:**828
Calcutta (India)
  Desai and, **2:**280, 281, 285
  Pareshnath Temple, **11:***1487*
  street scene, **7:***950*
  Tagore and, **11:**1486, *1487*,
    1488, 1493
Caldas (destroyer), **3:**418
California
  Huxley and, **5:**601, 604, 605,
    606
  Mann and, **7:**874
  Waugh and, **12:**1594, 1605
Calvino, Giovanna, **2:**152, 154
Calw (Germany), Hesse and, **5:**581,
    582, 583, 585
Camagüey (Cuba), Guillén and,
    4:517, 518, *519*, 520
Cambodia, Malraux and, **6:**841,
    847, 848, 860–61
Cambridge (England), Dangarembga
    and, **2:**268, 270, 274
Cambridge University
  Bloomsbury group and,
    12:1683

Desai and, **2:***279*, 280, 281
Forster and, **3:**320–21, 322, 323
Lewis and, **6:**806, 808
Murdoch and, **7:**969
Nabokov and, **7:***988*, 990
Rushdie and, **10:**132, 1319, *1322*
White and, **12:***1652*
Campion, Edmund, **12:***1592*, 1593
Camus, Catherine, **2:**162, 163, 176
Camus, Francine Faure, **2:**161, 162, 163, 176
Canada
Mowat and, **7:**927–36
Mukherjee and, **7:**939, 940, 941, 942
Richler and, **9:**1259–78
Roy and, **10:**1301–16
Canfield, Mary Grace, **5:***628*
Cannes Film Festival, **1:**15, *16*
Canterbury (England), as Conrad burial site, **2:**248, 250
Canton (China). *See* Guangzhou
Cape Town (South Africa), Coetzee and, **2:**225, 226, 229, 236, 240, 242
Caracas (Venezuela)
Carpentier and, **2:**184, 186
García Márquez and, **3:**411
Cárdenas, Lázaro, **3:**340
Caribbean area
Carpentier and, **2:**181–82, *189*, 192, 193
Césaire and, **2:**195, 196, 199, 200, 202
Guillén and, **4:**517–26
Kincaid and, **6:**747, 748–49, 750, 751, 752–62
Rhys and, **9:**1239, 1240, *1248*, 1250, 1254–56, 1257
Walcott and, **11:**1567–82
See also specific islands
Carl-Ferdinand University (Prague), Rilke and, **9:**1281, 1283
Carson, Charles, **9:**1194
Carysfort College (Dublin), Heaney and, **4:**563
Casarès, Maria, Camus relationship, **2:**163
Cassirer, Reinhold, **4:**464
Castiglione della Pescaia (Italy), Calvino and, **2:**152
Castro, Fidel, **3:***419*
Fuentes and, **3:**345, *347*, 348
García Márquez friendship, **3:**419, 428

Guillén and, **4:**519, 520
Neruda and, **8:**1068
Vargas Llosa and, **11:**1554, 1555
Catholicism. *See* Roman Catholicism
Cecil, David, Lord, **11:***1539*
censorship
Coetzee as critic of, **2:**225, 242, 244
in Ireland, **5:**641; **12:**1705, 1707
Joyce and, **5:**641, 656; **12:**1707
Kazantzakis and, **5:**707, 708, 716
Lawrence and, **6:**763, 766, 768, 775, *780*
Mahfouz and, **6:**849
Nabokov and, **7:**989
O'Connor and, **8:**1097–98, 1099
Osborne and, **8:**1134
Remarque and, **9:**1220
Richler and, **9:**1274
Chambers, Jessie, **6:**764, 765
Chambon area (France), Camus and, **2:**161, 162
Chaplin, Charlie, **5:**605; **10:**1338, *1365*
Charbotte, Marcel, **10:**1305
Charles, Prince of Wales, **10:***1330*
Charter 77 (Czech document), **4:**539, 541, 552
Chernikov (Russia), Conrad and, **2:**246
Chiang Kai-shek, **6:**854, *855*, *858*, 859
Chile
Allende and, **1:**41–58
Camus and, **2:**163
Neruda and, **8:**1055–70
China
Auden and Isherwood visit to, **1:***61*, 62, 63
Chou Shu-jen (Lu Xan) and, **2:**205–24
Gao Xingjian and, **3:**378–88
herbal medicine, **2:***219*
Malraux and, **6:**847, 848, 851, 854, *855*, 856–59
refugees, **2:***215*
rural families, **2:***219*
traditional culture, **2:**207, *210*, 211, 215, 216, 217, 218–19, 223
Chinese Communist Party, **3:**380, 381, *385*

Chinese language
Chou and, **2:**208, 210–11, 217, 223
Gao Xingjian and, **3:**384
Chinese New Woodcut Movement, Chou and, **2:**213–14
Chou En-lai, **6:**854
Christ Church (Oxford)
Auden and, **1:**60, 62, 63
Library, **11:***1539*
Christianity
Achebe and, **1:**22, 31–32, 33, 35
Auden and, **1:**60, 61, 62, 63, 65
Kazantzakis and, **5:**703, 706, 707, 708, 709, 710, 711, 712, 715, 716, 717
Lewis and, **6:**803, 805, 806, *806*, 810, 811, *812*, 813, 818, 820–21; **11:***1534*
Rilke and, **9:**1285, 1287
Solzhenitsyn and, **10:**1406, *1407*, 1408–9, *1416*
See also Anglicanism; Pietism; Roman Catholicism
Churchill, Randolph, **12:**1593
Churchill, Winston, **10:***1364*
Citadel Press, **1:**28
Civil War (Spain). *See* Spanish Civil War
Clark Lectures (Cambridge), Forster and, **3:**323, 324
Clermont-Ferrand (France), Camus and, **2:**161, 162
Clotis, Josette, **6:**848, 849, 850
coal miners, **6:***774*
Cohn-Bendit, Daniel, **10:***1351*
Collins, Michael, **8:**1093, 1095, 1101
Colombia, García Márquez and, **3:**409, 410, 411, 412, 414, 415, 416, 418–19, 424
colonialism
Achebe and, **1:**21, 26–27, 30, *31*, 32
Césaire and, **2:**195, 196, 197, 198, 199, 200, 201, 202, 203, 204
Coetzee and, **2:**231, 232, 233, 234, *237*, 238, 239
Conrad and, **2:**259–60, 264; **8:**1021, *1080*, 1089
Dangarembga and, **2:**267, 271, 273, 274, 275
Dinesen and, **3:**304–5

Colonialism (*continued*)
Emecheta and, **3**:316–18
Forster and, **3**:330, 331–34
Guíllén and, **4**:517, 524, 525
Narayan and, **8**:1052
Ngũgĩ and, 1077; **8**:1072, 1082–83, 1090
Orwell and, **8**:1111, 1112, 1129
Rhys and, **9**:1240, 1246, 1248, 1250
Soyinka and, **10**:1421, 1422, *1423*, 1431, 1432–33
Tagore and, **11**:1489, 1490, 1492, 1494, 1498
Walcott and, **11**:*1568*, 1572, 1574, 1578
See also decolonization; post-colonialism
Colorado College, Oz and, **9**:1159, 1161
Columbia University
Abe honorary doctorate, **1**:15
Borges honorary doctorate, **1**:109
Donald Keene Center for Japanese Culture, **1**:*14*
García Lorca and, **3**:392, 398, 403, *404*
Walcott and, **11**:*1571*
comic strips, as Calvino influence, **2**:156
communism
Abe and, **1**:11, 12–13, 14, 15
Brecht and, **1**:128, 129, 130, *132*, 141
Calvino and, **2**:151, 154
Camus and, **2**:161, 162, 164
Carpentier and, **2**:182, 183, 186
Césaire and, **2**:198, 200, 203
Chou and, **2**:205, 216
Gao Xingjian and, **3**:380, 381
Guíllén and, **4**:519, 520, 522
Habibi and, **4**:527, 529, 530, 532
Hammer and Sickle (image), **7**:*1003*
Kazantzakis and, **5**:706
Lessing and, **6**:*788*, 789, 791, 792, 795, *796*
Murdoch and, **7**:969, 970
Vargas Llosa and, **11**:*1555*
See also anticommunism; Marxism
Communist Party of China, **3**:380, 381, *385*

Communist Party of Israel, **4**:530
Communist Party of Japan, **1**:12–13, 15
Conference of African Writers of English Expression (Makerere), **8**:1075
Confucius, **2**:223
Congo River
Conrad and, **2**:248, 249
as *Heart of Darkness* setting, **2**:259–60
Congress of Intellectuals, University of Concepción (Chile), **3**:346, 348
Conrad, Jesse George, **2**:247, 248, 249
consumer consumption, as Murakami theme, **7**:958, 959, 963
Coole Park (Ireland), **12**:1698, 1712
Cooper, Lady Diana, **12**:1596
Cornell University, Nabokov and, **7**:988, 1000
corrido (song), **3**:396, 397
Costaguana (Conrad fictional place), **2**:264
Coventry (England), Forster and, **3**:319, 323
Craig, Helen, **3**:*402*
Crete, Kazantzakis and, **5**:704, 705, 707, *708*, 709, 710, 711, 713–15, 716–17
criollismo movement, **1**:110, 112
Crisa, Erno, **6**:*780*
Crotty, Derbhie, **11**:*1469*
Cuala Press, **8**:1097
Cuba
Calvino and, **2**:149, 150, 154
Carpentier and, **2**:179, 180–81, 182, 183, 184, 186, 189, 191
Fuentes and, **3**:344, 345, *347*, 348
García Lorca and, **3**:392, 398
García Márquez and, **3**:411, 412, 419, 428
Guíllén and, **4**:517–26
rural village dancers, **2**:*180*
Vargas Llosa and, **11**:1554, 1555
See also Havana
Cuban revolution (1959)
Carpentier and, **2**:183, 184, 191
Fuentes and, **3**:344, 345, 348
García Márquez and, **3**:419

Guíllén and, **4**:519
Vargas Llosa and, **11**:1555
Cultural Revolution (China)
Chou Shu-jen (Lu Xun) and, **2**:209
Gao Xingjian and, **3**:378–79, 381, 385, 386, 387
Cunningham, Sarah, **3**:*402*
Cusack, Sorcha, **11**:*1469*
Czechoslovakia (Czech Republic)
Camus and, **2**:162, 177
Havel and, **4**:537–58
Kafka and, **5**:659, 660, 661, 662, 663
Rilke and, **9**:1279, *1281*, 1283
Czechslovakian Writers Congress, **1**:13

Dakar (Senegal), **1**:77, *78*, 79, *80*
Dalton, Timothy, **11**:*1526*
Damas, Leon-Gontran, Césaire friendship, **2**:196, 197, 202
Daneman, Paul, **1**:*97*
Danielewski, Tad, **10**:*1341*
D'Arcy, Father Martin, **12**:*1593*
Darin, Bobby, **1**:*135*
Darrieux, Danielle, **6**:*780*
Dassin, Jules, **5**:*708*
Davey, Thomas, **6**:*740*
Davidman, Joy, **6**:808, 809, 824
Davies, Marion, **10**:*1365*
Days of May (France; 1968), Sartre and, **10**:1338, *1349*, *1351*
Dean, John, **11**:*1459*
decolonization
Naipaul and, **8**:1021, 1023, 1028–30
Ngũgĩ and, **8**:1082–83
Soyinka and, **10**:1428, 1434, 1435
See also postcolonialism
de Gaulle, Charles, **2**:161; **10**:*1338*
Malraux and, **6**:845, 850, 851, 854
de Klerk, F. W., **4**:461, 472
Delhi (India), Desai and, **2**:278, 284, 285
Delhi University, Desai and, **2**:279, 280, 281
Dench, Judi, **7**:974, *974*
Denmark
Brecht and, **1**:128, 129
Dinesen and, **3**:293, 294–95, 296–98
Desai, Ashvin, **2**:280, 281

Deschevaux-Dumesnil, Suzanne,
  1:90, 91, 92
Deutsch, André, **9**:1262
Deutsche Film- und Fernseh-
  Akademie, **2**:270
Devine, George, **8**:1133
Diamant, Dora, **5**:662, 665, *666*
Diawara, Manthia, **8**:1076
Dietrich, Marlene, **9**:1220, 1221,
  1225, 1237
Dimitrov, George, **6**:849
Diop, Obeye, **1**:78
Doggart, Jimmy, **12**:*1683*
Domínguez Berrueta, Martín, **3**:392
Dominica, Rhys and, **9**:1239, 1240,
  1242, 1243, *1248*
Donald Keene Center for Japanese
  Culture (Columbia
  University), **1**:*14*
Doors (rock band), **5**:618
Drama Association of Nigeria, **10**:1423
Drew, Annie Richardson, **6**:748,
  752, 761–62
Drew, Devon, **6**:748, 750, 761–62
Dreyfuss, Richard, **9**:*1271*
Dublin (Ireland)
  Heaney and, **4**:563
  Joyce and, **5**:635, 636, 637, 639,
    640, 641, *642*, 648–51, 654,
    655
  Murdoch and, **7**:965, 966, 970
  Shaw and, **10**:1356–57, 1358,
    1364
  Synge and, **11**:1463, 1464, 1467
  Yeats and, **12**:1696–1716
Duckworth, George, **12**:1674, 1677
Duckworth, Gerald, **12**:1674
Duckworth, Stella, **12**:1674, 1675,
  1677
Duino Castle, **9**:1282, *1293*
Duvalier, François ("Papa Doc"), **4**:515
dystopian fiction
  Forster and, **3**:336
  Nabokov and, **7**:1002, 1005

East Africa. *See* Kenya
East Berlin (Germany), Brecht and,
  1:125, 129, 130, *132*, 139
Eastern philosophy
  Hesse and, **5**:581, 586, 589,
    598, 599
  Huxley and, **5**:604, 605–6
  See also Buddhism; Hinduism
Easter Rising (1916; Ireland), **5**:637;
  12:1698, 1699–1700, 1706,
  1710–11

École Normale Supérieure (Paris)
  Beckett and, **1**:89, 91
  Sartre and, **10**:1335, 1336
Eden Mills (Vermont), García Lorca
  and, **3**:403
Edinburgh (Scotland), Spark and,
  11:1445, 1448, 1454, 1456,
  1458
Edinburgh Festival, Fugard and,
  3:363
Éditions de Minuit, Les (publisher),
  1:90
Edwardian era, Forster and, **3**:330
Edward VII, King (Great Britain),
  3:330
Egypt
  Mahfouz and, **6**:825–44
  See also Cairo
Egyptian Museum (Cairo), **6**:*829*
Ehrlichman, John, **11**:1459
Eiffel Tower, **6**:*846*
Einaudi (publishers), Calvino and,
  2:150, 152, 154
Einstein, Albert, **7**:872; **9**:1205
  Tagore and, **11**:1492
elephant, **8**:*1046*
Elkaim, Arlette, **10**:1336, 1338
Emory University, **7**:940
England. *See* Great Britain
English Stage Company, **8**:1133
environmentalism, Mowat and,
  7:928, 931, 932, 935
epic theater (Brecht term), **1**:125,
  131–33
Eritrean-Ethiopian conflict, **6**:744
Eritreans, **6**:744
Espectador, El (newspaper), **3**:*410*,
  411, 412, 418
Esteban, Lilia, **2**:183
Eton school
  Huxley and, **5**:602, 604
  Orwell and, **8**:111, 1110
Everett, Rupert, **3**:428
exile
  Gao and, **3**:380, 381
  Guíllén and, **4**:519
  Joyce and, **5**:641
  Mann and, **7**:873, 874
  Nabokov and, **7**:987–88, 990
  Neruda and, **8**:1060
  Remarque and, **9**:1220,
    1222–23, 1224
  Soyinka and, **10**:1424, 1425,
    1426, *1428*
existentialism
  Abe and, **1**:14

Camus and, **2**:163, 166
Hesse and, **5**:586, 600
Ionesco and, **5**:622, 624, 625,
  626
Sartre and, **10**:1333, 1337–38,
  1344–45, 1351
expatriatism
  Mansfield and, **7**:902
  Mukherjee and, **7**:937, 939–52
Express, L' (journal), **2**:163

Fabian socialism
  as Mahfouz influence, **6**:829
  Shaw and, **10**:1355, 1358,
    1359, *1361*, 1376
  Wells and, **10**:*1361*; **12**:1632,
    1633, 1637, 1638
Fairleigh Dickinson University,
  Emecheta and, **3**:312
Falk, Peter, **11**:1566
Falla, Manuel de, García Lorca
  friendship, **3**:391, 394
fallas (Spanish ritual bonfires),
  9:*1260*, 1261–62, 1264
fantasy
  Calvino and, **2**:149, 152
  Dinesen and, **3**:302, *303*
  Lewis and, **6**:813, 814–18
  Tolkien and, **11**:1529, 1534,
    1535–37, 1542–49
  See also magic realism; science
    fiction
Farlay Mowat (environmental flag-
  ship), **7**:930
fascism
  Pirandello and, **9**:1203
  See also antifascism; Nazism
Fedderly, Greg, **1**:75
feminism. *See* women's issues
Feuille, La (Geneva newspaper),
  1:114
Fiennes, Ralph, **6**:*730*
Finch, Peter, **4**:510
Finch-Hatton, Denys, **3**:296, 297,
  299, 301, 304
Finney, Albert, **8**:1133
First International Congress of Black
  Intellectuals and Artists
  (Paris), **2**:*197*
First World War. *See* World War I
Fischer, Bram, **4**:468, *469*, *475*
Focus (magazine), **2**:269
folklore
  Yeats and, **12**:1696, 1702,
    1708, 1709–10
  See also mythology; oral tradition

Fonda, Jane, **3**:*355*

Foot, Michael, **10**:*1364*

Ford, Ruth, **3**:*402*

Forster, Alice Whichelo (Lily), **3**:320, 321–22, 323

Fort-de-France (Martinique), **2**:*106*
   Césaire and, **2**:196, 198, 200, 201

Forum (poetry magazine), **11**:1448, 1449

France
   African colonialism, 1.78. *See also* Algeria
   Calvino and, **2**:156
   Camus and, **2**:159, 161, 162, 163, 172
   Carpentier and, **2**:180, 182, 184, 186, 191
   Césaire and, **2**:196–98, 200, 201, 202
   Conrad and, **2**:247, 248, 262
   Fuentes and, **3**:343, 344
   Gao Xingjian and, **3**:380, 381, 384
   Ionesco and, **5**:621, 623, 624, 626–27
   Kazantzakis and, **5**:708
   Lawrence and, **6**:766
   Malraux and, **6**:845–62
   Owen and, **8**:1142–43
   Sartre and, **10**:1333–53
   See also Paris

Franco, Francisco, **5**:706; **6**:849; **8**:1112

Franconia College (New Hampshire), **6**:*749*

Frankel, Eduard, **7**:969

French Canada, Roy and, **10**:1301–16

French Indochina, **6**:847, *860*

French language
   Bâ and, **1**:78, 79, 80
   Beckett and, **1**:87, 90, 91, 95, 96, 98, 101, 102
   Borges and, **1**:114, 120
   Gao Xingjian and, **3**:380

French National Assembly, Césaire and, **2**:198

French Resistance
   Beckett and, **1**:90, 91
   Malraux and, **6**:845, 848, 850
   Sartre and, **10**:1335–36, *1337*, 1349–50

French Revolution, **2**:192

Freudian psychology, Auden and, **1**:61

Frias, Miguel, **1**:42, 43, 44, 46

Fuentes Lemus, Carlos, **3**:*341*

Fuentes Lemus, Silvia, **3**:*341*, 344

Fuente Vaqueros (Spain), García Lorca and, **3**:389, 390, 398

Fugard, Betty Potgieter, **3**:360, 361, 362, 366, 374

Fugard, Lisa, **3**:361, *366*

Fugard, Sheila Meiring, **3**:361, 362

Fujimori, Alberto, **11**:1555, *1558*

Gable, Clark, **10**:*1365*

Gabriel, Archangel, **7**:982, *983*

Gaelic language, **11**:1466; **12**:1698, 1704–5

Gaelic League, **12**:1706

Gaitán, Jorge Eliécer, **3**:424

Galileo, **1**:140; **8**:1022

Gam, Rita, **10**:*1341*

Gandhi, Indira, **6**:851; **11**:1489

Gandhi, Mohandas
   on Shaw, **10**:*1364*
   Tagore and, **11**:1488, *1490*, 1492, 1498

Ganges River, **8**:*1050*

Ganzhou (Jiangxi Province, China), Gao Xingjian and, **3**:378, 381

Garbo, Greta, **5**:605; **9**:1202, 1220, 1221

García, Alan, **11**:1555

García Bacha, Mercedes, **3**:411, 419

gardening, Kincaid and, **6**:750

Garzanti (publishers), Calvino and, **2**:152

Gautama Buddha, **5**:586

Generation of '27 (Spain), **3**:390

Geneva (Switzerland), Borges and, **1**:105, 106–7, 108, 109, 114, 120

German culture, as Desai influence, **2**:278, 283, 285

Germany
   Auden and, **1**:61, 62, 66
   Brecht and, **1**:125–42
   Dangarembga and, **2**:270
   Desai and, **2**:285
   Hesse and, **5**:581, 582, 583, 584, 585, 586, 587, 588
   Mann and, **7**:869–90
   Mansfield satire and, **7**:901–3
   post-World War I conditions, **7**:872
   Remarque and, **9**:1217
   Rilke and, **9**:1282, 1287

Gidwani, Kitu, **10**:*1391*

Girton College (Cambridge), Desai and, **2**:*279*, 280, 281

Glass, Philip, **6**:789

Glover, Danny, **3**:367

go (Japanese game), **5**:*699*

Goddard, Paulette, **9**:1221, 1223, *1231*

Goddard, Robert, **12**:1648

Goethe Festival (1949), **7**:873

Gogary, Oliver St. John, **5**:637

Golding, Ann Brookfield, **4**:439, 444

Goldwyn, Samuel, **10**:*1365*

Gollancz, Victor, **8**:1112, 1130

Gonne, Maud, **11**:1466, 1467; **12**:1697, 1698, 1699, 1700, *1701*, 1702, 1708, 1711, 1716

Gonne-Stewart, Iseult, **12**:1698, 1700

Gordon, William ("Willie"), **1**:44, 46, 47, 48, 57

Goree Island, **1**:*78*

Gordon, William ("Willie"), **1**:44, 46, 47, 48, 57

Granada (Spain), García Lorca and, **3**:390, 392, 399

Grasset, Bernard, **6**:848

Graves, David, **4**:479, 480

Great Britain
   Auden and, **1**:59–76
   Coetzee and, **2**:227
   colonialism, **1**:27, 32, 33, 34, 35, 37–38; **8**:1072, 1073, *1089*, 1111, 1112, 1129; **9**:1240, 1248; **11**:1489, 1490, 1494, 1498, 1572, 1574
   Conrad and, **2**:245, 247, 248, 250, 262
   Dangarembga and, **2**:268, 270, 271, 274
   Desai and, **2**:279, 280
   Emecheta and, **3**:310, 311, 312, 318
   First World War poets, **8**:1146–47
   Forster and, **3**:319–38
   Golding and, **4**:437–56
   Graves and, **4**:477–94
   Greene and, **4**:496–516
   Huxley and, **5**:601–18
   Lawrence and, **6**:763–84
   Lessing and, **6**:789–93, 796
   Lewis and, **6**:803–24
   Murdoch and, **7**:965–85
   Naipaul and, **8**:1015, 1016, 1017, 1022

Orwell and, **8:**1109–30
Osborne and, **8:**1131–40
Owen and, **8:**1141–50
Rhys and, **9:**1241–58
Richler and, **9:**1262
Rushdie and, **10:**1319,
    1320–21, 1323, 1324, 1328
Shaw and, **10:**1357–65
Soyinka and, **10:**1422, 1424,
    1425, 1426, 1427, 1429
Spark and, **11:**1447, 1448,
    1449, 1458
Tolkien and, **11:**1529–50
Victorianism, **12:**1682
Waugh and, **12:**1589–1606
Wells and, **12:**1629–50
White and, **12:**1652, 1652–53,
    1655
Woolf and, **12:**1673–94
See also Irish nationalism
Greece, Kazantzakis and, **5:**703–18
Greek nationalism, **5:**705–6
Greek tragedy, **2:**235; **10:**1429
Greene, Leon, **1:***141*
Greene, Vivian Dayrell Browning,
    4:497, 503
Grein, J. T., **10:**1359
griot musical tradition, **1:**83
Group Areas Act of 1950 (South
    Africa), **3:**364–65
Group Theatre (New York City),
    Auden and, **1:**61, 62
Grupo Minorista, Carpentier and,
    2:181, 183, 186
Guadalupe Basilica (Mexico City),
    4:*499, 513*
Guangzhou (formerly Canton)
    (China)
    cavalry patrol, **6:***856*
    Chou and, **2:**211
Guinness, Sir Alec, **12:***1605*

Habash, George, **5:**685, *688*
Hadrian's Wall, **11:***1541*
Hagen, Uta, **10:***1372*
Haifa (Israel), Habibi and, **4:**526,
    527–28, 530, 532, 534–35,
    534
haiku
    Auden and, **1:**64
    Takamura and, **11:**1504
Haiti
    Carpentier and, **2:**186, 188,
        189, 191, 192
    Césaire and, **2:**202, 204

Greene and, **4:**503, 515
Haldeman, H. R., **11:**1459
Hamer, Max, **9:**1242, *1244*
Harare (Zimbabwe), Dangarembga
    and, **2:**268, 269
Harris, Richard, **9:***1185*, 1195
Harris, Rosemary, **12:***1688*
Harrison, Rex, **10:**1367
Harvard University
    Borges honorary doctorate,
        1:109
    Heaney and, **4:**562, 563, *564*
    honorary degree recipients,
        7:872
    Lessing honorary degree, **6:**791
    Museum of Comparative
        Zoology, **7:**988
    O'Connor and, **8:**1095
    Solzhenitsyn commencement
        speech, **10:**1406
    Soyinka honorary doctorate,
        10:1424
    Yehoshua and, **12:**1720, 1721
Havana (Cuba), **2:**181
    Calvino and, **2:**149, 150, 152,
        154
    Carpentier and, **2:**179, 180,
        181, 182, 183
Havard, Robert Emlyn, **11:**1538
Havel, Olga Splichalová, **4:**537,
    538, 538–39, 541, 542, 544,
    546, 548
Headley, Lena, **12:***1686*
Heaney, Marie Devlin, **4:**561, 562,
    563
Heard, Gerald, **5:**604, 605, 606
Hearst, William Randolph, **5:**616;
    10:*1365*
Hebrew language, **9:**1163
Hebrew University
    Oz and, **9:**1159, 1160, 1161
    Yehoshua and, **12:**1719, 1720,
        1721
Hendricks, Barbara, **1:***75*
Henrique Ureña, Pedro, **1:**114,
    115
Henze, Hans Werner, **1:***76*
herbal medicine, **2:***219*
Hershey, Barbara, **11:**1566
Hertfordshire (England), Forster
    and, **3:**320
Hesse, Maria Bernoulli, **5:**583, 584,
    585, 588, 589
Hesse, Martin, **5:**583, *584*, 590
Hié, Simone, **2:**161, 162
Hindi language, **2:**278–79

Hinduism
    Hesse and, **5:**586
    Huxley and, **5:**605
    Naipaul on, **8:**1032
    Narayan and, **8:**1037, *1041,*
        1043, 1044–45, *1050,* 1053
Hira, Mikijiro, **1:***17*
Hiraoka, Azusa, **7:**908, 909, 910
Hiraoka, Mitsuko, **7:**909, 910, 911
Hiraoka, Natsuko, **7:**908, 920
Hiraoka, Shinzue, **7:**908, 920
Hirohito, Emperor (Japan), **7:**912
Hitler, Adolf, **1:***128,* 131; **2:**203;
    7:872, 889, 969; **8:**1112,
    1124
Hodges, Beryl, **4:**479, 480, 481
Hofmeyr, Jan Hendrik, **9:**1180,
    1183, 1184
Hogarth Press, **7:**896; **12:**1676,
    1677, 1687
Holland, Agnieszka, **4:**557
Holocaust
    Auschwitz, **9:***1236*
    Keneally's *Schindler's Ark* on,
        6:725, *733, 736, 737,*
        738–40
    Remarque on, **9:**1224, 1230
    Richler and, **9:**1268–69
Holstentor (Lübeck), **7:***871*
Honganji Temple (Tokyo), **7:***915*
Hopkins, Anthony, **3:**335; **4:**502
Horniman, Annie, **12:**1705
Hours Press, **1:**93
House Committee on Un-American
    Activities, Brecht and, **1:***132,*
    141
Houseman, John, **1:***134*
Hovde, Bryan J., **5:***603*
Howard, Leslie, **10:**1366, 1367
Howard, Trevor, **4:***508,* 510
Hu'an (Chou's wife), **2:**211
Hubble, Edwin, **5:**605
Hue (Indochina), **6:***860*
Hughes, Mrs. Ted, **4:***567*
Hurt, William, **2:***173*
Huxley, Ellen Hovde, **5:***603*
Huxley, Laura Archera, **5:**604, *605,*
    606
Huxley, Leonard, **5:**602
Huxley, Maria Nys, **5:**603, 604, 606
Huxley, Matthew, **5:***603,* 604
Huxley, Thomas Henry
    Aldous Huxley relationship,
        5:602, *606*
    as Wells influence, **12:**1630,
        1638

Hyde-Lees, Georgie, **12:**1698, *1699,*
1700, *1713,* 1714–15

Ibo people, **1:**21, 22, 23, 24, 25, 33
Ibrahim, Abd al-Aziz, **6:**826, 827
Iceland, Auden visit, **1:**61, 62, 66
Igbo people, **3:**309, 310, 313, 314,
315–16, 318
Ihalmiut people, **7:**929, 933–34
Imán (journal), **2:**182
immigrant experience, Mukherjee
and, **7:**943, 944, 945,
946–49, 950, 952
Inca civilization, Neruda and,
8:1059, 1063, *1064,* 1066
Independent Union of Czechoslovak
Writers, **4:**539
India
Conrad and, **2:**255
Desai and, **2:**277–81
Forster and, **3:**322, 323, 326,
330, 331–34
Hesse and, **5:**581, 582, 584,
586, 589, 593–94, 600
immigrants in United States,
7:*943*
Mukherjee and, **7:**937–52
Naipaul and, **8:**1016, 1021,
1022, 1032
Narayan and, **8:**1035–54
Orwell and, **8:**1110, 1111,
1113, 1115
Rushdie and, **10:**1317, 1318,
1319–20, 1321, 1322,
1323, 1324, 1326, 1328,
1331
Sidhwa and, **10:**1377–98
Tagore and, **11:**1485–1500
Inklings (literary club), **6:**808;
11:1538–41
Innsbruck (Austria), Camus and,
2:162
International Brigade (Spanish Civil
War), **9:***1265, 1266,* 1278
Inuit people
Mowat and, **7:**929, 930, 931,
933–34
raven image, **9:***1276*
Roy and, **10:**1314
Ionesco, Rodica Bunileanu, **5:***620,*
621, 623, 625, 626
Iráklion (Crete), Kazantzakis and,
5:703, 707, *708*
Iran, fatwa against Rushdie,
10:1317, 1320–21, *1323,*
1324

Ireland
Beckett and, **1:**87–89, 91, 95
distinguished writers, **12:**1704
Heaney and, **4:**561–74;
12:1704
Joyce and, **5:**635–58; **12:**1704
Murdoch and, **7:**965, 966, 970
O'Connor and, **8:**1093–1108;
12:1704
Shaw and, **10:**1355–56;
12:1704
Synge and, **11:**1463–84;
12:1704
Yeats and, **12:**1695–1716
See also Dublin; Irish national-
ism; Northern Ireland
Irish civil war, **12:**1700, 1703,
1713–14
Irish Literary Revival, **12:***1697,*
1698, 1704–7
distinguished writers, **12:**1704
O'Connor and, **8:**1095, 1097,
1099, 1101
Irish Literary Theatre, **11:**1466;
12:1698, 1699, 1705
Irish nationalism
exiles in Australia, **6:**744–45
Joyce's view of, **5:**636, 637, 641
Synge and, **11:**1466, 1478
Yeats and, **12:**1697,
1699–1700, *1701,* 1703,
1704, 1706–7, 1710–11,
1716
Irish National Theatre Society,
11:1466, 1467
Irish Rebellion (1916). *See* Easter
Rising
Irish Renaissance. *See* Irish Literary
Revival
Irish Statesman (literary magazine),
8:1095, 1096
Irons, Jeremy. **12.***1600*
irony
Coetzee and, **2:**243
Habibi and, **4:**531
Murakami and, **7:**958
Islam
Bâ and, **1:**77, 78, 79, 84–85
fundamentalist fatwa against
Rushdie, **10:**1317, 1320–21,
1323, 1324
Naipaul's books on, **8:**1017,
1021, 1023, 1030–32
Israel
Habibi and, **4:**527–36
kibbutz, **9:***1158, 1163*

Oz and, **9:**1157–78
Yehoshua and, **12:**1717–26
See also Arab-Israeli conflict;
Palestinians
Italian Riviera, Calvino and, **2:**150
Italy
Calvino and, **2:**149–58
Forster and, **3:**326, 328, 330
Lawrence and, 767; **6:**766
Mann and, **7:**870, 873, 875,
876, 882–83
Pirandello and, **9:**1199–1216
Spark and, **11:**1448, 1450, 1458
Ivory, James, **2:***283;* **3:***331*
Izu Peninsula, 700; **5:***694,* 696

Jack, Robbie, **3:***374*
Jackson, Glenda, **6:***778;* **11:**1459
Jackson, Peter, **11:***1544, 1546*
Jacobi, Derek, **4:***490*
Jahin, Salah, **6:**835
Japan
Abe and, **1:**11–20
Calvino and, **2:**152, 156
Chou and, **2:**207, 210–11, 215,
216
Kawabata and, **5:**693–702
Mishima and, **7:**907–26
Murakami and, **7:**953–64
Takamura, **11:**1501–10
Japan Communist Party, **1:**12–13, 15
jazz, Brecht and, **1:***127,* 128, 132
Jerusalem, **12:***1723*
Yehoshua and, **12:**1718, 1720,
1723
Jesenká-Polale, Milena, **5:**662, 665,
666
Jesus, **5:**716; **10:***1407*
Jews. *See* Judaism
Joan of Arc, **1:**133; **10:**1372–73
Johnson, Van, **4:***514*
Jones, Daniel, **11:**1519
Jones, James Earl, **9:***1185,* 1195
Joseph Conrad (ship), **2:***246*
Josephson, Brian, **11:***1492*
Joyce, Stanislaus, **5:**638, 644
Joyce Museum, **5:***637*
Judaism
Kafka and, **5:**665, 673
Richler and, **9:**1260, 1266,
1267, 1268–69, 1271–72,
1277–78
See also anti-Semitism; Holocaust

Kafka, Hermann, **5:**660–61, *663*
Kafka, Julie, **5:**660, *661, 663*

Kahn, Jonathan, **7**:*921*
Kamel, Mustapha, **6**:826
Kani, John, **3**:362, 363, *366*, *369*
Kano (Nigeria), **1**:*84*
Kappus, Franz Xaver, **9**:1293
Karachi (Pakistan), Sidhwa and, **10**:1377, 1378, *1383*
Karen Coffee Company (Kenya), **3**:296, 297
Karloff, Boris, **11**:*1527*
Karori (New Zealand), Mansfield and, **7**:892, 895, 896, 903–4
Kashmir (India), **10**:1388, *1397*
Kasuali (Desai fictional village), **2**:286
Katherine Mansfield Museum (Wellington, New Zealand), **7**:*892*
Kazantzakis, Anastasia, **5**:704, *705*
Kazantzakis, Eléni, **5**:704, *705*
Kazantzakis, María, **5**:704, *705*
Kazantzakis, Mihalis, **5**:*704*, 710
Keaton, Buster, **1**:91
Kelly, P. J., **1**:*103*
Keneally, Judith Martin, **6**:728, 730, 744
Kennedy, Jacqueline, **6**:850
Kennedy, John F., **6**:813, 850
Kenya
    Dinesen and, **3**:295, 296, 297, *305*
    Ngũgĩ and, **8**:1071–92
Kerr, Deborah, **4**:*514*
Keshet (Israeli journal), **9**:1159
Khomeini, Ayatollah, **10**:1317, 1320–21, *1323*, 1328
Khrushchev, Nikita, **8**:1060; **10**:1403, 1405, *1416*
kibbutz (Israel), **12**:*1721*
Kikuyu culture (Kenya), Ngũgĩ and, **8**:*1072*, 1073, 1074, 1077, 1082, 1083, 1086, *1089*, 1090
King's College (Cambridge University)
    Forster and, **3**:320–21, 322, 323
    Rushdie and, **10**:132, 1319, *1322*
Kingsley, Ben, **6**:*730*, *737*
Kiowa Ranch (New Mexico), Lawrence and, **6**:768, *769*, *771*
Kissinger, Henry, **11**:1459
Kiswahali language, **8**:*1083*
Klopstock, Robert, **5**:662, 665
Knight, G. Wilson, **10**:1429

Knox, Ronald, **12**:1594
Kobe (Japan) rickshaw runner, **7**:*954*
Kōbō Abe Studio, **1**:13, 15
Kodama, María, **1**:108, 109, 115
Korda, Alexander, **9**:1182; **12**:1597, *1634*, 1649
Korda, Zoltan, **9**:1194
Korzeniowski, Apollo (Conrad's father), **2**:246, 248
Kristofferson, Kris, **7**:923
Kubrick, Stanley, **6**:737; **7**:989, 994
Kuomintang (China), **6**:847, 848, 854
Kyoto (Japan), Murakami and, **7**:953, 954

Ladd, Alan, **4**:*502*
Ladies' Home Journal (magazine), **3**:298
Laemmle, Carl, **9**:*1218*
Lagos (Nigeria)
    Emecheta and, **3**:309, 310, 312
    independence, **10**:*1425*
Lahore (Pakistan), Sidhwa and, **10**:1377, 1378, *1384*, 1386, 1388, 1397, 1398
Lahr, Chistopher, **12**:*1688*
Lakshmi, Padma, **10**:1322, *1330*, 1331
Lamont, Rosette, **5**:629
Lancaster, Burt, **12**:*1636*
Lang, Fritz, **1**:129, *130*
Lang, J. B., **5**:586
language
    Coetzee and, **2**:232, 234
    Murdoch and, **7**:969, 980
    Ngũgĩ and, **8**:1082–83
    Orwell and, **8**:1117, 1127, 1129
    Rhys and, **9**:1248–49, 1250
    See also specific languages
Larkin, Hugh, **6**:744
Latin America
    Allende and, **1**:41, 48–49, 54
    boom generation, **1**:105; **3**:346–47, 348; **11**:1557
    Borges and, **1**:105–24
    Calvino and, **2**:152, 156
    Carpentier and, **2**:179, 182, 184, 186, 187, 189
    Conrad and, **2**:247, 264
    Fuentes and, **3**:339–58
    García Márquez and, **3**:409, 410, 411, 412, 414, 415, 416, 418–19, 424

magic realism and, **2**:185, 187; **3**:345, 347, 348, 356–57, 409, 416–17, 420, 421, 422
Neruda and, **8**:1055–70
political emphasis of writers, **3**:348
real maravilloso style and, **2**:179, 182, 185, 187, 188, 189
Vargas Llosa and, **11**:1551–66
See also specific countries
Laugharne (Wales), Thomas and, **11**:*1517*, *1518*, *1519*, 1523
Laughton, Charles, **1**:129–30, *131*
Lawrence, Arthur, **6**:764, 766, 770, 773
Lawrence, Emily Una, **6**:*764*
Lawrence, Frieda von Richthofen, **6**:765, 766, 767, 768, 769, *771*, 782
Lawrence, George, **6**:764
Lawrence, Lettice Ana, **6**:*764*
Lawrence, Lydia Beardsall, **6**:764, 766, 770, 782, 783
Lawrence, T. E., **4**:479, 480, 487, 491, 492–93; **6**:861
Lawrence, William Ernest, **6**:*764*
League of Left-Wing Writers (China), Chou and, **2**:208, 211
Lean, David, **3**:334; **4**:493
Leary, Timothy, **5**:618
Lebanon, Kanafani and, **5**:685–86, *688*
Lee, Canada, **9**:*1193*, 1194
Lee, George Vandaleur, **10**:1356
Leeds University
    Ngũgĩ and, **8**:1074, 1075
    Soyinka, **10**:1422, 1424, 1425, 1429
    Tolkien and, **11**:1531, 1532
Left Book Club, **8**:1112
Leichardt, Ludwig, **12**:1654, 1665
leitmotiv technique, **7**:878
Lemmon, Jack, **8**:*1139*
Lenglet, John, **9**:1241, 1242
Lenin, Vladimir, **5**:710; **7**:989; **8**:1122, 1125; **10**:*1413*; **12**:1639
Lenya, Lotte, **1**:*126*, *138*
Leoncio Prado Military Academy (Peru), Vargas Llosa and, **11**:1552, 1554, 1560
lepidopterology, **7**:988, 990
Lerner, Alan J., **10**:1366, 1367
Lessert, Margarita, **2**:182, 183

Lessing, Gottfried Anton Nicolai, **6**:789, 791
Levi, Yitzak, **5**:665
Lewis, Albert, **6**:804, 805
Lewis, Joy Davidman, **6**:808, 809, 824
Lewis, Warren Hamilton
    C. S. Lewis and, **6**:804–5, 806, 808
    Inklings club and, **11**:1538, *1539*, 1540
Liberty Movement (Peru), **11**:1554, 1555
Lincoln, Abraham, **9**:1193
Little Carib Theatre (Trinidad Theatre Workshop), **11**:1569
Llona Barros, Francisca, **1**:42, *45*, 57
Llona Cuevas, Agustín, **1**:42, 45, 52, 54, 57
Llosa, Patricia, **11**:1554
Loma de Tierra (Cuba), Carpentier and, **2**:181
Lombard, Karina, **9**:*1243*
London (England)
    Conrad and, **2**:259, 265
    Dangarembga and, **2**:269
    Emecheta and, **3**:310, 311, 312, 318
    Forster and, **3**:319, 321, 322, 323
    Huxley memorial service in, **5**:604, 606
    Mansfield and, **7**:892, 893, 894–95
    pub, **11**:*1516*
    Shaw and, **10**:1357–61
    as Spark influence, **11**:1458
    street musician, **11**:*1513*
    street scene, **7**:*894*
    Thomas and, **11**:*1513*
    Woolf and, **1**:1675; **12**:1673, 1676, 1677, 1682–85
London University, Emecheta and, **3**:311, 312
Longman Press, **1**:79
Low Memorial Library (Columbia University), **11**:*1571*
LSD. *See* psychedelic drugs
Luard, Clarissa, **10**:1321, 1322
Lübeck (Germany), Mann and, **7**:869, 870, 873
Lubyanka prison (Moscow), **10**:1401, *1403*
Lucan, Lord, **11**:1462
Luhan, Mabel Dodge, **6**:766, 768, *769*

Lumumba, Patrice, **2**:204
Lustgarten (Berlin), **1**:*128*
Luther, Martin, **5**:587
Lutheranism, **5**:587
Lu Xun Museum (Shanghai), **2**:209
Lyne, Adrian, **7**:994
Lyon, Sue, **7**:*991*

MacBride, John, **12**:*1708*, 1711
Macchu Picchu ruins, Neruda and, **8**:1059, 1063, *1064*, 1066
Machado, Gerado, **4**:519, 522
Macnamara, Caitlin. *See* Thomas, Caitlin Macnamara
Macondo (García Márquez fictional place), **3**:411, 413, 415, 420, 421, 425–26
Madras (India), **8**:*1037*
Madrid (Spain)
    Carpentier and, **2**:192
    García Lorca and, **3**:394
    Vargas Llosa and, **11**:1553
Magdalen College (Oxford), **6**:*809*
Magdeburg, Mechthild von, **5**:587
magic realism
    Allende and, **1**:41, 47–48, *49*, 52, 54, 56
    Calvino and, **3**:347
    Carpentier and, **2**:179, 182, 185, 186, *187*, 188, 189
    Fuentes and, **3**:345, 348, 356–57
    García Márquez and, **3**:347, 409, 416–17, 420, 421, 422
    Latin American boom writers and, **3**:347, 348
    Narayan and, **8**:1043, 1047–48
    Rushdie and, **3**:347; **10**:1326, 1328
Magpie Players, **7**:*966*
Maharajah College, Narayan and, **8**:*1038*, 1039
Mahfouz, Atiyyat Allah, **6**:828, 829
Mahler, Gustav, **7**:882
Majorca, Graves and, **4**:479, 480, 481, 487
Makerere University College (Kampala), **8**:1075
Malgudi (Narayan fictional town), **8**:1035, 1039, 1046, 1047, 1050–52
Malraux, Clara Goldschmidt, **6**:847, 848, 849, 850, 860
Malraux, Madeleine Lioux, **6**:850, *852*
Malraux, Pierre-Gauthier, **6**:850

Malraux, Vincent, **6**:850
Manchuria, Abe and, **1**:12, 15, 18
Mandela, Nelson
    Fugard and, **3**:363, 365
    Gordimer and, **4**:461, 464, 465, 472, *475*
    Paton and, **9**:1183, 1184, 1194
Manitoba (Canada), Roy and, **10**:1301, 1302, 1303–4, 1305, 1307, 1312–14, *1314*, 1315
Mann, Heinrich, **7**:870, 873, 875
Mann, Julia Bruhn da Silva, **7**:870, 875
Mann, Katja Pringsheim, **7**:871, 873, *874*, 876, 884
Mao Zedong (Mao Tse-tung), **2**:205, *207*, 209; **3**:379, *382*; **6**:854
maqamat (Arabic genre), **4**:534
Maritzburg College, Paton and, **9**:1180, 1183
Marseilles (France), Conrad and, **2**:247, 248
Marshall, Frances (later Partridge), **12**:*1683*
Martello tower (south of Dublin), **5**:*637*
Martin, Steve, **1**:*99*
Martín Fierro (literary review), **1**:115
Martinique, Césaire and, **2**:196, 198, 200, 201, *202*
Martyn, Edward, **11**:1466
Marxism
    Auden and, **1**:61
    boom writers and, **3**:348
    Brecht and, **1**:128, 129
    Carpentier and, **2**:179
    Césaire and, **2**:202
    Chou and, **2**:216
    Neruda and, **8**:1055, 1059, 1060, 1061, 1063, 1066
    Ngũgĩ and, **8**:1079
    Sartre and, **10**:1333, 1336, 1338, 1340, 1342
    Shaw rejection of, **10**:1359
    Solzhenitsyn and, **10**:1399–1406, *1410*, 1418–19
    See also communism
März (journal), **5**:585
Masaai warriors, **8**:*1083*
Mashita, Kanetoshi, **7**:912
Mason, James, **7**:991, 994
Massachusetts Institute of Technology
    Desai and, **2**:281
    Huxley and, **5**:606

Mastroianni, Marcello, **2:***169*; **9:***1205, 1210*

Mau Mau resistance movement, **8:***1072*, 1073, 1078, 1084, *1089*, 1090, *1091*

Max Mueller Bhavan (cultural center), Desai and, **2:**280, 281

Mayer, Louis B., **10:***1365*

May Fourth Movement (1919; China), Chou and, **2:**207–8, 211

Mayrena, Charles-Marie David, **6:**861

Mazhar, Ahmad, **6:**835

Mazoe Valley (Zimbabwe), **6:***801*

Mazumdar, Toni Nime, **2:**278, 283, 285

McCormack, Brian and Michael, **4:***566*

McElhone, Natascha, **12:***1686*

McGill University, Mukherjee and, **7:**939, 940, 941

Meagher, Thomas Francis, **6:**744

Mehta, Deepa, **10:**1382, *1386*, 1387

Menninger Foundation, Huxley and, **5:**606

Merchant, Ismail, **2:**283; **3:**331

mescaline, Huxley experiments with, **5:**604, 605–6, 610, 618

metafiction
    Coetzee and, **2:**231, 238
    Latin American boom and, **3:**347

Mexican Revolution, **3:**340, 345, 347–48, 349, 352, 355–56

Mexico
    Calvino and, **2:**152, 156
    Carpentier and, **2:**183
    Fuentes and, **3:**339–58
    García Márquez and, **3:**411, 412, 413, 414
    Greene and, **4:**498, *499*, 503, 512–13
    Huxley visit to, **5:**604

Mexico City (Mexico)
    Fuentes and, **3:**341, 343, 344, 345, 351–52
    García Márquez and, **3:**411, 414

Middleburg (South Africa), Fugard and, **3:**359, 360, 362

Middle East. *See* Arab-Israeli conflict; Arab nationalism; *specific countries*

Miles, Sarah, **7:**923

Miranda House (Delhi University), Desai and, **2:**279, 280, 281

modernism
    Beckett and, **1:**94–96
    British war poets and, **8:**1146
    Conrad and, **2:**251; **9:**1239
    Gao Xingjian and, **3:**382
    García Márquez and, **3:**409, 411
    Joyce and, **1:**95; **5:**635, 638; **7:**985; **9:**1249
    Mansfield and, **7:**894, 897–99, 902
    Nabokov and, **7:**985
    Rhys and, **9:**1239, 1249
    Rilke and, **9:**1279, *1280*, 1286
    Spark and, **11:**1447

Moes, Wladyslaw, **7:**876

Moffat, Gary, **5:**628

Mokae, Zakes, **3:**361, 362, *369*

Mombasa. *See* Kenya

Momento (magazine), **3:**419

Mondovi (Algeria), Camus and, **2:**159, 162

Monroe, Marilyn, **3:***300*

Montagnola (Switzerland), Hesse and, **5:**581, *584*, 585, 586

Montclair State College, Mukherjee and, **7:**940

Montreal (Canada)
    Mukherjee and, **7:**939, 940, 941
    Richler and, **9:**1259–78
    Roy and, **10:**1301, 1303–4, 1305, 1307, 1309–11

Moore, Edward Courtnay Francis ("Paddy"), **6:**805

Moore, Maureen, **6:**806

Moore, Minto (Janie King), **6:**805, 806, 808

moral philosophy, Murdoch and, **7:***967*, 969, 972

Morante, Laura, **9:***1210*

Morrell, Lady Ottoline, **5:**603

Morrice, Gertrude, **12:**1664

Morrison, Jim, **5:**618

Mostel, Zero, **5:**624, *631*

Mount Holyoke College, Desai and, **2:**281

Movement of Veterans and Patriots against Corruption (Cuba), Carpentier and, **2:**182

Mozart, Wolfgang Amadeus
    Auden *Magic Flute* libretto, **1:**75, 76
    as Shaw influence, **10:**1364

Mukden (Manchuria), Abe and, **1:**12, 15

Munich (Germany)
    Brecht and, **1:**127–28, 129, 133
    Rilke and, **9:**1282, 1283

Murakami, Yōkō, **7:**955, 956, 957

Musa, Salama, **6:**829

Mussolini, Benito, **8:**1112, 1124
    Pirandello and, **9:**1202, 1203

Mussoorie (India), Desai and, **2:**277, 278, 280

Mutare (Zimbabwe), Dangarembga and, **2:**268, 270

Muti, Ornella, **3:***428*

Mutiiri (Kikuyu journal), **8:**1074

Mutoko (Zimbabwe), Dangarembga and, **2:**267, 268, 270

My Fair Lady (musical), **10:**1366–67

Mysore (India), Narayan and, **8:***1038*, 1039, 1043

mysticism
    Hesse and, **5:**587, 589, 598
    Huxley and, **5:**604, 605–6, 608, 610, 618
    Lessing and, **6:**793, 799
    Rilke and, **9:**1281
    Yeats and, **12:**1703, 1714–15

mythology
    Lewis and, **6:**805, 822–23
    Soyinka and, **10:**1421, 1422, 1425, 1427, 1428, 1429
    Tolkien and, **11:**1535
    Yeats and, **12:**1697

Nabokov, Dmitri, **7:**988, *989*

Nabokov, Elena Ivanovich, **7:**986

Nabokov, Sergey, **7:**987, *988*

Nabokov, Vera Slonim, **7:**988, *989*, 990, *994*

Nabokov, Vladimir Dmitrievich, **7:**986

Nacional, El (Venezuelan newspaper), **1:**43, 46

Naipaul, Patricia Anne Hale, **8:**1016, 1018

Nakadai, Tatsuya, **1:***17*

Narnia (Lewis fictional place), **6:**818–20

Naryayan, Rajam, **8:**1039, 1040

Nasser, Gamal Abdel, **6:**831, 834, 842

Natal University College, Paton and, **9:**1180, 1183

National Aborigine Day (Australia), **12:***1610*

nationalist movements
    Arab, **2:**161, *165*; **6:**825, 829, 830, 833
    Greek, **5:**705–6
    See also Irish nationalism; Palestinians
National Liberation League of Palestine, **4:**530, 532
National Library (Buenos Aires), Borges and, **1:**108, 109, 112
National University of Colombia, García Márquez and, **3:**410, 412
National University of Mexico, Fuentes and, **3:**341, 343, 344
naturalism, Lawrence and, **6:**773
Nazism
    atrocities of, **9:**1230, 1232–33
    book-burning, **9:***1223*
    Nazi Insignia (image), **7:***1003*
    See also anti-Nazism; Holocaust
negritude movement, Césaire and, **2:**195, 196, 202
Nehru, Jawaharlal, **6:**851
Neruda, Delia del Carril, **8:**1059, 1060
Neruda, Matilde Urrutía, **8:***1057*, 1059, 1060, 1063
Newboult, Arthur, **8:***1142*
Newburgh (New York), García Lorca and, **3:**403
New Delhi (India). *See* Delhi
New Horn Press, **1:**79
New Japan Literature Association, **1:**13
Newman, John Henry, **11:***1452*
Newman, Nanette, **4:**479
New Mexico, Lawrence and, **6:**766, 768, *769*, *771*
New South Wales (Australia), **6:***726*
New Statesman (periodical), Naipaul and, **8:**1016
New Woodcut Movement (China), **2:**213–14
New York City
    Auden and, **1:**61, 62
    Calvino and, **2:**152
    Carpentier and, **2:**189, 190
    García Lorca and, **3:**392, *393*, 398, 403, *404*
New Yorker (magazine)
    Kincaid and, **6:**749, 750, 752, 758
    Nabokov and, **7:**988
    O'Connor and, **8:**1097, *1105*
    Spark and, **11:**1448, 1450

New York University, Ngũgĩ and, **8:**1074, 1076
New Zealand
    harbor, **7:***896*
    Mansfield and, **7:**891, 892–93, 895–96, 897, 899–900, 902, 903–5
    pastoral landscape, **7:***903*
Ngũgĩ, Nyambura, **8:**1074, 1075
Nicholson, Nancy, **4:**479, 480
Nietzsche, Friedrich, **5:**705
Nigeria
    Achebe and, **1:**21–40
    Emecheta and, **3:**309–18
    postcolonial writers, **2:**233
    Soyinka and, **10:**1421–27
Nigerian Civil War. *See* Biafran war
Nightingale, Florence, **12:**1685
Nixon, Richard, **6:**851; **11:**1459
Nobel ceremony (Stockholm), **8:***1020*
Noma Award, **1:**77, 79, *80*
Norsa sagas, **1:**66; **6:**805
North Africa, Camus and, **2:**159, 160, 161, 162, 163, 164, *165*, 166, 174, 176
Northern Ireland
    Heaney and, **4:**559–61, 563, 564, 567–68, 570–71
    Lewis and, **6:**803, 804
    violence, **4:***571*
Northwestern University, Ngũgĩ and, **8:**1074, 1075
"Norwegian Wood" (song), **7:***956*
Nottingham University, Lawrence and, **6:**765, 766
Nouvelles Éditions Africaines, **1:**79
November Revolution (1918), **9:**1282, 1283
Ntshona, Winston, **3:**362, 363
nuclear disarmament movement
    "Ban the Bomb" protest, **6:**792
    Lessing and, **6:**789, 791, 792
    Mowat and, **7:**930, 932
    White and, **12:***1654*, 1655, 1656
Nyoongahs (aborigines), Weller and, **12:**1610, 1611, 1614, 1617, 1620–22, 1624, 1627

Obasanjo, Olusegun, **1:**25
O'Brien, William Smith, **6:**744
obscenity charges. *See* censorship
O'Connell, Daniel, **6:**744, *745*
O'Connor, Evelyn Bowen Speaight, **8:**1096

O'Connor, Harriet Rich, **8:**1096
Ogun (deity), **10:**1427
Ogwugwu Afor Publishing Company, **3:**312
Okada, Eiji, **1:***16*
O'Kane, Patrick, **11:***1469*
Okike: An African Journal of New Writing, **1:**24
Olivier, Laurence, **5:**632; **8:**1133, *1139*
Olympia Press, **7:**989
Oman, **5:***690*
Ontario (Canada) landscape, **7:***928*
opera
    Auden and, **1:**74–76
    Wagnerian influences, **5:**650; **6:**805; **7:**876, 878, 886; **10:**1364, 1375; **11**1536
oral tradition
    Achebe and, **1:**27, 29, 33
    Bâ and, **1:**83
    Soyinka and, **10:**1422
Oran (Algeria), Camus and, **2:**161, 162, 172
Orinoco River, **2:***186*
    Carpentier and, **2:**186, 189, 190
Orwell, Eileen Maud O'Shaughnessy, **8:**1112, 1113, 1115
Orwell, Sonia Brownell, **8:**1115
Otago (ship), **2:**247, 248, 265
Oulipo (literary circle), Calvino and, **2:**151
Owen, Harold, **8:**1150
Oxford Union Library, **11:***1531*
Oxford University
    Auden and, **1:**60, 62, 63, 66
    Borges honorary degree, **1:**109
    Christ Church Library, **11:***1539*
    Golding and, **4:**439, 441, 444
    Graves and, **4:**480
    Greene and, **4:**497, 503
    Heaney and, **4:**563
    Huxley and, **5:**602, 604
    Inklings club, **6:**808; **11:**1538–41
    Lewis and, **6:**805–6, *807*, 808, *809*
    Magdalen College, **6:**809
    Malraux honorary degree, **6:***850*
    Murdoch and, **7:**969, 970
    Naipaul and, **8:**1015, 1017, *1018*, *1023*
    Orwell and, **8:**1110
    Oz and, **9:**1159, 1160

Tagore honorary degree,
11:1486, 1488
Tolkien and, **11**:1530,
1531–32, 1533, 1534,
1538–41
Waugh and, **12**:1590, 1592
Oxford University Press,
11:1538–39
Oz, Nily Zukerman, **9**:1159, 1161

pacifism
Hesse and, **5**:584, 587, 589
Huxley and, **5**:604, 605, 616
Woolf and, **12**:1678, 1680,
1693–94
paganism, Forster and, **3**:326, 330,
331
Page-Barbour Lectures, Auden and,
1:62
Pakistan
Rushdie and, **10**:1319, 1323,
1324, 1328, 1330
Sidhwa and, **10**:1377–98
Palestinians, **5**:*684*; **12**:1717
Habibi and, **4**:527–36
Kanafani and, **5**:683, 684–85,
689
Panama City (Panama), Fuentes
and, **3**:339, 340, 344
pan-Arabism, Kanafani and,
5:685–86
Pan no Kai (Pan Society), **11**:1502,
1505
Papas, Irene, **5**:715
Pareshnath Temple (Calcutta),
11:*1487*
Paris (France), **8**:*1112*
Beckett and, **1**:89, 90, 91, 93,
95
café, **1**:*88*
Calvino and, **2**:152, 154
Camus and, **2**:161, 162, 163,
174
Carpentier and, **2**:179, 182,
183, 184, 185, 193–94
Césaire and, **2**:196, *197*, 198,
202
Eiffel Tower, **6**:*846*
García Márquez and, **3**:412,
418, 430
Ionesco and, **5**:621, 623, 624,
656
Joyce and, **5**:637, 638, 639, *640*
Kazantzakis and, **5**:705, 707
liberation of, **2**:163
Nabokov and, **7**:988, 990

Orwell and, **8**:1111–12
Richler and, **9**:1260, 1262,
1264
Rilke and, **9**:1282, 1287
Sartre and, **10**:1335, 1336
street scene, **6**:*846*
student protests, **10**:*1349*, *1351*
Synge and, **11**:1465, 1467
as Takamura influence, **11**:1502
Vargas Llosa and, **11**:1553,
1554
Yehoshua and, **12**:1721
Parsis, Sidhwa and, **10**:1378–79,
1384, 1386, 1388, 1390,
1393, 1395, 1396
partisan resistance (Italy), Calvino
and, **2**:150, *151*, 154
Partridge, Ralph, **12**:*1683*, 1684
Pascal, Gabriel, **10**:1366, 1367
Passbook Law (South Africa), **3**:*361*,
363
Paton, Anne Hopkins, **9**:1183,
1184, 1197
Paton, Dorrie Francis Lusted,
9:1180, 1182, 1183, 1184,
1195
patriarchy, as Dangarembga theme,
2:271, *272*
Paula (Chilean journal), **1**:43
Paxinou, Katina, **3**:*402*
Payne-Townshend, Charlotte,
10:1358, *1360*, 1361
Peace Now movement (Israel), Oz
and, **9**:1159, 1161
Pearson, Clive, **12**:1593
Penrose, Alec, **12**:*1683*
Penrose, Frances, **12**:*1683*
People's Republic of China. *See*
China
Perón, Eva, **1**:*111*
Perón, Juan, **1**:107, 108, 109, *111*
Perth (Australia), **12**:*1608*
Peru
Macchu Picchu ruins, **8**:1059,
1063, *1064*, 1066
Vargas Llosa and, **11**:1551–66
Peshawar mutiny, **8**:*1052*
Pétain, Henri-Philippe, **10**:*1338*
Peter Cat (Tokyo jazz bar),
Murakami and, **7**:955, 957
Pfefferberg, Poldek, **6**:728, 736, 737
Philby, Kim, **4**:498
Phillips, Robin, **12**:1596
Pietism, Hesse and, **5**:582, 587, 588
Pilate, Pontius, **10**:*1407*
Pinochet, Augusto, **1**:43, *54*

Pirandello, Maria Antonietta
Portulano, **9**:1202, 1203–4
Plowright, Joan, **5**:632
Poetry Review, **11**:1447, 1448
Poetry Society (London), **11**:1447,
1448
Poitier, Sidney, **9**:*1193*, 1194
Poland, Conrad and, **2**:246, 248,
250, 262
political correctness
Naipaul and, **8**:1022–23
Orwell and, **8**:1117, 1127–28,
1129
Pollack, Oskar, **5**:661, 663
Popular Front for the Liberation of
Palestine, **5**:683, 686
Population Registration Act of 1950
(South Africa), **3**:364
pornography charges. *See* censor-
ship
Port Elizabeth (South Africa),
Fugard and, **3**:360, 368, *369*,
371–72
Portora Royal School (Ireland),
Beckett and, **1**:88–89, 91
postcolonialism
Achebe and, **1**:21; **2**:27
Camus and, **2**:166, 170
Coetzee and, **2**:225, 233–34
Dangarembga and, **2**:274
Mukherjee and, **7**:943, 945
Narayan and, **8**:1047, 1050–51
Rhys and, **9**:1251
Soyinka, **10**:1421, 1422, 1429,
1432–33, 1435–36
Walcott and, **11**:1567, 1574
See also decolonization
postmodernism, Murakami and,
7:961
potato famine (1840s), **12**:1705
Prague (Czech Republic), **9**:*1281*
Camus and, **2**:177
Havel and, **4**:537, 538, 539–40,
541, 552
Kafka and, **5**:659, 660, 661,
663, 665, *671*, 673, 680
Rilke and, **9**:1279, 1280–81,
1281, 1283
Prague Castle, **4**:*540*
Prague Circle, **5**:661, 663
Prague Spring (1967–68), **4**:539,
552
Prensa, La (literary review), **1**:115
Prensa Latina (Cuban news agency),
3:411, 412, 419
Pre-Raphaelites, **12**:1702

Présence africaine (journal), **2**:199, 200

Presley, Elvis, **10**:1324, 1331

Pribram, Ewald, **5**:661

Princeton University
  Mann and, **7**:873, 874
  Murakami and, **7**:956, 957
  Yehoshua and, **12**:1720, 1721

Prisma (literary review), **1**:108, 115

Proa (literary review), **1**:108, 115

Progressive Party of Martinique, Césaire and, **2**:198

Pryce, Jonathan, **11**:1526; **12**:*1684*, 1685

psychoanalysis
  as Carpentier influence, **2**:186
  Hesse and, **5**:164, 584, 585, 586, 589, 590, 595, 598, 600, 615
  as Woolf influence, **12**:1687

Punch and Judy shows, **5**:626

pychedelic drugs, Huxley and, **5**:604, 605–6, 610, *617*, 618

Qinghai (China), Gao Xingjian and, **3**:379

Quebec City (Canada), Roy and, **10**:1305, *1306*

Quebec separatists, **9**:1263, 1264, 1267

Queen's University (Belfast), Heaney and, **4**:560, 561, 562, 563

Quick, Diana, **12**:*1600*

Quinn, Anthony, **5**:715

Quinn, John, **12**:*1713*

Rangoon (Burma), **8**:*1111*

raven image, **9**:*1276*

Ray, Satyajit, **11**:1489

Rea, Stephen, **4**:564; **11**:1526

realism, Fuentes and, **3**:339

realismo màgico. See magical realism

Reality: A Journal of Liberal Opinion (South Africa), **9**:1183

real maravilloso (literary style)
  Carpentier and, **2**:179, 182, 185, 188, 189
  magical realism vs., **2**:187

Redford, Robert, **3**:*305*

Redgrave, Vanessa, **12**:*1686*

Reed, Oliver, **6**:*778*

Reeves, Keanu, **11**:1566

refugees, China, **2**:*215*

reincarnation, **7**:917

Reinhardt, Max, **1**:129

Renaud, Madeleine, **1**:92

Reshotovskaya, Natalya Alekseevna, **10**:1400, 1402, 1403, 1405

resistance movements (World War II)
  in France, **1**:90, 91; **6**:845, 848, 850; **10**:1335–36, *1337*, 1349–50
  in Italy, **2**:150, *151*, 154

Revista mexicana de literatura (journal), **3**:344, 345

Rhodesia. *See* Zimbabwe

Richards, Grant, **5**:648

Richardson, Tony, **7**:994

Richler, Catherine Boudreau, **9**:1262, 1264

Richler, Florence Wood, **9**:*1261*, 1262, 1264

Ring des Nibelungen, Der (Wagner opera cycle), **6**:805; **11**:*1536*

Ripstein, Arturo, **3**:*343*

Robben Island (South Africa), **3**:363

Rockefeller, John D., **11**:*1490*

Rodriguéz Espinosa, Antonio, **3**:391

Roman Catholicism
  Carpentier and, **2**:189, 190, 193
  Greene and, **4**:495, 496, 497, 498–99, 503, 506, 507, 510, 512
  Joyce and, **5**:*648*, 649–50
  Keneally and, **6**:726, 742, 744
  Northern Ireland and, **4**:561
  Rilke and, **9**:1287
  Spark and, **11**:1445, 1448, 1449, *1449*, 1452, 1453, 1454, 1456, 1457, 1457–58, 1458, 1459
  Waugh and, **12**:1589, 1592, 1593, 1594, 1595, 1597, 1599, 1600–1601, 1602, 1603

romance form, García Lorca and, **3**:397, 400–401

Romania, Ionesco and, **5**:619–34

Rome (Italy), Calvino and, **2**:152

Roodt, Darrell James, **9**:1195

Rooksnest (Forster home), **3**:320, 326

Roosevelt, Theodore, **12**:1639

Rostropovich, Mstislav, **10**:*1406*

Roussy, Suzanne, **2**:198, 200

Roy, Germain, **10**:*1302*

Roy, Mélina Landry, **10**:1302, 1304–5, 1307, 1314

Royal Court Theatre (London)
  Osborne and, **8**:1133, 1134

Shaw and, **10**:1361

Soyinka and, **10**:1422

Royal University (Dublin), Joyce and, **5**:636, 639, 646

Rugby school, Rushdie and, **10**:1319, 1321

Rungsted (Denmark), Dinesen and, **3**:293, 297

Rungstedlund (Dinesen estate), **3**:294, 296, 297, 298

Russell, Ken, **6**:771, *778*

Russia
  Conrad and, **2**:245, 247, 262
  Nabokov and, **7**:985, 986–87, 990
  Solzhenitsyn and, **10**:1399–1409
  See also Soviet Union

Russian Revolution (1917). *See* Bolshevik Revolution

Russo-Japanese War, Chou and, **2**:207

Rwanda, **8**:1021, 1023

Sadat, Anwar, **6**:833

Sadhana (journal), **11**:1488

St. Clair Morford, Albert, **12**:1596

Saint Lucia, Walcott and, **11**:1567, 1568, 1570, 1572, 1574, 1576–78

Saint Lucia Arts Guild, **11**:1569

St. Petersburg (Russia), Nabokov and, **7**:986–87, 990

Sakharov, Andrei, **10**:*1405*

Sakyamuni Buddha, **3**:*383*

Salmon, Christian, **10**:*1430*

samizdat literature, Havel and, **4**:548, 548–59

San Marcos University, Vargas Llosa and, **11**:1552, 1554, 1564–65

San Remo (Italy), **2**:*150*
  Calvino and, **2**:150, 154

Sanskrit language, **11**:1493

Santa Mónica de los Venados (Carpentier fictional place), **2**:190

Santería, Carpentier and, **2**:193

Santiago de las Vegas (Cuba), Calvino and, **2**:149, 150, 154

Saturday Night (magazine), **7**:930

Schaefer, Norbert, **3**:*368*

Schell, Maria, **4**:510

Schepisi, Fred, **6**:729

Schiller Theater (Berlin), **1**:93

Schindler, Oskar, **6:**733, 736–37, 738–40
  list of, **6:**738
Scholz, Elfriede (Remarque's sister), **9:**1221, 1224, 1230
science fiction
  Abe and, **1:**14
  Forster and, **3:**336
  Lessing and, **6:**793, 794, 797–99
  Lewis and, **6:**803, 806, 814, 815
  Wells and, **12:**1629, 1630–31, 1634, 1635–36, 1642–44, 1646–49
Scofield, Paul, **3:**363
Scorsese, Martin, **5:**716
Scotland, Spark and, **11:**1445, 1446, 1448, 1454, 1456, 1458
Scottsboro case (1931), **10:**1340, 1352
Sebastian, Saint, **7:**909, 920
Sellers, Catherine, **2:**163
Sellers, Peter, **7:**994
Sen, Amartya, **11:**1489
Sendai (Japan), Chou and, **2:**207, 211
Senegal, Bâ and, **1:**77–86
Senghor, Léopold Sédar, **2:**196, 197, 202, 203
Sens (France), **2:**159
Sepoy Mutiny, **8:**1052, 1053
September 11 (2001) terrorist attacks, Naipaul and, **8:**1023, 1032
Serpent Players (South Africa), **3:**363
Sethna, Maia, **10:**1391
Seville (Spain), Calvino and, **2:**152
Shakespeare and Company (Paris bookstore), **5:**638, 640
Shanghai (China), Chou and, **2:**205, 208, 209, 211
Shantiniketan school (Bengal), Tagore and, **11:**1488–89, 1497, 1500
Shaoxing (Zhejiang Province, China), Chou and, **2:**205, 206, 211
Sharpeville (South Africa) massacre, **3:**364
Shavi (Emecheta fictional place), **3:**317–19
Shawn, Allen (Kincaid's husband), **6:**750

Shirakabaha (White Birch Society), **11:**1502
Shona culture, **2:**268, 271
Shona language, **2:**268
Sichuan (China), Gao Xingjian and, **3:**380, 386
Sickles, Dan, **6:**729
Siena (Italy), Calvino and, **2:**149, 154
Sikhs, **10:**1388
Simplicissimus (German magazine), **7:**873, 875
Singer, Esther Judith (Chichita) (Calvino's wife), **2:**152, 154
Sinn Fein, **11:**1467
Sino-Japanese War, **1:**61, 62, 63
Sirk, Douglas, **9:**1226
Six-Day War (1967), **5:**687, 689; **6:**828, 834; **9:**1159, 1160, 1161
Slatina (Romania), Ionesco and, **5:**619, 620, 623
slavery
  Césaire and, **2:**196
  Hegel on, **2:**232
Sligo (Ireland), **12:**1700, 1709
Smith, Leslie Tilden, **9:**1241–42
Smith, Maggie, **11:**1455, 1456
Smith College, Desai and, **2:**281
Smits, Jimmy, **3:**355
socialism
  Mahfouz and, **6:**828–29, 833, 834
  Orwell and, **8:**1112, 1113, 1119, 1120, 1122, 1123, 1127, 1130
  Shaw and, **10:**1355, 1358, 1359, 1361, 1376
  Wells and, **12:**1632, 1633, 1637
  See also communism; Marxism
socialist realism, Lessing and, **6:**799
Soeurs Optimistes Internationales (Senegal), **1:**80
Solzhenitsyn, Yemolai, **10:**1405
Somerville College (Oxford), Murdoch and, **7:**969, 970
Sorbonne
  Borges honorary doctorate, **1:**109
  student protests (1968), **10:**1349, 1351
South Africa, **9:**1186
  Coetzee and, **2:**225–44
  Fugard and, **3:**359–76
  Gordimer and, **4:**457–76

  Lessing and, **6:**785, 791, 793, 800
  Paton and, **9:**1179–98
  See also apartheid
South African Liberal Party, **9:**186, 1179, 1182, 1183, 1184
South America. *See* Latin America; *specific countries*
Southeast Asia
  as Conrad setting, **2:**245, 247, 260
  Malraux and, **6:**841, 847, 848, 860–61
  See also Vietnam War
southern Africa. *See* South Africa; Zimbabwe
Southern Rhodesia. *See* Zimbabwe
Soviet Union
  Brecht and, **1:**129
  Calvino and, **2:**151
  Czech occupation by, **4:**538, 539–40, 541, 544, 546, 548–49
  East Berlin and, **1:**132
  Great Terror, **8:**1122
  Lessing on, **6:**788
  Lessing trip to, **6:**789
  Neruda's exile in, **8:**1060
  Orwell's views of, **8:**1113, 1115, 1117, 1120, 1122, 1125–27, 1128
  samizdat publications and, **4:**548–49
  Shaw and, **10:**1364
  Solzhenitsyn and, **10:**1399–1420
  Stalinist purges, **10:**1404
  See also Bolshevik Revolution; Russia
Spain
  Borges and, **1:**108, 110, 114–15, 120
  Calvino and, **2:**156
  Carpentier and, **2:**182, 183, 184, 191, 192
  García Lorca and, **3:**389–408
  Richler and, **9:**1260, 1261–62, 1264
  Vargas Llosa and, **11:**1553
Spanish Civil War
  Auden and, **1:**61, 62, 63
  Carpentier and, **2:**182
  García Lorca and, **3:**394, 398; **4:**522, 525
  Guillén and, **4:**519, 520, 525
  Kazantzakis and, **5:**706

Spanish Civil War (continued)
Malraux and, **6:**848, 849, 861
Murdoch and, **7:**969
Neruda and, **8:***1056,* 1060,
1061, 1064–65
Orwell and, **8:**1112–13, 1115,
1116, 1119, *1121,* 1122,
1124–25
as Richler influence, **9:***1265,*
1266, 1268–69, 1270, 1278
Spark, Sidney Oswald, **11:**1446–47,
1448
Spielberg, Steven, **6:**736
Splichalová, Olga. *See* Havel, Olga
Splichalová
Stalin, Joseph, **8:**1060, 1124, 1125,
1126, 1127, 1128; **10:**1325,
1352, *1400,* 1401, 1403, *1404,*
1410, 1415, *1416,* 1418
Stanford University, O'Connnor and,
8:1095, 1097
Stanley, Kim, **3:**402
State University of New York,
Buffalo, Coetzee and, **2:**227
Stephen, Adrian, **12:**1674, 1675,
1677, 1678, 1684
Stephen, Julia, **12:**1674, 1677
Stephen, Thoby, **12:**1674, 1675,
1677, 1683, 1684
Sterling, Jan, **8:***1128*
Stern, Betty, **9:**1231
Sterne, Morgan, **10:***1341*
Stewart, Patrick, **11:**1526
stock market crash (1929), **3:**403
Stone, Oliver, **10:***1430*
Strand Films, **11:**1514, 1515
Stravinsky, Igor, **1:**74, *75;* **5:**605
stream of consciousness
Joyce and, **5:**650
Kanafani and, **5:**689
Woolf and, **12:**1679
Streep, Meryl, **3:***305*
student protests (May 1968),
10:1338, *1349, 1351*
Sucre (Colombia), García Márquez
and, **3:**410, 412
Sufism, **6:**833
Lessing and, **6:**793, 799
Sugiyama, Yoko, **7:**911, 912
Sulaco province (Conrad fictional
place), **2:**264
Sultan Bibar Mosque (Cairo), **6:***837*
Sun Yat-sen, **6:**854
supernatural. *See* fantasy; magic re-
alism
Sur (literary review), **1:**115

surrealism
Carpentier and, **2:**182, *185,*
186, 187, 189
Césaire and, **2:**198, 199, 202
Coetzee and, **2:**235
Suso, Heinrich, **5:**587
Svetlova, Natalya, **10:**1402, 1405,
1406
Swadeshi movement, **11:**1489–90,
1494–96, 1498
Sweden, Dangarembga and, **2:**269
Swinton, Tilda, **12:**1680
Switzerland
Borges and, **1:**105, 106–7, 108,
109, 110, 114, 120
Brecht and, **1:**130
Hesse and, **5:**581, 582, 583,
584, 585, 586, 592–93, 595
Joyce and, **5:**635, 639
Mann and, **7:**869, 873, 874
Nabokov and, **7:**990, 994
Remarque and, **9:**1220, 1221,
1222, 1223
Rilke and, **9:**1282–83, 1283,
1284
Sword of Stalingrad, **12:***1603*
Sydney (Australia), **12:***1653*
Keneally and, **6:**725, 726, 728
Whale Beach, **6:**727
White and, **12:**1654
symbolism
Dinesen and, **3:**299
Fugard and, **3:***368,* 369, 371,
373, 374, 375
García Lorca and, **3:**395–97,
402
Lawrence and, **6:**773–74, 778,
780, 781, 782
Mann and, **7:**876, *877,* 889
Yeats and, **12:**1703, 1715
Yehoshua and, **12:***1719*
symbolist poets, **7:**902
syncretism, Carpentier and, **2:**182
Synge, Kathleen, **11:***1464, 1465,*
1467, 1468

Tagore, Kadambari, **11:**1486, 1487,
1488
Taiwan, Gao Xingjian and, **3:**380
Takamura, Chieko Naganuma,
11:1501, 1502–3, 1505,
1506, 1507, 1508–9
Tambo, Oliver, **4:**465
tanka
Auden and, **1:**64
Takamura and, **11:**1504

Taos (New Mexico), Lawrence and,
6:766, 768, *769, 771*
Teatro d'Arte, Il (Rome), **9:**1203
Tel Quel (literary circle), Calvino
and, **2:**151
Temps modernes, Les (journal)
Camus and, **2:**163, 166
Sartre and, **10:**1338
terrorism
as Camus theme, **2:**161, *165*
Colombian *la violencia,* **3:**419,
424, 428, *429*
as Conrad theme, **2:**265
Naipaul on, **8:***1023,* 1032
Tokyo subway attack, **7:***956,*
957, 958
Teshigahara, Hiroshi, **1:***16, 17*
Texas, Coetzee and, **2:**227
Theater am Schiffbauerdamm (East
Berlin), **1:**130
Theater on the Balustrade
(Czechoslovakia), **4:**538
Théâtre de Babylone (Paris), **1:**90
Theodorakis, Mikis, **5:**715
Thirty-sixers (Havel group), **4:**538
Thirty Years' War, **1:**137
Thomas, Aeronwy, **11:**1514, 1515
Thomas, Caitlin Macnamara,
11:1513, 1514, *1517,* 1519
Thomas, Colm, **11:**1514, *1515,*
1516
Thomas, Llewelyn, **11:**1514, 1515
Thompson, Emma, **3:***335;* **12:***1684,*
1685
Thoor Ballylee, **12:**1712, *1713*
Thornton, Marianne (Forster's aunt),
3:320, 323
Thurn und Taxis-Hohnlohe,
Princess Maria von, **9:**1282,
1293
Tiananmen Square protests (1989;
Beijing), **3:**380, 381, 388
Time (magazine), Lewis cover story,
6:*812*
Ting, Samuel C. C., **8:***1020*
Tinkers (traveling people), **11:***1483*
Tlatelolco square (Mexico City)
massacre, **3:**349
Tokyo (Japan)
Chou and, **2:**211
metro system terrorist attack,
7:*956,* 957, 958
Mishima and, **7:**907, 908
nightlife section, **7:***955*
Tokyo University
Abe and, **1:**12

Borges honorary doctorate,
1:109
Kawabata and, 5:694, 696
Mishima and, 7:709, 710, 911
Tolkien, Edith Bratt, 11:1530, 1531,
1532, 1534, 1537
Tonbridge School (Kent, England),
3:320
Torrent, The (journal), 2:211, 213
totalitarianism, Orwell's novels on
evils of, 8:1109, 1115, 1116,
1120, 1127–28
Toussaint-Louverture, 11:*1575*
transmigration of souls, 7:917
Tree, Beerbohm, 10:1366
tree of literature (Coole Park),
11:*1466*
Trieste
Joyce and, 5:638
Rilke and, 9:1282
Trinidad, 8:*1015, 1017*
Naipaul, 8:1013–34
Walcott and, 11:1567, 1569,
1570, 1571, 1573, 1581
Trinity College (Dublin)
Beckett and, 1:89, 91
O'Connor and, 8:1097
Synge and, 11:1464–65, 1467
Tristan und Isolde (Wagner opera),
7:876, 886
Tropics (journal), 2:198, 199, 200
Trotsky, Leon
Malraux and, 6:849
Orwell's view of, 8:1122, *1123,*
1125, 1126, 1128
Rilke and, 9:1281
Sartre and, 10:1340, 1352
Troubles, the (Northern Ireland),
4:561, 563, 567–68
Trowell, Garnett, 7:893, 895
Trujillo, Rafael, 11:1566
T. S. Eliot Memorial Lectures
(University of Kent), Auden
and, 1:62
Tübingen (Germany), Hesse and,
5:583, 585, 588
Tung Chee-tiwa, 3:*380*
Turin (Italy) Calvino and, 2:150
Turpin, Kenneth, 6:*850*
Tuscany (Italy), Calvino and, 2:152
Tutu, Desmond, 4:475
Twiggy (model), 9:*1273*

Uganda, 8:1023
Ugandan National Theatre
(Kampala), 8:1075

Ukraine, Conrad and, 2:245, 248
Ulster. *See* Northern Ireland
ultraismo (literary movement),
Borges and, 1:108, 110,
114–15, 120
Umtali (Rhodesia), Dangarembga
and, 2:273
Unilateral Declaration of
Independence (Rhodesia),
2:273, 274
Unità, L' (newspaper), 2:151
United Fruit Company (UFC),
3:424
United Kingdom. *See* Great Britain
United Nations Relief and
Rehabilitation
Administration, 7:969, 970,
973
United States
Achebe and, 1:23, 25
Allende and, 1:44, 46, 55–56,
57–58
Auden and, 1:59, 62, 63, 67,
71–72, 74
Brecht and, 1:129–30, *132,*
133–34, 141
Calvino and, 2:152
Coetzee and, 2:227, 229, 242
Desai and, 2:*279,* 280, 281
Dinesen visit to, 3:297, 298, *300*
Forster visits to, 3:323
Fuentes and, 3:340–41, 343,
348
Fugard and, 3:363
García Lorca and, 3:392, *393,*
398, 403, *404*
García Márquez and, 3:411,
412, 413–14
Havel and, 4:539, 541
Heaney and, 4:561, 562
Huxley and, 5:604, 605–6
immigrants from India, 7:*943*
Lawrence and, 6:766, 767, 768,
769, 771
Mann citizenship, 7:873, 874
Mukherjee and, 7:939, 940,
941, 942, 948
Murakami and, 7:956
Nabokov and, 7:988–89, 990,
997
Ngũgĩ and, 8:1074, 1075, 1076
O'Connor and, 8:1095, 1097,
1098
Oz and, 9:1159, 1161
Remarque and, 9:1220, 1221,
1223

Rushdie and, 10:1321, 1322
Sidhwa and, 10:*1378,* 1380,
1382
Solzhenitsyn and, 10:1399, 1402,
1406
Soyinka and, 10:1425, 1426,
1429
Spark and, 11:1450, 1458
Tagore and, 11:*1490*
Thomas reading tours, 11:1514,
1516
Walcott and, 11:1567, 1569,
1570, 1571, 1573
Waugh and, 12:1592, 1594,
1605
Wells tour of, 12:1639
Yehoshua and, 12:1720, 1721
Universal Pictures, 9:*1218*
University College (Ibadan)
Achebe and, 1:22–23, 24
Soyinka and, 10:1422
University College (Nairobi), Ngũgĩ
and, 8:*1073,* 1074, 1075,
1083
University College (Oxford),
Naipaul and, 8:1015
University of Bern, Hesse and,
5:585
University of Bonn
Mann and, 7:874
Pirandello and, 9:1202
University of Bucharest, Ionesco
and, 5:621
University of Calabar, Emecheta
and, 3:312, 313
University of Calcutta, Mukherjee
and, 7:939, 940
University of California (Berkeley)
Heaney and, 4:561, 562
Mukherjee and, 7:940, 941
University of California (Santa
Barbara), Huxley and,
5:606
University of Cape Town, 2:*226*
Coetzee and, 2:226, 227, 229
Fugard and, 3:361, 362
University of Cartagena, García
Márquez and, 3:411, 412
University of Chicago, Yehoshua
and, 12:1720, 1721
University of Concepción (Chile),
Fuentes and, 3:346, 348
University of Cuba, Carpentier and,
2:184
University of Florence, Calvino and,
2:150

University of Granada, García Lorca and, 3:391, 392, 398
University of Haifa, Yehoshua and, 12:1720, 1721
University of Havana, Carpentier and, 2:183
University of Ibadan, Soyinka and, 10:1422, 1423, *1424*
University of Ife, Soyinka and, 10:1423
University of Iowa Writer's Workshop, Mukherjee and, 7:939, 940
University of Kent, Auden T. S. Eliot Memorial Lectures, 1:62
University of Minnesota Press, 1:134
University of Nigeria (Nsukka), Achebe and, 1:24
University of Palermo, Borges honorary doctorate, 1:109
University of Rome, Borges honorary doctorate, 1:109
University of Texas (Austin), Coetzee and, 2:229
University of the West Indies, Walcott and, 11:1568, 1570, *1572*
University of Venice, Borges honorary doctorate, 1:109
University of Virginia, Auden Page-Barbour lecture, 1:62
University of Zimbabwe, Dangarembga and, 2:269, 270, 274
Urquidi, Julia, 11:1553, 1554, *1555*, 1565
Uruguay, Camus and, 2:163
Ustinov, Peter, 7:990
utopianism
    Emecheta and, 3:317–18
    Wells and, 12:1649
    See also dystopian fiction
Uttar Pradesh (India), Desai and, 2:278
Uwa ndi Igbo: A Journal of Igbo Life and Culture, 1:24

Valencia (Spain), Richler and, 9:*1260*, 1261–62, 1264
Valmont (Switzerland), Rilke and, 9:1279, 1283, 1284
Vance, Courtney B., 3:*366*
vanguardismo (vanguard movement)
    Carpentier and, 2:181
    Guillén and, 4:518
Vatican City, 11:*1449*

Vaz Dias, Selma, 9:1242
Vedantism, 5:605
Vedrenne, J. E., 10:1361
Vega region (Spain), García Lorca and, 3:390–91
Velez, Lupe, 9:1220, 1223
Velvet Revolution (Czechoslovakia), 4:540, 541
Venezuela, 2:*184*
    Allende and, 1:43, 44, 46
    Carpentier and, 2:183, 184, 186, 189, 190
    García Márquez and, 3:411, 419, 424
Venice, Mann and, 7:876, 882–83
Venice Film Festival, Calvino and, 2:152
Venizélos, Eleuthérios, 5:705, 706
Verdi, Giuseppe, 10:1364
Verrières (chateau), 6:850, *851*
Versailles Treaty (1919), 2:207
Vichy government (France), 10:1349–50
Vicos Voco (journal), 5:585
Victorianism, 12:1682–83, 1684, 1691
Vietnam War, Coetzee and, 2:227, 229, 231
Villa, Pancho, 3:340
Vilmorin, Sophie de, 6:848, 851
violencia, la ("the violence") (Colombia), 3:419, 424, 428, *429*
Visva-Bharati University, Tagore and, 11:1488, 1489
Vitkevich, Nikolai, 10:1401
Vivos Voco (journal), 5:585, 586
Vologda (Russia), Conrad and, 2:246
Volta Cinema theater, 5:639

Wafd Party (Egypt), 6:833
Wagner, Richard
    as Joyce influence, 5:650
    as Lewis influence, 6:805
    as Mann influence, 7:876, 878, 886
    as Shaw influence, 10:1364, 1375
    Tolkien and, 11:*1536*
Wales, Thomas and, 11:1511–28
Walston, Lady Catherine, 4:*514*
War of a Thousand Days (1899; Colombia), 3:416
War Requiem (musical composition), 8:1147

Watergate scandal, 11:1457, 1459
Waugh, Harriet, 12:1592
Waugh, James, 12:1592
Waugh, Laura Herbert, 12:*1591*, 1592, 1593
Waugh, Margaret, 12:1592, *1594*
Waugh, Septimus, 12:1592
Waugh, Teresa, 12:1592
Weaver, Harriet Shaw, 5:638
Weigel, Helene, 1:127, 129, *134*, *138*
Weill, Kurt, 1:125, 128, 132, *135*, *138*, 140; 9:*1191*
Welch, Mary, 3:*402*
Welles, Orson, 3:300; 5:632; 12:1648
Wellington (New Zealand), 7:*892*, *893*, 895
    Katherine Mansfield Museum, 7:*892*
Wells, Amy Catherine Robbins, 12:1631, 1633
Wells, Frank Richard, 12:1633
Wells, George Philip, 12:1633
Wesleyan University, Naipaul and, 8:1017
West, Elizabeth, 10:1321, 1322
Westenholz, Mary Bess (Dinesen's aunt), 3:294, 301
West Indies. *See* Caribbean area
Westman, Nydia, 1:*103*
Whale, James, 9:*1222*
whale endangerment, 7:*932*
whimsical tales, Forster and, 3:336
Wiata, Inia Te, 1:*141*
Wilberforce, Samuel, 5:*606*
Wilby, James, 12:*1605*
Williams, Robin, 1:*99*
Williamson, Nicol, 8:1134
Winters, Shelley, 7:*994*
Wisdom, Frank, 6:789, 791
Wohryzek, Julie, 5:662, 665
wolves, 7:*935*
women's issues
    Allende and, 1:47, 48, 49, 50, *51*, 52, 54, 55
    Bâ and, 1:79–80
    Chou and, 2:221, *222*
    Coetzee and, 2:244
    Dangarembga and, 2:271, 272, 273
    Desai and, 2:277, 282, 284, 286
    Emecheta and, 3:309, *313*, 314
    García Lorca and, 3:395, 401–2, 404–6

Lessing and, **6:**791–92, 796, 799–800

Mukherjee and, **7:**945, 946–48

Rhys and, **9:**1251

Woolf and, **12:**1673, 1680, 1692–94

Wood, Elijah, **11:***1544*

wood-blockcut printing, **2:**213–14

Woodthorpe, Peter, **1:***97*

Worcester (South Africa), Coetzee and, **2:**226

World Hello Day, **4:***566*

World Union of Jewish Students, **12:**1721

World War I, **4:***493;* **9:***1219*

Brecht and, **1:**126

British propaganda poster, **8:***1144*

Chou and, **2:**207

Conrad and, **2:**250

Forster and, **3:**322, 323

gas attack, **8:***1148*

Graves and, **4:**477, 478, 480, 482, 487, 491, 493–94

Hesse and, **5:**584, 585, 586, 589, 598

impact on European civilization of, **8:**1147

Lawrence and, **6:**765, 766, 767, 775

Lewis and, **6:**805, 808

Mann and, **7:**871–72

Mansfield and, **7:**894, 895

modernism and, **7:**897

Owen and, **8:**1141, 1143–50

Pirandello and, **9:**1203

poets of, **8:**1141, 1143, 1145, 1146

as Remarque subject, **9:**1217, 1218–19, 1220, 1221, 1224, 1227–30, 1231

Rilke and, **9:**1282, 1283, *1287*, 1293

Scottish regiment, **8:***1145*

Tolkien and, **11:**1529, 1531, 1532, 1536, 1537

trenches, **9:***1227*

Wells and, **12:**1633, 1639

Ypres battle, **8:***1149*

World War II

Abe and, **1:**12

Beckett and, **1:**90, 91

Brecht and, **1:**128–30, 137, 139

Calvino and, **2:**150, *151,* 153, 156

Camus and, **2:**161, 162, 163, 172

Carpentier and, **2:**183

Césaire and, **2:**198, 200, 203

Dinesen and, **3:**296, 297, 298

Golding and, **4:**437, 438, 439, 444, 446, 449, 451, 454, 455

Greene and, **4:**498

Ionesco and, **5:**621, 626

Japanese kamikaze attacks, **7:***910*

Kawabata and, **5:**696

Keneally and, **6:**726, 736–37, 738–40

Malraux and, **6:**850

Mishima and, **7:**909–10

Mowat and, **7:**928, *929,* 930

Murdoch and, **7:**969

O'Connor and, **8:**1097

Orwell and, **8:***1113*

Osborne and, **8:**1132

Remarque and, **9:**1220, 1221, 1223, 1224

Sartre and, **10:**1335–36, *1337,* 1339–40, 1349–50

Solzhenitsyn and, **10:**1400, *1401,* 1402, *1410*

Spark and, **11:**1446–47, 1448

Takamura and, **11:**1503

Thomas and, **11:**1515, 1526

Waugh and, **12:**1592, 1593–94, 1603

Wells and, **12:**1634, 1639, *1648,* 1649

White and, **12:**1653, 1655

Woolf and, **12:**1678, 1693–94

See also Holocaust; Nazism

Wyspiansky, Floryan, **7:**893

Yai, Olabiyi, **4:***521*

Yale University

Fugard and, **3:**363

Ngũgĩ and, **8:**1074, 1076

Yamada, Machiko (Machi Abe), **1:**12, 15

Yeats, Jack, **12:**1696

Yeats, John Butler, **12:**1696, 1709, *1709*

Yehoshua, Rivka Kirsninski, **12:**1718, 1720

Yoknapatawpha County (Faulkner fictional place), **3:**411, 425

Yom Kippur War (1973), Oz and, **9:**1159, *1161*

Yoruba people, **3:***310*

Soyinka and, **10:**1421, 1422, 1423, *1423,* 1427, 1429, 1431, *1432,* 1437

Young Annam movement, **6:**860

Zaghloul, Saad, **6:**826

Zaire (formerly Belgian Congo)

Conrad on, 249, 259–60; **2:**248

Naipaul on, **8:**1021, 1023

Zambona, Jutta, **9:**221, 1220, 1221

Zambuko (Zimbabwean drama group), **2:**269

Zen, Gao and, **3:**386

Zia ul-Haq, Mohammad, **10:***1394*

Zimbabwe (formerly Rhodesia), **6:**787, *801*

Dangarembga and, **2:**267–76

Lessing and, **6:**786–87, 789, 791, 794, 799

Spark and, **11:**1446–47, 1448

Zionism, **12:**1721

Zoff, Marianne, **1:**127, 129

Zorbás, Giorgos, **5:**705, 708, 710, *710,* 714

Zoroaster, **10:***1384*

Zoroastrianism, **10:**1378–79, *1384,* 1386, 1388, 1390, 1393, 1395, 1396

Zurich (Switzerland)

Joyce and, **5:**635, 638, 639

Mann and, **7:**873

Comprehensive Index of Writers

Numbers in **bold** indicate volumes.
Page numbers in *italic* indicate illustrations or illustration captions.
Page numbers in **bold** refer to full articles.

Abe, Kōbō, **1:11–20**
  "Akai mayu," **1:**14
  awards and honors, **1:**11, 13, 15
  background and early life,
      1:12–13
  Box Man, The, **1:**20
  "Crime of S. Karma, The," **1:**19,
      20
  Dai-yon kampyoki, **1:**14, 20
  Face of Another, The, **1:**17–18
  Face of Another, The (screenplay),
      1:13, 17
  Friends, **1:**18–19
  Friends (screenplay), **1:**13
  Ghost Is Here, The, **1:**19–20
  Hako otoko, **1:**20
  highlights in life, **1:**15
  influences on, **1:**18
  Inter Ice Age Four, **1:**14, 20
  Kabe, **1:**13, 19
  Kangaroo Notebook, **1:**15
  list of works, **1:**19
  Moetsukita chizu, **1:**14
  Owarishi michi no shirube ni, **1:**12,
      15
  "Red Cocoon," **1:**14
  Ruined Map, The, **1:**14
  Ruined Map, The (screenplay),
      1:13, 17
  Tanin no kao, **1:**17–18
  themes and issues, **1:**14–16, 18–19
  Tomoclachi, **1:**18–19
  Tōō o yuku, **1:**13
  Walls, **1:**13, 19
  Woman in the Dunes (screenplay),
      1:13, 15, *16,* 17
  Woman in the Dunes, The, **1:**11,
      13, 15, *16*–17, 18
  Yūrei wa koka ni iru, **1:**19–20
Achebe, Chinua, **1:21–40; 2:**233
  Aka Weta (edited with
      Udechukwu), **1:**24

Anthills of the Savannah, **1:**24, 25,
      27, 28, 37, 38–39
Arrow of God, **1:**24, 26, 37–38
  awards and honors, **1:**24
  background and early life,
      1:22–24
*Beware Soul Brother and Other
      Poems,* **1:**24
Chike and the River, **1:**28
  children's stories, **1:**28–29
  as Dangarembga influence, **2:**274
Drum, The, **1:**29
  as Emecheta influence, **3:**316
Flute, The, **1:**29
Girls at War and Other Stories,
      1:24
  highlights in life, **1:**25
Home and Exile, **1:**24, 33
*Hopes and Impediments: Selected
      Essays, 1965–1987,* **1:**24
How the Leopard Got His Claws
      (with Iroaganachi), **1:**28
  influences on, **1:**33
  list of works, **1:**36
Man of the People, A, **1:**24, 27,
      39–40
No Longer at Ease, **1:**24, 27,
      32–36
  themes and issues, **1:**26, 30,
      32–33
Things Fall Apart, **1:**25, 26, 27,
      30–32, 33, 37
Trouble with Nigeria, The, **1:**24, 25
Ackerman, John, **11:**1527
AE (George Russell), **8:**1085, 1101
Aeschylus, **10:**1348
Aesop, **8:**1015
Agnon, S. Y., **9:**1159, 1161;
      12:1719
Alberti, Rafael, **3:**390
Alcott, Louisa May, **10:**1386, *1387*
Aldiss, Brian, **6:**793

Aleixandre, Vicente, **3:**390
Algren, Nelson, **10:**1343
Allain, Marie–Françoise, **4:**496
Allende, Isabel, **1:41–58**
  awards and honors, **1:**44
  background and early life,
      1:42–43
Daughter of Fortune, **1:**44, 46, 48,
      55–56, 57
Eva Luna, **1:**44, 46
  highlights in life, **1:**44
House of the Spirits, The, **1:**41, 44,
      45, 47, 48, 50–52, 53, 54, 56
Infinite Plan, The, **1:**46, 47, 48,
      50, 57–58
  influences on, **1:**42, 54
  list of works, **1:**50
  literary legacy of, **1:**48–49
Of Love and Shadows, **1:**46, 48,
      54, 56
Paula, **1:**42, 44, 46, 48, 52–53,
      54, 55, 57
Portrait in Sepia, **1:**56–57
Stories of Eva Luna, The, **1:**44, 46
  themes and issues, **1:**47–48, 50,
      55, 56
Alvi, Nadira, **8:**1017
Andersen, Hans Christian, **7:**909,
      920; **8:**1015
Anderson, Sherwood, **9:**1161
Andrezel, Pierre (Dinesen pseudo-
      nym), **3:**296, 297, 298
Angelou, Maya, **2:**274
Anouilh, Jean, **5:**624
Anscombe, Elizabeth, **6:**812
Aqqad, Mahmoud al-, **6:**830
Aristotle, **1:**122
Arnold, Matthew, **5:**602, 606
  poetic devices, **1:**72
Ashbery, John, **9:**1290
'Ashri, Fathi al-, **6:**830
Auden, W. H., **1:59–76; 11:**1447

About the House, **1**:64

Age of Anxiety, The: A Baroque Eclogue, **1**:63, 65, 66

Another Time, **1**:64, 71

background and early life, **1**:60–61

Bassarids, The (libretto with Kallman), **1**:76

Collected Poems, **1**:67

Collected Shorter Poems 1927–1957, **1**:67

"Communist to Others, A," **1**:61

Dance of Death, The, **1**:61

Double Man, The, **1**:65

Dyer's Hand, The, **1**:62

Elder Edda, The: A Selection from the Icelandic (translation with Taylor.), **1**:66

Elegy for Young Lovers (libretto with Kallman), **1**:76

Enchafèd Flood, The, **1**:62

Forewords and Afterwords, **1**:68

For the Time Being, **1**:60, 65

highlights in life, **1**:62

"If all our acts are conditioned behaviour," **1**:63

influences on, **1**:60, 61–62, 64, 65, 66

Inklings club and, **11**:*1539*

"In Praise of Limestone," **1**:67, 72–74

Journey to a War (with Isherwood), **1**:*61*, 62, 63

Letters from Iceland (with MacNeice), **1**:61, 62, 65

"Letter to Lord Byron," **1**:65

list of works, **1**:67

Look Stranger!, **1**:69

Love's Labour's Lost (libretto with Kallman and Nabokov), **1**:76

"Lullaby," **1**:64

Magic Flute, The: An Opera in Two Acts (libretto with Kallman), **1**:75–76

"Metalogue," **1**:76

"New Year Letter," **1**:65

Nones, **1**:72

"On the Circuit," **1**:63, 66

On This Island, **1**:64

opera libretti, **1**:74–76

Paid on Both Sides, **1**:66

Paul Bunyan: An Operetta in Two Acts (libretto), **1**:74

Poems, **1**:*60*, 62, 64, 69

"Postscript: Astrafiammante to the translators" (with Kallman), **1**:76

"Proem," **1**:76

"Protestant Mystics, The," **1**:68

Rake's Progress, The: A Fable (libretto with Kallman), **1**:74, 75, 76

Rilke's influence on, **9**:1285–86

"Sea and the Mirror, The: A Commentray on Shakespeare's *The Tempest*," **1**:65

Secondary Worlds, **1**:62, 76

"Secret Agent, The," **1**:66, 67, 69, *70*

"Short Ode to a Philologist, A," **1**:66

"Summer Night, A," **1**:67, 68–69

"Thanksgiving, A," **1**:63

Thomas and, **11**:1447, 1515

"Unknown Citizen, The," **1**:67, 71–72

verse forms, **1**:69, 72, 74

"World of Opera, The," **1**:76

Austen, Jane, **7**:*944*

Huxley screenplay for *Pride and Prejudice*, **5**:605, 608

as Mukherjee influence, **7**:944, 947

Bâ, Mariama, **1:77–86**

awards and honors, **1**:77, 79, *80*

background and early life, **1**:78–79

influences on, **1**:83

list of works, **1**:82

Scarlet Song, **1**:79, 80, 81, 82, 85, 86

So Long a Letter, **1**:77, 78–79, *80*, 81, 82, 84–86

themes and issues, **1**:81, 82–83, 84

Baker, George, **11**:1515

Ballantyne, R. M., **4**:446

Balzac, Honoré, as Fuentes influence, **3**:345, 354

Barfield, Owen, **6**:806, 810; **11**:1538

Barnes, Djuna, **9**:1249

Barrie, J. M., **12**:1630–31

Barthes, Roland, **4**:475

Baum, Oskar, **5**:663

Bayley, John, **7**:969, 970, *971, 972*

Beauvoir, Simone de, Sartre relationship, **10**:1335, 1336, 1337, 1338, *1342, 1343*, 1346, *1346*, 1348

Beckett, Samuel, **1:87–104**; **12**:*1705*

All That Fall (radio play), **1**:91, 92

awards and honors, **1**:87, 90, 91, 92; **12**:1704

background and early life, **1**:88–90

bilingualism of, **3**:300

as Camus influence, **3**:366

Catastrophe, **4**:540

as Coetzee influence, **2**:227

Dream of Fair to Middling Women, **1**:89–90, 94

Endgame, **1**:91, 92, *93*, 96, 102–3

Film (screenplay), **1**:91

as Gao influence, **3**:386

Happy Days, **1**:91, 92, *93*

Havel and, **4**:540, 552

highlights in life, **1**:91

influences on, **1**:95; **4**:567

Krapp's Last Tape, **1**:91, 92, 103–4

Malone Dies (*Malone meurt*), **1**:90, 100, 101

Molloy, **1**:90, 95–96, *98*, 100, 101

More Pricks Than Kicks, **1**:90, 91, 94

Murphy, **1**:90, 91, 94, 101

narrative technique, **1**:96

Night and Dream, **1**:91

Not I, **1**:91

Pirandello as influence, **9**:1208

"siege in the room" of, **1**:90, 91, 101

Stirrings Still, **1**:91

themes and issues, **1**:93, 97–98

Trilogy, The: *Molloy; Malone Dies; The Unnamable*, **1**:90, 91, 95, 96, 100–102

Unnamable, The, **1**:90, 96, 100, 101–2

Waiting for Godot, **1**:87, 90, 91, 92, 95, 96, 97–100, 102, 103; **3**:386, 387

Watt, **1**:91, 101

"What Is the Word," **1**:91

Whoroscope, **1**:89, 91, 93–94

Beerbohm, Max, **10**:*1371*

Bell, John, **8**:1150

Bell, Quentin, **12**:1675, 1676, 1678, 1684

Belloc, Hilaire, **8**:1043

Bellow, Saul, **8**:1014; **9**:1163

Benét, Stephen Vincent, **8**:1043

Bennani, Benjamin, **5**:690
Bennani, Catherine Warner, **5**:690
Bennett, Arnold, **12**:*1678*
Benstock, Bernard, **5**:646
Bentley, Eric, **1**:134, 139
Bergson, Henri, **5**:705, 710; **12**:1604
Bien, Peter, **5**:711, 715
Bierce, Ambrose, **3**:355
Bioy Casares, Adolfo, **1**:105, 108, 114, 115
Bjurström, Carl-Gustav, Camus and, **2**:164, 166
Blair, Dorothy, **1**:79
Blair, Eric Arthur. *See* Orwell, George
Blaise, Clark, Mukherjee and, **7**:939, 940, 941, *941*, 944, 949–50
Blake, William, **5**:618; **6**:769
Blixen, Karen. *See* Dinesen, Isak
Bloom, Harold, **7**:971
Bly, Robert, **9**:1290
Boccaccio, Giovanni, **9**:1216
Bode-Thomas, Modupe, **1**:79
Boland, Eaven, **12**:1704
Böll, Heinrich, **10**:*1406*
Borges, Guillermo Juan (cousin), **1**:115
Borges, Jorge Luis, **1:105–24**
   "Abencaján el Bojarí, Dead in His Labyrinth," **1**:117
   "Aleph, The," **1**:117, *118*
   Aleph, The (Aleph, El), **1**:107, 117, 119, 120, 122
   "Allusions," **1**:119
   Artifices, **1**:116
   "Averroës' Search," **1**:122, *123*
   awards and honors, **1**:108, 109, *109*
   "Babylon Lottery, The," **1**:122
   background and early life, **1**:106–7
   "Borges and I," **1**:121
   Calvino and, **2**:152
   "Circular Ruins, The," **1**:117, 119
   collaborative works, **1**:114–15
   "Cyclical Night, The," **1**:121
   "Dead Man, The," **1**:117
   "Death and the Compass," **1**:116–17, 119
   "Deutsches Requiem," **1**:122
   "Dialogue of the Dead," **1**:122
   Dreamtigers, **1**:119, 121, 122, 123
   "Dreamtigers," **1**:119

"Emma Zunz," **1**:117
Fervor of Buenos Aires (Fervor de Buenos Aires), **1**:107, 108, 110, 115
Ficciones, **1**:107, 116–17, 119, 120, 121–22
"Forms of a Legend," **1**:121
"Funes the Memorious," **1**:116
Garden of Forking Paths, The, **1**:107, 116, 120
"Garden of Forking Paths, The," **1**:117, 119
genres and work, 112; **1**:110, 112
"Hacedor, El," **1**:119
"Happy Prince, The" (translation of Wilde), **1**:114, 120
highlights in life, **1**:108
"Immortal, The," **1**:117
influences on, **1**:120
"Intruder, The," **1**:117
"Library of Babel, The," **1**:116, 119
list of works, **1**:113
Luna de enfrente Inquisiciones, **1**:115
"Maker, The," **1**:119
"Martín Fierro," **1**:123
Muerte y la brújula, La, **1**:109, 120
"New Refutation of Time, A," **1**:121
Personal Anthology, A, **1**:121
"Pierre Menard, Author of Don Quixote," **1**:116
Poems (Poemas), **1**:107
"South, The," **1**:107, 112, 120
"Story of the Warrior and the Captive Woman, The," **1**:117
"Sur, El," **1**:107, 112, 120
Tamaño de mi esperanza, El, **1**:115
"Tango, The," **1**:121
themes and issues, 119; **1**:116, 117, 120, 121
"Theologians, The," **1**:117
"Three Versions of Judas," **1**:121–22
"Tlön, Uqbar, Orbis Tertius," **1**:116, 117
"Two Kings and the Two Labyrinths, The," **1**:117
"Veiled Mirrors, The," **1**:119
Bowen, Marjorie, **4**:496
Brandes, Georg, **3**:301
Brecht, Bertolt, **1:125–42**
   "Alabama Song" (with Weill), **1**:*138*

artistic legacy of, **1**:133–34
awards and honors, **1**:129
background and early life, **1**:126–27
"Ballad of Mack the Knife, The" (with Weill), **1**:*135*
"Before the Flood," **1**:126
Caucasian Chalk Circle, The, **1**:126, 133, 141–42
Drums in the Night, **1**:127
Edward the Second (with Feuchtwanger), **1**:*128*
epic theater and, **1**:125, 131–33
as Gao influence, **3**:386
Good Person of Setzuan, The, **1**:133, 139–40
Hangmen Also Die (screenplay), **1**:129, *130*
influences on, **1**:126, 133
"Legend of the Dead Soldier, The," **1**:126, 127
Life of Galileo, The, **1**:129, 130, *131*, 132, *134*, 140
list of works, **1**:136
Mother Courage and Her Children, **1**:129, 130, 137–39
politics and, **9**:1223
Rise and Fall of the City of Mahagonny, The (with Weill), **1**:*127*, 128, 133, *138*, 140–41
St. Joan of the Stockyards, **1**:132, 133
"Song of the Great Capitulation," **1**:137
Soyinka and, **10**:1427, 1429
themes and issues, **1**:125, 135, 137, 139
Threepenny Opera, The (with Weill), **1**:125, 128, 129, 133, 134, 135–37
Trommeln in der Nacht, **1**:127
"Vor der Sintflut," **1**:126
Brennar, Yosef Haim, as Oz influence, **9**:1163
Brenner, Rachel Feldhay, **9**:1268
Breton, André
   as Carpentier influence, **2**:186
   Césaire and, **2**:199
Brod, Max, Kafka friendship, **5**:659, 662, 663, 664, *666*, 668, 673, 674, 676
Brontë, Charlotte
   Huxley screenplay for *Jane Eyre*, **5**:605, 608
   as Kincaid influence, **6**:752

as Rhys influence, **9:**1248–49, 1254, 1256

Brontë, Emily, **6:**752

Brooke, Rupert, as Paton influence, **9:**1180

Browning, Elizabeth Barrett, **12:**1681

Rilke's German translation of, **9:**1287

Browning, Robert, **12:**1681

Bruno, Giordano, **5:**650

Buck, Pearl, **3:***300*

Bulgakov, Mikhail, **10:**1325

Burnouf, M. E., **3:***322*

Byron, Lord (George Gordon), **2:**241

Callaghan, Morley, **9:**1262

Calvino, Italo, **2:149–58**

"Adventure of a Soldier, The," **2:**153

"Albino Gorilla, The," **2:**156

"All at One Point," **2:**155

"At Daybreak," **2:**155

awards and honors, **2:**150, 152, 154

background and early life, **2:**150

Baron in the Trees, The, **2:**153–54

Borges and, **2:**152

"Cheese Museum, The," **2:**156

Cosmicomics, **2:**151, 154, 155–56

Crow Comes Last, The, **2:**156

"Dinosaurs, The," **2:**155

"Distance of the Moon, The," **2:**155

Fiabe italiane, **2:**151

genres and works, **2:**153–54

Giornata d' uno scrutatore, La, **2:**156

highlights in life, **2:**154

If on a Winter's Night a Traveler, **2:**151

influences on, **2:**151, 156, 157–58

Invisible Cities, **2:**151, 154, 157–58

Italian Folktales, **2:**151

journalism career, **2:**149, 151

"Learning to be Dead," **2:**157

Lezioni americane: Sei proposte per il prossimo millennio, **2:**152

"Light-Years, The," **2:**155

list of works, **2:**157

magic realism and, **3:**347

Marcovaldo, or the Seasons in the City, **2:**153, 156

"Marcovaldo al supermarket," **2:**153

Palomar, **2:**154, 156–57, 158, *158*

Path to the Spiders' Nest, The, **2:**150, 153, 154

political activism, **2:**151

"Sign in Space, A," **2:**155

Six Memos for the Next Millennium, **2:**152

"Spiral, The," **2:**155

themes and issues, **2:**153–54, 155, 156

travels, **2:**152

Watcher, The, **2:**156

"Without Colors," **2:**155

Campbell, Roy, **11:**1539

Camus, Albert, **2:159–78**

"Adulteress, The," **2:**176

awards and honors, **2:**159, 162, 163, 164, 176

background and early life, **2:**160–61, 164

Caligula, **2:**161, 162, 163, 171

Cross Purposes (The Misunderstanding), **2:**162, 177

death in sports car crash, **2:**159, 163

as Desai influence, **2:**283

Exile and the Kingdom, **2:**163, 176

extended metaphor technique, **2:**166–67

Fall, The, **2:**159, 161, *161,* 162, 163, 167, 174–76

First Man, The, **2:**163, 176–77

as Fugard influence, **3:**366

"Guest, The," **2:**176

Happy Death, The, **2:**177

highlights in life, **2:**162

"Hope and the Absurd in the Work of Franz Kafka," **5:**667

"Hôte, L'," **2:**176

influences on, **2:**161, 162, 163, 164, 165, 166, 172

journalism career, **2:**159, 161, 162, 163

Kafka as influence on, **5:**667

list of works, **2:**171

Misunderstanding, The (Cross Purposes), **2:**162, 177

"Mute, The," **2:**176

"Myth of Sisyphus, The," **1:**162; **2:**161, 162

Myth of Sisyphus, The, **5:**667

Plague, The, **2:**159, 161, 162, 163, 166, 167, 172–74, *173,* 176

Possessed, The (Les possédés), **2:**162, 163

Rebel, The, **2:**162, 163, 166, 174

"Renegade, The," **2:**176

"Stone That Grows, The," **2:**176

Stranger, The, **2:**159, 161, 162, 164, 166, 167, 168–72, *169,* 177

theatrical work, **2:**162, 163, *167,* 177

themes and issues, **2:**159, 164–66, 170, 172, 174

translation of, **2:**168–69

Cansinos-Assens, Rafael, **1:**114–15

Capote, Truman, Forster as influence on, **3:**326

Capuana, Luigi, **9:**1202, 1207

Carey, Peter, **6:**735

Carpenter, Humphrey, **11:**1539, 1540–41

Carpentier, Alejo, **2:179–94**

awards and honors, **2:**183, 184

background and early life, 180–82

Baroque Concert, **2:**183

Chase, The, **2:**183, 184, 185, *185*

Ecué-Yamba-O, **2:**182, 183, 193

Explosion in a Cathedral, **2:**183, 184, 191–93

Harp and the Shadow, The, **2:**183

highlights in life, **2:**183

"High Road of Saint James , The," **2:**187, 193

influences on, **2:**179, 180, 181–82, 186

journalistic career, **2:**182, 185, 281

"Journey Back to the Source," **2:**187, 193

Kingdom of This World, The, **2:**183, 184, 187, *187,* 188–89

list of works, **2:**191

Literatura y conciencia política en América Latina, **2:**183

Lost Steps, The, **2:**183, 184, 187, 189–90

Music in Cuba, **2:**183

radio broadcasting by, **2:**182, 184, 185

real maravilloso and, **2:**179, 182, 185, 188, 189

Reasons of State, **2:**183, 193–94

Rites of Spring, The, **2:**183

themes and issues, **2:**188, 189, 191

Tientos y diferencias, **2:**183

Carpentier, Alejo (*continued*)
   *War of Time: Three Short Stories
     and a Novella*, **2**:183, 184, 193
Carrington, Dora, Bloomsbury
   Group and, **3**:*320*
Carroll, Lewis
   as Murdoch influence, **7**:967,
     973, 980
   as Waugh influence, **12**:1598
Carver, Raymond, **7**:958
Cary, Joyce, **1**:33
Cervantes, Miguel de
   as Borges influence, **1**:116, 120
   as Conrad influence, **2**:262
   as Fuentes influence, **3**:345, 354,
     357
   as García Lorca influence, **3**:401
Césaire, Aimé, **2**:**195–204**
   Aimé Césaire: The Collected Poetry,
     1:200; **2**:200
   *And the Dogs Were Silent: A
     Tragedy*, **2**:200
   awards and honors, **2**:200
   background and early life,
     2:196–98
   Complete Works, **1**:200; **2**:200
   Discourse on Colonialism, **2**:200,
     201, 202–3
   highlights in life, **2**:200
   influences on, **2**:202
   journalism career, **2**:196, 199,
     200, 203
   Letter to Maurice Thorez, **1**:200;
     2:200
   list of works, **2**:203
   *Notebook of a Return to the Native
     Land*, **2**:195, 198, 200, 201–2,
     203
   political life, **2**:198
   Season in the Congo, A, **2**:204
   *Tempest, A: After the Tempest of
     Shakespeare*, **2**:195, 199, 204
   themes and issues, **2**:201, 203
   Tragedy of King Christophe, The,
     2:195, 199, 204
Chacel, Rosa, **3**:390
Chaucer, Geoffrey, **11**:1538
Chekhov, Anton
   as Desai influence, **2**:283
   as O'Connor influence, **8**:1101
   as Osborne influence, **8**:136
   as Shaw influence, **10**:1375
Chesteron, Gilbert Keith, **8**:1043;
   12:1600
Chifunyise, Stephen, **2**:269
Chinodya, Shimmer, **2**:269, 270, 275

Chou Shu-jen, **2**:**205–24**
   "After Death," **2**:223
   "Ah Q zhenzhuan," **2**:212,
     219–21, 223
   background and early life,
     2:206–7
   Brief History of Chinese Fiction, A,
     2:211
   Call to Arms, **2**:211, 212,
     215–16, 218, 218–19, 219
   "Diary of a Madman," **2**:211–12,
     213, 215, 216–18, 219, 221
   as Gao influence, **3**:386
   highlights in life, **2**:211
   "Huaijiu," **2**:210
   influences on, **2**:210, *212*, 216
   "Kong Yiji," **2**:212, 223
   list of works, **2**:217
   "Literature on the Eve of
     Revolution," **2**:212
   "Medicine," **2**:218–19
   New Woodcut Movement and,
     2:213–14
   "New Year's Sacrifice," **2**:212,
     221–22, *222*
   Old Stories Retold, **2**:210, *210*,
     216, 223–24
   "Passerby, The," **2**:223
   political activities, **2**:207–8, 211
   "Power of Mara Poetry, The,"
     2:210
   Preface to *Call to Arms*, **2**:212,
     215–16, 218, 218–19, 219
   "Remembrance of the Past," **2**:210
   "Shadow's Farewell, The," **2**:223
   themes and issues, **2**:212, 215,
     216, 218, 219–20, 221
   "True Story of Ah Q, The,"
     2:212, 219–21, 223
   Wild Grass, **2**:212, 223
   "Zhufu," **2**:212, 221–22
Claussen, Sophus, **3**:301
Coetzee, J. M., **2**:**225–44**
   academic posts, **2**:227, 229
   Age of Iron, **2**:229, 231
   awards and honors, **2**:225, 229,
     231, 235, 240
   background and early life,
     2:226–27
   *Boyhood: Scenes from Provincial
     Life*, **2**:229, 242, 243, *243*
   Disgrace, **2**:226, *226*, 228, *228*,
     229, 231, 234, 240–42
   Dusklands, **2**:227, 229, 231, 234
   Foe, **2**:229, 231, 234, 237, *237*,
     238

   *Giving Offense: Essays on
     Censorship*, **2**:242, 244
   highlights in life, **2**:229
   influences on, **2**:227, 231, 232
   In the Heart of the Country, **2**:229,
     231
   Life and Times of Michael K, The,
     2:229, *230*, 231, 235–36, 238
   list of works, **2**:236
   Master of Petersburg, The, **2**:231
   themes and issues, **2**:233–34,
     235, 238–39, 240
   Waiting for the Barbarians, **2**:229,
     231, 232, 234, 238–40
Coetzee, Jacobus (Coetzee ancestor),
   2:227
Coghill, Nevill, **11**:1538
Coleridge, Samuel Taylor, **3**:308
Connolly, Cyril, **12**:1603
Conquest, Robert, **8**:1022
Conrad, Joseph, **2**:150, **245–66**;
   3:293
   Almayer's Folly, **2**:248, 249, 255
   artistic creed of, **2**:255
   "author's notes" series, **2**:255
   background and early life,
     2:246–47
   as Calvino influence, **2**:150
   Chance, **2**:248, 250, 252, 25229
   "Duel, The," **2**:262
   films based on works of, **2**:249
   as Greene influence, **4**:509
   Heart of Darkness, **2**:49, 245,
     248, 249, 250, 259–60;
     8:1021, *1080*
   highlights in life, **2**:248
   influences on, **2**:262
   Inheritors, The (with Ford), **2**:249
   "Karain," **2**:253
   "Lagoon, The," **2**:253
   Laughing Anne and One Day More,
     2:250, *250*
   list of works, **2**:252
   literary friendships, **2**:249
   Lord Jim, **2**:245, 248, 250, 252,
     260–63; **8**:*1080*
   modernism and, **2**:251; **9**:1239
   Naipaul and, **8**:1013, 1019–20,
     1021, 1023, 1024
   narrative technique, **2**:245,
     251–52, 264, 265
   Nature of a Crime, The (with
     Ford), **2**:249
   as Ngũgĩ influence, **8**:*1080*, 1089
   Nigger of the "Narcissus", The,
     2:250, 253, 255–58

Nostromo, **2:**248, 250, 252, 264, 265; **8:**1020
One Day More, **2:***250*
Outcast of the Islands, An, **2:**255
Personal Record, A, **2:**257
"Return, The," **2:**253
Romance (with Ford), **2:**249
Rover, The, **2:**251, 262
sea experiences, **2:**247, 248, 249, 255, 262, 265
Secret Agent, The, **2:**248, 250, 252, 264–65
"Secret Sharer, The," **2:**248, 250, 263–64, 265
Shadow Line, The, **2:**248, 250, 265–66
Suspense, **2:**250, 262
themes and issues, **2:**251, 252–54, 255, 256, 257, 258, 259, 260–61, 262, 263; **4:**446, 470
Tomorrow, **2:***250*
"Typhoon," **2:**250, 253
Under Western Eyes, **2:**248, 250, 265
"Youth," **2:**250
Cooper, James Fenimore, as Conrad influence, **2:**262
Corkery, Daniel, **8:**1101
Cortázar, Julioi, **3:**346–47
Crane, Stephen, Conrad friendship, **2:**248, 249
Crick, Bernard, **8:**1120
Crozier, Eric, **3:***321*
Cummings, E. E., **3:***300*
Cunninghame Graham, R. B., Conrad friendship, **2:**248, 249
Cushman, Keith, **6:**782
Cynewulf, **11:**1530–31

Daly, Ita, **8:**1103
Dangarembga, Tsitsi, **2:267–76**
awards and honors, **2:**267, 269, 270, *272*
background and early life, **2:**268–69
Baines Avenue Way, **2:**268
as film director, **2:**267, 270, 274, *275–76*
highlights in life, **2:**270
influences on, **2:**274
"Letter, The," **2:**269
list of works, **2:**275
Lost of the Soil, The, **2:**269
Nervous Conditions, **2:**267, 269, 270, 271, 272, 273–75

Out of Exile, **2:**268
as playwright, **2:**268, 269, 270, 271, 274
She No Longer Weeps, **2:**269, 270
themes and issues, **2:**271, 272, 273
Third One, The, **2:**269
Tobias Makombe, **2:**268
Dante Alighieri
as Golding influence, **4:***455*
as Heaney influence, **4:**567, 573
as Kazantzakis influence, **5:**710
as Solzhenitsyn influence, **10:**1419
Darío, Rubén
as García Lorca influence, **3:**392
as Guillén influence, **4:**522
as Neruda influence, **8:**1058
Darwin, Charles, **5:***606;* **11:**1464; **12:**1630
Davis, Jack, **12:**1609, 1617
Day-Lewis, Cecil, Auden and, **1:**60, 62
Defoe, Daniel
as Camus influence, **2:**172
as Coetzee influence, **2:**231, 234, 237, 238
Denham, Michael Aislabie, **11:**1543
De Quincey, Thomas, **6:**782
Desai, Anita, **2:277–86**
awards and honors, **2:**277, 278, 280, 281, 286
background and early life, **2:**278–81
Baumgartner's Bombay, **2:**280, 281, 282, 283, 285–86
Clear Light of Day, **2:**277, 278, 280, 281, 282, 284–85
Cry, the Peacock, **2:**280, 281, 282
Diamond Dust: Stories, **2:**281, 286
Fasting, Feasting, **2:**277, 280, 281, 282, 283, 286
films based on works of, **2:**279
Fire on the Mountain, **2:**280, 282, 283, 286
highlights in life, **2:**280
In Custody, **2:**277, 280, 281, 282, 283
influences on, **2:**278, 283, 285
Journey to Ithaca, **2:**281, 283
list of works, **2:**285
themes and issues, **2:**277, 282, 283, 284, 285, 286
Village by the Sea, The, **2:**280, 281, 286

Voices in the City, **2:**281, 282
Where Shall We Go This Summer?, **2:**282
Desai, Kiran (daughter), **2:**281
DeSalvo, Louise, **6:**775
Desani, G. V., **10:**1325
Descartes, René, **1:**93
Dickens, Charles
as Conrad influence, **2:**262
as Fuentes influence, **3:**354
as Greene influence, **4:**509
as Kincaid influence, **6:**752
as Lessing influence, **6:**793
as Naipaul influence, **8:**1024, 1025
Orwell on, **8:**1116
as Paton influence, **9:**1180
as Shaw influence, **10:**1357, *1361*
as Sidhwa influence, **10:**1386
as Soyinka influence, **10:**1422
Waugh's literary use of, **12:**1604–5
Dickens, Monica, as Emecheta influence, **3:**316
di Giovanni, Norman Thomas, **1:**108, 115
Dinesen, Isak, **3:293–308**
in Africa, **3:**295–96, 299, 301, 304–5
Albondocani (unfinished work), **3:**307
Anecdotes of Destiny, **3:**298, 299, 306–7
Angelic Avengers, The, **3:**297, 298
"Babette's Feast," **3:**300, 306–7
background and early life, **3:**294–95
"Cardinal's First Tale, The," **3:**307
Carnival: Entertainments and Posthumous Tales, **3:**298
"de Cats Family," **3:**295
"Deluge at Norderney, The," **3:**302, 304
"Dreamers, The," **3:**302, 304
"Dreaming Child, The," **3:**300
Ehrengard, **3:**295, 298
"Ex-Africa," **3:**297
films based on works of, **3:**295, 300, 301, 305, *306*
genres and works, **3:**299–301
"Hermits, The," **3:**295, 297
highlights in life, **3:**297
"Immortal Story, The," **3:**300
influences on, **3:**301, 302
"Kitosch's Story," **3:**304, 305

Dinesen, Isak (*continued*)
    Last Tales, **3**:298, 307
    Letters from Africa, **3**:298, 304
    list of works, **3**:296
    literary legacy of, **3**:298, 300–301
    "Monkey, The," **3**:302
    "Old Chevalier, The," **3**:302
    Out of Africa, **3**:293, 296, 297, 298, 299, 301, 304–5
    "Poet, The," **3**:302, 304
    "Roads of Life, The," **3**:304
    "Roads Round Pisa, The," **3**:302, 304
    "Sailor-Boy's Tale, The," **3**:307–8
    Seven Gothic Tales, **3**:293, 296, 297, 299, 302, *303*, 304
    Shadows on the Grass, **3**:298
    "Sorrow-Acre," **3**:306
    "Supper at Elsinore, The," **3**:301, 302
    "Tempests," **3**:301
    themes and issues, **3**:299–300, 304
    translations and, **3**:298
    visit to United States, **3**:297, 298, *300*
    Winter's Tales, **3**:296, 297, 299, 306
Dinesen, Wilhelm (father), **3**:294, 297, 301
Donelson, Linda, **3**:298, *299, 300, 305*
Donne, John
    as Oz influence, **9**:1159, 1163, 1166
    Thomas compared with, **11**:1518
Doolittle, Hilda (H. D.), **8**:1062
Dos Passos, John, as Richler influence, **9**:1271
Dostoyevsky, Fyodor
    as Abe influence, **1**:18
    as Camus influence, **2**:162, 163
    as Coetzee influence, **2**:231
    as Hesse influence, **5**:586, 596, 598
    as Kafka influence, **5**:673
    as Lessing influence, **6**:793
    as Remarque influence, **9**:1231
Drieu la Rochelle, Pierre, **6**:850
Drómhnaill, Nuala Ni, **12**:1704
Drozhzhin, Spiridon, **9**:*1284*
Dujardin, Édouard, **5**:650
Dumas, Alexandre, as Vargas Llosa influence, **11**:1559
Dunn, Nell, as Emecheta influence, **3**:316

Dyson, Henry Victor (Hugo), **6**:806; **11**:1540

Eckhart, Meister, **5**:587
Eco, Umberto, **1**:116
Eddison, Eric Rucker, **11**:1539
Eliot, George, as Lessing influence, **6**:793
Eliot, T. S.
    García Lorca and, **3**:*393*
    Graves and, **4**:480, 481
    as Greene influence, **4**:*509*
    Mansfield and, **7**:895, *900*, 902
    modernism and, **1**:95; **8**:1146; **9**:1239, 1286
    as Ngũgĩ influence, **8**:1089
    Spark and, **11**:1447
    Waugh and, **12**:1604
Emecheta, Buchi, **3**:**309–18**
    Adah's Story, **3**:311, 318
    awards and honors, **3**:312
    background and early life, **3**:310
    Bride Price, The, **3**:310, 311, 313
    Destination Biafra, **3**:*311*, 312
    Double Yoke, **3**:312, 313, *316*
    genres and works, **3**:313–14
    Head above Water, **3**:311, 312, 318
    highlights in life, **3**:312
    influences on, **3**:316
    In the Ditch, **3**:311, 312, 313, 316, 318
    Joys of Motherhood, The, **3**:309, 313, 315–16
    Kehinde, **3**:312, 318
    list of works, **3**:316
    Moonlight Bride, The, **3**:314
    Naira Power, **3**:312
    New Tribe, A, **3**:312
    Nowhere to Play, **3**:314
    Rape of Shavi, The, **3**:312, 316–18
    Second-Class Citizen, **3**:311, 312, 313, 318
    Slave Girl, The, **3**:313
    sociology career, **3**:311, 318
    themes and issues, **3**:*311*, 313, 314, 315, 316–17
    Wrestling Match, The, **3**:314
Emerson, Ralph Waldo, **3**:331
Engels, Friedrich, as Ngũgĩ influence, **8**:1075, 1089
Enright, D. J., **8**:1150
Erikson, Erik H., **8**:1138
Esquirol, Etienne, **9**:*1208*
Euripides, **1**:76; **10**:1348
    as Soyinka influence, **10**:1422, 1425, 1427, 1429

Fanon, Frantz
    as Dangarembga influence, **2**:275
    as Ngũgĩ influence, **8**:1075, 1089
Faris, Faris (pseud.). *See* Kanafani, Ghassan
Faulkner, William
    as Fuentes influence, **3**:345, 346, 354
    as Fugard influence, **3**:366
    as García Márquez influence, **3**:411, 413, 425
    as Kanafani influence, **5**:689
    Nobel Prize lecture, **11**:1580
    as Oz influence, **9**:1158
    as Soyinka influence, **10**:1429, 1433
    as Vargas Llosa influence, **11**:1559
Fernández, Macedonio, **1**:115
Feuchtwanger, Lion, **1**:127, 129; **9**:1223
Fielding, Henry, **8**:*1133*, 1134
Finneran, Richard, **12**:1711
Firbank, Ronald, **12**:1598
Fisher, Dorothy Canfield, **3**:*303*
Fitzgerald, F. Scott, Murakami Japanese translations of, **7**:957, 958, 963
Flaubert, Gustave
    as Borges influence, **1**:120
    as Conrad influence, **2**:262
    as Kafka influence, **5**:673
    Sartre biography of, **10**:1343
    as Vargas Llosa influence, **11**:1559
Ford, Ford Madox, **5**:*638*
    Coetzee thesis on, **2**:227
    Conrad friendship, **2**:248, 249
    Rhys relationship, **9**:1241, 1242, 1258
Forster, E. M., **3**:**319–38**; **8**:1129
    Abinger Harvest, **3**:323
    "Albergo Empedocle," **3**:323
    Aspects of the Novel, **3**:323, 324
    awards and honors, **3**:322, 323
    background and early life, **3**:320–22
    "Celestial Omnibus, The," **3**:330, 336, *337*
    Curate's Friend, The, **3**:326
    as Desai influence, **2**:283
    films based on works of, **3**:321, 327, 331, 334, *335*
    genres and works, **3**:324–25, 336
    highlights in life, **3**:323

homosexual novel and, **3**:326
Howards End, **3**:320, 322, 323, 326, 330, 334, *335*, 336
influence of, **3**:326; **7**:944
influences on, **3**:330
Life to Come, The, **3**:323, 327
list of works, **3**:333
Longest Journey, The, **3**:320, 323, 330
"Machine Stops, The," **3**:336
Maurice, **3**:321, 322, 323, 327
as Mukherjee influence, **7**:944
Nordic Twilight, **3**:323
Oz compared with, **9**:1174–75
Passage to India, A, **2**:283; **3**:322, 323, 326, 330, 331–34; **7**:944; **8**:1129; **9**:1174–75
Richler and, **9**:1261
Room with a View, A, **3**:320, 323, 326, 328, *329*, 330, 331, 333
Story of a Panic, The, **3**:326
themes and issues, **3**:319, 324, 326–27, 328, 331–32, 334
travel and, **3**:321–22, 326, 330
Two Cheers for Democracy, **3**:323
Woolf and, **12**:*1678*, 1682
Foucault, Michel, **2**:234
Fox, Adam, **11**:1540
Freud, Sigmund
    as Carpentier influence, **2**:186
    Cruz and, **3**:355
    as Joyce influence, **5**:650
    Nabokov's view of, **7**:992
    Pirandello's worldview and, **9**:1205
    on Rilke, **9**:*1280*
    as Sartre influence, **10**:1340
    as Woolf influence, **12**:1687
Friar, Kimon, **5**:711, 716
Friel, Brian, **4**:564
Froebenius, Leo, **2**:196, 197
Fry, Christopher, **8**:1131
Fuentes, Carlos, **3**:*339–58*; **11**:1557
    Aura, **3**:339, 344, 345, 356–57, 358
    awards and honors, **3**:344
    background and early life, **3**:340–41, 343
    Buried Mirror, The, **3**:344
    "Cervantes, or the Critique of Reading," **3**:344, 345
    "Chac Mool," **3**:*342*
    Change of Skin, A, **3**:344, 345
    Christopher Unborn, **3**:344
    Death of Artemio Cruz, The, **3**:344, 345, 347, 352, *353*, 354–55

diplomatic career, **3**:340, 341, 343, 344
film reviews and technique of, **3**:345
films based on works of, **3**:341, *343*, *355*
genres and works, **3**:346–48
Good Conscience, The, **3**:344, 345
highlights in life, **3**:344
Holy Place, **3**:344, 345
Hydra Head, **3**:344
influences on, **3**:345, 354
Latin American boom and, **3**:346–47
list of works, **3**:352
Masked Days, The, **3**:344
"Memory Lapses," **3**:354
"New Hispanic American Novel, The," **3**:344, 345, 348
Old Gringo, The, **3**:*340*, 344, 345, 355–56
politics and, **3**:347–48, 349
Terra Nostra, **3**:339, 344, 345, 354, 357–58
themes and issues, **3**:347–48, 349, 351, 352, 355–56
Where the Air Is Clear, **3**:339, 344, 345, 347, 351–52, 354
Years with Laura Díaz, The, **3**:344, 345, 349–50
Fugard, Athol, **3**:*359–76*
    antiapartheid activism of, **3**:362–63
    awards and honors, **3**:359, *363*
    background and early life, **3**:360–62
    Blood Knot, The, **3**:361–62, 366
    Boesman and Lena, **3**:359, 362, 366, *367*
    Captain's Tiger, The, **3**:362, 363, 374
    Dimetos, **3**:362, 363
    films based on works of, **3**:361
    genres and works, **3**:364–67
    highlights in life, **3**:362
    influences on, **3**:366
    Island, The, **3**:363
    Klass and the Devil, **3**:362
    Lesson from Aloes, A, **3**:359, 362, 363, *365*, 371–73, 375
    list of works, **3**:371
    literary legacy of, **3**:366–67
    Master Harold…and the Boys, **3**:359, 360, 362, 363, 365, 366, 368–71

My Children! My Africa!, **3**:362, 363, *366*
My Life, **3**:363
No-Good Friday, **3**:361, 362
Nongogo, **3**:361, 362
Playland, **3**:362, 363, 373
politics and, **3**:365
Road to Mecca, The, **3**:362, 363, 371
Sizwe Bansi Is Dead, **3**:361, 363
Sorrows and Rejoicings, **3**:362, 363, 375
Statement plays, **3**:360, 362, 363
Statements after an Arrest under the Immorality Act, **3**:363
theater and, **3**:361, 363, 364, 367
themes and issues, **3**:365–66, 368, 372, 373
travels, **3**:361, 362
Valley Song, **3**:362, 363, 373–74
Furuta, Sōichi, **11**:1506, 1507

Gallant, Mavis, **9**:1260
Galsworthy, John, Conrad friendship, **2**:248, 249, *250*
Ganetti, Elias, **1**:*126*
Gao Xingjian, **3**:*377–88*
    awards and honors, **3**:377, 380, 381
    background and early life, **3**:378–79
    Between Life and Death, **3**:388
    Bus Stop, The, **3**:379, 382, 385–86, 387, 388
    exile in France, **3**:380, 381, 384
    Fugitives, The, **3**:381
    genre and works, **3**:382, 384
    Hanye de xingchen, **3**:381
    highlights in life, **3**:381
    influences on, **3**:386
    list of works, **3**:384
    "Mother," **3**:384
    One Man's Bible, **3**:381, 382, 384, 388
    Other Shore, The, **3**:382
    Shengsijie, **3**:388
    Soul Mountain, **3**:379, 381, 382, 384, 386–87, 388
    Stars on a Cold Night, **3**:381
    themes and issues, **3**:385, 386
    Without Isms, **3**:384
    "Without Isms," **3**:384
García Lorca, Federico, **3**:*389–408*
    background and early life, **3**:390–91

García Lorca, Federico (*continued*)
   Blood Wedding, **3:**394, 397, 398,
     406
   Book of Poems, **3:**398
   Butterfly's Evil Spell, The, **3:**398
   Canciones, **3:**408
   "Caracola," **3:**408
   Casa de Bernarda Alba, La, **3:**389,
     395, 401–3
   "Ditty of First Desire," **3:***391*
   Doña Rosita the Spinster, **3:**397
   films based on works of, **3:**391,
     411, *428*
   genres and works, **3:**392, 394,
     395–97
   as Guillén influence, **4:**522, 525
   Gypsy Ballads, **3:**397, 399, 400, 401
   highlights in life, **3:**398
   House of Bernarda Alba, The,
     3:389, 395, 401–3
   Impressions and Landscapes, **3:**392
   influences on, **3:**391–92, 394,
     403, 410, 411, 415
   "Lagarto está llorando, El," **3:**408
   list of works, **3:**399
   literary legacy of, **3:**397
   Mariana Pineda, **3:**395, 398
   Neruda and, **8:**1059, 1060
   "Ode to Salvador Dali," **3:**397
   "Ode to Walt Whitman," **3:**394
   Poet in New York, **3:**392, 394,
     403–4
   politics and, **3:**414
   "Preciosa y el aire," **3:**399
   Shoemaker's Prodigious Wife, The,
     3:394, 406, *407*, 408
   significance of, **3:**389–90
   Songs, **3:**408
   themes and issues, **3:**397, 401,
     402, 403, 406
   "Unfaithful Wife, The," **3:**401
   Yerma, **3:**394, 404, 405, 406
García Márquez, Gabriel, **3:409–30**;
   11:1557
   as Allende influence, **1:**54
   Autumn of the Patriarch, The,
     3:411, 412, 414, 428
   awards and honors, **3:**347, 409,
     412, 413, 414, *415*
   background and early life,
     3:410–11, 418
   Big Mama's Funeral, **3:**411, 412,
     415, 426
   Chronicle of a Death Foretold,
     3:412, 414, 426, 428
   films based on works of, **3:**411

Fuentes collaboration, **3:***343*, 345
General in His Labyrinth, The,
   3:412, 426
genres and works, **3:**415–17
highlights in life, **3:**412
In Evil Hour, **3:**411, 412, 415,
   418, 419, 424, 428, 429, 430
influences on, **3:**410, 411, 415,
   418, 424, 425, 428
journalism career, **3:***410*, 412,
   414, 418, 419
Kafka as influence on, **5:**667
Latin American boom and, **3:**347
Leaf Storm, **3:**411, 412, 415,
   425–26
list of works, **3:**416
Love and Other Demons, **3:**412
Love in the Time of Cholera,
   3:412, 414, 422, 423, 425
magic realism and, **3:**347, 409,
   416–17, 420, 421, 422
No One Writes to the Colonel,
   3:411, 412, 415, 418, 426,
   427, 429
Of Love and Other Demons, **3:**412,
   426
One Hundred Years of Solitude,
   3:347, 409, 412, 413, 416,
   417, 420–22, 424, 426
politics and, **3:**413, 414, 418–19
as Rushdie influence, **10:**1325
screenwriting by, **3:**411, 414
Strange Pilgrims, **3:**412
themes and issues, **3:**420, 422,
   429
"Third Resignation, The," **3:**415
travels of, **3:**418, 419
Garnett, Edward, Conrad friend-
   ship, **2:**249
Gay, John
   Brecht's *Beggar's Opera* version,
     1:135
   Havel's *Beggar's Opera* version,
     4:558
   Soyinka's *Beggar's Opera* version,
     10:1427
Genet, Jean, Sartre biography of,
   10:1343
George, Henry, **10:**1358
Gibbon, Edward, **12:**1605–6
Gilbert, Stuart, Camus translation
   by, 168–69
Gilman, Charlotte Perkins, **3:**317
Ginsberg, Allen, **7:***993*; **9:**1260
   as Oz influence, **9:**1161
Glasgow, Ellen, **2:***247*

Glasheen, Aldeline, **5:**658
Glass, Colleen, **12:**1612
Goethe, Johann Wolfgang von
   Dinesen and, **3:**302
   Havel and, **4:**554
   Hesse and, **5:**596
   Mann and, **7:**872, 874, 888, 889
   as Remarque influence, **9:**1231
Gogol, Nikolay, **2:**217; **7:**991
Golding, William, **4:437–56**
   awards and honors, **4:**437, 438,
     441, 444, *445*
   background and early life,
     4:438–39
   Brass Butterfly, The, **4:**440, 444
   Break My Heart (radio play),
     4:440
   Close Quarters, **4:**445, 456
   Darkness Visible, **4:**445, 448,
     455–56, 456
   Double Tongue, The, **4:**441, 444
   Egyptian Journal, An, **4:**439
   Fire Down Below, **4:**445, 456
   Free Fall, **4:**447, 454
   highlights in life, **4:**444
   Hot Gates, The, **4:**440
   influences on, **4:**446
   Inheritors, The, **4:**442, 447, 453
   list of works, **4:**450
   literary legacy of, **4:**446
   Lord of the Flies, **4:**437, 439–40,
     441, 442, *443*, 444, 446, 447,
     448, 449–51
   Lord of the Flies (Golding),
     7:922–23
   Miss Pulkinhorn (radio play),
     4:440
   Pincher Martin, **4:**447, 451–52,
     454
   Pyramid, The, **4:**448, 455
   Rites of Passage, **4:**441, 444, 445,
     456
   Scorpion God, The, **4:**441
   Spire, The, **4:**442, 444–45,
     454–55
   themes and issues, **4:**442, 447,
     449, 451, 453
Gordimer, Nadine, **4:457–76**
   antiapartheid activism of, **4:**457,
     458, 459–60, 461, 462, 464
   awards and honors, **4:**457, 461,
     464
   background and early life,
     4:458–59
   Burger's Daughter, **4:**461, 463,
     468–70, *475*

Conservationist, The, **4:**461, 464,
    467–68
"Essential Gesture, The," **4:**475
Essential Gesture, The, **4:**473, 475
Face to Face, **4:**464
highlights in life, **4:**464
House Gun, The, **4:**461, 463,
    472–73
influences on, **4:**459, 470
July's People, **4:**461, 462, 463,
    470–72
Late Bourgeois World, The, **4:**461
list of works, **4:**472
"Living in the Interregnum,"
    4:475
Lying Days, The, **4:**459, 460–61
My Son's Story, **4:**461
Occasion for Loving, An, **4:**461
Pickup, The, **4:**461, 463, 476
Sport of Nature, A, **4:**461, 463,
    475–76
themes and issues, **4:**462, 467,
    468, 470, 472
Writing and Being, **4:**460
"Writing and Being" (Nobel Prize
    lecture), **4:**470
Gordon, E. V., **11:**1531, 1532
Graham, Alastair, **12:**1593
Grahame, Kenneth, **11:**1542, 1548
Gramsci, Antonio, **4:**471
Granville Barker, Harley, **10:**1361
Grass, Günter, **10:**1325
Graves, Robert, **4:477–94**
    background and early life, **4:**478
    *Claudius the God and His Wife
        Messalina,* **4:**477, 479, 480,
        482, 484, 488–91
    Complete Poems, **4:**486–88
    Country Sentiment, **4:**486
    "Dead Fox Hunter, The," **4:**487
    "Frog and the Golden Ball, The,"
        4:488
    "Goliath and David," **4:**487
    Good-Bye to All That, **4:**477, 478,
        479, 480, 491, 493–94
    Green Sailed Vessel, The (spoken-
        word album), **4:**487
    highlights in life, **4:**480
    I, Claudius, **4:**477, 479, 480,
        488–91
    influences on, **4:**478, 479, 480,
        487
    King Jesus, **4:**491
    Lawrence and the Arabs, **4:**480,
        492–93
    list of works, **4:**484–85

literary legacy of, **4:**482
Love Respelt, **4:**488, *489*
My Head! My Head!, **4:**480, 484
Over the Brazier, **4:**480
Owen and, **8:**1143, 1145, 1147
"Rocky Acres," **4:**486
themes and issues, **4:**482, 487,
    488–89
"Welsh Incident," **4:**482
White Goddess, The, **4:**477, 480,
    481, 484, 487, 491–92
Greene, Graham, **4:495–516**
    Babbling April, **4:**497
    background and early life,
        4:496–98
    Brighton Rock, **4:**495, 498, 500,
        503, 505–7
    Brighton Rock (screenplay), **4:**497,
        502
    Burnt-Out Case, A, **4:**499, 500,
        503, 510–12
    Captain and the Enemy, The,
        4:495, 503
    Catholic trilogy, **4:**498–99
    characteristics of style of, **4:**500
    cinematic technique of, **4:**500,
        502; **6:**854
    Comedians, The, **4:**499, 503, 515
    Comedians, The (screenplay),
        4:497, 502
    End of the Affair, The, **4:**499, 500,
        502, 513, *514,* 515
    Fallen Idol, The, **4:**497, 502
    Fallen Idol, The (screenplay),
        4:502
    films based on works of, **4:**497,
        502, *502,* 508, 510, *514*
    Gun for Sale, A (*This Gun for
        Hire*), **4:**500, *502*
    highlights in life, **4:**503
    "Hint of an Explanation, A,"
        4:500
    Honorary Consul, The, **4:**499, 503
    Human Factor, The, **4:**499
    influences on, **4:**496, 509
    as Keneally influence, **6:**734, 739
    Lawless Roads, The (*Another
        Mexico*), **4:**498, 513
    list of works, **4:**506
    literary legacy of, **4:**502–3
    on *Lolita,* **7:**989
    Lost Childhood, The, **4:**496
    Man Within, The, **4:**496, 497, 503
    Narayan and, **8:**1039–40, 1042,
        1043, 1052
    Our Man in Havana, **4:**499

Our Man in Havana (screenplay),
    4:497, 502
Power and the Glory, The, **4:**498,
    512–13
Quiet American, The, **4:**499, 500,
    502
park compared with, **11:**1445
Stamboul Train (*Orient Express*),
    4:497, 498, 503
Tenth Man, The (screenplay),
    4:502
themes and issues, **4:**500, 502,
    505, 507, 510; **6:**773
Third Man, The, **4:**502
Third Man, The (screenplay),
    4:497, 502
Travels with My Aunt, **4:**500,
    502
Ways of Escape, **4:**506, *508*
Gregg, Veronica Marie, **9:**1245
Gregory, Lady Augusta
    O'Connor and, **8:**1097
    Synge and, **11:**1466, 1467,
        1469, 1477, *1479*
    Yeats and, **12:***1697,* 1698–99,
        1702, 1705, 1706, *1707,*
        1712, 1714, 1716
Grillparzer, Franz, **5:**673
Groden, Michael, **5:**656
Guillén, Jorge, **3:**390
Guillén, Nicolás, **4:517–26**
    awards and honors, **4:**520
    background and early life,
        4:518–19
    Collected Works, **4:**520
    Daily Daily, The, **4:**520, 526
    Dove of a Popular Flight, The,
        4:519, 525–26
    Elegies, **4:**519, 525–26
    Elegy to Jesús Menéndez, **4:**519
    Great Zoo, The, **4:**526
    Heart and Mind, **4:**518
    highlights in life, **4:**520
    I Have, **4:**520, 526
    influences on, **4:**522
    list of works, **4:**525
    Love Poems, **4:**520
    Motives for Son (*Motivos de Son*),
        4:518–19, 520, 523
    Serrated Wheel, The, **4:**520
    *Soldier Miguel Paz and Sergeant
        José Inés,* **4:**519
    Sóngoro Cosongo: Mulatto Poems,
        4:519, 520, 523–24
    *Songs for Soldiers and Sones for
        Tourists,* **4:**519

Guillén, Nicolás (*continued*)
  Spain: Poem in Four Notes of Anguish and One of Hope, **4**:519, 525
  Sunday Sun, **4**:520
  themes and issues, **4**:523, 524, 525, 526
  Through the West Indian Sea Sails a Paper Boat, **4**:520
  West Indies, Ltd., **4**:519, 524–25
  Whole Son, The, **4**:519, 525
Gunston, Leslie, **8**:1142

Habibi, Imil, **4**:*527–36*
  awards and honors, **4**:530, 532
  background and early life, **4**:528–30
  highlights in life, **4**:532
  Ikhtayyi, **4**:532, 535
  influences on, **4**:534
  literary style of, **4**:531–32
  Optimist, The, **4**:534
  Secret Life of Saeed, the Ill-Fated Pessoptimist, The, **4**:*529*, 530, 532, 533–35
  Sextet of the Six Days, **4**:531–32, 535–36
  themes and issues, **4**:533, 535
  "Um al Rubabeeka," **4**:*530*
Habiby, Emile. *See* Habibi, Imil
Haggard, H. Rider, **4**:509
Hakim, Tawfiq al-, **6**:827, 830, 832, 836
Hamer, Richard, **1**:*109*
Haqqi, Yehya, **6**:830
Hardy, Thomas, **11**:1526
Harper, George Mills, **12**:1711
Hart, Moss, **10**:1366
Havel, Václav, **4**:*537–58*
  Art of the Impossible, The, **4**:544
  Audience, **4**:539, 541, 550
  awards and honors, **4**:539, 541, *543*
  background and early life, **4**:538
  Beggar's Opera, The, **4**:539, 541, 558
  as Czech Republic president, **4**:540, 541, 542, 544
  Disturbing the Peace (interview with Hvízdala), **4**:546–47
  Garden Party, The, **4**:538, 541, 544, 556
  highlights in life, **4**:541
  Increased Difficulty of Concentration, The, **4**:541, 544, 557–58

influences on, **4**:552
Largo Desolato, **4**:540, 541, 544, 557
Letters to Olga, **4**:537, 544, 546
Memorandum, The, **4**:538, 539, 541, 556–57
political dissent by, **4**:539–40, 541, 543, 544, 546, 548
"Politics and Conscience," **4**:541, 544
"Power of the Powerless, The," **4**:541, 544
Protest, **4**:550, 552
samizdat literature and, **4**:548–49
Slum Clearance, **4**:541, 544
Sorry..., **4**:550
Temptation, **4**:540, 541, 544, 554–56
themes and issues, **4**:550, 554
Unveiling, **4**:541, 550, 552
Vaněk Plays, The, **4**:544, 550–54, 557
"Word about Words, A," **4**:544
H. D. (Hilda Doolittle), **8**:1062
Heaney, Seamus, **4**:*559–74*; **12**:*1705*
  "Act of Union," **4**:572
  "At a Potato Digging," **4**:569
  awards and honors, **4**:559, 561, 562, 563, *564*, *569*; **12**:1704
  background and early life, **4**:560–61
  Beowulf (translation), **4**:560, 562
  "Blackberry-Picking," **4**:569
  "Bog Queen," **4**:568
  "Churning Day," **4**:569
  "Clearances," **4**:*565*, 566
  Cure at Troy, The, **4**:562, 564
  "Death of a Naturalist," **4**:566–67
  Death of a Naturalist, **4**:561, 562, *564*, 565, 566, 569–70, 571
  "Digging," **4**:569–70
  Door into the Dark, **4**:561, 562, 565–66, 571
  "Early Purges, The," **4**:569
  Electric Light, **4**:562, 563
  Eleven Poems, **4**:559, 561, 562
  Field Work, **4**:562, 563, 566, 572
  Finders Keepers: Selected Prose, 1971–2001, **4**:564
  "For the Commander of the `Eliza'," **4**:569
  "Funeral Rites," **4**:572
  "Glanmore Sonnets," **4**:566
  on Gordimer's political activism, **4**:462

"Grauballe Man, The," **4**:568
Haw Lantern, The, **4**:562, 563, 566
highlights in life, **4**:562
influences on, **4**:567
list of works, **4**:570
"Man and Boy," **4**:573
"Markings," **4**:573
"Mossbawn: Two Poems in Dedication for Mary Heaney," **4**:571
Nobel Prize lecture, **4**:*571*
North, **4**:562, 563, 568, 570–72
"Personal Helicon," **4**:564, *568*, 570
"Pitchfork," **4**:573
poetic style, **4**:565–66
"Punishment," **4**:568, 572
Redress of Poetry, The, **4**:562
"Seed Cutters, The," **4**:571
Seeing Things, **4**:562, 563, 572–73
"Singing School," **4**:572
Spirit Level, The, **4**:562, 563
"Squarings," **4**:572
Station Island, **4**:562, 563, 567
"Sunlight," **4**:571
Sweeney Astray, **4**:560, 573–74
themes and issues, **4**:559, 569, 570–71, 572–73
"Whatever You Say, Say Nothing," **4**:572
Wintering Out, **4**:562, 571
Hegel, G. W. F., as Coetzee influence, **2**:232
Hemingway, Ernest
  as Gábriel Márquez influence, **3**:418, 428
  Mishima's suicide compared with, **7**:915
  as O'Connor influence, **8**:1101
  Rhys compared with, **9**:1249
  as Richler influence, **9**:*1266*, 1271
  on short story form, **7**:898
  as Vargas Llosa influence, **11**:1559
Hesse, Hermann, **5**:*581–600*
  awards and honors, **5**:581, 585, 586, 589, 591
  background and early life, **5**:382–83, 588–89
  Beneath the Wheel, **5**:585, 589, 591, 597–98
  Demian, **5**:586, 589, 591, 592–94, 595, 598
  films based on works of, **5**:587

"For Madmen Only," **5**:596–97
Gertrud (Gertrude), **5**:589, 591
Glass Bead Game, The, **5**:585, 586, 591, 600
highlights in life, **5**:585
Hour behind Midnight, An, **5**:585, 588
influences on, **5**:581, 586, 587, 589, 598, 600
Journey to the East, The, **5**:591, 598, 600
list of works, **5**:591
"Magic Theater," **5**:597
Morgenlandfahrt, Erzählung, Die, **5**:591, 598, 600
Narcissus and Goldmund, **5**:585, 586, 591, 598, 598–600, 599
Nürnberger Reise, Die, **5**:586
Peter Camenzind, **5**:583, 585, 587–88, 591, 592–93, 594
Rilke's influence on, **9**:1285–86
Romantische Lieder, **5**:585, 588, 591
Rosshalde, **5**:584, 589, 591
Siddhartha, **5**:585, 586, 589, 593–95
Steppenwolf, **5**:585, 586, 588, 589–91, 595–97
Stunde hinter Mitternacht, Eine, **5**:585, 588
themes and issues, **5**:587–88, 589, 590, 592–94, 595
travels of, **5**:583–84, 585
"Treatise, The," **5**:597
Trip to Nuremberg, The, **5**:586
Higgins, F. R., **8**:1097
Hilton, James, **3**:317
Hiraoka, Kimitaké. *See* Mishima, Yukio
Hobsbaum, Philip, **6**:773
Hobson, Harold, **1**:97, 99
Hoggart, Richard, **6**:780
Homer, **5**:717
as Joyce model, **5**:654–55
as Kazantzakis model, **5**:710, 717
as Soyinka influence, **10**:1429
Walcott's epic and, **11**:1571, 1576, *1577*, 1578
as White influence, **12**:1659, 1665
Hopkins, Gerard Manley, **11**:1518
Hörstmeier, Fritz, **9**:1219
Housman, A. E., Forster on, **3**:326
Hove, Chenjerai, **2**:269

Hueffer, Ford Madox. *See* Ford, Ford Madox
Hughes, Langston, **4**:*518*; **11**:1518
Hughes, Richard, **4**:446
Hughes, Ted, **4**:567
Hugo, Victor
as Borges influence, **1**:120
as Conrad influence, **2**:262
as Vargas Llosa influence, **11**:1559
Huidobro, Vicente, **8**:1062
Hunt, Hugh, **8**:1096
Husayn, Taha, **6**:827, 830
Huxley, Aldous, **5**:601–18; **6**:813
After Many a Summer Dies the Swan, **5**:608, 616–17
Antic Hay, **5**:603, 608
awards and honors, **5**:604, 606
background and early life, **5**:602–3
Brave New World, **5**:601, 604, 605, 608, 610, 612–14; **8**:1119
Burning Wheel, The, **5**:603, 604, 608
Crome Yellow, **5**:603, 604, 608, 615, 616, *616*
Doors of Perception, The, **5**:604, 608, 617–18
Eyeless in Gaza, **5**:604, 605, 608, 615–16
highlights in life, **5**:604
as Hollywood screenwriter, **5**:604, 605
influences on, **5**:606
Island, **5**:608, 614–15
Jane Eyre (screenplay), **5**:605, 608
list of works, **5**:608
literary legacy of, **5**:610
as Orwell influence, **8**:1119
Perennial Philosophy, The, **5**:604, 608
Point Counter Point, **5**:604, 605, 608, 611–12
Pride and Prejudice (screenplay), **5**:605, 608
themes and issues, **5**:609–10, 611, 612, 614
Those Barren Leaves, **5**:603, 608
Time Must Have a Stop, **5**:608, 617
Hvízdala, Karel, **4**:546, 546–47
Hyde, Douglas, **12**:1705

Ibsen, Henrik
as Joyce influence, **5**:637, 646, 650

as Osborne influence, **8**:136
Shaw on, **10**:1359, 1364
Synge's view of, **11**:1477
Ignatius Loyola, Saint, **5**:706
Ionesco, Eugène, **5**:619–34
Amédée, **5**:622, 624, 627
awards and honors, **5**:623, 624
background and early life, **5**:620–21, 625–26
Bald Soprano, The, **5**:619, 622, 623, 624, *625*, 627, 628–30
Chairs, The, **5**:622, 624, 627
"Colonel's Photograph, The," **5**:633
Elegies for Tiny Beings, **5**:623, 626
Exit the King, **5**:623, 624, 626, 627, 633–34
films based on works of, **5**:621
as Havel influence, **4**:554
Hermit, The, **5**:624, 627
highlights in life, **5**:623
influences on, **5**:626
Jack, or The Submission, **5**:622, 624
Journeys among the Dead, **5**:624
Killer, The, **5**:624, 626, 627, 632–33
Lesson, The, **5**:622, 623, 624, *625*, 627
list of works, **5**:624
Motor Show, The, **5**:622
No!, **5**:621, 626
Notes and Counter Notes, **5**:623, 624, 625, 626
Pedestrian of the Air, **5**:624, 626, 627, 632, 633
Present Past, Past Present: A Personal Memoir, **5**:623, 624
Rhinoceros, **5**:619, 621, 623, 624, 626, 627, 630–32, 633
themes and issues, **5**:627, 628–29, 630
Victims of Duty, **5**:622, 624
Iroaganachi, John, **1**:36
Isherwood, Christopher, Auden collaborations with, **1**:60, 61, 62, 63

Jacobsen, Jens Peter, **9**:1287, 1293
James, Henry, **10**:*1361*
Conrad friendship, **2**:249
as Desai influence, **2**:283
as Greene influence, **4**:509
as Lawrence influence, **6**:770
Jayyusi, Salma, **4**:535
Jhabvala, Ruth Prawer, **3**:331
as Desai influence, **2**:283

Jiénez, Juan Ramon, García Lorca
  and, **3**:391
Joyce, James, **4**:*509*; **5**:*635–58*;
  12:*1706*
  "After the Race," **5**:637, 649
  "Araby," **5**:648, 649
  background and early life,
    5:636–39
  Beckett and, **1**:89, 91, 95
  "Boarding House, The,"
    5:649
  Chamber Music, **5**:637, 638, 644,
    653
  "Circe" manuscript, **5**:*655*
  "Clay," **5**:649
  "Counterparts," **5**:649
  "Dead, The," **5**:648, 649, 650–51
  Dubliners, **5**:637, 638, 639, 640,
    641, 643, 648–51, 653;
    12:1707
  "Encounter, An," **5**:648, 649
  "Eveline," **5**:637, 649
  Exiles, **5**:640, 644, 645–47, 650,
    653
  expatriatism of, **5**:640
  Finnegans Wake, **1**:89, 91; **5**:635,
    639, 640, 643, 650, 653,
    656–58
  as Fuentes influence, **3**:346, 354
  as García Márquez influence,
    3:411, 428
  "Grace," **5**:649
  Habibi compared with, **4**:535
  as Heaney influence, **4**:567
  highlights in life, **5**:639
  "I hear an army charging upon
    the land," **5**:638
  influence of, **3**:346, 354, 411,
    428; **4**:567; **8**:1101; **10**:1429;
    11:1519, 1523
  influences on, **5**:644, 650
  innovations of, **5**:656; **12**:1704
  "Ivy Day in the Committee
    Room," **5**:649
  Kazantzakis compared with,
    5:711, 716, 717
  Lawrence compared with, **6**:770,
    773, 782
  list of works, **5**:653
  literary legacy of, **5**:635, 641,
    643; **12**:1704
  "Little Cloud, A," **5**:649
  Mansfield and, **7**:902
  modernism and, **1**:95; **5**:635,
    638; **7**:985; **9**:1249
  "Mother, A," **5**:649

  as O'Connor influence, **8**:1101
  "Oxen of the Sun" chapter, **5**:656
  "Painful Case, A," **5**:649
  poetry of, **5**:644–45
  Pomes Penyeach, **5**:644, 653
  *Portrait of the Artist as a Young
    Man, A*, **5**:635, 636, 637, 638,
    639, 640, 643, 646, 651–53,
    654; **6**:782; **11**:1523
  Rilke grouped with, **9**:1286
  Shaw and, **10**:*1371*
  significance of, **12**:1704, 1707
  "Sirens" chapter, **5**:656
  "Sisters, The," **5**:637, 648–50
  as Soyinka influence, **10**:1429
  Stephen Hero. See *Portrait of the
    Artist as a Young Man, A*
  themes and issues, **5**:648, 651,
    653
  as Thomas influence, **11**:1519,
    1523
  "Two Gallants," **5**:649
  Ulysses, **3**:428; **5**:635, 637, 639,
    640, *642*, 643, 645, 646, 650,
    653, 654–56, 717; **12**:1685,
    1704, 1707
  Walcott's *Omeros* and, **11**:1576
  Woolf's assessment of, **12**:1685
Jung, Carl
  as Auden influence, **1**:65
  as Carpentier influence, **2**:186
  as Hesse influence, **5**:586, 595,
    598, 600
  as Lessing influence, **6**:793
  as White influence, **12**:1655

Kafka, Franz, **5**:*659–82*, 711
  as Abe influence, **1**:18
  "Aeroplanes of Brescia, The,"
    5:662
  Amerika, **5**:662, 664, 673, 674,
    678–80
  awards and honors, **5**:662, 664
  background and early life,
    5:660–61, 663–64
  "Before the Law," **5**:670
  Betrachtung, **5**:662, 664, 676
  as Borges influence, **1**:120
  "Brief an den Vater," **5**:660–61,
    662
  "Burrow, The," **5**:662, 666
  "Cares of a Family Man, The,"
    5:668
  Castle, The, **5**:662, 665, 666,
    673, 674, 674–76, 676
  as Coetzee influence, **2**:236

  Country Doctor, A, **5**:662
  "Crossbreed, A," **5**:670
  "Description of a Struggle,"
    5:662, 664
  films based on works of, **5**:667
  as García Márquez influence,
    3:410, 411, 415
  "Great Wall of China, The,"
    5:662, 664, 670
  Havel and, **4**:538
  "Heizer, Der: Ein Fragment,"
    5:662, 664, 676
  highlights in life, **5**:662
  "Hunger Artist, A," **5**:662, 681
  *Hunger Artist, A (Hungerkünstler,
    Ein: Vier Geschichten)*, **5**:665,
    676, 681
  "Imperial Message, An," **5**:670
  influences on, **5**:673
  "In the Penal Colony," **5**:662,
    664, 680–81
  "Investigations of a Dog," **5**:662
  "Josephine the Singer," **5**:662,
    668
  "Judgment, The," **5**:662, 664,
    670, 673
  "Letter to His Father," **5**:660–61,
    662
  list of works, **5**:676
  literary legacy of, **5**:667
  Meditation, **5**:662, 664, 676
  "Metamorphosis, The," **3**:410;
    5:662, 664, *665*, 667, 668,
    670, 673, 676–78
  "New Advocate, The," **5**:670
  "On Parables," **5**:670
  "Poseidon," **5**:670
  Prozess, Der. See *Trial, The*
  "Report to an Academy, A,"
    5:662, 666, 668
  Schloss, Das. See *Castle, The*
  as Soyinka influence, **10**:1436
  "Stoker, The," **5**:662, 664
  themes and issues, **5**:666, 668,
    672, 674, 676–77, 680
  Trial, The, **2**:236; **5**:662, 664,
    666, 670, 672–74, 680, 681
  "Verwandlung, Die". See
    "Metamorphosis, The"
  "View from a Window, A," **5**:661
  as Yehoshua influence, **12**:1719
Kallman, Chester, Auden partner-
  ship, **1**:61, 62, 74, 75, 76
Kamban (ancient writer), **8**:1044
Kanafani, Ghassan, **5**:*683–92*
  'A'id ila Haifa, **5**:687, 689, 691

All That's Left to You, **5:**686, 689, 691, 692
assassination of, **5:**687
background and early life, **5:**684–86
"Hand in the Grave, A," **5:**692
highlights in life, **5:**686
influences on, **5:**689
list of works, **5:**691
Ma tabbaqa lakum. See All That's Left to You
Men in the Sun, **5:**683, 686, 688, 690–91
Return to Haifa, **5:**687, 689, 691
Rijal fi al-shams. See Men in the Sun
themes and issues, **5:**688, 690
Umm Saad, **5:**688, 691
Kaniuk, Yoram, **4:**531
Karl, Frederick, **5:**668
Katiyo, Wilson, **2:**269
Kavanagh, Patrick, **4:**567
Kawa, Ryoko, **7:**920
Kawabata, Yasunari, **5:693–702**
awards and honors, **5:**693, *695,* 696, 697; **7:**912
background and early life, **5:**694
Beauty and Sadness, **5:**696, 697, 698
"Dancing Girl of Izu, The," **5:**693, 694, 696, 698, 700
Decorations of the Emotions, **5:**694
"Diary of My Sixteenth Year," **5:**694
films based on works of, **5:**695
highlights in life, **5:**696
House of the Sleeping Beauties and Other Stories, The, **5:**696
How Many Rainbows, **5:**697
influences on, **5:**699
"Izu no odoriko." *See* "Dancing Girl of Izu, The"
"Jurokusai no nikki," **5:**694
Kanjo soshoku (screenplay), **5:**694
Koto, **5:**696, 697
list of works, **5:**701
Master of Go, The, **5:**699
"Mirror of an Evening Scene," **5:**695
Mishima and, **5:**697; **7:**912, 920
Niji ikutabi, **5:**697
Old Capital, The, **5:**696, 697
On Being a Woman, **5:**697
Onna de aru koto, **5:**697
Page of Madness, A (screenplay), **5:**694, 696

Palm-of-the-Hand Stories, **5:**698, 699, 702
"Shokonsai ikkei," **5:**696
Snow Country, **5:**693, 695, 696, 698, 699, 701, 702
Sound of the Mountain, The, **5:**696, 697, 698–99, 702
suicide of, **5:**697; **7:**920
themes and issues, **5:**698, 700, 701
Thousand Cranes, **5:**696, 697
Tokyo People (Tokyo no hito), **5:**697
Utsukushisa to kanashimi, **5:**696, 697, 698
"View of Yasukuni Festival, A," **5:**696
"Yugeshiki no kagami," **5:**695
Yukiguni. See Snow Country
Kazantzakis, Nikos, **5:703–18**
Anaforá stan Gréko, **5:**704
awards and honors, **5:**707, 708
background and early life, **5:**704–6
Buddha, **5:**706, 708
Capodistria, **5:**708
Christ Re-Crucified. See Greek Passion, The
Constantine Palaiologos, **5:**708
Day is Breaking, **5:**705, 712
films based on works of, **5:**705
Fraticides, The, **5:**711, 712, 718
Freedom or Death, **5:**704, 708, 710, 711, 712, 717–18
Ftohúlis tou Théu, O, **5:**708, 709, 717
Greek Passion, The, **5:**706, 708, 710, 711, 712, 715, 717
highlights in life, **5:**707
Hristós ksanastavrónetai, O. See Greek Passion, The
influences on, **5:**705, 710
Jardin des rochers, Le, **5:**506
Kapetán Mihális, O. See Freedom or Death
Kapodístrias, O, **5:**708
Konstandinos o Palaiológos, **5:**708
Ksimeróne, **5:**705, 712
Last Temptation of Christ, The, **5:**703, 707, 708, 711, 716
list of works, **5:**712
literary legacy of, **5:**711
Moscou a Crié, **5:**706
Odyssey, The: A Modern Sequel (Odissia), **5:**703, 706, 707, 711, 716–17

Ofis ke kríno, **5:**705
Prometheus (Promithéas), **5:**708
Report to Greco, **5:**704
Rock Garden, The, **5:**706
Saint Francis, **5:**708, 709, 717
Salvatores Dei: Askitikí, **5:**706, 709, 715
Serpent and Lily, **5:**705
themes and issues, **5:**709–11, 715
Toda-Raba, **5:**706
Vúdas, **5:**706, 708
Zorba the Greek, **5:**703, 705, 707, 708, 710, 711, 713–15, 716, 717
Keats, John, **11:**1518
Keene, Donald, **1:***14*
Keller, Gottfried, **5:**583
Keneally, Thomas, **6:725–46**
American Scoundrel, **6:**728
awards and honors, **6:**728, 736
background and early life, **6:**726–27
Bring Larks and Heroes, **6:**727, 728, 735
Chant of Jimmie Blacksmith, The, **6:**728, 729, 734, 735, 740–42
Chant of Jimmie Blacksmith, The (screenplay), **6:**729
Confederates, **6:**728
films and, **6:**727, 729–30, 732, 736
Gossip from the Forest, **6:**728, 734
Great Shame, The: And the Triumph of the Irish in the English-Speaking World, **6:**728, 734, 744, 745, 746
highlights in life, **6:**728
influences on, **6:**739
list of works, **6:**732
Our Republic, **6:**728, 730
Place at Whitton, The, **6:**726, 728
Schindler's Ark, **6:**725, 728, 731, 733, 736–37, 738–40
Survivor, The, **6:**728
themes and issues, **6:**732, 734, 738, 740–41
Three Cheers for the Paraclete, **6:**728, 742–44
Towards Asmara, **6:**744
Kermode, Frank, **11:**1453
Kerrigan, Anthony, **1:**121
Keynes, John Maynard, Bloomsbury Group and, **3:***320;* **12:**1682, 1685
Khater, Akram, **4:**535

Kierkegaard, Søren, **1**:63; **5**:616
Kincaid, Jamaica, **6**:747–62
    Annie John, **6**:750, 754–56
    At the Bottom of The River, **6**:749, 750, 758, 760–61
    Autobiography of My Mother, **6**:750, 756–58
    awards and honors, **6**:750, 761, 762
    background and early life, **6**:748–49
    "Gift, The," **6**:759
    "Girl," **6**:758, 760
    highlights in life, **6**:750
    influences on, **6**:751
    list of works, **6**:756
    Lucy, **6**:751, 752, 756, 761
    My Brother, **6**:750, 752, 753, 760, 761–62
    My Garden (Book), **6**:751–52
    Small Place, A, **6**:758, 760
    Talk Stories, **6**:751
    themes and issues, **6**:751, 754, 756, *759*
    "West Indian Weekend," **6**:751
    "When I Was Seventeen," **6**:749, 750
Kinnell, Galway, Rainer influence on, **9**:1290
Kipling, Rudyard
    as Calvino influence, **2**:156
    as O'Connor influence, **8**:1101
Kleist, Heinrich von, **5**:673
Knight, Stephen, **12**:1618
Koestler, Arthur, **10**:*1343*

Lai, Wally Look, **9**:1250
Laing, R. D., as Lessing influence, **6**:793
Lange, Norah, **1**:115
Langen, Albert, **5**:585
Langland, William, **1**:60, 64
Lask, Thomas, **9**:1166
Lawrence, D. H., **6**:763–84
    background and early life, **6**:764–65
    "Christening, The," **6**:773
    "Collier's Wife, A," **6**:773
    as Desai influence, **2**:283
    films based on works of, **6**:765, 771
    "Fish," **6**:770
    highlights in life, **6**:766
    Huxley friendship, **5**:604, 605, 612
    influences on, **6**:770

    Kazantzakis compared with, **5**:711, 716
    Lady Chatterley's Lover, **6**:763, 766, 767, 767–68, 768, 769, 770, 771, 777, 779–81
    list of works, **6**:777
    literary legacy of, **6**:771–72
    Love Poems and Others, **6**:765
    "Man and Bat," **6**:770
    Mansfield and, **7**:894, 902
    Movements in European History, **6**:766
    New Mexico ranch, **6**:768, 769
    as Ngũgĩ influence, **8**:1089
    as O'Connor influence, **8**:1101
    "Odour of Chrysanthemums," **6**:766, 773–74
    Orwell and, **8**:1119
    Plumed Serpent, The, **6**:766, 767, 767–68, 768, 781–82
    Pornography and Obscenity, **6**:766
    "Prussian Officer, The," **6**:782
    Prussian Officer and Other Stories, The, **6**:766
    Psychoanalysis and the Unconscious, **6**:766
    Rainbow, The, **6**:763, 766, 770, 771, 775–77, 782
    "Rocking-Horse Winner, The," **6**:782
    St. Mawr, **6**:768
    "Sick Collier, A," **6**:773
    "Snake," **6**:770–71
    Sons and Lovers, **6**:764, 765, 766, 769, 770, 773, 782–84
    "Strike Pay," **6**:773
    Studies in Classic American Literature, **6**:766, 768
    symbolism and, **6**:773–74, 778, 780, 781, 782
    themes and issues, **6**:769, 770, 773–74, 775, 777, 779, 780
    Trespasser, The, **6**:782
    White Peacock, The, **6**:764, 765, 766, 770, 782
    Women in Love, **6**:763, 766, 767–68, 769, 771, 777–79, 782
L'Engle, Madeleine, **6**:813
Leopardi, Giacomo
    Pirandello and, **9**:1205, 1207, 1215, 1216
    Synge translations of, **11**:1472
Lermontov, Mikhail, **7**:991
Lessing, Doris, **6**:785–802

African Laughter, **6**:789
awards and honors, **6**:791
background and early life, **6**:786–87, 789
"Black Notebook," **6**:796
"Blue Notebook," **6**:796
Briefing for a Descent into Hell, **6**:792
Canopus in Argos series, **6**:789, 791, 793, 796, 797–99
Children of Violence series, **6**:790, 791, 794, 795
Diaries of Jane Somers, The, **6**:789, 796–97
Diary of a Good Neighbour, The, **6**:791
Documents Relating to the Sentimental Agents in the Volyen Empire, **6**:798
film and television scripts, **6**:793
films based on works of, **6**:787, 793
Five, **6**:799
Four-Gated City, The, **6**:792, 793, 794, 795
Going Home, **6**:789
Golden Notebook, The, **6**:785, 789, 791, 792, 796–97, 797
Grass Is Singing, The, **6**:785, 789, 791, 793, 800, *801*
highlights in life, **6**:791
"Hunger," **6**:799
influences on, **6**:793, 799
Landlocked, **6**:794
list of works, **6**:799
Making of the Representative for Planet 8, The, **6**:798
Man and Two Woman, A, **6**:799
Marriages between Zones Three, Four and Five, The, **6**:798
Martha Quest, **6**:794
"Old Chief Mshlanga, The," **6**:799
Playing the Game (with Adlard), **6**:789
Play with a Tiger, **6**:791
Proper Marriage, A, **6**:794
"Red Notebook," **6**:796
Ripple from the Storm, A, **6**:794
Shikasta, **6**:792, 798
Sirian Experiments, The, **6**:798
Summer before the Dark, The, **6**:791
themes and issues, **6**:790, 794, 796, 797–98

This Was the Old Chief's Country, **6:**789, 799

"To Room 19," **6:**799–800

Under My Skin, **6:**789

Walking in the Shade, **6:**789

Wind Blows Away Our Words, The, **6:**789

"Yellow Notebook," **6:**796

Lessing, Theodor, **7:**876

Levitt, Morton P., **5:**711

Lewis, C. S., **6:803–24**

  Abolition of Man, The, **6:**811, 818

  Allegory of Love, The, **6:**806

  Auden and, **1:**63

  background and early life, **6:**804–6

  Borges and, **1:***120*

  Christian apologetics and, **6:**806, 810–11, *812,* 813, 820–21; **11:***1534*

  Chronicles of Narnia, The, **6:**806, 808, 810, *812,* 813, *816,* 818, *819,* 820; **11:**1538, 1540

  English Literature in the Sixteenth Century, **6:**806

  Essays Presented to Charles Williams, **11:**1540

  films based on works of, **6:**805

  Great Divorce, The, **6:**821–22

  highlights in life, **6:**808

  influences on, **6:**816; **11:**1540

  Inklings club and, **11:**1538, 1539, 1540

  legacy of, **6:**813

  Lion, the Witch and the Wardrobe, The, **6:**808, 813, 818, 820; **11:**1538

  list of works, **6:**811

  Miracles, **1:**63; **6:**806

  Narnia chronicles . *See Chronicles of Narnia, The*

  Out of the Silent Planet, **1:***120;* **6:**808, 811, 814–17

  Perelandra, **6:**813, 814, *815,* 816–17; **11:**1540

  Pilgrim's Regress, The, **6:**806, 808, 810, 813

  Problem of Pain, The, **6:**806; **11:**1540

  Screwtape Letters, The, **6:**806, 820–21; **11:**1533

  space trilogy, **6:**813, 814–18

  Surprised by Joy, **6:**806

  That Hideous Strength, **6:**813, 814, *815,* 817–18; **11:**1540

  themes and issues, **6:**810–11, 813, 814, 818

  Till We Have Faces: A Myth Retold, **6:**806, 813, 822–24

  Tolkien friendship, **6:***772, 804,* 806, 810, *810,* 816; **11:**1532, 1533, *1534,* 1538, 1539, 1540, 1543, *1549*

  "Williams and the Arthuriad," **11:**1540

  Williams friendship, **6:**806, 816; **11:***1541*

Lewton, Val, **11:**1526

Llosa, Mario Vargas. *See* Vargas Llosa, Mario

Loewe, Frederick, **10:**1366, 1367

London, Jack, as Orwell influence, **8:**1119

Longley, Michael, **4:**561, *568*

Lorca, Federico García. *See* García Lorca, Federico

Lowell, Amy, **7:**902; **8:**1062

Lublinski, Samuel, **7:**876

Lu Hsün. *See* Chou Shu-jen

Lu Xun. *See* Chou Shu-jen

Macdonald, George

  as Lewis influence, **6:**816, 822

  as Tolkien influence, **11:**1542, 1549

Machado, Antonio, **3:**391

MacLennan, Hugh, **9:**1262

MacNeice, Louis, **11:**1515

  Auden and, **1:**60, 61, 62

Mahfouz, Naguib, **6:825–44**

  Abath al-aqdar, **6:**825

  Adrift on the Nile, **6:**834, 835, 836

  Afrah al-qubbah, **6:**835

  Aish fi al-haqiqa, Al-, **6:**833

  Akhenaten: Dweller in Truth, **6:**833

  Arabian Nights and Days, **6:**833

  awards and honors, **6:**825, 828, 829–30

  Awlad haratina, **6:**825, 828, 838, 840–41

  background and early life, **6:**826

  Baqi min al-zaman sa'a, Al-, **6:**834

  Bayn al-qasrayn, **6:**832, 836, 842

  Bayt sayye'al-sum'a, **6:**831

  Beggar, The, **6:**833

  Beginning and the End, The, **6:**831, 836

  Bidaya wa nihaya, **6:**831, 836

Cairo Trilogy, The, **6:**825, 826, 828, 829, 830, *832,* 833, 834, 842–44

Children of Gebalawi, **6:**825, 828, 838–41

"Fear," **6:**831

Fountain and Tomb, **6:**835

Hadrat al-muhtaram, **6:**833

Hams al-junun, **6:**828

Harafish, The, **6:**838, *839*

highlights in life, **6:**828

Hikayat haritina, **6:**835

Hubb tahta al-matar, Al-, **6:**835

influences on, **6:**827, 830, 833, *835*

Journey of Ibn Fattouma, The, **6:**833

Karnak, Al-, **6:**831

Khan al-khalili, **6:**833, 835

"Khawf, Al-," **6:**831

Kifah Tiba, **6:**825, 828

Layali alf-layla, **6:**833

list of works, **6:**836

Lis wal-kilab, Al-, **6:**833

Malhamat al-harafish, **6:**838, *839*

Maraya, Al-, **6:**835

Midaq Alley, **6:**830, 833

Miramar, **6:**836, 842

Palace of Desire, **6:**830, 834, 842–43

Palace Walk, **6:***832, 836,* 842

Qahira al-jadida, Al-, **6:**830, 835

Qasr al-shawq, **6:**830, 834, 842–43

Qushtumur, **6:**835

Radubis, **6:**825, 828

Respected Sir, **6:**833

Rihlat ibn Fattouma, **6:**833

scriptwriting by, **6:**831, 835

Search, The, **6:**833

Shahhadh, Al-, **6:**833

Sugar Street, **6:**830, 843–44

Sukariyya, Al-, **6:**830, 843–44

Taht al-midhallah, **6:**828, 832

Tariq, Al-, **6:**833

Tharthara fawq al-Nil, **6:**834, 835, 836

themes and issues, **6:**830, 833, 838, 840

Thief and the Dogs, The, **6:**833

Thulathiyya, al-. See Cairo Trilogy, The

Time and the Place, The, **6:**834

Wedding Song, **6:**835

Wijhat nazar (newspaper column), **6:**831

Mahfouz, Naguib (*continued*)
  writing style of, **6**:832
  Zuqaq al-Midaq, **6**:830, 833
Mahon, Derek, **4**:561
Makward, Edris, **1**:*81*
Malamud, Bernard, **7**:944
Mallarmé, Stéphane, **7**:902
Malraux, André, **6**:845–62; **9**:1271
  awards and honors, **6**:848, 849
  background and early life,
    6:846–47
  as Camus influence, **2**:161, 162,
    163, 166
  cinematic fiction technique of,
    6:852–54, 858, 861
  Condition humaine, La. See *Man's
    Fate*
  Conquerors, The (*Les conquéants*),
    6:845, 847, 848, 853, 854,
    855, 856–58
  Days of Wrath, The, **6**:848, 849,
    861
  Démon de l'absolu, Le (unfinished
    novel), **6**:861
  Espoir, L', **6**:848, 849, 861
  highlights in life, **6**:848
  influences on, **6**:854
  list of works, **6**:857
  Man's Fate, **2**:166; **6**:845, 848,
    849, 852, 854, 855, 858–59,
    861
  Man's Hope, **6**:848, 849, 861
  Noyers d'Altenburg, Les, **6**:850
  Pantheon reburial of, **6**:848, 852,
    853
  Règne du malin, Le (unfinished
    novel), **6**:861
  Royal Way, The, **6**:848, 849,
    860–61
  Temps du mépris, Le, **6**:848, 849,
    861
  Temptation of the West, The (*La
    tentation de l'occident*), **6**:845,
    848, 854, 860
  themes and issues, **6**:855, 856,
    858
  Voie royale, La, **6**:848, 849,
    860–61
  Walnut Trees of Altenburg, The,
    6:850
Mann, Erika, **7**:873
Mann, Golo, **7**:873
Mann, Heinrich, **7**:870, 871–72,
  873, 876; **9**:1223
Mann, Monika, **7**:873
Mann, Stanley, **9**:1262

Mann, Thomas, **7:869–90**
  "Appeal to Reason, An," **7**:872
  "Appeli an die Vernunft, Ein,"
    7:872
  awards and honors, **7**:869, 872,
    873
  background and early life,
    7:870–72, 875
  *Bekenntnisse des Hochstaplers Felix
    Krull,* **7**:873, 874
  Beloved Returns, The (*Lotte in
    Weimar*), **7**:874
  Betrachtungen eines Unpolitischen,
    7:872, 873, 876
  Black Swan, The, **7**:873, 889
  *Buddenbrooks: The Decline of a
    Family,* **7**:869, 872, 873, 875,
    879–82, 883
  *Confessions of Felix Krull,
    Confidence Man,* **7**:873, 874
  Death in Venice, **7**:869, 870, 871,
    873, 876, 882–84, 889
  Doctor Faustus (*Doktor Faustus*),
    4:554; **7**:873, 874, 878, 888,
    889
  films based on works of, **7**:871
  "Frederick the Great and the
    Grand Coalition," **7**:873
  "Freud," **7**:872
  Friedrich und die grosse Koalition,
    7:873
  Geschichten Jaakobs, Die, **7**:874
  "Goethe," **7**:872
  Havel and, **4**:554
  Hesse and, **5**:588, 592
  highlights in life, **7**:873
  Holy Sinner, The, **7**:873
  influences on, **7**:875, 878, 888,
    889
  Joseph and His Brothers (*Joseph und
    seine Brüder*), **7**:874, 887, 889
  Joseph in Egypt (*Joseph in
    Agypten*), **7**:874
  Joseph the Provider (*Joseph der
    Ernährer*), **7**:874
  Junge Joseph, Der, **7**:874
  Kazantzakis compared with,
    5:711, 716
  leitmotiv technique of, **7**:878
  list of works, **7**:881
  Little Herr Friedemann, **7**:870,
    873, 876
  Lotte in Weimar (*The Beloved
    Returns*), **7**:874
  Magic Mountain, The, **7**:869, 876,
    884–86

Mario and the Magician (*Mario
    und der Zauberer*), **7**:872
Reflections of a Non-Political Man,
    7:872, 873, 876
Remarque and, **9**:*1223*
Royal Highness, **7**:887
Tales of Jacob, The, **7**:874
themes and issues, **7**:875, 879,
    882, 884
Three Essays, **7**:873
Tod in Venedig, Der. See *Death in
    Venice*
Tonio Kröger, **7**:870–71, 873
Tristan, **7**:871, 873, 886–87
"Wagner," **7**:872
Young Joseph, **7**:873, 874
Mansfield, Katherine, **7:891–906**
  background and early life,
    7:892–94
  "Bliss," **7**:905–6
  Bliss, and Other Stories, **7**:895,
    896
  "Garden Party, The," **7**:904–5
  *Garden Party and Other Stories,
    The,* **7**:895, 896, *900*
  "Germans at Meat," **7**:901–3
  highlights in life, **7**:895
  In a German Pension, **7**:893, 895
  influences on, **7**:902
  list of works, **7**:900
  modernism and, **7**:894, 897–99,
    902
  as O'Connor influence, **8**:1101
  "Prelude," **7**:895, 896, 903–4
  short story form and, **7**:897,
    898–99
  themes and issues, **7**:895–96,
    901, 903–4
  tuberculosis and early death of,
    7:891, 894, 895, 896
Marles, Gwilyn, **11**:1512
Márquez, Gabriel García. See García
  Márquez, Gabriel
Marr, David, **12**:1655, 1657
Marryat, Frederick, as Conrad influence, **2**:262
Martyn, Edward, **12**:1705
Marx, Karl
  as Brecht influence, **1**:128, 133
  as Fuentes influence, **3**:348
  Habibi and, **4**:529
  Nabokov's view of, **7**:992
  as Ngũgĩ influence, **8**:1075, 1089
  as Sartre influence, **10**:1340
  as Shaw influence, **10**:1358
Masaryk, Tomáš, **4**:552

Masefield, John, **11**:1449

Maugham, W. Somerset, as Huxley influence, **8**:1119

Maupassant, Guy de
  as Borges influence, **1**:120
  as Conrad influence, **2**:262
  Lessing television adaptations of, **6**:793
  as O'Connor influence, **8**:1101

Mazini, Abd al-Qadir al-, **6**:830

Mazumdar, Anita. *See* Desai, Anita

McCullers, Carson, **3**:*300*

McGahern, John, **8**:1103; **12**:1704

McKay, Claude, **9**:1250

Mehrez, Samia, **4**:535

Melly, Diana, **9**:1244

Melville, Herman, **3**:*321*
  as Oz influence, **9**:1158

Mendelson, Edward, **1**:67, 69

Mendoza, Plinio Apuleyo, García Márquez and, **3**:414, 419

Merriman, Brian, **8**:1096

Meyrink, Gustav, **1**:120

Millay, Edna St. Vincent, **11**:1518

Miller, Arthur, **6**:830

Milton, John
  as Golding influence, **4**:455
  as Kincaid influence, **6**:752, *761*

Mishima, Yukio, **7:907–26**
  background and early life, **7**:908–10
  Confessions of a Mask, **7**:907, 910, 911, *922*
  Five Modern No Plays, **7**:911
  Forbidden Colors, **7**:910, 911, 916, 923–25
  Hanazakari no mori, **7**:910, 911
  "Hanazakari no mori," **7**:909
  highlights in life, **7**:911
  influences on, **7**:909, 920
  Kawabati as mentor, **5**:695, *697*
  Kyoko's House, **7**:912
  list of works, **7**:922
  literary legacy of, **7**:915
  private army of, **7**:911, 912, *914*
  Runaway Horses, **7**:911, *913*
  Sailor Who Fell from Grace with the Sea, The, **7**:911, 913, 914, 915, 920–23
  Sea of Fertility, The (tetralogy), **7**:911, 912, 916
  Sound of Waves, The, **7**:907, 911, 912, 913, 915
  Spring Snow, **7**:911, 916–17
  suicide of, **5**:697; **7**:911, 912, 915

Taido (Young Samurai: Bodybuilders of Japan) (introduction), **7**:911

Temple of Dawn, The, **7**:911, 912

Temple of the Golden Pavilion, The, **7**:911, 912

themes and issues, **7**:913–15, 917, 918, 920, 922

Thirst for Love, **7**:907, 910, 911, 913–14, 915, 918–20

Voices of the Heroic Dead, **7**:*910*

Mistral, Gabriela, as Neruda influence, **8**:1056, 1062

Mitchell, Stephen, **9**:1293

Moliére, as Césaire influence, **2**:199

Mommsen, Theodor, **10**:1375

Moore, G. E., **12**:1683

Moore, Marianne, **3**:*300*

Morris, William, **6**:*816*

Morrison, Toni, as Dangarembga influence, **2**:274

Mowat, Farley, **7:927–36**
  Aftermath: Travels in a Postwar World, **7**:928
  And No Birds Sang, **7**:928
  awards and honors, **7**:930
  background and early life, **7**:928–29
  Born Naked, **7**:*930*
  Desperate People, The, **7**:929, 930
  Dog Who Wouldn't Be, The, **7**:936
  films based on works of, **7**:929
  highlights in life, **7**:930
  influences on, **7**:932
  list of works, **7**:934
  Lost in the Barrens, **7**:929, 930, 936
  My Discovery of America, **7**:932
  My Father's Son: Memories of War and Peace, **7**:928
  Never Cry Wolf, **7**:927, 929, 930, 935
  People of the Deer, **7**:927, 929, 930, 931, 933–35
  themes and issues, **7**:931, 933–34, 935

Mukherjee, Bharati, **7:937–52**
  awards and honors, **7**:937, 940, *941*
  background and early life, **7**:938–39
  Darkness, **7**:940, 941
  Days and Nights in Calcutta (with Blaise), **7**:940, 949–50
  Desirable Daughters, **7**:940
  highlights in life, **7**:940

Holder of the World, The, **7**:940, 943, 950, 952

influences on, **7**:944

Jasmine, **7**:940, 948–49

Leave It to Me, **7**:940

list of works, **7**:947

literary legacy of, **7**:945

"Management of Grief, The," **7**:*951*, 952

Middleman and Other Stories, The, **7**:*947*, 952

Sorrow and the Terror, The: The Haunting Legacy of the Air India Tragedy (with Blaise), **7**:940

"Tenant, The," **7**:940

themes and issues, **7**:942–43, 945, 946, 948

Tiger's Daughter, The, **7**:940, 943

Wife, **7**:940, 943, *944*, 946–48

Murakami, Haruki, **7:953–64**
  American pop culture and, **7**:958, 963
  awards and honors, **7**:955, 957
  background and early life, **7**:954–55
  "Conceptions of Travel in American Cinema," **7**:957
  Dance, Dance, Dance, **7**:959, 961–62
  Elephant Vanishes, The, **7**:963
  Hard-Boiled Wonderland and the End of the World, The, **7**:961
  highlights in life, **7**:957
  influences on, **7**:963
  Japanese translations of F. Scott Fitzgerald by, **7**:957, 958, 963
  Kaze no uta o kike, **7**:955, 957, 961
  list of works, **7**:961
  My Lost City (translation of Fitzgerald), **7**:957
  1973 nen no pinbooru, **7**:959
  Norwegian Wood, **7**:953, 954, 956, 957, 960–61
  themes and issues, **7**:958, 961–62
  "TV People," **7**:963
  Underground: The Tokyo Gas Attack and the Japanese Psyche, **7**:956, 958
  Wild Sheep Chase, A, **7**:953, 956, 957
  Wind-up Bird Chronicle, The, **7**:956, 957, 963–64

Murdoch, Iris, **7**:965–84
  "Agamemnon Class of 1939,"
    7:969
  awards and honors, **7**:965, 969,
    970, 982
  background and early life,
    7:966–67, 969
  Bell, The, **7**:970, 982–83
  Black Prince, The, **7**:965, 973,
    977, 978–80
  Fairly Honorable Defeat, A, **7**:974
  "Fate of the Daisy Lee, The,"
    7:967, 969
  films and, **7**:974
  Flight from the Enchanter, The,
    7:974, 980–82
  highlights in life, **7**:970
  influences on, **7**:967, 969, 973,
    975
  Jackson's Dilemma, **7**:971
  list of works, **7**:978
  literary legacy of, **7**:974
  Oedipus at Colonus (translation of
    Sophocles), **7**:969
  Philosopher's Pupil, The, **7**:973–74
  "Phoenix-Hearted, The," **7**:969
  Sacred and Profane Love Machine,
    The, **7**:965, 966, 970, 982
  Sandcastle, The, **7**:974
  Sea, the Sea, The, **7**:965, 970,
    975–76, 978
  Severed Head, A, **7**:967, 970, 974
  themes and issues, **7**:972, 973,
    975–76, 978–79, 980
  Under the Net, **7**:969, 970, 974,
    978, 980
  Unicorn, The, **7**:974
Murry, John Middleton, Mansfield
  and, **7**:891, 894, 895, 896
Myers, Jeffrey, **8**:1116

Nabokov, Nicolas, **1**:76
Nabokov, Vladimir, **7**:985–1006
  Ada or Ardor: A Family Chronicle,
    7:990, 994, *1004,* 1005
  background and early life,
    7:986–88
  Bend Sinister, **7**:992, 1002, *1003,*
    1005
  bilingualism of, **3**:300
  butterflies as interest of, **7**:*986,*
    987, 988, 990, 1000
  Conclusive Evidence. See Speak
    Memory
  Defense, The, **7**:992
  Despair, **7**:992

  Dinesen compared with, **3**:293,
    300
  Eugene Onegin (translation of
    Pushkin), **7**:989, 990
  Eye, The, **7**:994
  films based on works of, **7**:987,
    992, 994
  Glory, **7**:991, 994
  highlights in life, **7**:990
  Invitation to a Beheading, **7**:992
  on Kafka's legacy, **5**:667
  Kamera Obskura. See Laughter in
    the Dark
  King, Queen, Knave (Karol', Dama,
    Valet), **7**:992
  Laughter in the Dark, **7**:987, 990,
    991, 992, 994, 997, *999,*
    1005
  list of works, **7**:999
  Lolita, **7**:985, 988–89, 990, 991,
    992, 997–1000
  Lolita (screenplay), **7**:989, *991,*
    994
  Look at the Harlequins, **7**:990
  Mary (Mashen'ka), **7**:987, 991
  Naipaul on, **8**:*1023*
  Pale Fire, **7**:989, 992, 1002
  Pnin, **7**:989, 994, 1000–1002
  Podvig, **7**:991, 994
  Priglashenie na Kazin', **7**:992
  Real Life of Sebastian Knight, The,
    7:988, 990, 991, 994, 995–97
  Soglyadataj, **7**:994
  Speak, Memory, **7**:986, 988, 991,
    994, 995–96
  themes and issues, **7**:989,
    991–92, *993,* 995–96, 1000,
    1001
  Transparent Things, **7**:990
  Zaschita Luzhina, **7**:992
Naipaul, V. S., **2**:233; **8**:**1013–34**
  Among the Believers: An Islamic
    Journey, **8**:1017, 1021,
    1030–32
  Area of Darkness, An, **8**:1016
  awards and honors, **8**:1016,
    1017, 1018, *1020*
  Bend in the River, A, **8**:1017,
    1019, 1020, 1021, 1023,
    1025, 1028–30, 1032
  Beyond Belief, **8**:1021
  childhood and early life, **8**:115,
    117
  Enigma of Arrival, The, **8**:1016,
    1017, 1021, 1032
  Flag on the Island, A, **8**:1016

  Guerrillas, **8**:1016, 1019, 1020,
    1021, 1026–28, 1030, 1032
  Half a Life, **8**:1017, 1019, 1021,
    1023
  highlights in life, **8**:1016
  House for Mr. Biswas, A, **8**:1016,
    1018, *1019,* 1020, 1022,
    1024–26
  In a Free State, **8**:1016, 1018,
    1020, 1021, 1023
  India: A Wounded Civilization,
    8:1016
  influences on, **8**:1015, 1019–20,
    1024, 1032
  list of works, **8**:1025
  Loss of El Dorado, The, **8**:1016,
    1020
  Middle Pasaage, The, **8**:1016,
    1018, 1020
  Miguel Street, **8**:1016, 1018,
    1020
  Mimic Men, The, **8**:1016, 1019,
    1020, 1021, 1023, 1032
  Mr. Stone and the Knight's
    Companion, **8**:1016
  as Mukherjee influence, **7**:944
  Mystic Masseur, The, **8**:1016,
    1018, 1020
  Overcrowded Barracoon and Other
    Articles, The, **8**:1016
  political correctness and,
    8:1022–23
  "Reading and Writing," **8**:1032
  Reading and Writing: A Personal
    Account, **8**:1032, *1033*
  on Rhys, **9**:1251
  Suffrage of Elvira, The, **8**:1016,
    1018, 1020
  themes and issues, **8**:1019,
    1021–22, 1023, 1024, 1026,
    1028
  Turn in the South, A, **8**:1017
  Way in the World, A, **8**:1017,
    1021
  "Writer and India, The," **8**:1032
Narayan, R. K., **8**:**1035–54**
  Astrologer's Day and Other Stories,
    An, **8**:1040
  Bachelor of Arts, The, **8**:1042
  background and early life,
    8:1036–39
  Dark Room, The, **8**:1042,
    1048
  Emerald Route, The, **8**:1040
  English Teacher, The, **8**:1040,
    1042, 1047–49

Gods, Demons and Others, **8**:1042, 1044

Grandmother's Tale, The, **8**:1040, 1052–53

Guide, The, **8**:1039, 1042, 1050–51

highlights in life, **8**:1039

honors and awards, **8**:1035, 1039

Horse and Two Goats, A, **8**:1040

Indian Epics Retold, The, **8**:1044

influences on, **8**:1043

Lawley Road and Other Stories, **8**:1040

list of works, **8**:1048

Mahabharata, The: A Shortened Modern Prose Version, **8**:1042, 1044–45

Malgudi Days, **8**:1040

Man-Eater of Malgudi, The, **8**:1042, 1046–47

My Dateless Diary, **8**:1040

My Days, **8**:1040

Naga, **8**:*1042,* 1053

Ramayana, The: A Shortened Modern Prose Version, **8**:*1039,* 1042, 1044, 1045

Swami and Friends, **8**:1039, 1042, 1051–52

themes and issues, **8**:1040, 1041–42, 1046–47, 1050

Nemcová, Bozena, **5**:673

Neruda, Pablo, **1**:46; **8**:1055–70

Anillos, **8**:1058

awards and honors, **8**:1055, *1058,* 1059

background and early life, **8**:1056–58

"Canción de la fiesta, La," **8**:1057

"Canto de amor para Stalingrado," **8**:1060

Canto general, **8**:1060, 1061, 1063, 1066, 1069

"Canto general de Chile," **8**:1060

Captain's Verses, The, **8**:1059

Carpentier and, **2**:182

Ceremonial Songs, **8**:1069

"Cordilleras," **8**:1069

Elementary Odes, **8**:1061, 1062, 1069–70

Extravagaria, **8**:1059, 1060

as García Lorca influence, **3**:391–92, 394

Habitante y su esperanza, El, **8**:1058

Heights of Macchu Picchu, The, **8**:1063, 1064–66

highlights in life, **8**:1059

Hondero entusiasta, El, **8**:1058

influences on, **8**:1056, 1058, 1060, 1062

Isla Negra: A Notebook, **8**:1059, 1061

list of works, **8**:1065

Memoirs, **8**:1060

"Mis ojos," **8**:1057, 1062

"Muñoz Marín," **8**:1068–69

One Hundred Love Sonnets, **8**:1060, 1061

Residence on Earth, **8**:1058, 1059, 1061

"Song of Despair, A," **8**:1068

Song of Protest, **8**:1068–69

Spain in My Heart, **8**:1060

Tentiva del hombre infinito, **8**:1058

themes and issues, **8**:1061, 1063

Twenty Love Poems and a Song of Despair, **8**:1055, 1057–58, 1059, 1063, 1066–68

Twilight, **8**:1057

Ngũgĩ, James. *See* Ngũgĩ wa Thiong'o

Ngũgĩ wa Thiong'o, **8**:**1071–92**

background and early years, **8**:1072–73, 1075

Black Hermit, The, **8**:1074

as Dangarembga influence, **2**:274

Decolonising the Mind: The Politics of Language in African Literature, **8**:1074, 1076, 1082, 1090

Detained: A Writer's Prison Diary, **8**:1074, 1076

Devil on the Cross, **8**:1074, 1075, 1092

on Dinesen, **3**:305

Grain of Wheat, A, **8**:1074, 1075, 1078–79, 1084–86

highlights in life, **8**:1074

Homecoming: Essays on African and Caribbean Literature, Culture and Politics, **8**:1074

influences on, **8**:*1080,* 1089, 1089–90

I Will Marry When I Want, **8**:1074, 1075

list of works, **8**:1081

Matigari, **8**:1076

Mother, Sing for Me, **8**:1076

Moving the Centre: The Struggle for Cultural Freedoms, **8**:1076

Penpoints, Gunpoints, and Dreams:

Towards a Critical Theory of the Arts and the State in Africa, **8**:1076

Petals of Blood, **8**:1074, 1075, 1079, 1081, 1086, *1087,* 1088, 1090

politics of language and, **8**:1082–83

River Between, The, **8**:1074, 1075, 1078, 1090, 1092

Secret Lives, **8**:1074, 1075

themes and issues, **8**:1078, 1084, 1086

Trial of Dedan Kimathi, The (with Mugo), **8**:1074, 1075

Weep Not, Child, **8**:1074, 1075, 1078, 1090, *1091*

Writers in Politics: A Reengagement with Issues of Literature and Society, **8**:1074, 1076, 1082

Niebuhr, Reinhold, **1**:63, 65

Nietzsche, Friedrich

as Chou influence, **2**:210, 212, 216

as Hesse influence, **5**:582, 583, 586, 596, 598

as Kazantzakis influence, **5**:707, 709–10

as Mann influence, **7**:878

as Remarque influence, **9**:1231

Niven, Alastair, **6**:772

Novalis, Jean Paul, **5**:596

Nwapa, Flora, as Emecheta influence, **3**:316

O'Brien, Edna, **12**:1704

O'Brien, Flann, **12**:1704

O'Brien, Kate, **1**:95; **12**:1704

Ocampo, Victoria, **1**:115

O'Casey, Sean, **8**:1097; **12**:1699, 1706–7, *1707*

O'Conner, Teresa F., **9**:1246

O'Connor, Frank, **8**:**1093–1108**; **12**:1704

Art of the Theatre, The, **8**:1096

awards and honors, **8**:1097

background and early life, **8**:1094–95

Big Fellow, The, **8**:1096

Bones of Contention and Other Stories, **8**:1096, 1108

Collection Two, **8**:1097

Common Chord, The, **8**:1096, 1097

Crab Apple Jelly, **8**:1096

Domestic Relations, **8**:1097

O'Connor, Frank (*continued*)
   Dutch Interior, **8:**1096, 1097
   "Face of Evil, The," **8:**1101
   "First Confession," **8:**1106–7
   Fountain of Magic, The (translation), **8:**1096, *1102*
   Guests of the Nation, **8:**1096, 1097
   "Guests of the Nation," **8:**1104–5
   highlights in life, **8:**1096–97
   influence of, **8:**1103
   influences on, **8:**1101
   In the Train (with Hunt), **8:**1096, 1107–8
   Invincibles, The (with Hunt), **8:**1096
   Irish Miles, **8:**1096
   Lament for Art O'Leary, A (translation), **8:**1099
   list of works, **8:**1103
   Little Monasteries, The, **8:**1097
   "Little Mother, The," **8:**1107
   Lonely Voice, The, **8:**1097
   "Majesty of the Law, The," **8:**1108
   Midnight Court, The (translation), **8:**1096, 1099
   Mirror in the Roadway, The, **8:**1097
   More Stories, **8:**1096
   Moses' Rock, **8:**1096
   "My Da," **8:***1105*
   "My Oedipus Complex," **8:**1099, 1105–6
   "Old Fellows," **8:**1101
   Only Child, An, **8:**1097
   Saint and Mary Kate, The, **8:**1096
   Statue's Daughter, The, **8:**1096
   Stories of Frank O'Connor, The, **8:**1096
   themes and issues, **8:**1099, 1104, 1105, 1106
   Three Tales, **8:**1096
   Time's Pocket, **8:**1096
   Traveller's Samples, **8:**1096, 1097, *1106*
   "What's Wrong with the Country?," **8:**1108
   Wild Bird's Nest, The (translation), **8:**1096
Odets, Clifford, **9:***1225*
O'Faolain, Sean, **8:**1097, 1108
O'Flaherty, Liam, **8:**1097; **12:**1704
Ogawa, Mimei, **7:**909
Okigbo, Christopher, **1:**28
O'Neill, Eugene, as Fugard influence, **3:**366

Orwell, George, **6:***772;* **8:1109–30**
   Animal Farm, **8:**1109, 1113, 1115, 1116, 1117, 1119, 1120, 1122, 1125–27
   anticommunism of, **8:**1113, 1115, 1117, 1120, 1122–23, 1125–27
   background and early life, **8:**1110–12
   Burmese Days, **8:**1111, 1112, 1115, 1129
   Clergyman's Daughter, A, **8:**1112, 1115
   Collected Essays, **8:**1129
   Coming Up for Air, **8:**1113, 1115
   Down and Out in Paris and London, **8:**1112, 1115, 1119
   dystopian fiction and, **7:**1002
   "Hanging, A," **8:**1111, 1129
   highlights in life, **8:**1115
   Homage to Catalonia, **8:**1109, 1113, *1117,* 1119, *1121,* 1122, 1124–25
   influences on, **8:**1119
   Keep the Aspidistra Flying, **8:**1112, 1115
   Lion and the Unicorn, The, **8:**1115
   list of works, **8:**1117
   1984., **7:**1002. 8.1109; **8:**1115, 1116, 1117, 1119, 1120, 1122, 1127–28
   politics and, **8:**1109, 1113, 1115, 1116, 1117, 1119, 1120, 1122–29
   "Politics and the English Language," **8:**1117, 1129
   "Politics vs. Literature: An Examination of *Gulliver's Travels,*" **8:**1120
   Road to Wigan Pier, The, **8:**1109, 1112, 1115, 1117, 1120, 1122, 1130
   "Shooting an Elephant," **8:**1111, 1129
   style of, **8:**1117
   "Such Were the Joys," **8:**1110
   themes and issues, **8:**1117, 1124, 1128
   "Why I Write," **8:**1117, 1120
Osborne, John, **8:1131–40**
   Almost a Gentleman: An Autobiography 1955–1966, **8:**1134
   awards and honors, **8:***1133,* 1134, *1135*

   background and early life, **8:**1132
   Better Class of Person, A: An Autobiography 1929–1956, **8:**1134
   Déjàvu, **8:**1134, 1140
   Entertainer, The, **8:**1131, *1132,* 1133, 1134, 1135–36, 1139
   films based on plays, **8:**1133
   highlights in life, **8:**1134
   Hotel in Amsterdam, The, **8:**1136
   Inadmissible Evidence, **8:**1131, 1134, 1135, 1136, 1138
   influences on, **8:**1136
   Look Back in Anger, **8:**1131, 1132, 1133, 1134, 1135, 1137–38, 1140
   Luther, **8:**1131, *1132,* 1133, 1134, 1136, 1138, 1139
   Patriot for Me, A, **8:**1131, 1134, 1136, 1139–40
   themes and issues, **8:**1137, 1138
   Time Present, **8:**1134, 1135, 1136
   Tom Jones (screenplay), **8:***1133,* 1134
   West of Suez, **8:**1134, 1135, 1136
Owen, Wilfred, **8:1141–50**
   "Anthem for Doomed Youth," **8:**1149
   background and early years, **8:**1142–43
   Collected Letters of Wilfred Owen, **8:**1150
   Dolce et decorum est, **8:**1148–49
   Graves and, **4:**478, 494
   highlights in life, **8:**1143
   influences on, **8:**1143, 1145, *1146,* 1147
   list of works, **8:**1147
   Poems, **8:**1148–50
   "Show, The," **8:**1147
   "Strange Meeting," **8:**1149
   Wilfred Owen; Selected Letters, **8:**1150
Oz, Amos, **9:1157–78**
   background and early life, **9:**1158, 1160–61
   Black Box, **9:**1161
   Don't Call It Night, **9:**1165, 1169, *1170,* 1171–72, 1174
   Elsewhere, Perhaps, **9:**1165
   Fima, **9:***1159*
   Hill of Evil Counsel, The, **9:**1161
   honors and awards, **9:**1157, 1159, 1161
   influences on, **9:**1158, 1160, 1161, 1163

list of works, **9**:1172

"Modest Attempt to Set Forth a
Theory, A," **9**:1166, 1167

My Michael, **9**:1157, 1159, 1160,
1164, 1165, 1168–69

"Nomad and Viper," **9**:1174–77

Panther in the Basement, **9**:*1172*

Perfect Peace, A, **9**:1169, 1171,
1172, *1173*, 1174

themes and issues, **9**:1161–63,
1165, 1168, 1169

Under This Blazing Light, **9**:1166,
1167

"Way of the Wind, The,"
9:1166–67, *1176*, 1177

Where the Jackels Howl, **9**:1159,
1161, 1162, 1174, 1177

Padilla, Herberto, **3**:*347*, 348
Pallister, Janis L., **2**:202
Pascal, Roy, **5**:671
Pasternak, Leonid and Boris, **9**:1281
Patočka, Jan, **4**:552
Paton, Alan, **9**:**1179–98**

Ah, but Your Land Is Beautiful,
9:1183, 1184, 1186, 1197

antiapartheid activism of, **9**:1179

background and early life,
9:1180–81

Cry, the Beloved Country, **9**:1179,
1180, 1181, 1182, 1183,
1186, 1187, 1189, 1190,
1191, 1192–95, 1197

"Debbie Go Home," **9**:1195

films based on works of, **9**:1181

highlights in life, **9**:1183

Hofmeyr, **9**:1183, 1184

influences on, **9**:1180, 1186–90

Instruument of Thy Peace, **9**:1183

Kontakion for You Departed,
9:1180, 1195

*Land and People of South Africa,
The*, **9**:1183

"Life for a Life," **9**:1195

list of works, **9**:1192

"Long View, The" (article series),
9:1183

"Meditation for a Young Boy
Confirmed," **9**:1197

Mkhumbane, **9**:1183

politics and, **9**:118, 184, 1179,
1180, 1182, 1186–87

"Rebuilding," **9**:1192

religious faith of, **9**:1186, 1187,
1188–89

"Search, The," **9**:1190

Songs of Africa, **9**:1197

Sponono, **9**:1183

Tales from a Troubled Land,
9:1195

"To a Picture," **9**:1183

Too Late the Phalarope, **9**:1182,
1183, 1186, 1195, *1196*,
1197

Towards the Mountain (w, Paton),
9:1188

"Trial and Reconciliation,"
9:1190, 1192

"Wasteland," **9**:1195

Paz, Octavio, on Fuentes, **3**:351, 357
Peters, John G., **11**:1506–7, 1510
Petrarch, Synge translations of,
11:1472
Phillips, William, **6**:*786*
Pinter, Harold

Dinesen screenplay by, **3**:300

Ionesco as influence on, **5**:619

Joyce's *Exiles* production by,
5:646–47

Pirandello, Luigi, **9**:**1199–1216**

awards and honors, **9**:1199,
1202

background and early life,
9:1200–1203

"Ciaula Discovers the Moon,"
9:1214–15, 1216

films based on works of, **9**:1201

Game of the Parts, The, **9**:*1203*

Henry IV, **9**:*1200*, 1202, 1203,
1205

highlights in life, **9**:1202

influences on, **9**:1207–8

Jar, The, **9**:1215–16

Late Mattia Pascal, The, **9**:1202,
1203, 1209–11

"Limes of Sicily, The," **9**:1203

list of works, **9**:1211

Mountain Giants, The, **9**:1204

Naked Masks, **9**:1203

Novelle per un anno, **9**:1203

On Humor, **9**:1209

Other Son, The, **9**:1206–7

*Right You Are, If You Think You
Are*, **9**:1203, 1208

*Six Characters in Search of an
Author*, **9**:1199, 1202, 1203,
1204, 1211–14, 1216

themes and issues, **9**:1209–10

"Vice, The," **9**:1203

worldview of, **9**:1205, 1206

Piscator, Erwin, **1**:133
Plath, Sylvia, **9**:1251

Plato

as Murdoch influence, **7**:969,
973

as White influence, **12**:1659

Plunkett Greene, Gwendoline and
Olivia, **12**:1593

Plutarch, **10**:1375

Poe, Edgar Allan

as Abe influence, **1**:18

as Borges influence, **1**:120

Kanafani compared with, **5**:692

Popper, Karl, **11**:*1559*

Pound, Ezra

Joyce published by, **5**:638

Mansfield and, **7**:895, 897, 902

modernism and, **1**:95; **7**:897;
8:1146

as Neruda influence, **8**:1062

Spark's advocacy of, **11**:1447

as Tagore advocate, **11**:1497

as Yeats influence, **12**:1709

Proust, Marcel, **5**:711; **7**:985

Beckett book on, **1**:89

as Latin American boom writers
influence, **3**:346

as Remarque influence, **9**:1231

Prudentius, **6**:821

Pushkin, Aleksandr, Nabokov translation of, **7**:989, 990, 991,
994

Pynchon, Thomas, on García
Márquez, **3**:422, 424

Queneau, Raymond, **5**:624
Quinn, John, **5**:*638*

Radley, Paul, **12**:1610
Ragusa, Olga, **9**:1205
Rattigan, Terrence, **8**:1131
Read, Herbert, as Greene influence,
4:*509*
Remarque, Erich Maria, **9**:**1217–38**

All Quiet on the Western Front,
9:1217, *1218*, 1219, 1220,
1221, 1222, 1224, 1227–30,
1231, 1233, 1235

Arch of Triumph, **9**:1221, 1224,
1225, 1237

awards and honors, **9**:1221

background and early life,
9:1218–19, 1221

Black Obelisk, The, **9**:1221, 1224

films based on works of, **9**:1219,
1226

Flotsam, **9**:1220, 1224, 1237

Full Circle, **9**:1221

Remarque, Erich Maria (continued)
  Heaven Has No Favorites, **9:**1221
  highlights in life, **9:**1220–21
  influences on, **9:**1231
  Letzte Akt, Der (screenplay),
    9:1219, 1224
  list of works, **9:**1232
  literary legacy of, **9:**1224, 1226
  Night in Lisbon, The, **9:**1221,
    1224, 1237
  Road Back, The, **9:**1220, 1222,
    1224, 1231, 1235
  Shadows in Paradise, **9:**1221,
    1224, *1232,* 1233–35, 1237
  Spark of Life, **9:**1221, 1224,
    1230, 1232–33, 1235, *1236*
  themes and issues, **9:**1224,
    1227–28
  Three Comrades, **9:**1220, 1224,
    1235
  Time to Love and a Time to Die, A,
    9:1221, 1224, *1226,* 1235,
    1237
  Traumbude, Die, **9:**1220, 1221
  *Von der Freuden und Mühen der
    Jugendwehr,* **9:**1220
Reyes, Alfonso, Borges and, **1:**114,
  115
Rhys, Jean, **9:1239–58**
  After Leaving Mr. Mackenzie,
    9:1258
  awards and honors, **9:**1244
  background and early life,
    9:1240–43
  "Day They Burned the Books,
    The," **9:**1240, 1257
  films based on works of, **9:**1241
  "Goodbye Marcus, Goodbye
    Rose," **9:**1257
  Good Morning, Midnight, **9:**1242,
    1246, 1248, 1249, 1252,
    1253, 1254
  highlights in life, **9:**1242
  influences on, **9:**1248
  Left Bank and Other Stories, The,
    9:1242, 1257
  "Let Them Call It Jazz," **9:**1257
  list of works, **9:**1249
  literary perspective on, **9:**1250–51
  Quartet: A Novel, **9:**1242, 1257–58
  Sleep It Off Lady, **9:**1243
  *Smile Please: An Unfinished
    Autobiography,* **9:**1242,
    1243–44
  themes and issues, **9:**1244, 1245,
    1246, 1250, 1251, 1252

tombstone, **9:***1244*
"Vienne," **9:**1257
Voyage in the Dark, **9:**1240, 1242,
  1246, 1248, 1257
Wide Sargasso Sea, **9:**1239,
  1240, 1242, 1243, 1246,
  1248–49, 1250, 1251,
  1254–56
Richardson, Elaine Potter. *See*
  Kincaid, Jamaica
Richler, Mordecai, **9:1259–78**
  Acrobats, The, **9:**1260, 1261,
    1262, 1264, *1265,* 1266,
    1267, 1270–71, 1277
  *Apprenticeship of Duddy Kravitz,
    The,* **9:**1266, 1271–72
  *Apprenticeship of Duddy Kravitz,
    The* (screenplay), **9:**1261,
    1264, *1271*
  awards and honors, **9:**1259,
    1263, 1264
  background and early life,
    9:1260–62, 1266
  Choice of Enemies, A, **9:***1265,*
    1267, 1277
  Cocksure, **9:**1262, 1263, 1264,
    1273–74
  films based on works of, **9:**1261
  Fun with Dick and Jane (screen-
    play), **9:**1264
  highlights in life, **9:**1264
  *Home Sweet Home: My Canadian
    Album,* **9:**1264
  *Hunting Tigers under Glass: Essays
    and Reports,* 1264
  Incomparable Atuk, The, **9:**1263,
    1272–73
  influences on, **9:***1265,* 1266,
    1271
  Jacob Two-Two and the Dinosaur,
    9:1264
  *Jacob Two-Two Meets the Hooded
    Fang,* **9:**1264
  Joshua Then and Now, **9:**1264,
    1265, 1277–78
  Joshua Then and Now (screen-
    play), **9:**1261, 1263, 1264
  journalism career, **9:**1262, 1264,
    1266
  Life at the Top, **9:**1262, 1264
  list of works, **9:**1267
  *Notes on an Endangered Species
    and Others,* **9:**1264
  St. Urbain's Horseman, **9:**1262,
    1263–64, *1265,* 1266,
    1274–75, 1277

as scriptwriter, **9:**1262, 1265,
  1277
"Shades of Darkness: Three
  Impressions," **9:**1261
Shovelling Trouble, **9:**1264
Solomon Gursky Was Here,
  9:1263, 1264, 1275–76
Son of a Smaller Hero, **9:***1265,*
  1266, 1267, 1277
Street, The: A Memoir, **9:**1263,
  1264
themes and issues, **9:**1262,
  1263–64, 1270, 1271, 1275
This Year in Jerusalem, **9:**1263
Richter, Johann Paul Friedrich (Jean
  Paul), **5:**582
Riding, Laura, Graves relationship,
  4:479, 480, 487, 494
Rilke, Rainer Maria, **9:1279–94**
  as Abe influence, **1:**18
  "Angel, The," **9:**1294
  Auguste Rodin, **9:**1283, 1292
  background and early life,
    9:1280–82
  Book of Hours, The, **9:**1282, 1283,
    1288, 1290, 1293, 1294
  Book of Images, **9:**1283
  Duino Elegies, **9:**1279, 1283,
    1286–87, 1288, 1289, 1290,
    1292, 1293, 1294
  highlights in life, **9:**1283
  influence of, **1:**18; **9:**1285–86,
    1290
  influences on, **9:**1287
  *Lay of the Love and Death of the
    Cornet Christoph Rilke, The,*
    9:1293
  Letters to a Young Poet, **9:**1292–93
  Life and Songs, **9:**1281, 1283
  list of works, **9:**1289
  literary legacy of, **9:**1285–87
  New Poems, **9:**1282, 1283, 1294
  *Notebooks of Malte Laurids Brigge,
    The,* **9:**1279, 1282, 1283,
    1288–90, 1293
  "Panther, The," **9:**1294
  Sonnets to Orpheus, **9:**1279, 1283,
    1288, 1292, 1293
  themes and issues, **9:**1285
Robbe-Grillet, Alain, **6:**832
Robinson, Lennox, **8:**1101
Rodriguez Monegal, Emir, **1:***110*
Roethke, Theodore, **11:**1515
Roh, Franz, **2:**185; **3:**417
Rossetti, Christina, **11:**1518
Roy, Gabrielle, **10:1301–16**

awards and honors, **10**:1301, 1304, 1305, *1307*, 1312, 1315
background and early life, **10**:1302–3
"Capuchin from Toutes-Aides, The," **10**:1313–14
Cashier, The, **10**:1305, 1307, 1310–12
Children of My Heart, **10**:1305, 1315
Enchantment and Sorrow: The Autobiography of Gabrielle Roy, **10**:1305, 1314, *1315*
"Gadabouts, The," **10**:1313
highlights in life, **10**:1305
influences on, **10**:1307, 1314
list of works, **10**:1308
"Luzina Takes a Holiday," **10**:1313
Road past Altamont, The, **10**:1307
"School on the Little Water Hen, The," **10**:1313
Street of Riches, **10**:1305, 1307, 1312–13
themes and issues, **10**:1306, 1309–10
Tin Flute, The, **10**:1301, 1303, 1304, 1305, 1307, 1309–10
Where Nests the Water Hen, **10**:1305, 1307, 1313–14
Windflower, **10**:1314
Runeberg, Nils, **1**:121–22
Rushdie, Salman, **10**:1317–32
awards and honors, **10**:1317, 1320, 1321, 1322
background and early life, **10**:1318–20
East, West, **10**:1321, 1322
Fury, **10**:1321, 1322, 1324, 1330–31
Grimus, **10**:1320, 1321, 1330
Ground beneath Her Feet, The, **10**:1321, 1322, 1324, 1331
Haroun and the Sea of Stories, **10**:1321–22, 1331
highlights in life, **10**:1321
Imaginary Homelands, **10**:1321
influences on, **10**:1325, 1331
Islamist fatwa against, **10**:1317, 1320–21, *1323*, *1324*, 1328
Jaguar Smile, The: A Nicaraguan Journey, **10**:1321, 1331
list of works, **10**:1326
magic realism and, **3**:347
Midnight's Children, **10**:1317, *1318*, 1320, 1321, 1324–25, 1326–28, 1331
Moor's Last Sigh, The, **10**:1322, 1324, 1325, 1331
Mukherjee compared with, **7**:944
"Over the Rainbow," **10**:1319, 1331
Satanic Verses, The, **10**:1317, *1318*, 1320, 1321, 1323, 1324, 1325, 1328, *1329*, 1331
Shame, **10**:1320, 1321, 1324, 1330
themes and issues, **10**:1323–24, 1326, 1328
Wizard of Oz, The, **10**:1321, 1331
Russell, Bertrand, **7**:895
Russell, George, **8**:1095, 1101

Sackville-West, Vita, **12**:1676, 1677, 1678
Šafařik, Josef, **4**:552
Salinger, J. D.
Golding's success compared with, **4**:446
as O'Connor influence, **8**:1101
Saramago, Jorge, **10**:*1430*
Saro-Wiwa, Ken, **1**:22; **2**:233
Sartre, Jean-Paul, **10:1333–54**
Autres, Les. See *No Exit*
awards and honors, **10**:1333, 1338, 1341, 1350
background and early life, **10**:1334–35
Being and Nothingness, **10**:1335–36, 1338, 1344–45
Brecht-Weill collaboration and, **1**:*135*
Camus and, **2**:163
Condemned of Altona, The, **10**:1338, 1340, 1353
Devil and the Good Lord, The, **10**:1353
Dirty Hands, **10**:1340, 1352
Être et le néant, L'. See *Being and Nothingness*
existentialist philosophy of, **10**:1344–45
Flies, The, **10**:1336, 1340, 1348–50
highlights in life, **10**:1336
Huis clos. See *No Exit*
influences on, **10**:1340
list of works, **10**:1347
Mains sales, Les, **10**:1340, 1352

as Murdoch influence, **7**:969, 970, 973
Nausea (La Nausée), **10**:1333, 1336, 1337, 1338, 1340, 1341, 1346–48
No Exit, **10**:1335, 1336, 1340, 1341, 1350–52
themes and issues, **10**:1337–38, 1339–40, 1346, 1348–49, 1350
as Vargas Llosa influence, **11**:1559
Sassoon, Siegfried
Graves and, **4**:478, 494
Owen and, **8**:1143, 1145, *1146*, 1147, 1148, 1149
Satō, Hiroaki, **11**:1506, 1507
Schikaneder, Emanuel, **1**:75
Schopenhauer, Arthur, **7**:878
Schreiner, Olive, **6**:793
Schweitzer, Albert, **5**:582
Scott, Sir Walter
as Achebe influence, **1**:33
as Mahfouz influence, **6**:827, *835*
as Paton influence, **9**:1180
Sevendsen (later Selborn), Clara (Dinesen translator), **3**:298
Shakespeare, William
Auden and, **1**:65, 76
as Césaire influence, **2**:199, 203, 204
as Conrad influence, **2**:262
as Dinesen influence, **3**:301
Forster on, **3**:326
Huxley and, **5**:614
Joyce and, **5**:641, 647
as Kincaid influence, **6**:752
Lawrence compared with, **6**:782
as Murdoch influence, **7**:975, 979
as Oz influence, **9**:1166
as Shaw influence, **10**:1357, 1364, 1375
as Soyinka influence, **10**:1429
Thomas and, **11**:1518
as Walcott influence, **11**:1573, 1574
Shaw, George Bernard, **10:1355–76**; **11**:*1466*
Apple Cart, The, **10**:1365
Arms and the Man, **10**:1360, 1362
As Far As Thought Can Reach, **10**:1375
awards and honors, **10**:1358; **12**:1704, *1705*

Shaw, George Bernard (*continued*)
background and early life,
10:1356–59
Back to Methuselah, **10**:1358,
1361, 1365, 1375–76
Caesar and Cleopatra, **10**:1360,
1363, 1374–75
Candida, **10**:1360, 1362–63
Captain Brassbound's Conversion,
10:1360
Devil's Disciple, The, **10**:1360,
1363
Doctor's Dilemma, The, **10**:1355,
1361, 1363, 1375
Emecheta and, **3**:318
Fabian Essays in Socialism,
10:1359
"Farfetched Fables," **10**:1365
Getting Married, **10**:1363
*Gospel of the Brothers Barnabas,
The*, **10**:1375
Heartbreak House, **10**:1355,
1358, 1361, 1363, 1375
highlights in life, **10**:1358
influences on, **10**:1358, 1364
"In Good King Charles's Golden
Days," **10**:1365
*Intelligent Woman's Guide to
Socialism and Capitalism, The*,
10:1355, 1358, 1361, 1376
In the Beginning, **10**:1375
John Bull's Other Island, **10**:1363
list of works, **10**:1369
Major Barbara, **10**:1355, 1361,
1363, *1369*, 1370–72
Man and Superman, **10**:1355,
1358, 1360, 1363, 1364,
1368–70
Man of Destiny, The, **10**:1360
Misalliance, **10**:1363
Mrs. Warren's Profession, **10**:1360,
1362, 1373–74
music criticism by, **10**:1357, 1359
as Narayan influence, **8**:1043
as Orwell influence, **8**:1119
Perfect Wagnerite, The, **10**:1364
Philanderer, The, **10**:1360, 1362
Plays Pleasant and Unpleasant,
10:1358, 1360
Pygmalion, **10**:1355, 1358, 1361,
1363, 1366–67
Quintessence of Ibsenism, The,
10:1359
Saint Joan, **10**:1355, 1358, 1361,
1365, 1372–73
Sanity of Art, The, **10**:1364

themes and issues, **10**:1368–69
Thing Happens, The, **10**:1375
Three Plays for Puritans, **10**:1358,
1360
Too True to Be Good, **10**:1365
*Tragedy of an Elderly Gentleman,
The*, **10**:1375
Why She Would Not, **10**:1362
Widowers' Houses, **10**:1358,
1359–60, 1362
You Never Can Tell, **10**:1360,
1363
Shawn, William, Kincaid and,
6:749, 750, 752
Shelden, Michael, **4**:496
Sidhwa, Bapsi, **10:1377–98**
American Brat, An, **10**:1380,
1382, 1385, 1393–95
awards and honors, **10**:1380,
1382
background and early life,
10:1379–80
Bapsi Sidhwa Omnibus, **10**:1380
Bride, The, **10**:1379, 1382, 1386,
1389, 1396–98
Cracking India, **10**:1377, *1378*,
1380, 1382, 1385, *1386*,
1387, 1388, 1390–91, *1392*,
1393
Crow Eaters, The, **10**:1379–80,
1385, 1393, 1395–96
highlights in life, **10**:1380
Ice-Candy-Man . See *Cracking India*
influences on, **10**:1386, *1387*
list of works, **10**:1387
"New Neighbors," **10**:1388–89
themes and issues, **10**:1385,
1390, 1393
Sigal, Clancy, **6**:789, 791
Silko, Leslie Marmon, **5**:690
Sinclair, Emil (Hesse pseud.), **5**:584,
586, 589, 598
Sinclair, Upton, **4**:459
Sirin (Nabokov pseud.), **7**:987
Sitwell, Edith, **11**:1513, 1514
Sjöstrand, Östen, **4**:*569*
Smart, Christopher, **1**:69
Solzhenitsyn, Aleksandr,
10:1399–1420
August, 1914 **10**:*1417*
awards and honors, **10**:1399,
1402, 1405, 1406
background and early life,
10:1400–1401
Cancer Ward, **10**:1403, 1408,
1412–18, 1419

Christian faith, **10**:1406, *1407*,
1408–9, *1416*
exile of, **10**:1406
First Circle, The, **10**:1401, 1419
Gulag Archipelago, **10**:*1400*,
1402, 1405–6, 1419–20
highlights in life, **10**:1402
"Incident at Krechetovka Station,
An," **10**:1418–19
influences on, **10**:1414
list of works, **10**:1417
"Matryona's House," **10**:1418
*One Day in the Life of Ivan
Denisovich*, **10**:*1400*, 1401,
1402, 1403, 1408, 1410–12,
1414, 1419
as political prisoner, **10**:1401,
1402, 1403, *1410*, 1411,
1412, 1414
return to Russia by, **10**:1399,
1402, 1406, *1408*, *1414*
themes and issues, **10**:1407–8,
1410, 1412
We Never Make Mistakes, **10**:1418
"World Split Apart, A," **10**:1402
Somers, Jane (Lessing pseud.),
6:789, 791
Sophocles
as García Márquez influence,
3:425
Heaney translations of, **4**:562,
564
Mishima updating of, **7**:920
Murdoch translation of, **7**:969
Sartre retelling of, **10**:1348
Synge's updating of, **11**:1480
Southern, Terry, **9**:1260
Soyinka, Wole, **10:1421–38**
Aké, **10**:1428, 1431–32
awards and honors, **10**:1421,
1422, 1424, 1426, *1427*
Bacchae of Euripides, The,
10:1425, 1427, 1429
"Cobweb's Touch in the Dark, A,"
10:1436
Dance of the Forests, A, **10**:1423,
1424, 1427
Death and the King's Horseman,
10:1427
as Emecheta influence, **3**:316
Evening without Décor, An,
10:1422
exile of, **10**:1424, 1426
"Four Archetypes," **10**:1436
"Fourth Stage, The," **10**:1429
"Gulliver," **10**:1429, 1436

"Hamlet," **10**:1429, 1436
highlights in life, **10**:1424
"Hunt of the Stone," **10**:1436–37
influences on, **10**:1422, 1429
Interpreters, The, **10**:1423, 1424,
    1428, 1429, 1432–33
Jero's Metamorphosis, **10**:1425
"Joseph," **10**:1429, 1436
Kongi's Harvest, **10**:1425, 1427
Lion and the Jewel, The, **10**:1423,
    1427, 1437
list of works, **10**:1433
*Man Died, The: Prison Notes of
    Wole Soyinka,* **10**:1423, 1424,
    1425, 1428, 1434
*Myth, Literature, and the African
    World,* **10**:1425
Ogun Abibiman, **10**:1428
Open Sore of a Continent, The,
    10:1424, 1426, 1434–36
as political prisoner, **10**:1423,
    1424, 1425, *1426,* 1434
"Purgatory," **10**:1436
return to Nigeria by, **10**:1424,
    1426, *1428*
Road, The, **10**:1427
Season of Anomy, **10**:1424, 1428
Shuttle in the Crypt, A, **10**:1429,
    1436–37
Strong Breed, The, **10**:1425,
    1427
Swamp Dwellers, The, **10**:1422,
    1424, 1427
themes and issues, **2**:233;
    10:1431, 1432, 1434–35
Trials of Brother Jero, The,
    10:1425, 1427, 1437
"Ulysses," **10**:1429, 1436
Wonyosi, **10**:1427, 1429
Spark, Muriel, **11**:1445–62
Abbess of Crewe, The, **11**:1445,
    1447, 1457–59
Aiding and Abetting, **11**:1450,
    1462
awards and honors, **11**:1448,
    1449, 1450
background and early life,
    11:1446–47
Ballad of Peckham Rye, The,
    11:1453
Catholic conversion of, **11**:1449,
    1453, 1458
Comforters, The, **11**:1448, 1449,
    1458, 1459–60
Doctors of Philosophy, **11**:1448
Driver's Seat, The, **11**:1462

Fanfarlo and Other Verse, The,
    11:1449
films based on works of,
    11:1445, 1447
Girls of Slender Means, The,
    11:1447, 1450
highlights in life, **11**:1448
Hothouse by the East River, The,
    11:1450
influences on, **11**:1458
list of works, **11**:1456
Loitering with Intent, **11**:1447
Mandelbaum Gate, The, **11**:1450
Memento Mori, **11**:1461–62
Not to Disturb, **11**:1462
Only Problem, The, **11**:1458
Prime of Miss Jean Brodie, The,
    11:1445, 1446, 1448,
    1454–56, 1458
Public Image, The, **11**:1458
Robinson, **11**:1460
"Seraph and the Zambesi, The,"
    11:1449
themes and issues, **11**:1454,
    1457
Spender, Stephen
    Auden and, **1**:60, 62
    Thomas and, **11**:1513
Stein, Gertrude
    as expatriate, **9**:1250
    modernism and, **7**:897; **9**:1249
Stephen, Adeline Virginia. *See*
    Woolf, Virginia
Stephen, Leslie, **12**:1674–75, 1677,
    1683
Stephens, Edward, 1*11465*
Stephens, James, **8**:1095, 1097
Stevenson, Robert Louis
    as Achebe influence, **1**:33
    as Greene influence, **4**:509
    as Murdoch influence, **7**:967,
        973
    as Thomas influence, **11**:1526
Stoppard, Tom, **10**:1424
    Ionesco as influence, **5**:619
    Largo Desolato screenplay by,
        4:557
Stowe, Harriet Beecher, **9**:1193,
    1194
Strachey, Lytton
    Bloomsbury Group and,
        3:*320*
    Woolf and, **12**:1675, 1678,
        1682, 1683, 1684, 1685
Swift, Jonathan
    as Achebe influence, **1**:33

as Orwell influence, **8**:1119,
    1120
Oz compared with, **9**:1167
as Soyinka influence, **10**:1429,
    1436
Synge, John Millington, **1**:95;
    11:1463–84
    Abbey Theatre and, **12**:1705–6
    Aran Islands, The, **11**:1466
    background and early life,
        11:1464–66
    Collected Works, **11**:1466
    "Curse, The," **11**:1472
    "Danny," **11**:1472, *1473*
    Deirdre of the Sorrows, **11**:1469,
        1471, 1481
    "End of the Book," **11**:1472
    "Glencullen," **11**:1472
    highlights in life, **11**:1467
    influences on, **11**:1477
    *In the Shadow of the Glen. See
        Shadow of the Glen, The*
    "I've Thirty Months," **11**:1473
    list of works, **11**:1480
    "On an Anniversary," **11**:1473
    Playboy of the Western World, The,
        11:1463, 1466, 1467, 1468,
        1469, 1471, 1472, 1477,
        1478–81, 1484; **12**:1698,
        1699, *1702,* 1703, 1704,
        1706, 1715, 1716
    Poems and Translations, **11**:1472
    poetry of, **11**:1472–73
    "Question, A," **11**:1472–73
    realism of, **11**:1469
    Riders to the Sea, **11**:1463, 1465,
        1467, 1471, 1474–75;
        12:1709
    Shadow of the Glen, The, **11**:1463,
        1466, 1467, *1470,* 1471,
        1475–78
    as Soyinka influence, **10**:1429
    themes and issues, **11**:1469–80,
        1474, 1475, 1477, 1478–79
    Tinker's Wedding, The, **11**:1471,
        1483–84
    "To the Oaks of Glencree,"
        11:1473
    translations by, **11**:1472
    Well of the Saints, The, **11**:1463,
        1467, 1471, 1481–83, 1484
    When the Moon Has Set,
        11:1466
    Yeats friendship, **12**:*1697,* 1698,
        1699, *1702,* 1703, 1704,
        1706, 1707, 1714

Tagore, Dwijendranath, **11**:1486
Tagore, Rabindranath,
    11:1485–1500
    "Amar Sonar Bangla," **11**:1493
    awards and honors, **11**:1485,
      1486, 1488, 1489, 1497,
      1498
    background and early life,
      11:1486–89
    Chhelebela, **11**:1486
    "Creative Unity," **11**:1492
    "East and West," **11**:1492
    Ghare-Baire, **11**:1490, 1492,
      1494–96
    Gitanjali, **11**:1489, *1495*,
      1496–98
    highlights in life, **11**:1488
    Home and the World, The,
      11:1490, 1492, 1494–96
    influences on, **11**:1498
    "Jana Gana Mana Adhinayaka,"
      11:1493
    Jiban Smriti, **11**:1486
    Kabikahini, **11**:1487
    list of works, **11**:1495
    "Meaning of Art, The," **11**:1491
    My Boyhood Days, **11**:1485
    My Reminiscences, **11**:1485
    "Parrot's Training, The," **11**:1499
    Parrot's Training and Other Stories,
      The, **11**:1499
    "Poet's School, A," **11**:1499–1500
    Post Office, The, **11**:1498–99
    Rabindrasangit (song), **11**:1493
    "Religion of the Artist, The" (lec-
      ture), **11**:1491
    Song Offerings, **11**:1489, *1495*,
      1496–98
    themes and issues, **11**:1491–92,
      1494, 1496–97, 1498, 1499
    as visual artist, **11**:1490, *1493*
    writing style of, **11**:1492–93
Tagore, Swarnakumari, **11**:1486
Tailhade, Laurent, **8**:1143
Takamura, Kōtarō, **11:1501–10**
    background and early life,
      11:1502
    Brief History of Imbecility, A,
      11:1503, 1505, 1507, 1510
    Brief History of Imbecility, A (trans-
      lated by Satō), **11**:1506
    Chieko and Other Poems of
      Takamura Kōtarō (translated
      by Satō), **11**:1506
    Chieko Poems, The (translated by
      Peters), **11**:1506–7

"Chieko Riding the Wind,"
    11:*1509*
Chieko shō, **11**:1501, 1503,
    1505, 1506, 1507, 1508–9,
    1510
Chieko shō sono go, **11**:1501,
    1503, 1505, 1506, 1507,
    1509
Chieko's Sky (translated by
    Furuta), **11**:1506, 1507
"Decadence," **11**:*1503*
Dōtei, **11**:1501, 1503, 1505,
    1506, 1508, 1510
editions and English translations
    of, **11**:1505–7
"Fountain of Mankind," **11**:*1504*
Hakufu, **11**:1504
highlights in life, **11**:1505
influences on, **11**:1502, 1508
Kiroku, **11**:1505, 1510
list of works, **11**:1507
Ōinaru hi ni, **11**:1505, 1510
Ojisan no shi, **11**:1505, 1510
sculpture by, **11**:1502, 1504,
    1505, 1508
Tenkei, **11**:1503, 1505
themes and issues, **11**:1508,
    1509
Tangye Lean, Edward, **11**:1538
Taylor, Paul B., **1**:66
Taymour, Mahmoud, **6**:830
Tennyson, Alfred, Lord, as Soyinka
    influence, **10**:1422, 1436
Thackeray, William Makepeace, as
    Waugh influence, **12**:1598,
    1600
Theroux, Paul, Naipaul and, **8**:*1023,*
    1024
Thomas, Dylan, **11:1511–28**
    Adventures in the Skin Trade,
      11:1524, 1527–28
    "And Death Shall Have No
      Dominion," **11**:1514
    "Author's Prologue," **11**:1521
    background and early life,
      11:1512–14
    Child's Christmas in Wales, A,
      11:1524–26
    Collected Letters, **11**:*1518*
    Collected Poems of Dylan Thomas,
      1934–1952, The, **11**:1514,
      1516, 1520–21
    Deaths and Entrances, **11**:1514,
      1515, 1526
    Doctor and the Devils, The (screen-
      play), **11**:1526, *1527*

"Do Not Go Gentle into That
    Good Night," **11**:1511, 1516,
    1520, 1521
18 Poems, **11**:1512, 1513, 1514,
    1518, 1526
"Fern Hill," **11**:1524, 1526
highlights in life, **11**:1514
"If I Were Tickled by the Rub of
    Love," **11**:1526
influences on, **11**:1519, 1523,
    1526
"In My Craft or Sullen Art,"
    11:1515, 1526
list of works, **11**:1521
literary legacy of, **11**:1518–19
Map of Love, The, **11**:1514, 1515
New Poems, **11**:1514
*Portrait of the Artist as a Young
    Dog*, **11**:1514, 1523–24,
    1525, 1527
themes and issues, **11**:1517–18,
    1521, 1523–25
25 Poems, **11**:1513–14
Under Milk Wood (radio play),
    11:1514, 1516, *1517*, 1521,
    1522, 1523, 1525
"Winter's Tale, A," **11**:1515
World I Breathe, The, **11**:1514
Thomas, Ludwig, **5**:585
Thomas Aquinas, **5**:650
Thurman, Judith, **3**:305
Tillich, Paul, **1**:63
Tindall, William York, **5**:644
Tolkien, Christopher (son),
    11:1532, 1533, 1535, 1540,
    1541, 1546
Tolkien, J. R. R., **11:1529–50**
    Adventures of Tom Bombadil, The,
      11:1532, 1534, 1535, 1538
    "Ainulindalë," **11**:1547, 1548
    "Akallabêth," **11**:1548
    Auden and, **1**:66
    background and early life,
      11:1530–31
    *Beowulf: The Monsters and the
      Critics*, **11**:1532, 1533
    Book of Lost Tales, The, **11**:1532,
      1533, 1547
    "Chaucer as Philologist: The
      Reeve's Tale," **11**:1533
    "Errantry," **11**:1538
    Farmer Giles of Ham, **11**:1532,
      1533, 1548
    Fellowship of the Ring, The,
      11:1531, 1543
    "For W. H. A.," **1**:66

highlights in life, **11**:1532

History of Middle-earth, The, **11**:1533, 1535, 1540, 1547

Hobbit, The, **1**:66; **11**:1529, 1532, 1533, 1534, 1535, 1536, 1537, 1542–43, 1544, 1545, 1548, 1549

influences on, **6**:816; **11**:1537

Inklings club and, **11**:1538–41

invented languages by, **11**:1536, *1537*

"Leaf by Niggle," **11**:1534, 1548–49

Lewis friendship, **6**:772, *804*, 806, 810, *810*, 816; **11**:1532, 1533, *1534*, 1538, 1539, 1540, 1543, *1549*

list of works, **11**:1545

Lord of the Rings, The, **1**:66; **6**:806, *810*; **11**:1529, *1530*, 1532, 1533, 1535, 1536, 1537, 1538, 1540, *1541*, 1542, 1543–47, 1548, 1549

Monsters and the Critics and Other Essays, The, **11**:1536

"Music of the Ainur, The," **11**:1547

"Notion Club Papers, The," **11**:1540

"Of the Rings of Power and the Third Age," **11**:1548

"On Fairy-Stories," **1**:66; **11**:1532, 1533, 1534, 1536, 1540

"Quenta Silmarillion: The History of the Silmarils," **11**:1547–48, 1549

Return of the King, The, **11**:1543

Roverandom, **11**:1535

"Secret Vice, A," **11**:1536

Silmarillion, The, **11**:1529, 1531, 1532, 1533, 1535, *1546*, 1547–48

Sir Gawain and the Green Knight (edited with Gordon), **11**:1531, 1532, *1533*

Smith of Wootton Major, **11**:1532, 1534, 1549

themes and issues, **11**:1542, 1543–44, 1547

Tree and Leaf, **11**:1532, 1534, 1536, 1548

Two Towers, The, **11**:1543

Unfinished Tales, **11**:1535

"Valaquenta," **11**:1547

"Voyage of Éarendel the Evening Star, The," **11**:1547

Tolstoy, Leo
  as Lessing influence, **6**:793
  Rilke and, **9**:1281, *1284*
  as Vargas Llosa influence, **11**:1559

Trevor, William, **8**:1103

Turgenev, Ivan, as O'Connor influence, **8**:1101

Tvardovsky, Aleksandr, **10**:*1416*

Twain, Mark, as Borges influence, **1**:120

Tynan, Kenneth, **6**:*807*; **8**:1133

Udechukwu, Obiora, **1**:24

Unamuno, Miguel de, **5**:706

Updike, John, **7**:992

Vaculík, Ludvík, **4**:548

Valéry, Paul, **7**:975

Vargas Llosa, Mario, **11:1551–66**
  Aunt Julia and the Scriptwriter, **11**:1552, 1558, 1559, 1565–66
  awards and honors, **11**:1554, 1560
  background and early life, **11**:1552–53
  Captain Pantoja and the Special Service, **11**:1558–59
  Conversation in the Cathedral, **11**:1557
  Death in the Andes, **11**:1558
  Feast of the Goat, The, **11**:1554, 1558, 1566
  Flight of the Inca, The, **11**:1552
  García Márquez and, **3**:414
  Green House, The, **11**:1553, 1554, 1557, 1564–65
  Huida del Inca, La, **11**:1552
  influences on, **11**:1559
  In Praise of the Stepmother, **11**:1559
  Jefes, Los, **11**:1553, 1554
  list of works, **11**:1562
  Notebooks of Don Rigoberto, The, **11**:1559
  Paraíso en la otre esquina, El, **11**:1554
  presidential candidacy of, **11**:1551, *1552*, 1553, 1554, 1555, *1556*, 1557
  Real Life of Alejandro Mayta, The, **11**:1558
  Storyteller, The, **11**:1558, 1562–64

themes and issues, **11**:1557–59, 1560, 1562–63

Time of the Hero, The, **11**:1553, 1554, 1557, 1559, 1560, 1560–62

Vázquez, María Esther, **1**:108

Velasco, Luis Alejandro, **3**:418

Verga, Giovanni, **9**:1207

Verlaine, Paul, **7**:902

Verne, Jules, as Borges influence, **1**:120

Vico, Giambattista, **5**:650

Villon, François, Synge translations of, **11**:1472

Vilmorin, Louise de, **6**:848, 849, 850, 851

Virgil
  as Heaney influence, **4**:573
  Walcott epic and, **11**:1576, 1577, 1578

Voltaire, **4**:534

Wain, John, **11**:1539, 1540–41

Walcott, Derek, **11:1567–82**
  Antilles, The: Fragments of Epic Memory, **11**:1580–81
  awards and honors, **11**:157, *1568*, 1570, 1571, 1580
  background and early life, **11**:1568–70
  Castaway, The, **11**:1570
  Dream on Monkey Mountain, **11**:1569–70, 1578–80
  Henri Christophe, **11**:1569, 1570, *1575*
  highlights in life, **11**:1570
  In a Green Night, **11**:1569
  influences on, **11**:1572, 1573
  list of works, **11**:1580
  as Ngũgĩ influence, **8**:1089
  Odyssey, The (Homer; adaptation), **11**:1571
  Omeros, **11**:1571, 1576–78
  themes and issues, **11**:1576, 1578
  Twenty-five Poems, **11**:1570

Walcott, Roderick, **11**:1568, 1570, 1571

Walker, Alice, **2**:274

Ward, Mrs. Humphrey, **5**:602

Ward, Matthew, **2**:168–69

Wassermann, Jakob, **5**:588

Watkins, Vernon, **11**:1519, 1521

Waugh, Alec (brother), **12**:1590, 1598

Waugh, Arthur (father), **12**:1590, 1598

Waugh, Auberon (son), **12:**1592, 1593

Waugh, Evelyn, **12:1589–1606**
background and early life, **12:**1590–91
Black Mischief, **12:**1592, 1593
Brideshead Revisited, **12:**1589, 1592, 1593, 1594, 1595, 1596, 1597, 1598, 1599–1602, 1604, 1605
Decline and Fall, **12:**1591, 1592, 1595, 1596, 1598, 1604
Edmund Campion, **12:**1592, 1593
films based on works of, **12:**1591, 1594, *1596*, 1597
Handful of Dust, A, **12:**1592, 1596–97, 1604–5
Helena, **12:**1592, 1594, 1605–6
highlights in life, **12:**1592
influences on, **12:**1598
Labels, **12:**1592
list of works, **12:**1601
literary legacy of, **12:**1597–98
Love among the Ruins, **12:**1592, 1595
Loved One, The, **12:**1592, 1594, 1597, 1605
Men at Arms, **12:**1592, 1602, 1603
Ninety-two Days, **12:**1592
Officers and Gentlemen, **12:**1592, 1602, 1603
Ordeal of Gilbert Pinfold, The, **12:**1592, 1594
PRB: An Essay on the Pre-Raphaelite Brotherhood, **12:**1591
Remote People, **12:**1593
Robbery under Law: The Mexican Object-Lesson, **12:**1592, 1593
Roman Catholic conversion of, **12:**1593
Scarlet Woman, The (screenplay), **12:**1591, 1597
Scoop, **12:**1592, 1593, *1598*, 1604
Scott-King's Modern Europe, **12:**1592
Spark compared with, **11:**1445
Sword of Honour, The trilogy, **12:**1589, 1592, 1594, 1596, 1597, 1602–4
themes and issues, **12:**1596, 1597, 1599, 1602, 1603
Unconditional Surrender (The End of the Battle), **12:**1592, 1602–4

Vile Bodies, **12:***1590*, 1591, 1592, 1595, 1596, 1597
Waugh in Abyssinia, **12:**1592, 1593
When the Going Was Good, **12:**1592
Webb, Beatrice, **10:**1359, *1360*
Webb, Sidney, **10:**1359, *1360*
Weil, Simone, **7:**973
Weller, Archie, **12:1607–28**
"All the Pretty Little Horses," **12:**1618
awards and honors, **12:**1610, 1611, 1612
background and early years, **12:**1608–9
Cooley, **12:**1614, 1616, 1627
crime fiction, **12:**1618–19
Day of the Dog, The, **12:**1607, 1610, 1611, 1612, 1616, 1618, 1620–22
"Dead Dingo," **12:**1609, 1611, 1617
Dead Roses, **12:**1618
Going Home, **12:**1611, 1611–12, 1612, 1614, 1624, 1627
"Going Home," **12:**1624, 1626–27
highlights in life, **12:**1611
influences on, **12:**1617
"Johnny Blue," **12:**1627
Land of the Golden Clouds, **12:**1611, 1613, 1616, 1618, 1622–24
list of works, **12:**1620
Nidjera, **12:**1612
"Pension Day," **12:**1627
Purple Dreams, **12:**1611
"Saturday Night and Sunday Morning," **12:**1618, 1627
Songs of the Sea, **12:**1618
"Story of Frankie…My Man, The," **12:**1611
Sunset and Shadows, **12:**1611, 1612
themes and issues, **12:**1614, 1620–21, 1622–23
Wells, H. G., **10:***1361*; **12:1629–50**
Ann Veronica, **12:**1632, 1637
Anticipations, **12:**1632, 1633, 1639
"Art of Staying at the Seaside, The," **12:**1631
background and early life, **12:**1630–31
"Beautiful Suit, The," **12:**1641

as Borges influence, **1:**120
"Cone, The," **12:**1640
Conrad friendship, **2:**248, 249
"Country of the Blind, The," **12:**1640–41
"Door in the Wall, The," **12:**1641
"Empire of the Ants, The," **12:**1636, 1640
Experiment in Autobiography, **12:**1633
films baseed on works of, **12:**1631
First Men in the Moon, The, **12:**1632
"Flowering of the Strange Orchid, The," **12:**1641
Food of the Gods, The, **12:**1632
Forster and, **3:**336
Future in America, The, **12:**1639
highlights in life, **12:**1633
History of Mr. Polly, The, **12:**1632, 1636
"Inexperienced Ghost, The," **12:**1641
influences on, **12:**1638
In the Days of the Comet, **12:**1632
Invisible Man, The, **12:**1631, 1635
Island of Dr. Moreau, The, **12:**1631, 1635
Kipps: The Story of a Simple Soul, **12:**1631, 1632
list of works, **12:**1644
Love and Mr. Lewisham, **12:**1631, 1636
"Magic Shop, The," **12:**1640
Mind at the End of Its Tether, **12:**1634
Modern Utopia, A, **12:**1632, 1649
Mr. Britling Sees It Through, **12:**1633, 1639
"Mr. Skelmersdale in Fairyland," **12:**1641
as Naipaul influence, **8:**1024
New Machiavelli, The, **12:**1639
New Worlds for Old, **12:**1637
as Orwell influence, **8:**1119
Outline of History, The, **12:**1629, 1633, *1637*
"Pearl of Love, The," **12:**1641
Russia in the Shadows, **12:**1639
science fiction, **12:**1630–31, 1635–36, 1638, 1642–44, 1646–47, 1648–49
"Sea Raiders, The," **12:**1640
Shape of Things to Come, The, **12:**1633, *1634*, 1648–49

short stories by, **12**:1640–41

"Star, The," **12**:1636, 1640

themes and issues, **12**:1642, 1644

Time Machine, The, **12**:1629, 1631, 1633, 1639, 1642–44, 1646

Tono-Bungay, **12**:1629, 1632, 1633, 1644–46

War in the Air, The, **12**:1632

War of the Worlds, The, **12**:1631, 1635–36, 1646–48

Wife of Sir Isaac Harman, The, **12**:1637

World of William Clissold, The, **12**:1633, 1639

World Set Free, The, **12**:1632

Weltsch, Felix, **5**:663

Werfel, Franz, **5**:663

West, Anthony, **12**:*1632*

West, Rebecca, **12**:*1632*, 1633

White, Edmund, **3**:326

White, Patrick, **12**:**1651–72**

Aunt's Story, The, **12**:1653, 1659, 1664–65

awards and honors, **12**:1651, *1652*, 1655, 1656, *1657*, 1667, 1669

background and early life, **12**:1652–53

Big Toys, **12**:1663

Bread and Butter Women, **12**:1662

Burnt Ones, The, **12**:1655

Eye of the Storm, The, **12**:1656

Flaws in the Glass: A Self-Portrait, **12**:1655, 1656, 1671–72

Four PLays, **12**:1662

Ham Funeral, The, **12**:1662, *1663*

Happy Valley, **12**:1653, 1655

highlights in life, **12**:1655

influences on, **12**:1655, 1659, 1665

as Keneally influence, **6**:735, 739

list of works, **12**:1669

literary legacy of, **12**:1661

Living and the Dead, The, **12**:1653

Memoirs of Many in One, **12**:1655

Netherwood, **12**:1663

Night of the Prowler, The, **12**:1663

Patrick White Letters (edited by Marr), **12**:1657

Patrick White Speaks, **12**:1657

Ploughman and Other Poems, The, **12**:1652, 1655, 1662

poetry and plays, **12**:1662–63

Return to Abyssinia, **12**:1662

Riders in the Chariot, **12**:1659, 1667–69

School for Friends, The, **12**:1662

Season at Sarsaparilla, The, **12**:1655, 1662

Signal Driver: A Morality Play for the Times, **12**:1663

Solid Mandala, The, **12**:1655, 1670–71

themes and issues, **12**:1658–59, 1664, 1665, 1667, 1669

Thirteen Poems, **12**:1655, 1662

Three Uneasy Pieces, **12**:1657

Tree of Man, The, **12**:1653, 1654, 1670

Twyborn Affair, The, **12**:1656, 1671

Voss, **12**:1654, 1655, 1659, 1665–67

White, William Allen, **7**:872

Whitman, Walt, **3**:334

as Borges influence, **1**:120

as García Lorca influence, **3**:393, 394, *399*, 403

Thomas Compared with, **11**:1518

Wiesel, Elie, **9**:1268

Wiggins, Marianne, **10**:1321, 1322

Wilde, Oscar

Borges translation of, **1**:114, 120

as Mishima influence, **7**:920

sexuality scandal and, **3**:326

Williams, Charles

Auden and, **1**:61, 62, 63

Lewis and, **6**:806, 816; **11**:*1541*

Tolkien and, **11**:1538, 1539, 1540, *1541*, 1543–44

Williams, William Carlos, **8**:1062; **9**:1294

Wilson, Edmund, public quarrel with Nabokov, **7**:989, 990

Wilson, Paul, **4**:544

Winter, Joe, **11**:1498

Wittgenstein, Ludwig, as Murdoch influence, **7**:969, 973

Wodehouse, P. G., **12**:1598

Woodcock, George, **9**:1266

Woolf, Leonard, **12**:1675–76, 1677, 1678, *1683*, 1685

Woolf, Virginia, **12**:**1673–94**

background and early life, **12**:1674–75

Between the Acts, **12**:1677, 1687, 1691–92

Bloomsbury Group and, **3**:*320*; **12**:1673, 1676, 1677, 1682–85

Common Reader, The:, **12**:1677, 1680–81

experimentation and form and, **12**:1679–81

films based on works of, **12**:1675

Flush, **12**:1681

as García Márquez influence, **3**:411

highlights in life, **12**:1677

influences on, **12**:1687

Jacob's Room, **12**:1677, 1678

Kew Gardens, **12**:1677

list of works, **12**:1689

Mansfield friendship, **7**:895, 896, *898*, *902*

Mark on the Wall, The, **12**:1677

modernism and, **7**:897; **9**:1249

Monday or Tuesday, **12**:1677

Mrs. Dalloway, **9**:1163, 1166, 1167; **12**:1676, 1677, *1679*, 1686–89

Night and Day, **12**:1677

Orlando, **12**:1677, 1678, *1680*, 1681, 1687

as Oz influence, **9**:1163

Roger Fry: A Biography, **12**:1677

Room of One's Own, A, **12**:1677, 1680, 1692–93

suicide of, **12**:1677, 1678

themes and issues, **12**:1673, 1680, 1686, 1689, 1692

Three Guineas, **12**:1677, 1678, 1681, 1693–94

To the Lighthouse, **9**:1163; **12**:1676, 1677, 1678, *1679*, *1688*, 1689–90

Voyage Out, The, **12**:1676, 1677

Waves, The, **12**:1677, 1680

Years, The, **12**:1677

Wordsworth, William, **11**:1449

Beckett and, **1**:95

poetic devices, **1**:69, 72

Wyndham, Francis, **9**:1242, 1244

Xenophon, **7**:975

Yeats, William Butler, **12**:**1695–1716**

as Achebe influence, **1**:32

"Among School Children," **12**:1713

automatic writing and, **12**:1698, *1699*, 1700, 1714–15

Yeats, William Butler (continued)
awards and honors, 12:1695, 1697, 1698, 1700, 1704
background and early life, 12:1696–97
"Beautiful Lofty Things," 12:1714
"Black Tower, The," 12:1714
Cathleen Ni Houlihan, 12:1698, 1699, 1715–16
Celtic Twilight, The, 12:1696
"Church and State," 12:1703
Collected Works of W. B. Yeats, The (Finneran and Harper, ed.), 12:1711
Countess Cathleen, The, 12:1699, 1702, 1705
"Easter 1916," 12:1700, 1710, 1712
"Everlasting Voices, The," 12:1710
Fairy and Folk Tales of the Irish Peasantry, 12:1696
Full Moon in March, A, 12:1715
as Heaney influence, 4:567, 573
"He Mourns for the Change That Has Come upon Him and His Beloved, and Longs for the End of the World," 12:1702
"He Wishes for the Cloths of Heaven," 12:1710
"He Wishes His Beloved Were Dead," 12:1710
highlights in life, 12:1698
"Hosting of the Sidhe, The," 12:1709
"Host of the Air, The," 12:1709
influences on, 12:1701, 1709
Island of Statues, The, 12:1697
Joyce and, 5:637, 638
as Keneally influence, 6:739
King of the Great Clock Tower, The, 12:1715
"Lake Isle of Innisfree, The," 12:1702

Land of Heart's Desire, The, 12:1698, 1715
Last Poems and Two Plays, 12:1714
list of works, 12:1711
"Meditations in Time of Civil War," 12:1700, 1713–14
Michael Robartes and the Dancer, 12:1710–12, 1714
"Municipal Gallery Revisited, The," 11:1477; 12:1714
mythic subjects of, 11:1469
"Nineteen Hundred and Nineteen," 12:1713, 1714
O'Connor and, 8:1096, 1097, 1101, 1102
Poems, 12:1701
"Prayer for My Daughter, A," 12:1712
Purgatory, 12:1715
Rilke grouped with, 9:1286
Rose, The, 12:1701
"Sailing to Byzantium," 12:1712, 1713
"Second Coming, The," 1:32; 12:1695, 1703, 1712, 1715
"September 1913," 12:1703
"Song of the Faeries," 12:1697
"Stolen Child, The," 12:1702
"Sweet Dancer," 12:1714
Synge friendship, 11:1465, 1466, 1467, 1477, 1479; 12:1697, 1698, 1699, 1702, 1703, 1704, 1706, 1707, 1714
Tagore's poetry and, 11:1486, 1488, 1489, 1496–97
themes and issues, 12:1708–9, 1710, 1712
theory of poetry of, 12:1696
"To Be Carved on a Stone at Thoor Ballylee," 12:1713
"Tower, The," 12:1703, 1712–13
Tower, The, 12:1712–14
Vision, A, 12:1703, 1714–15

"Voices," 12:1697
Wanderings of Oisin and Other Poems, The, 12:1698
"What Then?," 12:1714
Wind among the Reeds, The, 12:1697, 1701, 1702, 1708–10
"Wisdom of the King, The," 12:1701
Yehoshua, A. B., 12:1717–26
awards and honors, 12:1717, 1720
background and early life, 12:1718–19
Between Right and Right, 12:1720, 1721
"Death of the Old Man," 12:1718–19, 1720
"Facing the Forests," 12:1726
Facing the Forests, 12:1726
films based on plays of, 12:1719
Five Seasons, 12:1720, 1723
highlights in life, 12:1720
influences on, 12:1718, 1719, 1723
Journey to the End of the Millennium, A, 12:1720
Late Divorce, A, 12:1720, 1722
Liberating Bride, The, 12:1720
list of works, 12:1725
Lover, The, 12:1720, 1722–23
Mr. Mani, 12:1717, 1718, 1720, 1722, 1723, 1724–25
Open Heart, 12:1720, 1725–26
themes and issues, 12:1722–23, 1724, 1725
Yokomitsu, Riichi, 5:694
Yu Dafu, 2:211

Zamatin, Eugene, 8:1119
Zhou Shuren. See Chou Shu-jen
Zhou Zhangshou. See Chou Shu-jen
Zola, Émile, as Ngũgĩ influence, 8:1089